Autism Spectrum Disorder

Sara Miller McCune founded SAGE Publishing in 1965 to support the dissemination of usable knowledge and educate a global community. SAGE publishes more than 1000 journals and over 800 new books each year, spanning a wide range of subject areas. Our growing selection of library products includes archives, data, case studies and video. SAGE remains majority owned by our founder and after her lifetime will become owned by a charitable trust that secures the company's continued independence.

Los Angeles | London | New Delhi | Singapore | Washington DC | Melbourne

2nd Edition

Autism Spectrum Disorder

Characteristics, Causes and Practical Issues

Jill Boucher

Los Angeles | London | New Delhi
Singapore | Washington DC | Melbourne

Los Angeles | London | New Delhi
Singapore | Washington DC | Melbourne

SAGE Publications Ltd
1 Oliver's Yard
55 City Road
London EC1Y 1SP

SAGE Publications Inc.
2455 Teller Road
Thousand Oaks, California 91320

SAGE Publications India Pvt Ltd
B 1/I 1 Mohan Cooperative Industrial Area
Mathura Road
New Delhi 110 044

SAGE Publications Asia-Pacific Pte Ltd
3 Church Street
#10-04 Samsung Hub
Singapore 049483

Editor: Luke Block
Editorial assistant: Lucy Dang
Production editor: Imogen Roome
Proofreader: Leigh C. Timmins
Marketing manager: Lucia Sweet
Cover design: Wendy Scott
Typeset by: C&M Digitals (P) Ltd, Chennai, India
Printed in the UK

Library of Congress Control Number: 2016947067

British Library Cataloguing in Publication data

A catalogue record for this book is available from the British Library

ISBN 978-1-4462-9566-3
ISBN 978-1-4462-9567-0 (pbk)

At SAGE we take sustainability seriously. Most of our products are printed in the UK using FSC papers and boards. When we print overseas we ensure sustainable papers are used as measured by the PREPS grading system. We undertake an annual audit to monitor our sustainability.

TABLE OF CONTENTS

PREFACE

My main aim in writing this book is to provide an account of autism that people with little or no specialist knowledge will find comprehensible and digestible, but which at the same time offers more advanced readers a clear summary of existing knowledge with pointers to more detailed reading. In brief, the book is intended as both an introduction and a source. I have tried to keep in mind trainee practitioners, whether careworkers or classroom assistants, teachers, therapists, psychologists, social workers, nurses or doctors whose practice involves working with people with autistic spectrum disorder (ASD) and/or their families; also undergraduate and graduate students who need a crib before embarking on more detailed and specialised reading relevant to their essay, dissertation or thesis. I should like to think that some parents whose child has just received a diagnosis of autism might find 'dipping and skimming' this book answers some of their immediate questions.

I also wanted to write an account that was as impartial as I could make it. There are many books that present an author's particular 'take' on autism, and these can contribute greatly to advanced discussion of the nature, causes, treatment, etc. of autism. However, they do not make good starting points, and – unless several such books are read – they can leave the reader with an incomplete or biased understanding.

There are some other underlying principles or themes that may make the book a little different from some others. In particular, I try to put current views into the perspective of a continuing search for answers, in which much can be learned from past research and much remains to be learned in the future. I try to present research and practice as working together to make life as good as possible for people with autism, their families and other carers, whilst accepting some differences in aims and priorities. I have worked both as a practitioner and as a researcher and know that co-operation is beneficial for all concerned. Similarly, where there is a controversy I try to present opposing evidence and arguments fairly, rather than taking sides one way or the other. Finally, much of the illustrative material in the book is provided by people with ASD themselves, either within disguised descriptions or with their own or their families' agreement. I am grateful to all those individuals and families whose stories, drawings, etc. are included.

Two practical points. First: the book covers more material than most beginning students will need, and lecturers/tutors should use the text selectively according to their student group. For example, for students on some vocational courses, some or all the chapters in Part II might be omitted. For students on non-vocational psychology courses or undertaking postgraduate research, Part III could be made optional reading.

Secondly: terminology in the autism field is a sensitive issue, and preferred terms reflect current societal trends as well as 'where the person is coming from'. I try to take a middle line, avoiding medical-model terms (e.g. 'mental retardation', 'patient', 'symptom') as far as possible, at the same time avoiding extremes of political correctness, not least because PC terminology changes all the time. I have always advised students to be sensitive to the preferred terminology of the person they are talking to, and adjust their own terminology accordingly ('When in Rome…'). I can't do that in a book, and am aware that the terminology I use will not please all readers: it is a 'no win' situation, as concluded by Kenny et al. (2015). Occasional footnotes are used within the main text to explain my usage of some terms where clarification may be helpful.

ABOUT THE AUTHOR

Jill Boucher is Professor of Developmental Psychology at City, University of London. Initially she trained and worked as a speech and language therapist. Within a few years, however, the need to better understand the brain, and those malfunctions of the brain that cause communication and language impairments, led her to retrain and pursue an academic career as a neuropsychologist. After some years spent teaching and researching at the University of Warwick, she moved to Sheffield University to supervise an existing vocational course for speech and language therapists. She subsequently played a critical role in developing a multidisciplinary Department of Human Communication Sciences at Sheffield, where research and practice are equally valued and mutually beneficial. The conviction that practitioners and researchers must work collaboratively to improve the lives of people with ASD, and to help families and others who support and provide for them, informs the approach taken in the present book.

PART I

WHAT IS AUTISM?

HISTORICAL BACKGROUND

AIMS

The main aim of this chapter is to provide a context within which to set current attempts to answer the question 'What is autism?' Underlying aims are: first, to counteract the view that the past has nothing to tell us about autism, by demonstrating that early definitions and descriptions of autism prefigure those in use today; and secondly, to convey the fact that – in our present incomplete state of knowledge and understanding – what is published and read about autism today will take its place in 'the history of autism' tomorrow.

EARLY CASE REPORTS

'Autism' has almost certainly always existed in human populations. However, autism was not recognised as a distinct condition until the mid-twentieth century. Prior to that, less able people with autism were included within an undifferentiated group of those who were described as simpletons, or imbeciles, or feeble-minded (people were not sensitive to stigmatising language in those days). More able people with autism – those who acquired language and did at least reasonably well at school – were merely seen as loners and eccentrics.

A few reports of individuals whom we might now recognise as autistic survive from as early as the eighteenth century. Notable amongst these are reports of feral children, that is to say children who had been abandoned by their parents but who had managed to survive in the wild. The earliest well-documented case of a feral child is that of the 'Wild Boy of Aveyron', found in the late 1780s at about the age of 12, living like an animal alone in a forest. Victor, as the boy was named by those who rescued him, had no language, nor was he responsive to human beings. Significantly, Victor never became responsive to other people despite the fact that from the time of his rescue until the time that he died in middle age he was kindly cared for, and energetic attempts were made to educate him (Frith, 1989). Other detailed accounts of children who might nowadays be diagnosed with autism spectrum disorder (ASD) survive from the nineteenth century (Waltz & Shattock, 2004).

THE FIRST ATTEMPTS TO IDENTIFY AUTISM AS A DISTINCT CONDITION

Kanner's and Asperger's Seminal Accounts

Autism was first identified by an American psychiatrist named Leo Kanner in a paper published in 1943 entitled 'Autistic disturbances of affective contact'. One year later an Austrian medical student called Hans Asperger published a paper entitled 'Die Autistischen Psychopathen im Kindesalter' ('Autistic Psychopathy in Childhood') (Asperger, 1944/1991). The individuals described by Kanner and by Asperger in their separate papers differed from each other in some respects. However, there was also considerable overlap between the descriptions, as is clear from Box 1.1.

Box 1.1 Kanner's and Asperger's early descriptions

KANNER *'Early infantile autism'*	ASPERGER *'Childhood autistic psychopathy'*
Profound lack of affective [i.e. emotional] contact with others.	Severe impairment of social interaction, shown in odd, inappropriate behaviour rather than aloofness and indifference.
Intense resistance to change in routines. Fascination with manipulating particular objects, but not using them for correct function.	All-absorbing, narrow interests, often to the exclusion of other activities.
	Imposition of repetitive routines on self and others.
Muteness or abnormalities of language.	Good grammar and vocabulary but inappropriate use of speech.
Superior rote memory and visual-spatial skills.	A tendency to engage in monologues on special interests.
	Limited or inappropriate non-verbal communication.
	Motor clumsiness.
	'Mischievous' behaviour.

Kanner's paper was immediately influential in English-speaking countries. However, Asperger's paper was not brought to the attention of English-speaking researchers for nearly 40 years (Wing, 1981) and was not readily available in English until 1991. For 40 years, therefore, answers to the question 'What is autism?' were largely shaped in English-speaking countries by Kanner's original descriptions, although Asperger's paper was influential in psychiatric circles in parts of Europe.

Two Blind Alleys

From the 1950s onwards, more and more children were brought to the attention of practitioners on account of their socially withdrawn behaviour, delayed or absent language, and other unusual behaviours. Kanner's concept of 'early childhood autism' was not yet widely known about or accepted, and two groups of puzzled professionals tried to describe and understand these children, and to fit them into their existing categories of childhood disorder – and failed.

Autism as a form of neurosis

Psychoanalysts and psychotherapists who were asked by desperate parents to help their problem child concluded that autism was a form of **neurosis**[1] caused by disturbed mother–child relationships (Mahler, 1952; Bettelheim, 1967). The stigmatising and unjustifiable term 'refrigerator mother' indicates the supposed origins of the impaired relationship.

By the 1970s, this theory had been disproved by studies showing that people with autism have significant abnormalities of brain structure and function (Hutt et al., 1965; Rutter et al., 1967). It was also appreciated that infants with autism are extremely difficult to mother normally because they are socially unresponsive. It is, after all, not easy to **bond** with a child who doesn't look at you, doesn't smile or hold out their arms to be picked up, and who dislikes being cuddled. Thus any disturbance of early mother–child relationship can be traced back to the autistic infant's odd and unrewarding behaviour rather than the mother's 'coldness'.

Autism as a form of psychosis

Some medically-minded psychiatrists, on the other hand, conceived of autism as a **psychotic** condition with a physical, brain-related cause (e.g. Bender, 1956). It was mistakenly thought that the odd behaviours of young children with autism were early manifestations of schizophrenia, and they were accordingly diagnosed as cases of **childhood schizophrenia**, or **childhood psychosis**. These medically-minded practitioners were very concerned with issues of definition and diagnosis, and in the UK a committee was set up under the chairmanship of Dr Mildred Creak to establish a set of diagnostic criteria for 'childhood schizophrenia'. The result was what became known as 'Creak's Nine Points', listed in Box 1.2.

Box 1.2   Creak's 'Nine Points'

1   Gross and sustained impairment of emotional relationships.
2   Serious retardation, with islets of normal or exceptional intellectual function.
3   Apparent unawareness of personal identity.
4   Pathological preoccupation with particular objects.
5   Sustained resistance to change.
6   Abnormal response to perceptual stimuli.
7   Acute and illogical anxiety.
8   Speech absent or underdeveloped.
9   Distorted motility [movement] patterns.

(Creak, 1961: 889–890)

It worth noting that there is not one of Creak's Nine Points that would not be accepted today as descriptive of the problems of individuals with what is now

---

[1]Words or phrases in bold type on first occurrence can be found in the Glossary.

called 'autism spectrum disorder' (ASD), except that point 8 applies only to a proportion of people with ASD. Moreover, all of the issues raised in the Nine Points continue to be discussed by diagnosticians and researchers and will come up as topics at various points in this book. This demonstrates the continuity between early theorists' attempts to define and describe autism and those of the present day.

However, the suggestion that children with autism were suffering from childhood schizophrenia was disproved by a study of a large group of children, all of whom had been diagnosed as suffering from 'childhood schizophrenia/psychosis' (Kolvin, 1971). Kolvin found that only those children whose development was essentially normal until the school years showed the hallucinations, delusions and other behavioural abnormalities associated with schizophrenia. By contrast, those children whose abnormal behaviours were apparent before the age of three conformed to Kanner's (1943) description of 'early infantile autism'. Moreover, whereas the parents of the late-onset group showed an unusually high incidence of schizophrenia or **schizoid personality disorder**, this was not the case for parents of children in the early-onset group. Kolvin referred to the early-onset group as having 'infantile psychosis' as opposed to 'late-onset psychosis'. From the early 1970s, therefore, the conflation of autism with childhood schizophrenia ceased. Nevertheless, the relationship between autism and schizophrenia/schizoid personality has remained a topic of interest (King & Lord, 2011).

Back to Kanner

Developments within the field of childhood disorders

These early attempts at description and definition did not take place in a vacuum. On the contrary, they were part of an increasing concern with children's mental health and educational needs which occurred during the third quarter of the last century. And as more became known about the kinds of psychological[2] and behavioural problems that can occur in childhood, it became easier to see what autism *is not*.

In particular, by the mid-1970s it was not only clear that autism is *not* a form of neurosis or psychosis, it was also clear that autism is *not* just a form of intellectual disability comparable to, for example, **Down syndrome**; it is *not* the result of inappropriate learning (which was at one time suggested – see Ferster, 1961); it is *not* just the result of an exceptionally severe language-learning problem (which was also suggested – see Rutter et al., 1971; Churchill, 1972).

Developments relating to autism

At the same time, research into autism itself burgeoned in response to the increasing numbers of children being referred to child development clinics with the kinds of behaviour described by Kanner. The first academic journal devoted to

---

[2]The term 'psychological' is used in this book to refer to all mental faculties, from sensation, perception and emotional experience through to attention, learning and memory, thinking and reasoning, language and literacy, decision-making and action. The term 'cognitive' is reserved for those mental faculties that subserve learning, thinking, reasoning, etc.

research in this field appeared in 1971 (called '*The Journal of Autism and Childhood Schizophrenia*', soon to be changed to '*The Journal of Autism and Developmental Disorders*', as it is known today). Publication of a specialist journal reflected widening acceptance of Kanner's claim that autism is a condition in its own right, and sets of proposed diagnostic criteria for autism began to appear in the English-language literature. The most influential were those of Rutter (1968) in the UK and of Ritvo and Freeman (1977) for the National Society for Autistic Children in the USA.

All the above developments paved the way for the first official recognition of autism as a distinct condition, nearly 40 years after Kanner first described it – as outlined next.

THE FIRST OFFICIAL DEFINITIONS

Successive editions of the American Psychiatric Association's *Diagnostic and Statistical Manual of Mental Disorders* and of the World Health Organisation's *International Classification of Diseases* are internationally recognised as offering the most authoritative classification schemes and diagnostic criteria for health disorders. The *Diagnostic and Statistical Manual* covers mental disorders only, and is most widely used in the States. However, it is also commonly used by researchers in other English-speaking countries who may wish to publish articles in American journals. The *International Classification of Diseases* covers all forms of disease and is used world-wide by members of the medical professions and by health policy professionals. It is the system of choice in Europe, including the UK.

There are more similarities than differences in the classification schemes and diagnostic criteria for autism given in these two influential publications. However, 'autism' was recognised earlier in editions of the *Diagnostic and Statistical Manual* (DSM) than in editions of the *International Classification of Diseases* (ICD). Because of its wider usage in English-speaking countries, the historical development of formal definitions of 'autism' outlined below is based on definitions in successive editions of the DSM. A short account of ICD descriptions of 'autism' follows the account of successive DSM definitions.

Diagnostic and Statistical Manual (DSM) Definitions

DSM-III (American Psychiatric Association (APA), 1980)

'Infantile autism', as it was then called, was first formally recognised as a distinct condition in 1980, in the third edition of the *Diagnostic and Statistical Manual of Mental Disorders*. The condition was defined in terms of four diagnostic criteria:

- Lack of responsiveness to others.
- Impaired language and communication skills.
- Bizarre responses to aspects of the environment.
- Early onset (prior to 30 months).

DSM-III-R (APA, 1987)

Just one year after the first official definition of autism was published in DSM-III, Wing (1981) published a paper on '**Asperger's syndrome**', which made Asperger's description of children with 'autistic psychopathy' accessible to English-language readers for the first time. Wing's paper was influential, not just because Wing herself was a highly respected clinician and academic in the field, but also because what she wrote in that paper was instantly recognised by many clinicians and others as matching their own experience. In her paper, Wing described individuals known to her who had the problems of social relating, communication and behavioural flexibility described by Kanner, but who did not have significant language impairments, nor were they less intelligent than average. Indeed, some had precociously large vocabularies and were highly intelligent. Wing suggested that these able people should be described as having 'Asperger's syndrome'.

When a revised edition of DSM-III, known as DSM-III-R (APA, 1987) appeared, Wing's suggestion was not acted upon. However, the emphasis on impaired language as a necessary criterion for what was now named **autistic disorder** was reduced. Absent or delayed language development was mentioned in the list of the kinds of impairments of communication that might sometimes be associated with autism, but was no longer seen as an essential characteristic without which a diagnosis of autism should not be made. Thus, nearly 50 years after Asperger published his paper, people with social impairments and restricted interests, but with normal language and learning abilities, could be diagnosed with 'autistic disorder'. However, a diagnosis of **Asperger disorder** was not officially sanctioned until the next edition of the DSM, as outlined next.

DSM-IV (APA, 1994)

DSM-IV moved away from conceptualising autism as a single, or '**unitary**', mental health condition, albeit one encompassing an extremely broadly defined and varied group of individuals, as in DSM-III-R. In place of a unitary concept of autism, DSM-IV identified a set of **pervasive developmental disorders (PDDs)**. These were: **autistic disorder, Asperger disorder, pervasive developmental disorder not otherwise specified (PDD-NOS), childhood disintegrative disorder**, and **Rett syndrome**.

Rett syndrome and childhood disintegrative disorder may be characterised by some autistic-like behaviours. However, both these disorders are by definition degenerative conditions with a poor **prognosis**. Although regression occasionally occurs in individuals with the three other forms of PDD (see Chapter 5), continued degeneration is not typical. In the years following the publication of DSM-IV, it therefore became customary to group autistic disorder, Asperger disorder and PDD-NOS as subtypes of autism, leaving question marks over the relationship of Rett syndrome and childhood disintegrative disorder to autism. Diagnostic criteria for all three autism subtypes included social interaction impairments and restricted and repetitive behaviours. Autistic disorder was to be distinguished from Asperger disorder by the presence of language impairments in the former but not the latter condition. PDD-NOS was to be distinguished from the other two conditions by the fact that the social interaction impairment and restricted and repetitive behaviours occurred in mild or atypical form.

DSM-IV-TR (APA, 2000)

DSM-IV was updated in a 'Text Revised' (TR) edition in 2000. In DSM-IV-TR, diagnostic criteria for the three autism subtypes were largely unchanged, although some additional detail was given concerning behaviours that might help to identify cases of PDD-NOS or of Asperger disorder.

International Classification of Diseases (ICD) Definitions

The tenth edition of the *International Classification of Diseases* (ICD-10) published in 1992 by the World Health Organisation (WHO) provided diagnostic criteria for use by clinicians, and the edition published in 1993 provided diagnostic criteria for use by researchers. The research criteria were slightly more detailed and precise than the clinical definitions, reflecting the fact that researchers need to be as certain as possible that the diagnosis really is appropriate, whereas clinicians may need to take a more inclusive approach to diagnosis.

ICD-10, like DSM-IV, conceptualised autism as a set of subtypes coming under the broad heading of PDDs. Suggested names for subtypes differed from those in DSM-IV, being **childhood autism** (instead of 'autistic disorder'), Asperger's syndrome (instead of 'Asperger disorder') and **atypical autism** (instead of 'PDD-NOS'). However, diagnostic criteria for the three subtypes were essentially the same as those in DSM-IV, although behaviours that might be associated with 'Asperger syndrome' were more fully described.

An extended and updated edition of ICD diagnostic criteria and descriptions is due for publication in 2018 following an extended period of consultation and drafting. Those in charge of this process have stated that they aim to align ICD-11 with the latest edition of the DSM (described in the next chapter) as closely as possible. However, there are likely to be slight differences, as in previous editions. Readers interested to follow progress on the development of ICD-11 prior to publication should look for the acronym iCAT, standing for 'internet Collaborative Authoring Tool' on the WHO website.

SUMMARY

Likely cases of autism were occasionally reported from as early as the eighteenth century. However, the first detailed descriptions of autism based on clinical observation were those of Kanner (1943) and Asperger (1944/1991). Asperger's work, written in German, did not become well known in the English-speaking world until the early 1980s; and for 40 years Kanner's view that autism was always associated with language and learning impairments was universally accepted.

Initially, autism was conceptualised as either a form of neurosis associated with inadequate mothering, or as a form of psychosis synonymous with childhood schizophrenia. Both these views had been abandoned by the 1970s in the face of contrary evidence. There was then a return to Kanner's original view that autism is a brain-based, neurodevelopmental condition characterised by a distinctive set of behavioural abnormalities. This view was officially recognised when 'infantile autism' was included in the third edition of the *Diagnostic and Statistical Manual of Mental Health Disorders*, published in 1980. Shortly afterwards, Asperger's work became known, and it was realised that autism-related conditions included people with normal language and intelligence. However, Asperger syndrome as a subtype of autism was not recognised in the diagnostic manuals until the 1990s.

CURRENT CONCEPT
AND DEFINITION

AIMS

The main aims of this chapter are: (1) to give an account of the latest attempt to define and characterise what is now officially named 'autism spectrum disorder'; (2) to outline some of the reasons why this change in name, and other major changes to the definition and description of 'autism', have been made; (3) to indicate some of the objections that may be made to some of these changes; and (4) to indicate how DSM-5 diagnostic criteria and descriptors may apply in practice to a very diverse group of people. An underlying aim of the chapter is to emphasise that because we don't know enough to be able to say definitively what autism *is*, the concept and definition will undoubtedly change again in future years.

INTRODUCTION

Giving a name to anything, such as a kind of tree, an emotion, a colour, a mental health condition, involves agreeing on what the named thing *is*. Naming something is driven by the need to communicate about it, although the reasons why we may need or want to communicate about something are extremely varied. In the case of a mental health condition, the pressure to communicate about it is driven first and foremost by the need to identify the distinctive set of behavioural anomalies or difficulties adversely affecting a particular group of people, so as to develop ways in which their difficulties may be prevented, overcome or alleviated. (For elaboration of these reasons, see Chapter 11, especially the section entitled 'Why Diagnose?')

Sometimes we need to name something tentatively before we can say definitively what it is, improving our understanding over possibly long periods of time. Moreover, improved understanding may result in re-naming something, so as to better represent an updated concept of what the named thing is. For example, astronomers used to refer to what's-out-there-in-space as 'the ether', whereas nowadays astrophysicists might refer more specifically to 'dark matter' (though they are still not able to say exactly what dark matter actually is). The terms used to refer to what in this book is generally called 'autism' are of this kind: from 'childhood schizophrenia/psychosis' to 'early childhood/infantile autism' to 'pervasive developmental disorders' including Asperger syndrome, autistic disorder and PDD-NOS – these are all terms that have in turn been superceded.

This terminological instability results from the fact that autism presents as a complex behavioural condition which we are as yet unable to fully understand or explain, despite the considerable progress that has been made since it was first tentatively identified. Nevertheless, we are getting better at characterising the kinds of behaviour that invariably or commonly occur in the group of people that clinicians and others see as 'autistic'. This progress is reflected in the latest attempt to characterise what autism *is* and to establish evidence-based guidelines for the diagnosis of individuals who are autistic.

In the next section, these guidelines are presented first. Justifications for the latest changes made to the diagnostic terminology and criteria for autism will then be outlined. Objections to some of these changes will be considered. The chapter ends with two thumbnail sketches of real-life individuals, both of whom qualify for a diagnosis of autism spectrum disorder (ASD) despite the diversity of their **manifest behaviours**.[1]

DSM-5 CONCEPT AND DEFINITION

Diagnostic Criteria for Autism Spectrum Disorder

After extensive consultation and deliberation by mental health experts over a 14-year period, a fifth edition of the *Diagnostic and Statistical Manual of Mental Disorders* (DSM-5 – note use of the Arabic numeral) was published by the American Psychiatric Association in 2013.

In DSM-5 the concept of 'autism' was radically changed from the concept that had underpinned the definition of autism in DSM-IV (1994) and DSM-IV-TR (2000) (see Chapter 1). DSM-5 diagnostic criteria for what is now termed 'autism spectrum disorder' are shown in Box 2.1.

Changes from DSM-IV to DSM-5

Seven major changes were made, as outlined below.

1. Whereas DSM-IV had conceptualised autism as a set of related but diagnostically distinct subtypes of 'pervasive developmental disorders', DSM-5 abandoned the PDD-subtypes concept, returning to the earlier notion of autism as a single mental health condition, now referred to as 'autism spectrum disorder'('ASD').
2. For a diagnosis of ASD, behaviour must be significantly impaired in two, instead of three, major ways. Specifically: what were described separately in DSM-IV as 'social interaction impairments' and 'communication impairments' are now combined as 'deficits in social communication and social interaction' (see A. under 'Diagnostic criteria' in Box 2.1).
3. Restricted and repetitive behaviour remains as an essential element in the diagnostic criteria for ASD (see B. under 'Diagnostic criteria' in Box 2.1). However, sensory behaviours are now included as one of the most common forms of restricted, repetitive behaviours (RRBs) (see B.4 under 'Diagnostic criteria' in Box 2.1). Sensory anomalies were not mentioned in DSM-IV, although mentioned in earlier definitions.
4. Diagnostic criteria for ASD are now supplemented by **descriptors**. These concern (a) the *severity* of the criterial impairments or anomalies; and (b) the *presence of any additional diagnosable conditions or special circumstances*, referred to as **specifiers**.
5. Delayed or impaired language is listed as a possible specifier instead of being included as a possible manifestation of 'communication impairment'.

---

[1]Words or phrases in bold type on first occurrence can be found in the Glossary.

6. It is explicitly recognised that the behaviours essential for a diagnosis of ASD, although present from early childhood and retrospectively identifiable, may not 'become fully manifest' and a cause for concern until 'demands exceed limited capacities'.

7. A new diagnostic category, termed **social communication disorder**, is introduced. This diagnosis is intended to apply to individuals who have the socio-emotional-communicative (SEC) impairments and anomalies typical of ASD, but not the RRBs.

Box 2.1   DSM-5 diagnostic criteria and descriptors for autism spectrum disorder

Diagnostic Criteria: All four criteria, A, B, C, and D must be met for a diagnosis of ASD to be made.

A. Persistent deficits in social communication and social interaction across multiple contexts, as manifested by all three of the following, currently or by history (NB: examples are illustrative, not exhaustive).

1. Deficits in social-emotional reciprocity, ranging, for example, from abnormal social approach and failure of normal back-and-forth conversation; to reduced sharing of interests, emotions, or **affect**; to failure to initiate or respond to social interactions.
2. Deficits in nonverbal communicative behaviors used for social interaction, ranging, for example, from poorly integrated verbal and nonverbal communication; to abnormalities in eye contact and body language or deficits in understanding and use of gestures; to a total lack of facial expressions and nonverbal communication.
3. Deficits in developing, maintaining, and understanding relationships, ranging, for example, from difficulties adjusting behavior to suit various social contexts; to difficulties in sharing imaginative play or in making friends; to absence of interest in peers.

B. Restricted, repetitive patterns of behavior, interests, or activities as manifested by at least two of the following:

1. Stereotyped or repetitive speech, motor movements, or use of objects (such as simple motor stereotypies, echolalia, repetitive use of objects, or idiosyncratic phrases).
2. Excessive adherence to routines, ritualized patterns of verbal or nonverbal behavior, or excessive resistance to change (such as motoric rituals, insistence on same route or food, repetitive questioning or extreme distress at small changes).
3. Highly restricted, fixated interests that are abnormal in intensity or focus (such as strong attachment to or preoccupation with unusual objects, excessively circumscribed or perseverative interests).
4. Hyper- or hypo-reactivity to sensory input or unusual interest in sensory aspects of environment (such as apparent indifference to pain/heat/cold, adverse response to specific sounds or textures, excessive smelling or touching of objects, fascination with lights or spinning objects).

C. Symptoms must be present in early childhood (but may not become fully manifest until social demands exceed limited capacities).

D. Symptoms together limit and impair everyday functioning.

Descriptors: Severity Levels and Specifiers

Severity of socio-communicative impairments:

Level 1: 'Requiring support': Without supports in place, deficits in social communication cause noticeable impairments. Has difficulty initiating social interactions and demonstrates clear examples of atypical or unsuccessful responses to social overtures of others. May appear to have decreased interest in social interactions.

Level 2: 'Requiring substantial support': Marked deficits in verbal and nonverbal social communication skills; social impairments apparent even with supports in place; limited initiation of social interactions and reduced or abnormal response to social overtures from others.

Level 3: 'Requiring very substantial support': Severe deficits in verbal and non-verbal social communication skills cause severe impairments in functioning; very limited initiation of social interactions and minimal response to social overtures from others.

Severity of restricted, repetitive behaviors (RRBs):

Level 1: 'Requiring support': RRBs cause significant interference with functioning in one or more contexts. Resists attempts by others to interrupt RRB's or to be redirected from fixated interest.

Level 2: 'Requiring substantial support': RRBs and/or preoccupations or fixated interests appear frequently enough to be obvious to the casual observer and interfere with functioning in a variety of contexts. Distress or frustration is apparent when RRBs are interrupted; difficult to redirect from fixated interest.

Level 3: 'Requiring very substantial support': Preoccupations, fixated rituals and/or repetitive behaviors markedly interfere with functioning in all spheres. Marked distress when rituals or routines are interrupted; very difficult to redirect from fixated interest or returns to it quickly.

Specifiers

- with or without accompanying intellectual impairment
- with or without accompanying language impairment
- associated with known medical or genetic condition or environmental factor
- associated with another neurodevelopmental, mental, or behavioral disorder
- with catatonia
- onset (eg with regression) is to be described

(APA, 2013, with permission)

WHY THE CHANGES?

In what follows, justifications for each of the seven major changes outlined above are considered in turn. There follows a short section summarising possible criticisms of the DSM-5 concept and criteria for ASD.

Why Abandon Subtypes in Favour of a 'Spectrum'?

Fuzzy boundaries

The major problem with the subtypes concept was that it proved difficult in practice to make unambiguous distinctions between the three putative subtypes of autism. As a result, the diagnostic labels were inconsistently applied (Happé, 2011). The distinction between 'autistic disorder' and 'Asperger disorder' ('Asperger syndrome' (AS) as it became more commonly known) was particularly problematic in practice. According to DSM-IV, the presence or absence of impaired language ability is critical to the distinction (see Chapter 1). However, there is currently no evidence of a clear cut-off point between autistic disorder and AS in terms of language ability. Rather, there is a **continuum** of language abilities from superior in some individuals through to good average, to low average, to mild impairment in others, down to moderately, severely, and finally profoundly impaired in yet other individuals. Intelligence, or what will more usually be referred to in this book as 'learning ability' – which was also seen as critical to the distinction between autistic disorder and Asperger disorder – also lies on a continuum varying from superior to profoundly impaired, with all gradations in between.

The lack of clear boundaries between autistic disorder and AS meant that in practice the diagnostic labels were loosely used, with a bias towards inappropriate use of the Asperger label. This bias is understandable, because a diagnosis of AS had more positive connotations than a diagnosis of autistic disorder. The hopes and expectations of parents, teachers and others of a child diagnosed with AS were justifiably quite high in terms of likely ability to do well at school, attend university, find employment and live independently. And expectations are important because to some extent they are self-fulfilling. Similarly, self-esteem need not be adversely affected in an adult with a late diagnosis of AS, whereas a diagnosis of autistic disorder is harder to come to terms with. Understandable as it is, stretching the Asperger label to cover not only borderline cases, but sometimes cases fully meeting criteria for autistic disorder, reduced its meaningfulness and usefulness.

The label 'Asperger syndrome' was also over-used at what might be termed the 'top end' of the autism spectrum, where the boundary between autism and normality/**typicality** is unclear. The term gained a certain cachet from the representation in some popular films and books of people with AS as odd, quirky characters with amazing talents. The upside of the AS label was further enhanced in popular understanding by suggestions that very high-achieving individuals such as Einstein or the philosopher Wittgenstein may have been cases of AS. Thus the

'Asperger' label has risked becoming what Skuse (2011) refers to as 'autism for the middle classes', and what Wing – who first argued for recognition of 'Asperger syndrome' – has referred to as 'a political diagnosis' (quoted in Skuse, 2011).

Over-emphasis on the special abilities of the most able people warranting a DSM-IV diagnosis of AS, combined with under-emphasis of the many negative aspects of the diagnosis (such as vulnerability to bullying at school, and to social isolation, sexual frustration, and anxiety and depression in adulthood), undoubtedly contributed to over-use of the label in everyday speech, including incautious and potentially damaging usage in some instances (see Box 2.2). Whether or not this misrepresentation led to over-use of the label by some clinicians, contributing to the substantial increase over the last decade or two in the reported prevalence of autism-related disorders, is a moot point (see Chapter 5).

Box 2.2   'Shaun': Not autistic – just unhappy

Shaun was just 5;0 when his parents broke up after a tempestuous relationship. Shaun stayed with his mother, and his father was forbidden access to Shaun and his sister whilst being assessed for a mental health disorder. Shaun was considered too young to be told why he could not see his father, but he kept a photograph beside his bed and often asked why he couldn't see his daddy.

When Shaun started in the reception class of primary school, his mother mentioned that she and Shaun's father were separated, but did not give any details. She knew that Shaun was somewhat withdrawn, spending hours playing computer games or drawing imaginary monsters. And he had not yet brought home any friends to play after school. But he had a close loving relationship with her and he was gentle and caring with his baby sister. He was also well ahead of other children in the class in reading and maths, and never got into trouble for bad behaviour.

When attending the first parent-teacher evening, therefore, Shaun's mother expected to get a favourable assessment of Shaun's progress in his first term at school. Instead, the teacher suggested that he might have 'Asperger syndrome' and should be seen by an Educational Psychologist, a suggestion that came out of the blue to Shaun's mother, adding to her own emotional burdens and, indirectly, to Shaun's. Fortunately, after a preliminary assessment, the Educational Psychologist's opinion was reassuring. However, she suggested to Shaun's mother that she should be more open with Shaun's teacher concerning recent family problems, and enlist her help to draw Shaun out of his shell at school. This advice bore fruit. And as things settled down at home, and Shaun got to see his father on a regular basis, he became more outgoing at school, had a circle of good friends – and was happy!

Was the teacher wrong, therefore, to voice her suspicions? Probably yes, in view of the fact that Shaun was so new into school and she knew very little about his home background at this stage. She might have done better to have encouraged the mother to talk about why in her view Shaun was withdrawn at school, and to suggest a need to 'keep an eye on him', preparing cautiously for the possibility of a psychological assessment in the not too distant future.

Diagnostic instability

An additional though very different problem in applying the subtype labels was that individuals change – sometimes showing remarkable improvement; sometimes regressing (Seltzer et al., 2003). One individual – I'll call him Sam – known to me over many years, not only shifted from an authoritative DSM-IV diagnosis of 'autistic disorder' in early childhood to a diagnosis of 'Asperger syndrome' in later childhood, but now – as a young adult – no longer qualifies for any ASD-related diagnosis at all. How did this come about? I have to say that everything was in Sam's favour: a very early diagnosis; parents able to afford every possible kind of appropriate help; a supportive extended family; and parents themselves, both teachers, who became more expert than the experts in understanding autistic behaviour and who devoted themselves to helping Sam (cf. Orinstein et al., 2014). Other cases of **optimal outcome (OO)**, although rare, are now well documented (Fein et al., 2013). As in Sam's case, residual traces of ASD remain, but are so attenuated as not to warrant an ASD diagnosis (Tyson et al., 2014).

Advantages of the spectrum concept

The concept of autism as a spectrum made up of individuals having in common certain kinds of unusual or impaired behaviours, while varying widely in many critical ways, had been argued for as long ago as 1979, as described in Box 2.3.

Box 2.3   The Camberwell Study

In 1979, Wing and Gould published a report of a large-scale study of children with special educational needs (aka 'exceptional children') attending schools in the London area of Camberwell. In this study the clinician-researchers identified some children who had all the behavioural impairments originally described by Kanner (1943), including impaired language and low learning ability; other children who were more able in terms of language and learning abilities, but who were nevertheless 'autistic'; and some children who had some but not all of the behavioural impairments characteristic of autism. Wing and Gould did not see these roughly differentiable groups as clear-cut subtypes of autism. Instead, they wrote first of a *continuum* of autism-related problems, later preferring the term 'the autism spectrum' to refer to the varied forms that autism might take.

In their report of the Camberwell study, Wing and Gould stressed the importance of explicitly recognising that there is a continuum of severity with which autism-related behaviours occur; also that language ability and learning ability vary, covering the full range from entirely normal to profoundly impaired. Finally, Wing and Gould noted that some but not all of the children had additional physical disabilities, medical problems or developmental difficulties and that these, too, might be more or less severe.

In sum, Wing and Gould's report prefigured not only the DSM-5 concept of a spectrum of autistic disorders, but also the descriptors needed to provide a full account of each individual's problems and needs.

The term 'spectrum' allows for the fact that people whose behaviours conform to Asperger's descriptions are clearly very different from people conforming to Kanner's descriptions – as different from each other as the colours at opposite ends of the spectrum of visible light. At the same time, just as violet morphs into blue, then into green, yellow, orange and finally red, the word 'spectrum' captures the fact that there are no clear boundaries between the different forms that autism takes.

The term 'autism spectrum' was, in fact, increasingly commonly used from the 1990s onwards. Some clinicians and researchers preferred to use the term 'autism spectrum disorders' (plural), allowing for the possibility of the identification of discrete subtypes at some future time. Others used the term in its singular form, anticipating DSM-5 usage.

Why Only Two Core Impairments?

Social interaction and communication are inextricably related: all successful communication involves social interaction, whether directly or indirectly; and all truly social interaction involves communication of some kind or another. Certainly, communication can be unsuccessful and fail to achieve the intended interaction. For example, sending messages about humankind into space has not yet, so far as one can tell, achieved the aim of making social contact with aliens. Equally, not all interactions between people are social and therefore communicative. For example, two people might accidentally collide on a crowded street, thus physically interacting but not communicating. However, the overlap and mutual dependencies between social interaction and communication are far more compelling than the differences. That is why 'social interaction impairment' and 'communication impairment' needed to be merged.

Why are Sensory Anomalies Included?

'Abnormal response to perceptual stimuli' was listed as one of 'Creak's Nine Points' (see Box 1.2). Similarly, Ritvo and Freeman's (1977) definition of autism for the National Society for Autistic Children in the US included 'Abnormal responses to sensations: any one or a combination of sight, hearing, touch, pain, balance, smell, taste'. Again, the first official criteria for the diagnosis of autism published as DSM-III in 1980 included 'Bizarre responses to aspects of the environment'. Moreover, first-hand accounts of what it is like to be autistic invariably emphasise peculiarities of sensory-perceptual experience (see Box 3.4, in the next chapter). It is hard to understand, therefore, why sensory abnormalities were not mentioned in DSM-IV, and their re-inclusion in DSM-5 is logical and welcome.

Why Add 'Descriptors'?

Descriptors indicating the severity and complexity of any one individual's condition were introduced across most of the mental health disorders listed in DSM-5.

In the case of ASD, the combination of diagnostic criteria plus these two sets of descriptors is designed to be sufficiently broad to encompass the whole range of people with autism-related behaviours in all their diversity. The introduction of descriptors was also specifically intended to facilitate the development of appropriate, individualised treatment plans.

It remains to be seen how useful the addition of descriptors is in practice. However, official recognition of huge differences in the problems and needs amongst individuals with ASD is to be welcomed in that it helps to counteract any illusion of **homogeneity**, such as may be fostered by bringing together all forms of autism under the single heading of 'Autism Spectrum Disorder'.

Why the Changed Status of Impaired Language?

Until the publication of DSM-5, delayed or impaired language had always been mentioned either as a *necessary* component of a communication impairment (as in Kanner's early formulation) or as a *possible* component of the communication impairment (once Asperger's descriptions became well known). However, if impaired language is not invariably present in people with ASD, then it makes sense to list it as a specifier rather than under the umbrella of 'socio-communicative impairment'.

In making this change, the DSM-5 experts were again going along with a change that was already widely accepted in practice. In particular, it had become commonplace to describe individuals with the hallmark behaviours of autism, but with good language and intellectual abilities, as having 'pure' autism. By implication, those with additional language (and learning) problems were seen as having 'autism + additional problems'.

It may not be immediately obvious why 'communication' and 'language' are considered separable, or, to use the more technical term, '**dissociable**'. After all, human beings communicate via language, pre-eminently, using words and sentences. However, communication is something that we *do*, using spoken and written words, for sure, but also by gestures, facial expressions, body movements, flag-waving, smoke signals, pictorial signs… Language, on the other hand, is something that we *have*: a store of words (or signs) and their meanings; our knowledge of grammar. Asperger (1944/1991) captured this distinction perfectly when he noted that the individuals he was seeing in his clinic had 'good grammar and vocabulary but inappropriate use of speech'. More is said about this important distinction in Chapter 4.

Why Allow for Late Diagnosis?

It has become increasingly common over the last couple of decades for a diagnosis of ASD to be made quite late in childhood, or in adulthood. DSM-5 diagnostic criteria specifically allow for this (see under 'C' in Box 2.1), once again accepting, rather than initiating, a trend that is already well established in practice. Notice, however, that a diagnosis of ASD still requires that signs of autism have been present from quite early in childhood, even if identified only in retrospect.

The increase in late diagnosis undoubtedly largely reflects greater recognition of mild forms of ASD occurring in able individuals who compensate well, and who 'get by' socially – at least until some life event brings their autism-related problems under the spotlight. An academic colleague of mine was diagnosed at the age of 60, when his marriage finally broke up. Recognition of the role of his autistic tendencies in breaking up his marriage made the separation more comprehensible to both him and his wife, softening the elements of blame and recrimination experienced by both partners. Another case of late diagnosis, and the relief it brought to the individual involved, is described in Chapter 11, Box 11.2.

'Social Communication Disorder': What is it, and Why is it Mentioned?

DSM-5 diagnostic criteria for Social Communication Disorder (SCD) can be found on the internet and will not be detailed here. In brief, however, SCD is characterised by persistent difficulties in the social use of verbal and nonverbal communication sufficiently severe as to interfere with social relationships, academic achievement and occupational performance. Communication difficulties will have been present from a very early age, though often not noticed until a child enters school. SCD should only be diagnosed if an individual's communication impairment is not explicable in terms of some other diagnosable condition, such as **learning disability**, deafness, autism, or a speech or language impairment.

The experts who worked over several years to produce DSM-5 justified their introduction of this novel category of mental disorder as follows:

> The SCD diagnosis was needed to ensure that the unique needs of affected individuals are met. … Because the symptoms described in SCD were not defined in previous editions of DSM, many individuals with such symptoms may have been lumped under the 'not otherwise specified' category of 'pervasive development disorder'. This led to inconsistent treatment and services across different clinics and practices. Research shows that communication disorders are amenable to treatment, so identifying distinct communication problems are an important first step in getting people appropriate care. (http://dsm5.org/APA)

Although SCD was not defined in previous editions of the DSM, it had been recognised and well researched long before DSM-5 was published. 'Social communication' problems were first identified in children by Rapin and Allen (1983). These authors described such children as having 'conversational difficulties' or, to use the more technical term, problems of **pragmatics** (see Box 4.2). They suggested that these children also had problems with word meanings ('lexical semantics' – see Box 4.2), and suggested the name '**semantic-pragmatic disorder**' be used to identify children with this combination of problems. Subsequent research, however, showed that although the two types of problem sometimes occur together, they can occur separately and in the absence of the socio-emotional interaction impairments that are a necessary feature of autism (Bishop & Norbury, 2002; Botting & Conti-Ramsden, 2003). DSM-5 was therefore officially recognising a well-justified distinction.

OBJECTIONS TO THE CHANGES

At the time of writing, objections – or fears as to the consequences of – the changes to diagnostic criteria come from people in two interest groups in particular. The first of these consists of people with an existing subtypes diagnosis, and their families. The second group consists of professionals involved in work relating to autism, including some clinicians with responsibility for diagnosis, and also some researchers. The objections or reservations of these two groups are considered separately.

People with an Existing Subtypes Diagnosis, and their Families

Asperger syndrome   When DSM-5 was published in 2013 it was explicitly stated that people who already had a diagnosis of Asperger syndrome would retain that diagnostic label. This assurance did not, however, prevent some adults with the diagnosis from expressing dismay, mainly at the loss of a designation that had, for them, been the linchpin of their sense of identity. For example, one such person blogged: 'The psychiatric bible tells me I'm autistic but in my heart I will always have Asperger's.' Later in his blog this person expressed a sense of distaste and apprehension at being described as 'autistic', writing:

> Asperger's sufferers have been put under a new umbrella called 'autism spectrum disorder', which lumps us in with autistic people who, in some cases, lack the power of speech. . . . (Matthieu Vaillancourt, http://blogs.spectator.co.uk/2015/05)

Some parents of offspring with an existing AS diagnosis have also been vocal about their sense of loss. Elaine Nicholson, for example, writing in a newsletter for the charity 'Action for Aspergers', uses the term 'mourning' to describe how she feels at the loss of 'Asperger syndrome' as a diagnostic category. She, like Matthieu Vaillancourt, is also honest enough to voice fears of the stigmatisation she sees as associated with an 'autism' diagnosis (an unjustified fear according to a survey reported by Ohan et al., 2015).

By no means do all articulate adults with an AS diagnosis feel so negatively, however. Another AS blogger writes:

> I personally think it's a good thing. One of the reasons why I feel this way is that [the Asperger's diagnosis] just seems to have caused so much confusion. I feel that the difference between Aspergers and High Functioning Autism doesn't exist. (http://www.alexlowery.co.uk/)

It is important also to point out that some highly able people with ASD, who are themselves actively involved in understanding and publicising the condition, are happy to refer to themselves as 'autistics', arguing that it is their autism that makes them the people they are (for a discussion of autism-related terminology see Kenny et al., 2015).

It is also pertinent to point out that high-functioning people with ASD have over recent years formed a very strong community, referring to themselves as 'Aspies'. Aspies communicate with each other largely through social media. However, they also organise their own social gatherings and conferences, paying expert 'insider' attention to each other's social, communication and sensory vulnerabilities (for an engaging account see Silberman's award-winning book 'Neurotribes', 2015). Aspies form a powerful lobbying group, arguing with increasing success that they are 'different' but not 'disordered'. This informal, self-named community is not likely to disintegrate with the loss of the AS diagnostic label. So one hopes that individuals such as Matthieu Vaillancourt will in time identify themselves as being an Aspie, and cease to mourn.

Autistic disorder　Families of people with an existing diagnosis of 'autistic disorder' appear not to object to the implication that their offspring should now be referred to as being 'on the autism spectrum' or as having 'ASD' (Kenny et al., 2015). However, some parents have expressed fears that the inclusion of their child under the same diagnostic label as high-functioning people may lead to a reduction of services to the less able. This fear is based on the fact that investment in services for people at the top end of the spectrum produces greater measurable returns, not least economically, than investment for people at the lower end.

PDD-NOS　I have not identified any expressions of concern from individuals with a PDD-NOS diagnosis or their families. This may be because at least some people with this diagnosis would now qualify for a diagnosis of 'Social Communication Disorder', providing a more accurate and helpful description of their major problem than 'PDD-NOS'. There is, however, some concern amongst clinicians that people who might formerly have been diagnosed with PDD-NOS (or 'atypical autism', under ICD-10 criteria) will now go undiagnosed (see below).

Professionals, Especially Clinicians and Researchers

Objections to the change from a subtypes to a spectrum model　Tsai and Ghaziuddin (2014), amongst others, have argued vehemently in support of the subtypes model of ASD as enshrined in DSM-IV, citing numerous studies in which differences have been found between groups diagnosed with either AS or autistic disorder, or with AS or 'high-functioning autism'. Other clinicians and researchers, however, dispute the strength of the evidence (see, for example, Happé, 2011, cited earlier in the chapter).

Another objection to the change from subtypes to a spectrum concept of autism-related conditions is that if there are no longer diagnostic criteria differentiating putative subtypes of ASD, then it will become increasingly difficult for researchers to resolve disputes concerning the existence and validity of such subtypes. It is quite hard to argue with this point, although some authoritative researchers have offered reassurance (Grzadzinski et al., 2013).

Concerns about possible under-diagnosis   Of greater immediate concern is the possibility that DSM-5 criteria for 'Autism Spectrum Disorder' will fail to identify a significant proportion of individuals who would have received a diagnosis using DSM-IV criteria. This concern focuses on individuals with atypical autism who might have been diagnosed with PDD-NOS under DSM-IV criteria; also on high-functioning individuals with two but not all three of the socio-emotional-communicative impairments required for an ASD diagnosis in DSM-5. For representative articles expressing this concern see Mayes et al. (2014) and Tsai (2014). For reassurance relating to this concern, however, see Kent et al. (2013) and Huerta et al. (2012); also the overviews cited below.

Concern as to possible adverse effects on early diagnosis   In a paper published in 2015, Zander and Bölte reported a study the results of which suggested that diagnosis using DSM-5 criteria risked under-diagnosing ASD in toddlers and young children. A multi-centre study using 'gold standard' assessment procedures modified to reflect DSM-5 criteria strengthened this finding (de Bildt et al., 2015). Relatively able young children with 'milder' forms of ASD were particularly likely to be undiagnosed.

In Chapter 11, ongoing improvements to assessment tools, bringing them into line with DSM-5 criteria and increasing their sensitivity to ASD in young children, will be described. This is an example of ways in which some of the teething troubles associated with recent changes in diagnostic practice are likely to be addressed over the next few years. It may be the case, for example, that the requirement of having all three of the socio-emotional-communicative impairments specified in DSM-5 is relaxed. Clinicians with responsibility for diagnosing people for whom a diagnostic label is clearly needed, for whatever reason, will no doubt use their discretion in individual cases.

Accessible overviews of the advantages and disadvantages of the changes to autism diagnosis introduced in DSM-5 can be found in Halfon and Kuo (2013) (written for paediatricians) and by Hazen et al. (2013) (written for psychiatrists). Other useful summaries can be found in Lai et al. (2013) (predominantly positive) and in Volkmar and Reichow (2013) (somewhat more negative).

APPLYING THE CRITERIA IN PRACTICE

Generalised versus Manifest Behaviour

Descriptions of the criterial features of behaviour presented in diagnostic manuals are highly *generalised*. So, for example, under A.1. in DSM-5, it is stated that for a diagnosis of ASD to be appropriate there must be 'Deficits in social-emotional reciprocity, ranging, for example, from abnormal social approach and failure of normal back-and-forth conversation; to reduced sharing of interest, emotions, or affect; to failure to initiate or respond to social interactions'. But these phrases do not identify any actual, concrete instances of what might constitute, for example, 'abnormal social approach' or 'reduced sharing of emotions'. This is inevitable because diagnostic criteria are designed to apply equally to children and adults; to those with high intelligence and good language as well as to those with profound language and learning impairments; and to individuals with their own personalities and past experiences in all the different environments in which they might be observed – at home, at school, at work, on holiday, when well, when ill, etc. However, the need to generalise entails that the phrases used in the diagnostic manuals fail to convey the diversity of actual, *manifest* behaviour that might contribute to a diagnosis of ASD. Consider, for example, how the actual behaviour of the two children described in the following 'thumbnail sketches' qualifies both of them for a diagnosis of ASD:

Mandy, age 8 years observed in the school playground at break time Mandy is sitting on a swing, passively; this is where she is usually to be found at playtime. When another child approaches, she doesn't look at the child, but gets off the swing and moves to a corner of the playground with her back to the other children. She rocks from foot to foot. At one point she utters an odd squeal and flaps her hands excitedly, for no apparent reason. Then she begins to hit her own head with her hand. The adult on playground duty approaches, takes Mandy's hand to stop her hitting herself, and says: 'Did you want to have a swing, Mandy? Look, there's a swing free now.' Mandy removes her hand from the adult's and turns away saying 'free now'. But she doesn't go towards the vacant swing. Instead she runs off, with a clumsy gait, bumping into a smaller child who falls over and begins to cry. Mandy stops running, puts her hands over her ears and stands looking at the weeping child, with an uncomprehending, distressed expression on her face.

Damien, age 15 years, observed at home Damien is sitting at the dining room table, tracing a map of New Zealand with extreme care. He tells the observing adult that he is interested in geology, and asks, rhetorically: 'Do you know the difference between a fjord and a sound?' The adult smiles and says: 'That's a funny question! They're quite different sorts of things, aren't they?' Damien ignores the observer's response and continues with what he was going to say anyway, providing the textbook definitions of a fjord as opposed to a sound (as in Queen Charlotte Sound, in New Zealand). Damien's mother comes in carrying a tray with cutlery, plates, glasses, etc. to lay the table, and asks Damien to move his things and feed the dog before tea. Damien complies slowly, putting away his pencils, ruler, tracing pad, etc. carefully in different compartments of a drawer, while his mother waits to put the tray down. He then opens a tin of dog food, fills the dog's bowl, and puts it in the usual place, but does not call the dog in from the garden. He tells the observer that he is taking four subjects in his next set of school exams and expects to get top grades and go to university to study geology. The observer volunteers the information that her own son is, by chance, already studying geology at university, but Damien doesn't follow this up. Instead he asks: 'Did you know that New Zealand is 268,000 square kilometres in size, and two thirds the size of California?' When it is time for the observer to leave, Damien's mother says: 'See the lady to the door, Damien'. Damien rises reluctantly to his feet and walks behind the observer as far as the front door, immediately turning back without returning her wave.

DSM-5 attempts to capture some of the differences in the manifest behaviour of individuals, using 'severity' as a descriptor. It may be helpful in addition to consider the range of manifest behaviours indicative of autism in terms of qualitative differences in the kinds of behaviours that may be seen across the spectrum. Regarding socio-communicative abnormalities, for example, Wing (1996) identified four qualitatively different patterns of socio-communicative abnormalities, as summarised in Box 2.4.

Box 2.4   Wing's four types of autism-related social behaviour

The *aloof group* behave as though other people did not exist. They might, for example, obliviously bump into someone who is coming through a door towards them carrying a tray of drinks. They do not respond to, or willingly accept, social approaches from others. For example, an 'aloof' 4;0 year old will struggle to get free if picked up to sit on an adult's knee. An 'aloof' adult may get up and move away if another person sits on a seat beside them.

The *passive group* are not completely cut off from others. They accept social approaches but do not initiate social interaction. For example, if picked up to sit on an adult's knee, a 4;0 year old 'passive' child will not wriggle off the adult's lap, but will prefer to sit facing forwards, avoiding eye contact or face-to-face interaction. A 'passive' adult will tolerate having someone come to sit beside them, but will not initiate conversation.

The *active but odd group* make social approaches to other people, but do so in a peculiar one-sided fashion. Repetitive questioning is a feature of this group, who have the motivation to make social contact but do not have varied means of achieving this. So, for example, an 'active but odd' teenager or adult may approach a visitor to their school or college repeatedly asking 'What's your name?'… 'What's your name?'… A more able individual may monologue about their own special interest, regardless of the other person's attempts either to join in or to change the subject.

The *overly formal, stilted group* are highly able adolescents or adults who are excessively polite and formal. They try very hard to behave well and cope by sticking rigidly to the rules of social interaction.

Wing did not see her 'aloof', 'passive', 'active-but-odd' and 'stilted' descriptions as identifying discrete subgroups, but rather as typifying points along a continuum of socio-communicative abnormalities/oddities. Moreover, she stressed that – given appropriate intervention and support – individuals' behaviour often changes over time. For example, the 'aloof' child who buries her head in her arms to escape other people (e.g. Mandy) may become a 'passive' child who tolerates being touched, and who will hold the teacher's hand although never initiating contact herself. And the 'active-but-odd' adolescent who initiates conversation, even if clumsily (e.g. Damien), may in time learn the 'rules' of acceptable socio-communicative behaviour and achieve less self-centred, albeit somewhat 'stilted', interaction.

Similarly, restricted and repetitive behaviours may be described as lying along a continuum from self-stimulatory stereotypic movements (rocking, hand-flapping, biting the backs of the hands), through to pre-occupation with the manipulation of objects or materials (turning on light switches or taps; letting sand slide through the fingers; twiddling a drinking straw held very close to the eyes), to insistence on routines (e.g. for eating, dressing, the route taken to school) and maintenance of sameness (e.g. of the arrangement of furniture in a room), to repetitive utterances – idiosyncratic or ostensibly meaningful but inappropriately used, to restricted interests and strongly preferred topics of conversation (e.g. dinosaurs, railway timetables, military equipment), to the **adaptive** (i.e. constructively useful) amassing of factual knowledge relevant to certain areas of legitimate study, and 'one-track-mindedness' in pursuing a particular hobby or interest.

SUMMARY

The DSM-5 concept and diagnostic criteria for autism changed from those in DSM-IV in quite radical ways, including the following. First, the concept of subtypes of pervasive developmental disorder was abandoned in favour of the concept of autism as an indivisible spectrum of related conditions. Secondly, a diagnosis of autism spectrum disorder requires that two, rather than three, major behavioural anomalies are present, namely SECs and RRBs. Thirdly, behaviours coming under the heading of RRBs include hyper- and hypo-sensitivity to sensory stimuli. Fourthly, individuals satisfying the two basic criteria for ASD are differentiated by two groups of 'Determiners': the *severity* of SEC impairments and RRBs, and the absence or presence of additional *specifiers*. The most commonly occurring specifiers are recognised as being learning disability and language impairment. Other specifiers include various comorbid medical conditions. Finally, a condition to be known as 'Social Communication Disorder' is for the first time recognised in DSM-5 and differentiated from ASD. These changes, which were agreed upon by experienced clinicians in the field who consulted widely with other 'stakeholders' over an extended period, have had a mixed reception. Inevitably, it is those with the negative reactions who have been the most vocal in the first years following publication of DSM-5. In particular, some individuals with an existing diagnosis of Asperger syndrome, or who have committed much of their lives to working with and for people with AS, feel a sense of betrayal. There is also some evidence that DSM-5 criteria may be too restrictive, with the danger that some individuals who should be diagnosed with ASD are not identified using currently available assessment methods. To illustrate the difficulties of formulating diagnostic guidance that is sufficiently general to identify individuals from the bottom to the top of the spectrum, the chapter closes with 'thumbnail sketches' of two extremely different children whose behaviour in both cases satisfy DSM-5 criteria.

THE FULLER PICTURE:
SHARED CHARACTERISTICS

INTRODUCTION

EXPANDING THE DIAGNOSTIC DESCRIPTIONS
Social, Emotional and Communicative Impairments
Restricted, Repetitive Behaviours and Sensory-Perceptual Anomalies

SOME ADDITIONAL SHARED CHARACTERISTICS
Imagination and Creativity: Strengths and Weaknesses
Islets of Ability
Motor Skills: Strengths and Weaknesses
Impaired Sense of Self

SUMMARY

AIMS

The main aim of this chapter is to provide a more detailed account than has been given so far of what people on the autism spectrum have in common with each other, even when the actual manifestations of these characteristics vary across individuals and over time. Subsidiary aims are: (1) to ensure an appreciation of the complexity of the behavioural, physical and medical characteristics that may occur in individuals with a diagnosis of ASD; (2) to stress strengths as well as 'impairments' or 'anomalies'.

INTRODUCTION

Chapter 2 presented and discussed the latest attempt to identify the distinctive behaviours that people with ASD have in common with each other, behaviours that can be said to be **pathognomic**[1] of ASD. Although accepting that there are differences in the *severity* with which these pathognomic behaviours occur, and differences relating to *whether or not additional conditions are present*, DSM-5 presents a 'bare bones' answer to the question 'What is autism?' A fuller picture than has been presented so far is important for establishing 'What has to be explained' in Part II of the book, concerning causes of autism. It is also important for identifying and responding accurately and appropriately to the practical needs of individuals within the ASD population, to be discussed in Part III. In this chapter, therefore, the bare bones account of the diagnostic impairments will be fleshed out. Some other behavioural characteristics that people with ASD almost certainly share, but which are not mentioned in DSM-5, will also be described.

EXPANDING THE DIAGNOSTIC DESCRIPTIONS

Social, Emotional and Communicative Impairments

Impaired dyadic interaction[2]

The earliest signs that an individual may at some future time warrant a diagnosis of autism occur long before most of the socio-emotional-communicative (SEC) impairments described in DSM-5 are readily apparent. **Retrospective studies** of family videos, also **prospective studies** of infants at risk for autism, indicate that

---

[1]Words or phrases in bold type on first occurrence can be found in the Glossary.

[2]Another term used to refer to one-to-one social interactions in infancy is **primary intersubjectivity**, but 'dyadic interaction' will be used here. Similarly, the term 'triadic interaction' will be preferred to the alternative term, **secondary intersubjectivity.**

the earliest signs of **prodromal autism** are a lack of **dyadic interaction** behaviours such as making eye contact or responding to their own name.

Dyadic social interactions involve two people attending solely to each other. Typically developing babies' earliest social interactions are all of this one-to-one kind. So, for example, within the first two months of life typically developing infants smile in response to another's smile and hold another's face-to-face gaze as if entranced. They also involuntarily imitate other people's facial movements, such as opening the mouth or protruding the tongue. Within the first six months they engage in face-to-face lap play, initiating and turn-taking in **protoconversations** or games such as peek-a-boo, unconsciously synchronising their own sounds and movements with those of the other person (Trevarthen & Aitken, 2001; Sigman et al., 2004). Dyadic social interaction continues throughout life, typically occurring in the context of intimate relationships.

Prospective studies suggest that babies who will later be diagnosed with ASD have relatively normal one-to-one interactions with primary caregivers in their earliest months, but lose these some time between the ages of six months and 24 months (Zwaigenbaum et al., 2013; Jones et al., 2014). This age range corresponds to the range of ages-of-onset of ASD identified by parental report (see Chapter 5). Dyadic interaction never regains complete normality in people with ASD, although targeted intervention may ameliorate the impairments.

Impaired triadic interaction

Triadic interactions involve two people attending to the same thing: 'you, me, and X'. Within the first six months of life, typically developing infants will turn their heads to look where someone else is looking, a response known as **gaze following**. By the end of their first year, they will turn back to check where the other person is looking, demonstrating implicit (subconscious) awareness that something in the environment can be the object of **shared** or **joint attention** – 'What I see, you see', or 'What I find interesting/funny/scary, you may also find interesting/funny/scary'. In the first half of their second year they start to use **protodeclarative pointing** to draw someone else's attention to something of interest, as illustrated in Figure 3.1.

Children with ASD have long been known to lack these early mind-sharing behaviours (Curcio, 1978; Loveland & Landry, 1986), and an absence of joint attention behaviours, in particular a lack of protodeclarative pointing, is one of the most reliable early indications that a toddler is autistic (see Chapter 11).

Impaired mindreading

'**Mindreading**' is a broad term covering all kinds of insights and understandings of other people's minds, from an implicit (unconscious) appreciation that 'What I see, you see' (as illustrated in Figure 3.1), to the ability to reason consciously about what another person believes, knows, feels, wants etc., and to predict their behaviour accordingly.

The phrase '**theory of mind**' **(ToM)** is frequently used in the same broad sense as 'mindreading'. However, 'ToM' will be used narrowly here. Specifically, **implicit ToM** will be used to refer to *unconscious* knowledge of what another person may see, feel, know, etc. **Explicit ToM** will be used to refer to the *conscious* verbalisable

Figure 3.1 *Protodeclarative pointing and joint attention*

knowledge of what another person sees, etc. Explicit ToM ability brings with it the capacity to reason about the contents of another person's mind and to make a verbalisable prediction about their behaviour. Theory of mind tests, whether of implicit or explicit ToM, are widely known as '**false belief tasks**'. Over the years since the early 1980s when the first test of explicit ToM in typically developing children was reported, numerous versions of false belief tasks have been used. Most commonly these involve the acting out of scenarios using puppets or dolls, or verbally presented stories with illustrative drawings. Examples of tests used to assess explicit ToM and implicit ToM, respectively, are outlined in Box 3.1.

Studies of implicit ToM show that typically developing 1;0 year olds already have implicit ToM: they involuntarily glance towards the empty box (Onishi & Baillargeon, 2005; Kovács et al., 2010). By contrast, tests of explicit ToM are not passed by typically developing children until around the age of 4;0 years.

As has long been known, school-age children and adults with ASD struggle to succeed on tests of explicit ToM (Baron-Cohen et al., 1985; Yirmiya et al., 1998). More recently, direction-of-looking studies have shown that all individuals with an ASD diagnosis lack implicit ToM: even highly intelligent adults with ASD who can succeed on explicit ToM tasks by effortful reasoning (Happé, 1994) fail to look involuntarily towards where another person will mistakenly seek a hidden object (Senju et al., 2009; Schneider et al., 2013).

Box 3.1   Examples of test formats commonly used to assess (a) explicit ToM and (b) implicit ToM

(a) A test of explicit ToM

A doll-sized box and a basket, both with lids/covers, are placed side by side, a small distance apart.

A doll, 'Sally', enters, holding a marble.

Sally puts the marble into the basket, replaces the lid, and exits.

A second doll, 'Ann', enters, goes to the basket, takes out the marble and places it in the box, replaces both lids, then exits.

Sally returns.

The Tester asks the child: 'Where will Sally look for her marble?'

To give a correct answer, the individual being tested must consciously and explicitly know that Sally holds the false belief that the marble is in the basket where she placed it, and that she will therefore look for the marble in the basket. The individual being tested must also have sufficient language to understand and to respond to the test question.

(b) A test of implicit ToM

A mini-movie shown on a computer depicts a person (e.g. a teenage girl/young woman) facing the camera, looking onto a toy-sized 'stage' set up between them and the camera. There are two boxes on the stage, both with lids on.

A puppet enters and places a toy in one of the boxes and replaces the lid before exiting, watched by the girl. For several runs of the mini-film a 'chime' is then heard, after which the girl reaches in to retrieve the toy.

Once it has been established that the individual being tested (the 'testee') automatically (i.e. without thinking/unconsciously) *expects* the girl to reach towards the box where the toy is hidden and therefore *looks* towards that box when the chime is heard, the film changes, as follows.

After placing the toy in one or other of the boxes, the puppet returns and – unseen by the girl who has just turned her back to the camera – moves the toy to the other, previously empty, box, replacing both lids before exiting.

The girl turns round, the chime is heard, and an eye-tracking device on the computer records the testee's direction of looking: will they 'know' (at some unconscious level) that because the girl didn't see the toy being moved she has a false belief concerning the location of the toy? If so, the testee will *expect* the girl to reach into the wrong box, and they will therefore *involuntarily glance* at the now-empty box when the chime is heard.

Impaired emotion processing

To understand the pattern of emotion-processing abilities and disabilities in people with ASD it is necessary to establish some key terms and concepts. These are presented in Box 3.2.

Box 3.2 Terms used in the psychological study of emotion

Affect is a term used by psychologists to mean emotion.

Basic emotions are those that are universal in humans: happiness, sadness, anger, fear and disgust (surprise is sometimes included).

Complex emotions are those that are dependent on understanding how others see us, for example, pride, guilt, embarrassment.

Emotion contagion aka **contagious/affective empathy**[*] refers to the most primitive form of emotion processing, or affect processing, and consists of the involuntary sharing of others' basic emotions. Emotion contagion produces physiological changes such as increased heart rate, or sweating, which may be accompanied by involuntary behaviours such as laughing or crying along with the laughter or tears of another person. This 'infectious behaviour' can occur in the absence of knowing what the other person is laughing or crying about.

Cognitive empathy[*] is the term used to describe intuitive knowledge of the cause or 'content' of an experienced emotion: knowing what the emotion is *about*. The fact that experiencing an emotion can be differentiated from knowing what the emotion is about is evident from the common experience of waking in the morning with a sinking feeling but momentarily not knowing the cause of the feeling (e.g. the exam to be taken, the bad news received the previous day).

Alexithymia is a clinical condition characterised by lack of intuitive knowledge of the content of one's own emotions, and inability to identify or describe one's own emotions.

Sympathy[*] is sometimes used to refer to the desire to take action in response to the emotions of other people, for example, to alleviate their pain or to soothe their anger.

The empathising system is a term introduced by Baron-Cohen (2005: 2) to refer to 'The ability to identify another person's emotions and thoughts and to respond to these with an appropriate emotion'. Thus, the system comprises affective empathy, cognitive empathy, and sympathy, as defined above.

[*] 'Empathy' and 'sympathy' are often used loosely and interchangeably in everyday speech. Moreover, these terms may be differently defined in other specialist literatures. The definitions given here are those most commonly used in the autism literature.

The ability to *experience basic emotions* is intact in people with ASD: they smile when they are happy, cry when they are sad, scowl and shout when they are angry – even if the actual sounds they make, the facial expressions and bodily gestures they produce, are not always quite like those of other people (Yirmiya et al., 1989). By contrast, the ability to *identify the basic emotions of other people* from their facial expressions is generally impaired, especially for negative emotions. When others' facial expressions of emotion are correctly identified it is generally thought that success is achieved in ways that are qualitatively different from **neurotypical** processing of facial expressions (Harms et al., 2010).

The ability to *experience complex emotions*, or to *identify complex emotions in others*, is impaired (Baron-Cohen, 1991). Understanding complex emotions such as pride or embarrassment involves 'seeing ourselves as others see us', and people with ASD are not good at doing this (Capps et al., 1992). So, for example, many adolescents and adults with autism have to be taught that completing a task successfully may win praise, or that appearing in public in states of undress will embarrass others.

Emotion contagion/affective empathy has been shown to be unimpaired in individuals diagnosed with ASD (Blair, 1999; Ben Shalom et al., 2006). Children with autism are not oblivious to the emotion of others, and one screaming child in a room full of children with autism will produce signs of arousal and even distress in the other children. Similarly, experienced teachers will often say that children with autism whom they teach, even those who are quite severely learning disabled, are quick to pick up nervousness or apprehension in a novice teacher and, completely unconsciously, behave in an anxious or disorganised way as a 'contagious' response.

Cognitive empathy, on the other hand, is impaired (Jones et al., 2010; Mazza et al., 2014). Mandy, for example, one of the children described in the thumbnail sketches in Chapter 2, does not appear to understand that the child she knocks over is crying because she is hurt.

Sympathy is also, inevitably, impaired. Because people with ASD do not intuitively know what another person's emotion is about, they do not have the usual impulse to make an appropriate response. High-functioning individuals with ASD may consciously work out what another person's expressions of emotion are about, and they may act on what they know, consciously, to be an appropriate response – for example, offering to find a plaster for someone's bleeding finger. However, this process lacks the immediacy and intimacy of intuitive cognitive empathy and sympathy.

The problem of knowing what another person's emotion is about may extend to knowing what one's own emotion is about (Hill et al., 2004; Faran & Ben Shalom, 2008). This may explain why children with ASD ask questions such as 'Did I like it when I went on the bouncy castle?' or 'Was I frightened when I went on the aeroplane?' They may remember going on the bouncy castle or the trip on the aeroplane, but have no memory of whether it was frightening or fun. Inability to identify the content of one's own emotions causes *alexithymia* (Lombardo et al., 2007).

Fuller accounts than can be given here of emotion-processing abilities in ASD can be found in Gaigg (2012) and Hobson (2014).

Communication impairments

Communication is always, by definition, impaired in people on the autism spectrum, including the most able. It could not be otherwise, given that impaired social interaction is at the heart of autism, and communication is involved in almost every form of social interaction, as noted in Chapter 2.

It is important to appreciate that both the *means of communication* used by humans, and also *the rules for engaging in communicative episodes*, are impaired. The means of communication are language – whether spoken, written, signed, or conveyed in some other way – and nonverbal signals including facial expressions, body orientation and movements, gestures, and vocalisations such as laughing or crying. Speech prosody, i.e. the acoustic patterns of pitch, rhythm, etc. that help to convey meaning, as well as conveying states of mind and the emotions of speakers, may also be considered a form of communication (see Box 4.2). Language is sometimes but not always impaired across the spectrum. By contrast, the understanding and, to a lesser extent, the use of **nonverbal communication** signals is invariably impaired (Spezio et al., 2007; Peppé et al., 2011; Watson et al., 2013).

The rules and conventions for using language and nonverbal communication signals to communicate come under the heading of pragmatics (Leinonen et al., 2000; Perkins, 2007). Pragmatics is invariably impaired across the spectrum (for a short review, see the section on 'Language Use' in Kim et al. (2014). Some examples of the kinds of pragmatic impairments commonly observed in people with ASD are given in Box 3.3.

Mutism   In addition to the communication impairments that are universal in people with ASD, a communication impairment called **selective** or **elective mutism** occasionally co-occurs with autism. In this condition, which is not confined to people with ASD, the individual understands at least some spoken language, and in some cases may speak in some environments and situations, but not in others. So, for example, a child may speak at home but not at school; or with adults but not with other children. Selective/elective mutism is generally an anxiety-related or phobic condition (Cline & Baldwin, 2004). A rare minority of individuals with ASD have a form of mutism that appears to result from a physical difficulty in initiating and/or co-ordinating actions required for language output, regardless of whether speech, writing, signing or typing is used (Rapin, 1996). People with this kind of **pervasive mutism** can understand at least some spoken (and possibly written) language, but can only express themselves nonverbally.

Box 3.3   Examples of pragmatic impairments in people with ASD

Inappropriate topic initiation and topic maintenance, e.g. introducing a novel topic midway through a conversation and without warning; talking repetitively about their preferred topic even if their interest is not shared; not responding to a question; repeating questions which have already been answered.

Lack of conversational 'coherence', e.g. failing to identify what or whom they are talking about; recounting events in a disconnected order; making remarks that are irrelevant to the ongoing conversation.

Failure to take account of 'where the other person is coming from', e.g. recounting the story of a film to someone who they know has seen it; failure to modify their conversation when talking to a teacher as opposed to a classmate; making tactless and/or personal remarks.

Poor 'conversational rapport', e.g. ignoring conversational approaches from others; not paying attention when someone is talking to them; not looking at the person they are talking to.

Repetitiveness, e.g. using 'favourite' words, phrases or sentences, regardless of appropriacy; turning conversation to certain preferred topics and repeating information or views they have aired many times previously.

Restricted, Repetitive Behaviours and Sensory-Perceptual Anomalies

Restricted, repetitive behaviours

Two broad categories of restricted, repetitive behaviours (RRBs) are generally recognised: '**repetitive sensory-motor stereotypies**' (**RSMs**) and '**insistence on sameness**' (**IS**). RSMs referred to in DSM-5 can affect movements (e.g. hand-flapping), use of objects (e.g. lining up toys), or speech (e.g. **echolalia**). One important form of RSM not mentioned in DSM-5 is **self-injurious behaviours** (**SIBs**), such as head banging, eye-poking, or hand-biting. Forms of IS identified in DSM-5 cover a wide range of behaviours, all of which serve to effectively reduce novelty and promote predictability in the individual's immediate environment and experience.

It is recognised in DSM-5 that RRBs tend to change over time. For example, RSMs such as hand flapping or SIBs are common in young children with ASD but less common in adults, except those who are very low-functioning. Similarly, echolalia is quite common in young children but less common in adults, except those with very little language. Older as well as more able people with ASD are more likely to have IS behaviours which have adaptive value for the individual. So, for example, the habit of lining up toys may be replaced by routines such as always putting on clothes in the same order, or laying the family meal table in exactly the same way. Similarly, as comprehension improves, echolalia may be replaced by use of **formulaic** phrases and mono-loguing on a preferred topic (forms of IS). So the repetitiveness remains, but is manifested in different ways.

Sensory-perceptual anomalies

Sensory information may be understood as raw, or unelaborated, data from the senses, in contrast to **perception**, which involves the elaboration and interpreta-tion of sensory data – making sense of it. **Sensation** and perception are, however, so closely linked and interactive, including top-down influences from perception to sensation as well as bottom-up input from sensation to perception, that for present purposes the two will not be differentiated. In Chapter 9, however, where possible causes of sensory-perceptual anomalies in autism are considered, the dis-tinction will sometimes be made.

First-hand accounts of what it is like to be autistic invariably emphasise prob-lems to do with the processing of sensory-perceptual information. Some excerpts from first-hand accounts are shown in Box 3.4.

Impairments and anomalies of sensation in people with ASD have been demon-strated in research studies and are frequently commented on by parents and carers. Summaries of observations across the senses are given below.

Hearing   The prevalence of hearing impairment in ASD is uncertain, with some studies showing increased prevalence, while others report negative findings (Beers et al., 2014). People with intellectual disability, with or without autism, have higher rates of hearing impairment than the general population (McClimens et al., 2015), which may help to explain the discrepant findings on hearing loss across the spectrum in ASD.

Apart from increased incidence of hearing impairment (at least in less able people with ASD), certain hearing anomalies occur, corresponding to some of those reported in first-hand accounts (see Box 3.4). In particular, increased sensitiv-ity to sound, or **hyperacusis**, is quite frequently observed in people with autism (Rosenhall et al., 1999). Particular sounds may become the focus of a phobic resistance to certain places or situations, such as travelling on the underground, or going to an event where fireworks may be let off. Whether or not hyperacusis is, strictly speaking, a hearing problem is, however, open to question (Stiegler & Davis, 2010). Similarly, reported difficulties in discriminating speech against back-ground noise (Alcántara et al., 2004) may possibly be ascribed to an abnormality of **attention** as opposed to a hearing anomaly. Certain facets of the perception of sound may be better than those of ordinary people of similar age. For example, people with ASD have a better sense of musical pitch than people in the general population (Heaton et al., 1998).

Vision   Visual impairment in the sense of decreased visual acuity is relatively common in people with ASD (Pring, 2005). Certain anomalies of vision and visual perception also occur, as in the case of hearing. In particular, peripheral vision may be utilised to an unusual extent (Lord et al., 2000). Over-sensitivity

---

Box 3.4　First-hand accounts of sensory-perceptual experiences in very high-functioning individuals with autism-related characteristics

Darren White (quoted in White & White, 1987: 224) 'I was rarely able to hear sentences because my hearing distorted them. I was sometimes able to hear a word or two at the start and understand it and then the next lot of words sort of merged into one another and I could not make head or tail of it.... Sometimes when other kids spoke to me I could scarcely hear them, and sometimes they sounded like bullets. I thought I was going to go deaf. I was also frightened of the vacuum cleaner, the food mixer and the liquidiser because they sounded about five times as loud as they actually were. Life was terrifying...'

John van Dalen (quoted in Boucher, 1996: 84, 85) 'My way of perceiving things differs from that of other people. For instance, when I am confronted with a hammer, I am initially not confronted with a hammer at all but solely with a number of unrelated parts: I observe a cubical piece of iron near to a coincidental bar-like piece of wood. After that, I am struck by the coincidental nature of the iron and the wooden thing resulting in the unifying perception of a hammerlike configuration. The name "hammer" is not immediately within reach but appears when the configuration has been sufficiently stabilised over time. Finally, the use of a tool becomes clear when I realise that this perceptual configuration known as a "hammer" can be used to do carpenter's work.'

Temple Grandin (Grandin & Scariano, 1986: 32) 'Wool clothing is intolerable for me to wear. . . . I dislike nightgowns because the feeling of my legs touching each other is unpleasant.'

Jim Sinclair (reported in Cesaroni & Garber, 1991) 'Sometimes the channels get confused, as when sounds come through as colour. Sometimes I know that something is coming in somewhere, but I can't tell right away what sense it's coming through.'

Donna Williams (Williams, 1994: 22) 'In my dark cupboard ... the bombardment of bright light and harsh colours, of movement and blah-blah-blah, of unpredictable noise and the uncontrollable touch of others were all gone. Here there was no final straw to send me from overload into the endless void of shutdown.'

to visual stimuli also occurs. For example, some people with ASD prefer to watch television with the brightness turned down. Impaired processing of visual motion (seen movement) has been reported in several studies (Gepner & Mestre, 2002; Milne et al., 2005). Visual detail may be perceived in place of whole objects or scenes, making the perception of whole objects effortful and slow, as described by John van Dalen in Box 3.4. However, good perception of detail has some advantages: for example, it enables people with ASD to notice small changes in familiar surroundings, and to outperform people without autism in certain psychological tests. Further evidence of the processing of detail as opposed to wholes will be presented and discussed in Chapter 9. A comprehensive review of research on visual processing in ASD can be found in Dakin and Frith (2005).

Taste, smell and touch   Hypersensitivity to taste, smell and/or touch is not uncommon, according to parental reports and first-hand accounts. One girl with autism commented that nearly everyone has bad breath (Stehli, 1992). A child I worked with had a habit of approaching strangers and putting her face close to theirs in order to sniff them.

Pain   Sensitivity to pain, on the other hand, is generally considered to be low, making people with ASD vulnerable to injury, and it has been suggested that self-injurious behaviours are experienced as pleasurable self-stimulation, rather than as painful (Allely, 2013). However, see Moore (2014) regarding incidents of hyper- rather than hypo-sensitivity.

Synaesthesia and overload   Information from the various senses may be confused, as in the condition known as **synaesthesia,** where, for example, sound may be perceived in terms of colour, or colours may be perceived in terms of taste and smell (Baron-Cohen et al., 2013). Information arriving from the different sensory channels can also be experienced as confusing to the point of being overwhelming, as vividly described in the last quote in Box 3.4.

Over-focused attention   Wendy Lawson, a very able person with ASD, has suggested that people with ASD have **monotropic attention**, in the sense of only being able to attend to a limited range of sensory inputs at any one time (Murray et al., 2005). This suggestion is consistent with early studies reporting **over-selective attention** in people with ASD (Rincover & Ducharme, 1987) and is also consistent with some of the superior abilities noted above, such as unusual sensitivity to musical pitch and to visual detail. It might also help to explain why complex or multi-sensory inputs are experienced as confusing and overwhelming, leading to the defensive reaction of **shutdown** referred to by Donna Williams (Box 3.4) and endorsed in many other first-hand accounts. However, an understanding of the precise nature of processes associated with attention in ASD has proved elusive (Ames & Fletcher-Watson, 2010).

Comprehensive reviews of evidence on sensory-perceptual processing in people with ASD can be found in Iarocci and McDonald (2006) and Baranek et al. (2014).

Links between sensory-perceptual anomalies and repetitive restricted behaviours

The inclusion of sensory anomalies within the set of RRBs in DSM-5 was based on research showing that repetitive behaviours and sensory anomalies in ASD are related. This relationship had, in fact, been noted and discussed decades ago (see, for example, Hutt et al., 1964; Ornitz, 1976; Zentall & Zentall, 1983), but then dropped below the threshold of most researcher/theoreticians' attention until around the turn of the century. At that time, a review of sensory anomalies in ASD by O'Neill and Jones (1997) and empirical studies by Gal et al. (2002) and others brought this relationship back under the spotlight.

These researchers concluded that individuals who frequently engage in repetitive sensory-motor stereotypies (RSMs) may do so either to mitigate over-stimulation – '**sensory soothing**' – or to compensate for under-stimulation – '**sensory seeking**'. Subsequent research studies confirmed the relationship between RSMs and hyper- or hypo-sensitivity to sensory stimuli (e.g. Gabriels et al., 2008; Boyd et al., 2010). Other studies established relationships between hyper-sensitivity and anxiety (Pfeiffer et al., 2005; Green & Ben-Sasson, 2010; Green et al., 2012), and between anxiety and insistence on sameness (IS) (Spiker et al., 2011; Rodgers et al., 2012; Lidstone et al., 2014).

SOME ADDITIONAL SHARED CHARACTERISTICS

Imagination and Creativity: Strengths and Weaknesses

Data from the influential 'Camberwell Study' (see Box 2.3) showed that all children on the autism spectrum had 'impaired social interaction, communication, and imagination'. The impairment of imagination was hypothesised to entail an impairment of creativity, with the net result that behaviour in autism is abnormally repetitive and restricted in character. RRBs and 'impaired creativity' were, therefore, conceived as two sides of the same coin. Although attention has shifted towards emphasising RRBs, as opposed to problems of imagination and creativity, it is not in reality possible to separate one from the other. In what follows, therefore, some examples of impaired imagination and creativity are briefly outlined.

Pretend play

Children's pretend play, or 'pretence', is generally considered to be of two distinct kinds. The simpler, earlier-occurring kind of pretence involves play with miniature versions of real objects (e.g. moving a dinky car along the floor as if being driven; combing a doll's hair with a toy comb). This kind of play is generally known as **functional pretend play/pretence**. The later-occurring, more imaginative kind of pretence involves using objects as if they were something else (e.g. a stick as a gun; a broom as a ride-on horse), or behaving as if something were present or happening, when the imagined thing or event is absent (e.g. pretending to drink from an imaginary cup; pretending to be afraid of an imaginary lion; pretending to be a lion). This is sometimes called **symbolic pretend play/pretence**.

Early clinical observation of children with autism suggested that symbolic play is impaired (Wing et al., 1977), an observation subsequently confirmed in numerous experimental studies (see reviews by Jarrold et al., 1996; Jarrold et al., 2003). So, for example, typically developing children presented with a toy car plus a cardboard box or a matchstick and encouraged to 'Show me what you could do with these' often 'drive' the car into 'the garage'; or 'park' the car beside the 'petrol pump' to 'get petrol'. By contrast, children with ASD are more likely to pick up the car and put it onto or into the box, or place the car and the matchstick side by side (Lewis & Boucher, 1988). By the time DSM-IV was published in 1994, impaired symbolic play was included as one type of aberrant behaviour indicative of autism.

Functional pretend play is, by contrast, consistent with **mental age**. Moreover, in their tests of pretend play, Lewis and Boucher (1988) found that if children with ASD were *instructed* to 'drive the car into the garage' they turned the box onto its side and moved the car along the ground towards and into the box – just as children without ASD had done spontaneously when asked to 'Show me what you could do with these'. Similarly, if *instructed* to 'make the car get petrol' they held the matchstick on its end and 'parked' the car close up beside it. This inability to access ideas for, or to initiate, behaviour is referred to again in Chapter 9, in the section on RRBs.

Imagining the 'unreal' or 'impossible'

'Imagination' in its most basic sense of 'being able to think about, or to envisage, things that are unreal or impossible' has also been shown to be impaired. For example, one well-known test of this ability asks the person being tested to change some detail of a picture of a house to make the picture 'unreal' or 'impossible' (e.g. by putting the front door at first-floor level, or showing a chimney extending horizontally from the side of the house). Studies by Scott and Baron-Cohen (1996) and by Low et al. (2009) showed that children with autism are impaired on this task.

Imagining something that conflicts with reality is also involved in **counterfactual reasoning**. This kind of reasoning involves imagining how things might have been if A *had not* happened ('If I had not gone out in the rain I would not have got wet'), or if B *had* happened ('If I had taken an umbrella I would not have got wet'). Impaired counterfactual reasoning was at one time thought to offer a possible explanation of the failure of people with autism to pass explicit false belief tasks. However, the handful of studies that have tested counterfactual reasoning in autism suggest that this kind of imagining does not constitute a major problem, at least for higher-functioning individuals (see, for example, Scott et al., 1999; Begeer et al., 2009).

Generativity

The term **generativity** as used by psychologists refers to the ability to produce 'out of one's head' numerous varied and original words, drawings, ideas, etc. Generativity is commonly assessed using 'fluency' tests. These could involve asking someone to shut their eyes and say as many single words as they can within a given time – a test of **verbal fluency**; or asking them to 'draw as many different things as you can', testing **design fluency**; or asking someone to name as many uses of a brick or a piece of string as they can think of, assessing **ideational fluency**. Generativity is impaired in people with ASD when using the above

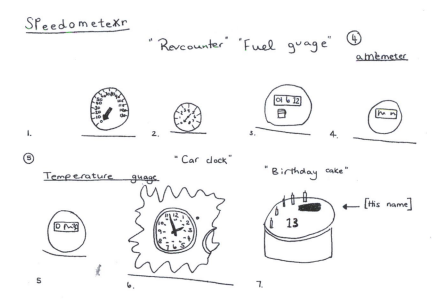

Figure 3.2 *A series of drawings by a boy with autism in response to requests to 'Draw something different from what you drew before', showing the tendency to produce a run of related pictures. In this case, the pictures are related by both category and shape*

type of 'open', or 'non-prompted' instruction; but is not impaired when a cue is provided, such as 'words beginning with /f/', or 'names of animals' (Boucher, 1988; Turner, 1999). Similarly, if the instructions for generating drawings do not stress that each new drawing should be 'quite different' from previous drawings, children with ASD can produce categorically related (e.g. different vehicles, or different fruits) or perceptually related (e.g. circular objects such as a face, a lollipop, a sun, a ball...) drawings as readily as children without autism (Lewis & Boucher, 1991; Liu et al., 2011) – see Figure 3.2.

Generativity is closely related to creativity, and despite experimental evidence of impaired generativity, some striking examples of spared generativity/creativity have been reported. For example, Hermelin and colleagues (summarised in Hermelin, 2001) reported improvisational ability in low-functioning individuals with ASD who could play the piano. Hermann et al. (2013), as well as Kasirer and Mashal (2014), have shown that adults diagnosed with 'Asperger syndrome' can generate novel metaphors better than their neurotypical peers. Examples of metaphors generated by these able individuals included comparing a feeling of success to 'Seeing the view from a mountain top', and a feeling of sadness to 'Offering a salad to someone from South America'(!). A poem written by a very high-functioning adult with ASD is reproduced in Box 3.5, partly to demonstrate unusual creative language ability, but also because the poem is so moving in itself. It is rightly well known, being frequently reproduced on the internet.

Box 3.5   'The Bridge' – by Jim Sinclair

I built a bridge
out of nowhere, across nothingness
and wondered if there would be something on the other side.
 I built a bridge
out of fog, across darkness
and hoped that there would be light on the other side.
 I built a bridge
out of despair, across oblivion
and knew that there would be hope on the other side.
 I built a bridge
out of helplessness, across chaos
and trusted that there would be strength on the other side.
 I built a bridge
out of hell, across terror
and it was a good bridge, a strong bridge,
a beautiful bridge.
 It was a bridge I built myself,
with only my hands for tools, my obstinacy for supports,
my faith for spans,
and my blood for rivets.
 I built a bridge and crossed it,
but there was no-one there to meet me on the other side.

(from Cesaroni & Garber, 1991)

Generalisations about 'lack of creativity and imagination' must also be tempered by the fact that some of the most creative people that the world has known – including scientists, musicians, philosophers and mathematicians – have had autism-related behavioural traits, and it has been speculated that some might have qualified for a DSM-IV diagnosis of 'Asperger syndrome'. As Lyons and Fitzgerald (2013) point out in an extended review of 'special gifts and talents' in people with autism: 'A significant challenge to ... perceived lack of creativity is the enormous achievement that some people with ASD show in creative and scientific fields.'

Examples of notably spared abilities, some occurring across the large majority or all individuals on the spectrum, some occurring only in rare, exceptional individuals, are considered next.

Islets of Ability

Relatively spared abilities across the spectrum

Uneven abilities are characteristic of people with autism across the spectrum. Even people with very low-functioning autism have some 'splinter skills', or islets of relatively good ability – i.e. things they can do significantly better than would be predicted by their overall level of functioning, even if not completely normally.

Pairs of closely related spared and impaired abilities are referred to in the autism literature as **fine cuts**. Fine cuts are theoretically important because they are informative about the causes of autism: if skill A is impaired but closely related skill B is unimpaired, this narrows down possibilities concerning the cause of the impairment of skill A. In what follows, some fine cuts are identified within the domains of social interaction, communication and **cognition**.

Spared social interaction ability: Attachment An important area of predominantly spared social ability is **attachment**. Attachment, as used in psychology, refers to the emotional bond between two people, especially between young children and their primary carers. Several studies have shown that young children with autism generally do form attachments to their primary carers, although there are some differences in the ways in which attachment is expressed, and less able children with ASD are less securely attached than more able children (Rutgers et al., 2004; Grzadzinski et al., 2014). Adults with ASD are less likely than neurotypical adults to form secure attachment relationships, but a minority do form such relationships. Moreover, adults with ASD are no less likely to form secure attachments than are adults with other mental health disorders (Taylor et al., 2008). The fact that attachment is frequently spared in people with ASD, at least in children, contrasts sharply with their social interaction impairments more generally.

Spared communicative ability: Protoimperatives Most individuals with autism, again excluding those who are most profoundly intellectually impaired, will communicate wants and needs intentionally, whether by using language, or by gesture (pointing to something they want), or by manipulating another person's hand towards a desired object or to carry out a desired action such as opening a door. Pointing at, or otherwise indicating, a desired object or action is called **protoimperative pointing**, because it constitutes a demand. Protoimperative or 'demand' communication contrasts with protodeclarative communication in which the intention is to share something of interest, as in Figure 3.1.

Spared cognitive abilities: Rote memory, fitting and assembly tasks, mechanical reading There are numerous spared, or relatively spared, cognitive abilities common to most or all individuals with ASD. Some of these were noted in the earliest descriptions of autism and included in some early definitions (see Chapter 1).

In particular, rote memory is generally spared, as is evident from children with ASD's good echoing ability, and their ability to memorise advertising jingles or tunes or (if able to acquire language) the words of songs or prayers. According to Miller (1999), rote learning is characterised by (i) primary concern with the physical aspects of a stimulus; (ii) high-fidelity representation of the original information; and (iii) little if any reorganisation of the information.

Spared, or relatively spared, visual-spatial reasoning and constructional skills – sometimes referred to as fitting and assembly tasks – are also well known, and occur even in individuals with profound learning difficulties and ASD (DeMyer et al., 1974).

'Mechanical reading', or **hyperlexia**, is another well-known peak ability (although some individuals with autism are dyslexic – see Chapter 4). In people with lower functioning autism, hyperlexia takes the classic form of an ability to read individual words accurately with no understanding of their meaning. In people with higher functioning autism, hyperlexia manifests as mechanical reading that is superior to reading comprehension (Grigorenko et al., 2002; Nation et al., 2006). Both hyperlexia and also **hypercalculia** were reported in a study by Jones et al. (2009).

Spared abilities in rare, exceptional individuals

A small minority of individuals on the autism spectrum have abilities that are very significantly superior to their overall level of function, and also significantly superior to abilities found in the general population. These rare individuals are referred to as **savants**, and their special talents are referred to as **savant abilities** (Hermelin, 2001; Happé & Frith, 2010; Treffert & Tammet, 2011). Most frequently, savant abilities involve feats of visual or musical perception and the exact reproduction of what has been seen or heard (Pring, 2008; Mottron et al., 2009); or feats involving estimation (of number, size, weight, etc.) or numerical calculation (Thioux et al., 2006; Soulières et al., 2010). Occasionally, however, some unusual form of savant ability occurs, as in the case of 'Grace', described in Box 3.6.

Box 3.6   'Grace': A young woman with a special talent for humour

Grace is a woman whose autism and moderate intellectual disability are combined with a striking capacity for verbal humour. Humour is not generally considered to be characteristic of people with ASDs, let alone jokes based on word-play, which makes Grace all the more unusual. Examples of her jokes are shown below.

Puns

'Here's the weavery looming up' (on approaching the weaving centre when showing a visitor around her residential village).
'Smashing windows' (when asked to write in a local church Visitors' Book).

Riddles

Question: 'What does the ant aerial get called?' Answer: 'Antenna'.
Question: 'What happens if a boa constrictor argues with another boa constrictor?' Answer: 'A boa war'.

Nonsense talk

(Describing two train passengers who were sitting when Grace had to stand, which she resented): 'There was a man chatting to a colly-girl with miniscule lips and sloping bum, while womping through a burger. God! I thought he was going to burst his trouser-buttons!'

(From Werth et al., 2001)

Comment

In high-functioning people with autism, spared and sometimes superior abilities greatly outnumber behavioural impairments and underlie the ability to live independently, to earn a living, and sometimes to achieve significant success in a particular field.

In low-functioning individuals, islets of ability, whether in the form of relatively spared abilities or in the form of savant abilities, provide possibilities for compensatory mechanisms, and may be maximised in ways that enable individuals to achieve success on tasks that they might otherwise struggle with. Spared abilities of any kind also enhance identity ('This is what I CAN do!'); and savant abilities may sometimes be harnessed (usually by a parent or other family member) to earn money for the individual, and even fame!

Motor Skills: Strengths and Weaknesses

'**Motor skills**' refer to body movement. The term covers a wide range of abilities involving not only nerves and muscles, but also an internalised self-image, or **body schema**, derived from **proprioceptive** and **kinaesthetic** awareness; also complex psychological processes of planning, temporal organisation and control. Fine motor skills, such as are involved in, for example, doing up buttons, typing or tap-dancing, involve a different set of underlying abilities from gross motor skills, such as walking or climbing stairs. Balance is important for some kinds of motor skills (e.g. riding a bike); hand–eye co-ordination for others (catching a ball). Well-learned, unconsciously executed movement patterns such as doing up buttons or climbing stairs utilise a partly different set of abilities from those required for novel willed actions such as fashioning a clay figure or negotiating an obstacle course.

Motor abnormalities of one kind or another are probably universal in ASD (Fournier et al., 2010; Bodison & Mostofsky, 2014). Gowen and Hamilton (2013) review available evidence relating to school-age children and adults, and report the following commonly observed impairments:

Muscular abnormality: reduced muscle tone, technically referred to as **hypotonia**.

Gross motor skills: unstable balance; impaired gait (people with ASD tend to walk clumsily and are poor at running); toe-walking (walking on the balls of the feet with the heels raised) is common in early childhood, and sometimes persistent; reduced co-ordination of locomotor skills (e.g. running to kick a ball).

Fine motor skills: slower than average repetitive hand or foot movements; slower and less than normally accurate movement alternation, for example, alternately flexing and extending an arm, or articulating the speech sounds /b/ and /k/ in rapid succession; poor ball skills (aiming and catching).

In addition to the above, various forms of **dyspraxia** have been reported, with higher rates (up to 75 per cent) in lower- as opposed to higher-functioning individuals (Dzuik et al., 2007; MacNeil & Mostofsky, 2012). Dyspraxia is an impairment of voluntary movement in the absence of hypotonia. It can differentially affect the limbs, hands or mouth areas. Someone with limb dyspraxia or **apraxia** may, without thinking, scratch the back of their neck if it itches, but have great difficulty in voluntarily bringing a brush or comb into contact with the back of their head to tidy their hair. Similarly, someone with oral apraxia may blow out a match or lick an ice-cream without thinking, but if asked to copy someone rounding their lips to make the sound 'oo', or if instructed to stick their tongue out, they struggle to achieve these movements voluntarily. Limb dyspraxia may contribute to the clumsiness commented on earlier in the chapter; and oral and manual dyspraxia contribute to language output problems (speech or manual signing) in some individuals (Seal & Bonvillian, 1997; Page & Boucher, 1998; Gernsbacher et al., 2008).

The ability of people with ASD to *imitate movements* has frequently been questioned. However, in a review of the evidence, Vanvuchelen et al. (2011) conclude that impaired imitation is not a universal characteristic of people with ASD, nor – when it does occur – is it specific to people with ASD (i.e. impaired imitation can occur with other conditions). It is probably the case, however, that one particular kind of imitation is universally affected in, and specific to, people with autism. Thus, a **meta-analysis** of studies of imitation in people with autism suggested that while object-oriented actions (such as pointing to a picture or picking up a spoon) are generally spared, the imitation of bodily actions not involving an object (such as touching one's nose with a finger or pulling a face) is severely impaired (Williams et al., 2004; Colombi et al., 2012). Similarly, acting on objects in ways that involve relationship with the body (e.g. holding a music box close to one ear) was shown to be impaired in a study by Meyer and Hobson (2004). Stewart et al. (2013) suggest that this kind of imitation impairment derives from a deficit in **self–other equivalence mapping** ('I must do to *my* nose what you did to *your* nose'; 'I must hold the music box up to *my* ear like you held it to *your* ear'). Strictly speaking, therefore, any universal and ASD-specific imitation impairment should not be seen as a movement problem, but rather as a problem associated with sense of self, and perhaps of appreciating equivalences between 'self' and 'other' (see below).

Despite the common – probably universal – occurrence of motor abnormalities of one kind or another in people with autism, some aspects of motor functioning are relatively unaffected in most individuals, and peaks of motor skill are occasionally observed. For example, Wing (1996) reported that some young children with autism, including some who are not particularly able, may be agile climbers with excellent balance and no apparent fear of heights (with potentially scary implications for parents and carers). Indeed, Kanner's (1943) original paper included reports of individual children with autism spinning objects skilfully and climbing 'gracefully'. Impaired and spared motor abilities often co-exist in the same individual. For example, Leary and Hill (1996) noted that 'the [autistic] individual who typically experiences severe difficulties with the most simple of movements may suddenly perform complex, skilled movements'. Similarly, Rinehart et al. (2006) reported that a less demanding motor task was worse performed than more demanding tasks, even by participants with an Asperger syndrome diagnosis.

Impaired Sense of Self

An 'apparent lack of personal identity' was listed in one of the earliest attempts to identify essential features of autistic behaviour (Creak, 1961 – see Box 1.2). However, interest in possible impairment of self-concept, or sense of self, lapsed for nearly three decades, possibly because impaired sense of self appears – superficially – incompatible with the egocentricity and self-absorption that give 'autism' its name. Moreover, studies showed that children with autism recognise themselves in a mirror at about the same age as children without autism, if overall ability is taken into account (Dawson & McKissick, 1984; Spiker & Ricks, 1984). This was, again mistakenly, taken as evidence of intact sense of self.

However, studies by Hobson and colleagues in the 1990s (Hobson, 1990, 1993; Lee & Hobson, 1998; see also Hobson et al., 2006) showed that although children and adolescents with mid- to lower-functioning autism could answer questions about their own physical attributes, their activities and abilities, they were impaired in their responses to questions about themselves as social beings, where it is important to be aware of how others see us. Hobson and colleagues interpreted their findings in terms of an impaired 'interpersonal self'. Also during the 1990s, Powell and Jordan (1993) suggested that people with ASD lack an 'experiencing self' that provides a personal dimension to ongoing events – the feeling that '*I* am doing this', or '*I* was there at the time'. Frith (2003) also noted the loss or impairment of an experiencing self, in her 'absent self' theory.

Increasing support for the suggestion that people with ASD, including the most able, have an impoverished sense of themselves comes from demonstrations of alexithymia, mentioned above; also from reports of impaired **autobiographical memory** (Crane & Goddard, 2008; Crane et al., 2009; Lind, 2010), and of the diminished salience of self-referential vocabulary (Lombardo et al., 2007; Yoshimura & Toichi, 2014). For extended reviews of the complex field of sense of self and its relation to sense of others in people with ASD, see Gallagher (2004), Lombardo and Baron-Cohen (2011) and Uddin (2011).

SUMMARY

Diagnostic criteria for ASD offer a 'bare bones' description of the core behaviours (SEC impairments and RRBs) necessary for a diagnosis of ASD to be made. A great deal more is known about these core behaviours – their individual components, their earliest manifestations and later trajectories – than can be stated in a diagnostic manual.

Within the group of SEC impairments, *social interaction* impairments are first evident as impaired dyadic relating; early forms of triadic social interaction, such as protodeclarative pointing and joint attention, are then affected, as are both implicit and explicit forms of theory of mind. Regarding *emotion processing*, the experience and expression of basic emotions is spared, as is 'contagious' or 'affective' empathy, whereas the experience and expression of complex emotions, and also 'cognitive empathy' and 'sympathy', are impaired. Regarding *communication*, both the means of communicating, especially nonverbally, and the rules for engaging in communication ('pragmatics') are impaired.

Within the set of RRBs, repetitive sensory-motor stereotypies (RSMs) tend to occur in younger or less able individuals with ASD, whereas insistence on sameness (IS) is more common in older and more able individuals. Sensory anomalies include heightened sensitivity to sound, taste and smell, but reduced sensitivity to pain. Perceptual abnormalities may include synaesthesia and monotropic attention. It has been suggested that RSMs may be responses either to excessive stimulation or to under-stimulation. IS has been linked to high levels of anxiety, which in turn may be a response to hypersensitivity and excessive stimulation.

Certain other facets of behaviour are almost certainly universally affected in individuals with ASD, adding to the range and complexity of shared characteristics across the spectrum. In particular, imagination and creativity, motor skills and sense of self are all impaired in certain ways or in certain circumstances, but not in others. In addition to these typically uneven capacities and characteristics, islets of ability occur, sometimes in the form of 'fine cuts', or as some relatively spared skill in an otherwise severely learning disabled individual, or – more rarely – as a true 'savant' ability.

THE FULLER PICTURE:
SOURCES OF DIVERSITY

AIMS

The aim of this chapter is first to ensure an appreciation of the fact that people on the spectrum are more different from each other than they are alike; and secondly to ensure that the sources of these differences are fully appreciated.

INTRODUCTION

The DSM-5 'Determiners' (see Chapter 2) are of critical importance in understanding ways in which subsets of people on the spectrum differ from each other. The first Determiner relates to the *severity* of each individual's SEC impairments and RRBs. Clear descriptions of the different degrees of severity characterising autism across the spectrum are given within the set of DSM-5 criteria reproduced in Box 2.1. In addition, examples of actual behaviour that might contribute to a diagnosis of ASD in a child with severe autism as compared to a child with relatively mild autism were provided towards the end of Chapter 2. Nothing more will be said in the present chapter concerning differences in severity. However, these differences are clearly crucial to understanding the ways in which people on the spectrum differ from each other.

The second Determiner included in DSM-5 is the set of possible *specifiers*. The most commonly occurring specifiers are:

- Learning disability.
- Language impairment.

These are listed in DSM-5 but not described in detail. Accounts of what are here referred to as the 'major specifiers' therefore form the bulk of this chapter.

There are, in addition, many other specifiers which, by their absence, or by their presence and range of severity, contribute to diversity among individuals on the spectrum. The majority of these additional specifiers fall under one or another of the following headings:

- Comorbid physical and medical conditions.
- Mental health problems.
- Neurodevelopmental conditions.
- Behavioural problems.

Brief accounts of several minor specifiers are included under these subheadings.

Finally, there is a short section emphasising the importance of individual differences in contributing to the diversity and individuality among people with ASD.

MAJOR SPECIFIERS

Learning disability and language impairment affect over half of those diagnosed autistic in the UK (Charman et al., 2010). For affected people themselves and those who care for them, these impairments can be more disabling and of more concern than the SEC impairments and RRBs. It is appropriate, therefore, to describe these disabilities first and in some detail. Specifiers coming under the heading of 'known medical or genetic condition or environmental factor' may also be of major significance to individuals and their families. However, such conditions are diverse and individually rare, and are considered more briefly under the heading 'Minor specifiers'.

Learning Disability

Learning ability may be analysed and described in two ways: first, in terms of 'intelligence' as assessed by **standardised**[1] intelligence tests (Mackintosh, 2011); and secondly, in terms of cognitive abilities such as attention, perception, memory and reasoning (Sparrow & Davis, 2000). Most of what is known about learning disability in people with ASD comes from studies of 'intelligence'. For this reason, some basic information about concepts of 'intelligence' and about methods of assessment is given first, followed by a section on what is known about the strengths and weaknesses of intelligence in people across the spectrum. Less is known about the cognitive strengths and weaknesses of learning disabled people with ASD, most research into cognitive abilities in autism having been carried out with high-functioning individuals. A brief subsection on cognitive abilities in lower-functioning individuals follows the discussion of intelligence.

Intelligence and intelligence tests

We all know what we mean when we say that someone is 'bright' or 'not so bright'. However, actually pinpointing what it is that makes people more or less intelligent is very difficult, and psychologists have argued about this for over a century (Mackintosh, 2011). Nevertheless, many intelligence tests are based on a broad distinction between acquired knowledge, or what is referred to as **crystallised intelligence**, as opposed to general reasoning ability and/or speed of thinking, referred to as **general** ('**g**') or **fluid intelligence**, which is predominantly (though not entirely) inherited. Broadly speaking, crystallised intelligence is reflected in tasks that assess **verbal abilities** and the kinds of knowledge acquired from experience and education, mainly via language; whereas fluid intelligence is reflected in tasks that assess **nonverbal abilities** such as pattern perception and visual-spatial reasoning.

The most widely used tests of intelligence are the Wechsler scales, comprising the Wechsler Adult Intelligence Scale (WAIS) (1999) and the Wechsler

---

[1]Words or phrases in bold type on first occurrence can be found in the Glossary.

Intelligence Scale for Children (WISC) (2004). These scales were first published in the US in the mid-twentieth century, but have been updated on a regular basis and published internationally in editions that take account of differences in language and culture. A summary of subtests comprising the Verbal and Performance (nonverbal) scales from the UK version of WISC-IV (Wechsler, 2004) is shown in Box 4.1. This Box also provides an explanation of how **intelligence quotients (IQs)** and mental ages (MAs) are calculated.

Box 4.1   The Wechsler Scales: Subtests and measures

Verbal Subtests

Information assesses general knowledge.

Vocabulary assesses the ability to define words.

Comprehension assesses knowledge of social and cultural conventions.

Arithmetic assesses mental arithmetic skills.

Similarities assesses the ability to say in what way two things are alike.

Digit Span tests the ability to repeat back a string of numbers in the correct order, and in the reverse order.

Performance (Nonverbal) Subtests

Picture Completion involves spotting the missing detail in a picture.

Picture Arrangement involves placing a set of small pictures in order, to tell a story.

Object Assembly is a timed jigsaw puzzle test.

Block Design involves using nine cubes, each with two red, two white, and two diagonally red and white faces, to copy a given red and white pattern; the test is timed.

Digit Symbol (adult scale) and *Coding* (children's scale) provides a symbol (e.g. square, oblique line) for each of the digits 1–9, to be written against a randomised string of digits within a given time.

Measures

Raw Scores are calculated for each subtest.

Standard Scores (SS) and *Full Scale IQ (FSIQ)* can be identified from the raw scores, using a Table representing how the participant's raw score rates in terms of the average for the general population in a given age range.

Verbal IQ (VQ/VIQ) can be identified as for FSIQ (above) using scores from Verbal subtests only.

Performance/nonverbal IQ (PQ/PIQ or NVQ/NVIQ) can be identified as for FSIQ (above) using scores from Performance subtests only.

Mental Age (MA) or *Age-Equivalent (AE)* is calculated by taking the individual's combined subtest scores and using a Table to identify the chronological age for which the score is the exact average. To ascertain Verbal MA (VMA), or Performance/ Nonverbal MA (NVMA), scores on the relevant set of subtests are used.

Intelligence test profiles in people with autism

The Wechsler scales have been used for many years to assess learning abilities in individuals with autism. Two reviews of early studies of lower-functioning individuals (excluding the least able, for whom the test is inappropriate) showed consistent discrepancies between **nonverbal IQ (NVQ)** and **verbal IQ (VQ)**, in favour of the former (Lincoln et al., 1995; Siegel et al., 1996). Moreover, the NVQ > VQ discrepancy was larger in the more severely learning disabled groups than in groups whose overall IQ was within the low–average range.

Since these reviews were published, increasing numbers of higher-functioning individuals with ASD have been diagnosed; the age range of groups tested has increased, with more studies of adults appearing; and the Wechsler tests themselves have been updated. A mixed age, mixed ability study by Mayes and Calhoun (2003) demonstrated the importance of both age and overall ability in determining patterns of findings on the Wechsler tests. Similarly, a study by Oliveras-Rentas et al. (2012; see also Dawson et al., 2007; Barbeau et al., 2013) demonstrated that differences in tests used can lead to significant differences in findings. Nevertheless, the following broad conclusions can be drawn:

- Intelligence test scores in people with autism are notably uneven. However, the unevenness has a somewhat different pattern in people with high-functioning autism as compared to people with lower-functioning autism. Specifically:
- Lower-functioning people with ASD generally have higher NVQs than VQs, although this discrepancy decreases with age.
- Higher-functioning individuals with autism have more evenly balanced verbal as opposed to nonverbal abilities, with considerable individual variation.

Typical profiles of Wechsler subtest scores for individuals with higher-functioning ASD compared to those with lower-functioning ASD are shown in Figure 4.1.

The fact that scores on most nonverbal ('performance') subtests are consistently better than scores on verbal subtests in lower-functioning individuals suggests that what makes some people with ASD 'less able' than others is mainly an impairment of crystallised intelligence, with fluid intelligence, or 'g', being less affected.

Cognitive abilities

As noted above, cognitive abilities in lower-functioning people with ASD are under-researched. However, lower-functioning individuals have, by definition, uneven sensory-perceptual processing, entailing unusual strength in attention to detail, generally at the expense of attending to wholes, as described in the previous chapter. Attention may be 'single channel' (monotropic), as also mentioned in Chapter 3. Visual-spatial reasoning is often a peak ability, middle-to-lower functioning ASD groups achieving normal levels of performance on relevant tests (Dawson et al., 2007). Speed of processing as assessed using an inspection-time task is also a peak ability (Scheuffgen et al., 2000). Performance on visual-spatial reasoning tests and on speed-of-processing tests are generally considered to assess fluid, or general intelligence ('g'). These findings therefore strengthen the conclusion that fluid intelligence is relatively

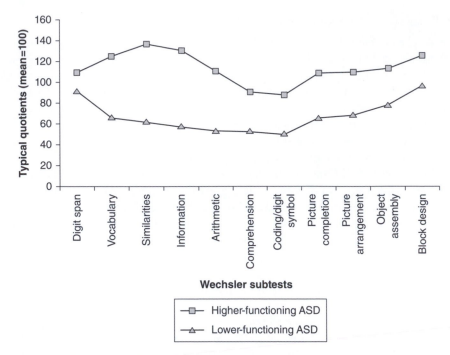

Figure 4.1 *Typical profiles of Wechsler subtest scores in lower- and higher-functioning individuals with ASD*

spared in lower-functioning autism, whereas crystallised intelligence is subaverage and sometimes very poor.

Language Impairment

Terminology

For a clear understanding of what is and what is not impaired across the spectrum, it is essential to be clear about what is meant by language, as opposed to communication; and about the distinction between language and speech. The first of these distinctions was touched on in the previous chapter, and is explained more fully in Box 4.2.

Impaired communication is a key component of the social interaction impairments diagnostic of autism, and was considered in some detail in the previous chapter. Impaired communication will not therefore be considered further here, where the focus is first on speech, then on language.

Speech across the spectrum

Speech in the large majority of high-functioning individuals with ASD is 'clinically normal', i.e. not warranting referral to a speech and language therapist. However, minor errors such as slightly lisped /s/ or incompletely rolled /r/ are quite common (Shriberg et al., 2001). Moreover, around 10 per cent of high-functioning

Box 4.2 Definitions of communication, language and speech

Communication

Communication is something that humans – and animals – *do*. They do it to convey, receive and share feelings, thoughts, information, etc. – or simply to oil social wheels or pass the time. Communication can be involuntary (e.g. yawning during a boring conversation), or voluntary (escaping from a boring conversation by making a verbal excuse).

Means of communication used by humans include language and nonverbal signals such as tone of voice, facial expression, body posture and gesture.

Pragmatics refers to the rules and conventions for using language and nonverbal communication signals to communicate.

Language

Language is something that humans *have*. Languages consist of a set of **symbols** (the words or signs), plus rules for combining symbols meaningfully. Linguistic knowledge can be stored in the brain, or described in dictionaries and grammar books.

Lexical semantics refers to the meanings of words or signs in a particular language.

Syntax refers to the grammatical rules for combining individual symbols meaningfully.

Morphology refers to the minimal meaningful components of a language, including 'semantic **morphemes**' such as 'and', 'but', 'or', as well as 'grammatical morphemes' such as /-ing/, /un-/, /'s/ /-ed/. **Morphosyntax** refers to the rules and conventions governing combinations of morphemes.

Phonology refers to knowledge of the sound system of spoken language, including knowledge of individual **phonemes** such as 'b', 't', 'th', 'sh', 'ee', 'ah', also knowledge of **phonotactics** – the rules and conventions for combining phonemes into meaningful words and phrases, such as (using the above phonemes): 'bath sheet'.

Speech

Speech is the output channel for spoken language, just as writing is the output channel for written language, and hand postures and movements are the main output channel for signing. Speech is a motor activity involving **articulation:** it is not part of the language system itself, any more than hearing – the input system subserving spoken language – is part of the language system. However, any impairment of phonology will be manifested in impaired speech. Phonological and articulatory impairments are therefore hard to tease apart. **Prosody** refers to the acoustic patterning of speech in terms of pitch, loudness, tempo and rhythm.

individuals have persistent, clinically significant phonological/articulatory errors (Rapin et al., 2009; Cleland et al., 2010).

In lower-functioning people with ASD, phonology/articulation is always impaired, but usually only to the same extent as in non-autistic individuals with a comparable degree of intellectual disability (Boucher, 1976; Kjelgaard & Tager-Flusberg, 2001). Thus, their phonological/articulatory abilities can be said to be 'Mental Age (MA) appropriate'.

Language

An abbreviated account of what is known about language and language impairment across the spectrum is given here. Full accounts can be found in Eigsti et al. (2011), Kelley (2011), Boucher (2012) and Kim et al. (2014).

In people with higher-functioning ASD Language is clinically normal in the most able people with ASD (those who warranted a diagnosis of 'Asperger syndrome' under DSM-IV definitions). That is to say that the vocabulary used is large and the grammar ostensibly correct (but see Tyson et al., 2014). However, the language used by individuals at the top end of the spectrum is somewhat pedantic and idiosyncratic, as noted by Asperger. For example, one able man I worked with some years ago used the phrase 'in a manner of speaking' repeatedly throughout his conversation – almost like a tic. There are difficulties in understanding non-literal uses of language, as in metaphor or sarcasm (Happé, 1995). There is also evidence of subtle differences in the content and organisation of the conceptual networks underlying linguistic meaning (Volden & Lord, 1991; Kelley et al., 2006; Bowler et al., 2008). This may help to explain why words and phrases may be used with unusually narrow or idiosyncratic meaning.

There are, in addition, some autistic children with normal nonverbal intelligence who acquire language later and more slowly than the typically developing child, with errors and immaturities persisting into the junior school years (Rapin & Dunn, 2003). Thereafter, however, their language is clinically normal.

In people with lower-functioning ASD A proportion of individuals with lower-functioning autism never develop meaningful language, displaying little or no understanding or use of speech, written language, gestures or signs. These individuals are generally severely or profoundly intellectually impaired, often with multiple physical as well as intellectual disabilities.

However, another group of individuals with ASD who never speak are not profoundly intellectually disabled, as shown by their relatively good self-care and daily living skills (Carter et al., 1998; Kraijer, 2000). They may also understand some language (Windsor et al., 1994). This rare subset of lower-functioning individuals may be described as having pervasive mutism, as described in the section on 'Communication', in Chapter 3.

More commonly, people with middle to low-functioning ASD acquire some useful but limited language. Language profiles in this group are very varied. This is partly because of differences in nonverbal (fluid) intelligence (Stevens et al.,

2000; Luyster et al., 2008); also because **comorbid** conditions such as hearing loss, epilepsy or **syndromic** medical disorder are commonly present, adding their own distinctive sets of speech and language problems to those characteristic of lower-functioning ASD, as described below.

Underlying the diversity of language profiles in lower-functioning individuals with some useful language, some common characteristics can, however, be perceived. These emerge only from large-scale group studies in which the diversity among individuals is outweighed by the shared characteristics of all the individuals in the group (see, for example, Rapin, 1996; Rapin & Dunn, 2003). Shared characteristics of what is later in the book referred to as the 'autism-specific language profile' include the following:

- Language impairment (when present) is **amodal**: in other words, it affects language in all modalities, whether spoken, gestural, signed, written or otherwise conveyed.
- The impairment is characterised first and foremost by problems of comprehension and meaning, i.e. **semantics.** In a review of early studies of language in young children with lower-functioning autism, Fay and Schuler (1980: 49) wrote 'the vocal product, whether echoic or otherwise noncommunicative, continues unimpinged by the meaning system'. Linguistic meaning for older or more able individuals tends to remain abnormally narrow and literal, revealing 'limited ability to integrate linguistic input with real-world knowledge' (Lord & Paul, 1997: 212).
- Impairments of grammar (syntax and morphology) are prominent in the preschool years (Eigsti et al., 2007) but are probably less persistent and pervasive than semantic impairments. Thus, in their authoritative review of 'Language and Communication in Autism', Kim et al. (2014: 241) conclude:

  > It seems very likely that syntactic development in children with autism is more similar than dis-similar to normal development. It proceeds at a slower pace and is related to developmental level more than to chronological age.

- However, the relative sparing of grammar is controversial, and of importance for explanations of language impairment in lower-functioning ASD, as will be discussed in Chapter 10.
- Expressive language (language output) may appear to be superior to comprehension as a result of the tendency to reproduce echoed or rote-learned chunks of language verbatim. For example, the phrase 'Time to go home' may be uttered when the bell rings at the end of afternoon school, or 'Do you want some juice' may be used to ask for a drink, echoing sentences frequently addressed to the individual. Truly productive language output is not superior to comprehension. Thus, a child using the echoed sentences in the examples above would be unlikely to produce spontaneous utterances recombining parts of those sentences, for example: 'Time' / 'for some juice' or 'Do you want' [meaning 'I want'] / 'to go home'.
- Expressive language is also characterised by some distinctive features. These include echolalia in younger or less able people; the use of idiosyncratic words or phrases and also **neologisms** (made-up words); and problems with **deixis/deictic** terms, the meaning of which is dependent on the speaker and the speaker's location in space and time, for example, 'you'/'me', 'here'/'there', 'now'/'then' (Bates, 1990). In addition, emotion-related words, and words referring to **mental states** are under-represented.

MINOR SPECIFIERS

Comorbid Physical and Medical Conditions

'Comorbidity' is a medical term that refers to the co-occurrence of two or more identifiable conditions where one is not an integral – i.e. invariable – component of the other. Several comorbid conditions appear to be related to ASD in the sense that they co-occur with autism more often than they occur in the general population, and therefore more often than can be explained in terms of normal variation. It is important to be aware that this need not imply that the rate of co-occurrence with ASD is high. **Tuberous sclerosis**, for example, which is described below, occurs in 0.01 per cent of the general population, but in approximately 2 per cent of all people with autism. Thus, none of the conditions described in this section is universally associated with ASD; few are as commonly associated with ASD as are intellectual disability or language impairment; and some are rare. The results of a population study reported by Levy et al. (2010) demonstrate that it is actually relatively rare for people with ASD *not* to have some additional diagnosed condition. This paper also demonstrates the very wide range of comorbid conditions that have been reported, only a selection of which are referred to below.

Some physical and medical conditions that co-occur with ASD more often than can be explained in terms of chance have been mentioned in previous chapters. In particular, the above-chance incidence of hearing and visual impairments, hypotonia and toe walking were mentioned in Chapter 3. In the section on 'Syndromic autism' in Chapter 7, certain other medical conditions are mentioned which are – albeit rarely – causally linked to ASD. These conditions include tuberous sclerosis, **Fragile X syndrome**, Down syndrome, **Turner syndrome** and **Prader-Willi** syndrome, among numerous others (Miles, 2011; Sztainberg & Zoghbi, 2016). In what follows, only some of the more common conditions that are not mentioned elsewhere in the book will be outlined.

Epilepsy Epilepsy occurs in an estimated 20–35 per cent of individuals with autism (Tuchman & Rapin, 2002), generally manifesting during adolescence in lower-functioning individuals (Matson & Neal, 2009).

Immune system disorders **Autoimmune disorders** occur when the immune system attacks normal body components as if they were foreign invaders. Some autoimmune disorders are well known and easy to identify, such as asthma, eczema, rheumatoid arthritis, and Type-1 diabetes. Other, less immediately detectable, immune disorders operate by producing antibodies that can cause biochemical and tissue abnormalities, as in the case of inflammatory bowel disease (see below). When brain chemistry and tissue are affected, there are consequences for behaviour. There are many anecdotal and some research reports of raised prevalence of autoimmune disorders in people with autism. However, these reports have yet to be confirmed in methodologically rigorous studies (see Krause et al., 2002, and Ashwood & Van de Water, 2004, for reviews).

Gastrointestinal disorders Gut and bowel disorders became a much-debated topic in the ASD literature when it was suggested that inflammatory bowel disease and ASD might result from administration of the measles, mumps and rubella (MMR) vaccines (Wakefield et al., 1998). The evidence for a raised prevalence of gastrointestinal disorders is in fact mixed. Symptoms such as abnormal stools, constipation, diarrhoea, food faddiness and excessive thirst (**polydipsia** in medical terminology) are commonly reported, all of which could be related to digestive problems (Erickson et al., 2005; Ibrahim et al., 2009). However, Buie et al. (2010) concluded that the rate of occurrence of gastrointestinal disorders in children with ASD, although high, was similar to the rate of occurrence in typically developing children, and generally responsive to treatment. It is probably true to say that the jury is out on this issue.

All the above medical conditions, and many others that can co-occur with autism, are characterised by unique sets of physical and behavioural anomalies and impairments, adding to the differences seen among individuals with ASD. In some individuals, the characteristics of the co-occurring syndrome mask the presence of autism, as in the child described in Box 4.3.

Mental Health Problems

Comorbid mental health problems are common in people with autism. However, prevalence estimates vary considerably according to the method used to identify such problems, the criteria used to identify individuals to be studied, the age at which groups are studied, and whether those studied are higher- or lower-functioning (Moss et al., 2015).

Studies of children and young people In a study in which mothers of children with ASD between the ages of 6;0 and 16;0 years were asked about their child, 54 per cent of higher-functioning children and 42 per cent of lower-functioning children were identified as suffering from 'depressed mood'; and 79 per cent of higher-functioning and 67 per cent of lower-functioning children were identified as 'anxious' (Mayes et al., 2011).

However, in a study in which clinicians formally assessed a large group of 8;0 year olds with ASD, including both lower- and higher-ability children, emotion-related conditions including anxiety and depression were found in only 9.2 per cent of the group. **Oppositional defiant disorder (ODD)** was diagnosed in 4 per cent of the children, and **obsessive compulsive disorder (OCD)** occurred in 2 per cent. Other mental health disorders, including psychoses, were rare, none occurring in more than 1 per cent of the children studied (Levy et al., 2010).

In later childhood the prevalence of comorbid mental health conditions increases. In a clinician-based study of 10;0–14;0 year olds of mixed ability, it was reported that 70 per cent of participants had at least one comorbid condition and 41 per cent had two or more. The most common psychiatric diagnoses were **social anxiety disorder** and ODD, which occurred in 29.2 per cent and 28.1 per cent, respectively, of the children studied (Simonoff et al., 2008).

Box 4.3   Craig: A child with multiple difficulties

Craig was initially diagnosed as having **Williams syndrome**, a rare genetic disorder usually characterised by overall intellectual disability in combination with hyper-sociability and good language. Williams syndrome, like Down syndrome, is easy to detect in early infancy because it is associated with distinctive facial features and also some health problems that may need early medical attention. It can also, like Down syndrome, be diagnosed using a physical test.

When I first met him at age eight years, Craig was very clearly a Williams syndrome child: in appearance, in some of the health problems he had, and also in the fact that he had marked intellectual disability. However, he had no language, either spoken or signed: in fact he could not even communicate using pictures – for example, pointing to a picture of a biscuit to ask for a biscuit; or to a picture of his coat if he wanted to go outside. Failure to acquire language is very unusual in a child with Williams syndrome, and in his junior school years Craig was found to meet DSM-IV criteria for autistic disorder. This did not mean that he had been wrongly diagnosed as having Williams syndrome. Rather, it showed that he suffered from Williams syndrome and ASD simultaneously. In addition to his ASD and Williams syndrome, Craig has a heart abnormality, dyspraxia and psoriasis, a truly unfair load.

When I last saw Craig some years ago, at age 15, however, he had finally learned to communicate using pictures. He was also as demonstratively affectionate towards his parents as he always was, which was probably what masked his ASD for so long.

(With thanks to Craig's parents for permission to publish this description.)

Studies focusing on a range of obsessive and compulsive behaviours in children with ASD show that although these types of behaviour are common, they are different in kind from those most typical of OCD, and may be more appropriately considered to be forms of RRBs (Zandt et al., 2007; Ruta et al., 2010). A range of self-injurious compulsive behaviours are considered below under the heading 'Behavioural problems'.

Studies of adults   A study of lower-functioning adults with ASD, in which clinicians were the assessors, reported relatively low rates of depression and anxiety (5 per cent and 4 per cent respectively), and a low rate of comorbid psychosis (1 per cent). However, the rate of 'problem behaviours' (**challenging**, aggressive or destructive behaviours) was high, at 38 per cent (Melville et al., 2008). More is said about such behaviours below.

In contrast to the relatively low rates in lower-functioning adults of mental health conditions other than problem behaviours, studies of high-functioning adults with ASD consistently show a startlingly high level of mental health conditions. Some of the findings from a study by Hofvander et al. (2009) are summarised in Table 4.1.

Similarly, Maddox and White (2015) found that 50 per cent of young adults with high-functioning ASD qualified for a diagnosis of social anxiety disorder. Kato et al. (2013) reported that 7.3 per cent of patients admitted to hospital following attempted suicide qualified for a diagnosis of ASD – an extremely high percentage

Table 4.1 Mental health conditions in high-functioning adults with ASD (reported by Hofvander et al., 2009)

Diagnosis	≥1 personality disorder	Mood disorder	Anxiety	OCD	Substance abuse	Psychoses	Impulse control disorder	Eating disorder
No. assessed	117	122	119	122	122	122	122	119
Percentage with the disorder	62	53	50	29	16	12	9	5

given that ASD occurs in only around 1 per cent of the population. A review of what is known about suicide in people with ASD can be found in Richa et al. (2014).

The fact that anxiety and depression are more common in people with high-functioning autism than in less able individuals reflects the fact that high-functioning individuals are more likely to have to cope with the normal world, with all its unpredictability and social demands. High-functioning adults with ASD are also aware that they are 'different' in ways that entail many difficulties and frustrations. Thus, the capacity for self-awareness and self-knowledge that is of such benefit in some ways can at the same time bring great unhappiness, which less able people with ASD are largely spared. An example of how desperate this unhappiness can be – especially in the absence of a diagnosis – is given in Box 4.4. The case of 'Mr A' also serves to illustrate the fact that comorbid psychiatric and mental health disorders can mask the underlying presence of ASD, making differential diagnosis difficult (Mazzone et al., 2012).

Neurodevelopmental Problems

Catatonia is mentioned as a specifier in DSM-5 diagnostic criteria for ASD (see Box 2.1). It may occur in up to 15 per cent of young adults with ASD (Kakooza-Mwesige et al., 2008). For descriptions and discussion of **catatonic states** in people with ASD, see Hare and Malone (2004) and Mazzone et al. (2014).

Hyperactivity, impulsivity and distractibility These also commonly co-occur with autism, with high levels of comorbidity of ASD with **attention deficit and hyperactivity disorder (ADHD)** reported in mixed-ability groups of children (Mayes et al., 2012; Van der Meer, Oerlemans et al., 2012) as well as in studies of adults (Hofvander et al., 2009; Mazzone et al., 2012). For a review of studies and discussion of the relationship between ASD and ADHD see Gargaro et al. (2011).

Dyslexia Precise rates of formally diagnosed **developmental dyslexia** in people with ASD are not established. However, reading comprehension is frequently poor across the spectrum, and although there is an unusually high proportion of individuals who are hyperlexic, as mentioned in the section on Islets of Ability in the previous chapter, there is also a high proportion of individuals with poor

---

Box 4.4 'Mr A': An able man with ASD and severe anxiety and depression

'Mr A', a 44-year-old married man in professional employment, was admitted as an emergency to the psychiatric department of an American hospital following a failed suicide attempt. He described himself as 'thoroughly depressed'. When interviewed by clinicians, Mr A answered questions with 'almost scripted' verbal responses, with little rhythmic variation in his speech. He showed little capacity for discussing his own and others' feelings, and recounted emotionally charged occurrences matter-of-factly, inappropriately smiling, and with his eyes fixed on the mouth of the interviewer, rather than the eyes.

Investigation of Mr A's early history revealed that he had always been socially awkward, with a poorly developed regard for the feelings of others, and a preoccupation with routine and rigidity. As an infant, he rebuffed his mother's affection and coddling. As a toddler, he engaged in independent or parallel but not reciprocal play, often playing intensely and exclusively with toy trucks. As a school-age child, he kept to himself and was picked on by other students for being different. While at college, Mr A had suffered from depression and anxiety, associated with heavy drinking and drug abuse, culminating in an unsuccessful suicide attempt. An inability to cope with opposition or frustration had in the recent past precipitated an assault on a fellow employee at work, and the immediate trigger for his recent suicide attempt was a similar violent outburst in a situation he couldn't handle, leading to his being fired from his job.

Mr A was subsequently diagnosed with ASD and, at the time of writing, is receiving multifaceted treatment for the problems associated with his condition. Mr A greatly appreciates knowing that he has ASD, remarking, 'It's helpful to at least know why I see or experience the world differently than what others seem to.'

(From Spencer et al., 2011, with thanks to the authors for permission to include this account)

---

mechanical reading ability as well as poor comprehension (Nation et al., 2006; Jones et al., 2009). In the study by Hofvander et al. (2009), selected data from which are reproduced in Table 4.1, the rate of clinically diagnosed dyslexia in high-functioning adults with ASD was reported to be 14 per cent.

Behavioural Problems

Self-injurious and other maladaptive behaviours   Self-injurious behaviours (SIBs), such as head banging, eye poking or hand-biting, quite commonly occur in learning disabled people generally (Collacott et al., 1998) but are most common in lower-functioning people with ASD (Richards et al., 2012). Self-injurious behaviours may be responses to a lack of external stimulation and/or high pain threshold or, conversely, to an excess of stimulation that the individual cannot process. Some

SIBs may result from internally generated compulsions such as occur in OCD. However caused, these behaviours are always an issue of serious concern, not least because SIBs can cause secondary health problems of bruising, bleeding and infection, resulting in additional distress. Health problems can also arise from habitual compulsive behaviours such as **pica** or **trichotillomania**.

Challenging behaviour   Challenging behaviour, like SIBs, can occur as a reaction to overstimulation, or as an expression of anger or frustration. Some people with autism may vent their anger or frustration on others, but this is rare. More commonly, challenging behaviour involves having a temper tantrum, active refusal to comply with reasonable requests, or antisocial behaviour such as spitting or screaming. Behaviours such as these may be judged by us to be '**maladaptive**', 'unwanted' or 'antisocial'. However, when such behaviours occur in severely intellectually disabled people who have little or no effective control over their own lives, and who have little or no means of communicating their own desires and preferences, the behaviours are more appropriately understood as expressive and communicative. So for example, hitting may express 'Go away: leave me alone'; spitting may express 'I'm frightened: get me out of here'. Such communicative acts are not, of course, intentional or under voluntary control, let alone 'naughty' or 'malicious'. (It takes some degree of insight to be naughty or malicious, and although more able children with autism may on occasion do things that they know will hurt or annoy, this is uncommon.) Many of the bizarre or undesirable behaviours that can occur in people with ASD should rather be seen as responses to being autistic, vulnerable to stress, powerless, and – in very young children or less able adults – with limited ability to communicate (Jordan & Powell, 1995).

Sleep disturbance   Sleep disorders are common in people with ASD, especially in those who are lower functioning (Souders et al., 2009; Mannion & Leader, 2014). There may be problems in getting to sleep at an appropriate time or problems of night-time waking. Abnormalities of rapid eye movement (REM) sleep in people with autism have been demonstrated in several studies (see, for example, Elia et al., 2000). Sleep disturbances are extremely wearing for parents and other close carers to cope with, and may create more problems for families than any other aspect of their child's autism.

INDIVIDUAL DIFFERENCES

A common stereotypic view of someone with autism is of a person who never looks you in the eye, who rocks or bangs their head on the wall, and who is generally 'out of it' to the extent that they are unmanageable and an embarrassment in public places. An alternative stereotypic view, largely derived from the kind of fictional presentations of ASD exemplified in the film *Rain Man* and the novel *The Curious Incident of the Dog in the Night-time*, is of a slightly quaint, quirky character with some amazing (savant) abilities (see comments in Chapter 2). Individuals fitting both these stereotypes can be found in reality. However, this alone emphasises the very great range of people who fit under the umbrella term 'autism'. It also illustrates just how wrong any one stereotypic view of people with ASD can be.

There is no reason, in fact, why people with autism should conform to any stereotype. Imagine a room full of people with hearing impairment, or who are of short stature. They would have certain things in common by virtue of the fact that they all have hearing impairment or a growth deficiency. However, in all other respects they would be different from each other: in detailed physical characteristics; in temperament and personality; in abilities, education and interests, likes and dislikes; all with different histories and formed by different experiences. Exactly the same is true of people with autism: they have a few things in common by virtue of the fact that they all have to a greater or lesser extent some specific impairments and some strikingly spared abilities. They may also share certain characteristics with some people with ASD but not with others: for example, impaired language, the physical characteristics associated with Down syndrome, or depressive tendencies. But in overwhelmingly more important respects, people with ASD are unique individuals. To quote Dr Stephen Shore: 'If you've met one person with autism, you've met one person' (*the-art-of-autism.com/favorite-quotes*). For a compelling account of the characteristics and causes of **heterogeneity** among people with ASD, see the book by Waterhouse (2013) entitled *Rethinking Autism: Variation and Complexity*.

SUMMARY

'Determiners' identified in DSM-5 are the *severity* of SEC impairments and RRBs, and the presence or absence of additional problems referred to as *specifiers*. These determiners make major contributions towards the diversity among individuals, all of whom warrant an ASD diagnosis.

Differences in severity are clearly described within DSM-5 criteria.

Of the specifiers listed, some degree of clinically significant learning disability and language impairment occurs in over half of all people with ASD. Within this group, language, rather than speech, is most commonly affected in tandem with lower than average levels of verbal – or 'crystallised' – intelligence. Nonverbal or 'fluid' intelligence is generally less affected, however, and in individuals who might be described as having 'middle-functioning ASD' fluid intelligence may be within the normal range. Language impairment is generally amodal, with comprehension and meaning (semantics) more severely and persistently affected than phonology or syntax. Pragmatics is always impaired, because it is primarily associated with *use* of language, that is to say with communication, rather than with the language system itself.

Various medical, mental health and neurodevelopmental and behavioural conditions occur in association with autism significantly more often than in the general population. Some of these conditions are strikingly common, affecting high-functioning adults in particular – for example, anxiety and depression. Other common conditions are more likely to occur in lower-functioning individuals – for example, epilepsy, behaviour problems or sleep disturbance. Some other comorbid conditions are rare, though still occurring more often than in the general population. Most of these rarer conditions are more likely to occur in, and to contribute to, low-functioning autism, and include various genetic syndromes. Some individuals with autism have multiple difficulties, of which ASD may not be the most important when considering the individual's needs.

Despite the complexity and variety associated with 'determiners', the largest contribution to diversity comes as in all human populations or subpopulations from individual differences of temperament and personality, educational opportunities and life experiences.

FACTS AND FIGURES: EPIDEMIOLOGY AND LIFESPAN DEVELOPMENT

AIMS

The main aim of this chapter is to provide factual information about autism in general, as opposed to information about the characteristics of people with ASD. A subsidiary aim is to add a longitudinal perspective to the picture established in previous chapters by looking at facts and figures concerning people with ASD from infancy to old age.

EPIDEMIOLOGY

'**Epidemiology**'[1] translates literally as 'the study of epidemics', and refers to the frequency of occurrence and the distribution of diseases or disorders in particular populations. The frequency of occurrence of autism will be considered first, followed by a section on the distribution of cases of autism across gender, race and social class.

Frequency of Occurrence of ASD

Frequency of occurrence can be calculated either in terms of **incidence** or in terms of **prevalence**, words with slightly different meanings when used by epidemiologists. Incidence refers to the number of new cases of a disease or disorder reported in a given period of time. Prevalence refers to the total number of cases of a disease or disorder in a specified population at a particular point in time. An easy way to remember this distinction is to think of incidence as referring to 'incidents', or 'happenings', that is to say new cases; whereas prevalence refers to a prevailing, or ongoing, situation.

There are some problems in calculating both the incidence and the prevalence of ASD. The problem for calculating incidence is that autism rarely if ever has a clear date of onset, and the process of identification and diagnosis may take a long time, or occur late in life. For this reason, the incidence of new cases in any one year, or even over a five-year period, is difficult to calculate with certainty.

The problem in calculating prevalence is the likelihood of underestimating the actual numbers of people with ASD. This is because some people who are autistic will not be diagnosed, perhaps because they are too young to have received a diagnosis, or because they are severely physically and intellectually disabled and their needs are dictated mainly by these handicaps rather than by their autism.

The problem in calculating the incidence of ASD is usually considered harder to overcome than the problem of calculating prevalence, which can be mitigated by calculating prevalence for an age group that specifically excludes very

---

[1]Words or phrases in bold type on first occurrence can be found in the Glossary.

young children, and by **screening** all individuals in that age group within the general population. To answer the question 'How common is autism?', therefore, measures of prevalence are generally preferred, and will be used in the figures quoted below.

In what follows it is important to bear in mind that studies of prevalence, also of the distribution of autism across gender, race and class, have not been carried out in some middle- and lower-income countries. Figures given below are therefore derived from studies carried out in affluent countries where the identification of individuals with autism is well established.

Rising prevalence estimates

Prior to the 1980s, 'Kanner's syndrome' or 'classic autism' was consistently estimated as affecting approximately 0.05 per cent of children in studies carried out in the US or the UK. From the 1980s, when it was recognised that autism often occurs in the absence of learning and language impairments, estimates of the prevalence of ASD began to rise. This is not surprising, because people who had not been included previously as they had normal language and intellectual ability now began to be diagnosed and included in prevalence estimates.

More surprising is the continuing rise in the estimated prevalence of ASD. In the early 2000s, three authoritative studies, including one by Baird and colleagues (Baird et al., 2000), put the prevalence at 0.6 per cent. Six years later, another paper by Baird and colleagues estimated prevalence as nearer to 1 per cent (Baird et al., 2006). Significantly, however, this rate applied only when a broad definition of autism was used, the estimated prevalence rate halving when narrower diagnostic criteria were used. In 2012, the authoritative Centers for Disease Control and Prevention in the US estimated the prevalence of ASD to be 1 in every 88 members of the population.

There has been a great deal of discussion as to what factors may be driving the increase in prevalence rate (see, for example, Hertz-Picciotto & Delwiche, 2009; Hill et al., 2014). There are two main possibilities. First, it could be the case that actual prevalence has not changed, but that rates of diagnosis have increased, for some or all of the following possible reasons:

- Changed diagnostic practices that could allow a much broader group of individuals than previously to be described as having ASD.
- Greater public awareness of autism through films, TV programmes and newspaper articles, reducing the likelihood that cases of ASD go undetected.
- Improved availability of health-related services that encourage families to bring their child to the attention of clinicians, or adults to self-refer.
- Greater willingness among clinicians to diagnose autism in individuals who have some other significant condition, for example, intellectual disability or Tourette's syndrome.
- Improved methods in prevalence studies, including more careful screening and ascertainment procedures.

Alternatively – or additionally – the actual prevalence of autism may be rising. This could only be established once the possible effects of all the factors listed above had been taken into account. When this has been done, some carefully conducted studies suggest that increased prevalence rates are more apparent than real (Elsabbagh et al., 2012; Hansen et al., 2015).

However, if established, a genuine rise in prevalence could be of considerable theoretical and practical importance. It would be *theoretically* important because, in view of the fact that the gene pool of a stable population does not change over decades, it could only be explained by relatively recently occurring environmental factors. This in turn would be of immense *practical* importance because environmental factors contributing to increased prevalence might be counteracted. Thus it might be possible to halt and subsequently to reverse any real rise in numbers of people with ASD. Environmental factors that may contribute to the increased prevalence of autism are discussed in Chapter 7.

Whether real or apparent, the perceived 'epidemic' of ASD and the associated costs led to a flurry of legislation in the US, the UK and elsewhere designed to 'combat' autism by allocating increased funding for early detection and intervention, as well as for research into causes and cures.

Distribution of Cases of ASD

Gender distribution

Autism spectrum disorder is widely held to be more common in males than in females by a ratio of approximately 4:1 (Fombonne, 1999), a ratio that has not changed significantly since the time of Kanner. However, this is a whole-spectrum average, which masks the fact that males diagnosed with ASD greatly outnumber females diagnosed with ASD at the high ability end of the spectrum, but by very much less at the low ability end of the spectrum.

Reasons for the excess of males over the whole spectrum, and for the differences in gender distribution from high-functioning to low-functioning autism, are not well understood. However, it is increasingly suggested that there may be many girls and women, especially at the more able end of the spectrum, who are currently undiagnosed and with un-met needs (Gould & Ashton-Smith, 2011). Failure to diagnose high-functioning girls and women may occur because autism-related manifest behaviours are different, or milder, in females as compared to males; or because social difficulties are better compensated for; or possibly because of an unconscious gender bias among diagnosticians (Dworzynski et al., 2012).

Geographical and racial differences

There is insufficient evidence at present to determine with any certainty whether there are any geographical or racial differences in the distribution of cases of autism. This is because of the lack of large-scale studies undertaken in middle- and lower-income countries. However, such studies are beginning to be undertaken (see the review by Elsabbagh et al., 2012) and over the next decade or so relevant data should become increasingly available.

With regard to racial differences, such evidence as there is comes from studies of populations that include a significant proportion of immigrant families, in whom increased prevalence rates are quite frequently reported (e.g. Barnevik-Olsson et al., 2010; Keen et al., 2010). However, this evidence is hard to interpret: groups studied tend to be quite small; immigrant populations are not necessarily representative of their original racial group; they are also subject to some exceptional environmental stressors.

Social class differences

A once common belief about autism was that it occurred more frequently in families with middle or high **socio-economic status (SES)** than in families with lower socio-economic status. This belief arose because wealthier families were more likely than less well-off families to obtain a diagnosis for their child in the 1950s and 1960s when autism was not universally recognised, and diagnostic and educational services for children with autism were both rare and expensive.

Many subsequent studies have, in the main, disproved this belief, while confirming that more children from higher SES families are diagnosed because of the greater knowledge and access to services of this parent group (Fombonne, 1999; Durkin et al., 2010). However, the study by Durkin et al. produced some slight evidence that children of higher-SES families may be somewhat more vulnerable to autism than children of parents in other social class groups, as once confidently believed. Further research is needed to settle this issue.

LIFESPAN DEVELOPMENT

Age of Onset

Idiopathic autism

Until relatively recently, it was usual to identify two patterns of onset in **idiopathic autism**: early onset autism, and late onset or **regressive autism**. However, a study reported by Ozonoff et al. (2011) suggested that three distinct patterns of onset can be identified:

- Early onset, in which socio-emotional-communicative behaviours are absent or odd within the first 18 months of life.
- Late onset/regressive autism, in which SEC behaviours and also language development are entirely typical in the first 18 months of life, but decline significantly, and sometimes rapidly, usually in the second half of the second year (Kern et al., 2014).
- Onset associated with 'plateau-ed' development, in which early SEC behaviours are similar to those of typically developing babies for the first 18 months or so, after which development slows down almost to a halt.

In a comprehensive review of studies of age and patterns of onset, Zwaigenbaum et al. (2013) go further than Ozonoff et al., concluding that there is a continuum of ages and stages of the appearance of autistic behaviours within the first 12 to 30 months of life.

In their review, Zwaigenbaum et al. summarise findings both from retrospective studies using home videos and from prospective studies in which 'at risk' babies have been studied from birth. Home videos of children subsequently diagnosed as autistic reveal that by the end of their first year, most (but not all) such children are less likely than typically developing 1;0 year olds to respond to their own names, to look at other people's faces or to follow another person's direction of looking or pointing. They are also averse to social touch. By 18 months there may be a noticeable absence of play and a continuing absence of interest in other people, including lack of joint attention behaviours such as protodeclarative pointing (illustrated in Figure 3.1). Speech is likely to be delayed. In cases where autism is preceded by a period of normal development, a significant decline in social, communicative, play and linguistic abilities is generally evident by the age of 3;0 years.

'Age of onset' suggests that at some point in time a person does not have autism, but at a later time they do have autism. As will be apparent from what has been said above, it is rarely possible to identify a precise date of onset. Occasionally, however, parents report that autism develops following an illness accompanied by fever and/or seizures, or that regression followed a stressful event such as a death in the family or the birth of a sibling. However, such reports are anecdotal and possibly unreliable (Ozonoff et al., 2011). It is therefore an open question as to whether regression, when it occurs, is spontaneous – that is to say, it occurs as a result of developmental changes within the child – or whether it is triggered by some environmental factor in a genetically vulnerable child; or, indeed, whether autism might result from some illness or trauma in a child with no genetic vulnerability – as considered next.

Acquired autism

In rare cases a school-age child or an adult may develop behaviours associated with autism following an illness, usually **herpes encephalitis**, that causes damage to certain areas of the brain (DeLong et al., 1981; Gillberg, 1986; Ghaziuddin et al., 2002). Cases of autistic-like behaviours developing after other kinds of focal brain damage in adults have also occasionally been reported (Umeda et al., 2010). Such individuals might be described as having **acquired autism**. However, because the symptoms of autism in these cases may subside after a time or be partial or atypical, the description **pseudo-autism** (or **quasi-autism**) is probably more appropriate.

The Developmental Trajectory: Continuities and Change

The phrase **developmental trajectory** refers to ways in which an individual develops and changes during their lifetime. The developmental trajectory of every individual is unique, not least for people with autism for all the reasons that were outlined in Chapter 4. Generalisations about people with autism must therefore always be tempered by recognition of their uniqueness as individuals. With that caveat in mind, some generalisations follow concerning some of the more common patterns of lifetime development and change.

Continuities

In some important ways people do not change. This is true for everyone, not just for people with autism. The continuous, or unchanging, characteristics of an individual's physical make-up, personality or intellectual potential are important because they partly determine how a person develops. Some stable characteristics that are particularly important in considering how a person with autism may develop are discussed below.

First, most – though not all – individuals who have been given an authoritative diagnosis of autism at one age will meet the criteria for autism if assessed again at a later age (Lord et al., 2006). Cases of recovery are occasionally reported, in the sense that an individual originally diagnosed with ASD no longer meets diagnostic criteria at a later age (Seltzer et al., 2003; Pellicano, 2012c; Fein et al., 2013). As with 'Sam', however, whom I described in the section on 'Diagnostic instability' in Chapter 2, residual traces of autism generally remain.

Secondly, intellectual and linguistic potential remain fairly constant from early childhood, to adolescence, through to adulthood, and largely determine the long-term outlook for each individual (Levy & Perry, 2011; Howlin et al., 2014). Thus, the autistic child with high IQ and good language at age 5;0 years is likely to do well at school and progress to higher education, a job and independent living. By contrast, the autistic child with below average IQ and limited language at age 5;0 is likely to require special education and to live (and to work, if at all) in sheltered settings in adulthood.

Positive change during development

Diminution of the severity of autistic behaviours The continuities that constrain the scope for normal development and normal life for people with ASD might be seen as the bad news for any parent whose child has just received a diagnosis. Set against this is the good news that, with a combination of maturation and early intervention, the majority of individuals can be expected to show fewer or milder signs of autism in adolescence and adulthood than they did when first diagnosed (Seltzer et al., 2003; see also McGovern & Sigman, 2005; Levy & Perry, 2011; Pellicano, 2012a,c).

Regarding SEC impairments, the tendency to treat people 'instrumentally' (e.g. taking a person's hand and placing it on the juice carton to ask for a drink) reduces except in the least able nonverbal individuals. Empathy, as expressed by offering comfort to others appropriately, generally increases, as does social approach behaviour and the capacity to share enjoyment (e.g. rough and tumbling with another child). The originally 'aloof' child may progress to 'passive' acceptance of physical contact with, or in interaction with, others; whereas the originally 'passive' child may start to initiate social contact, albeit inappropriately; and the originally 'active but odd' child (if high-functioning) may learn the rules and conventions of social interaction and conversation and interact reasonably well, though in a formal and somewhat 'stilted' manner (see Box 2.4).

Repetitive behaviours and behavioural inflexibility also reduce and change in kind over the years, except in the lowest-functioning individuals (Seltzer et al., 2003;

McGovern & Sigman, 2005). For example, motor stereotypies that are often prominent in young children with autism are generally less prominent in older children, who may develop more 'normal' repetitive behaviours such as always putting on their clothes in the same order or asking repetitive questions. This in turn may give way to having a preferred activity or interest, such as playing computer games, drawing or listening to music. In some individuals, a preferred activity or interest may become an asset if it can be shared with others and form the basis of a friendship, or if it can be utilised in some meaningful occupation or work in adult life.

Diminution of difficult or challenging behaviours Behaviour problems generally reduce with age, as the individual becomes better able to communicate their wants and needs and gains competencies and skills that help to reduce dependency and frustration. It is important to note, however, that reductions in challenging behaviours are less common in the least able individuals, especially those with comorbid epilepsy and self-injurious behaviours (Howlin et al., 2014).

Negative change that can sometimes occur

Adolescence constitutes a period of risk for children growing up with autism (Mesibov & Handlan, 1997). The deterioration may be transient, but in some cases it marks a regression in development or a plateau beyond which little further development occurs. Risk factors for severe behavioural deterioration in adolescence were studied by Périsse et al. (2010), and included low IQ, comorbid epilepsy, depression, and poor home support and care. It should be noted, however, that for some individuals (generally the more able), adolescence may constitute a period of improved social and intellectual functioning (Howlin, 2000).

There are other risk periods for people growing up with ASD, several of which are associated with environmental changes involving novelty and/or loss of structure. The transitions from one school to another, for example, or from school to college or from the parental home to an independent or residential setting, can all precipitate deterioration in behaviour, as can the loss of a parent or other attachment figure or similar traumatic life event. Such deterioration is usually temporary, however, and can be minimised by careful management (Sterling-Turner & Jordan, 2007; Faherty, 2008).

Cyclic changes can also cause unusually large variations in behaviour. Most commonly in women this is associated with menstruation (Kyrkou, 2005). However, seasonal changes or particular kinds of weather can also affect certain individuals for unknown reasons. One teenage boy with whom I used to work was often distressed and difficult during the winter months, although generally co-operative at other times of year. Teachers report that children with autism tend to 'get high' in windy weather – but this may be true for children in general.

Adult Outcomes

Parents of typically developing children generally hope that their offspring will do reasonably well at school; move from school to college, university or other training or go straight into work; maybe travel a bit, have fun, change jobs a few times; experiment with relationships for a while before settling down with a long-term partner to make a home, progress in a career, and eventually retire and enjoy reasonable health into old age. Judged by these criteria for successful adult outcomes, people with autism do not as a group do well. For example, a study by Howlin et al. (2004) of adults with nonverbal intelligence of 50 or above rated adult outcomes as 'Very good' in only 12 per cent of cases based on linguistic and educational attainment, employment status, friendships and the capacity to live independently. In the remaining 88 per cent, outcomes were 'Good' in 10 per cent, 'Fair' in 19 per cent and 'Poor' or 'Very poor' in 58 per cent. A similar range of outcomes is reported in large-group follow-up studies by Farley et al. (2009) and Anderson et al. (2013). Some brief factual information about adult outcomes in key areas is given below. In Part III of this book, more will be said about the many practical issues relating to these topics.

Post-secondary education

People with high-functioning autism may do well at school and easily obtain a place at college or university. However, such individuals may struggle to complete their courses for a variety of reasons, including social difficulties and problems of self-organisation in a relatively unstructured environment (Wei et al., 2013). Others, however, obtain their degree, and the most academically able may in fact excel within their year group (two out of 68 adults in the Howlin et al.'s 2004 study cited above had obtained PhDs).

People with middle-functioning autism frequently remain in education as young adults, taking courses in colleges that offer learning support. This extension of education can be valuable in developing vocational and life skills, and it can also cushion the transition from school student to adult status (Taylor & Seltzer, 2011). The least able individuals may remain in school until the late teen years and have no further formal education, although they are likely to receive training to improve their self-care and daily living skills within supportive settings.

Employment

The same small minority of high-functioning individuals who do well educationally may find paid employment that utilises their abilities and education, often in careers to do with computers, engineering, accountancy or academic research (Howlin et al., 2004). However, entry into employment, or holding down a job, may not be easy because of social clumsiness or other autism-related behaviours (Hurlburt & Chalmers, 2004). Success in entering and maintaining employment is also dependent on cultural factors, including the amount of support provided by various agencies (Jordan, 2001). Once in work, however, people with autism are often viewed as particularly conscientious and reliable employees (Howlin et al., 2005).

A minority of middle-functioning people with ASD also find paid employment in normal environments, tending to work in jobs that are routinised and require relatively little social interaction, such as gardener, kitchen assistant, assembly line worker or supermarket trolley collector (Howlin et al., 2004). Here again, entry into work may be supported, and in some cases support may be maintained in the long term (Gerhardt et al., 2014). Some other middle- and lower-functioning individuals work as volunteers, for example in charity shops; or they work for pocket money on schemes run by their local autism support group, for example growing and selling garden produce.

For the least able and especially those from low-income families, entry into any form of consistent employment or occupation is rarely achieved because of the level of sustained support required (Shattuck et al., 2012) Nevertheless it can be achieved, as illustrated in the account of Nancy, in Box 5.1.

Box 5.1   Nancy: An example of successful supported work arrangements for a woman with significant autism

Nancy is in her early 40s and has significant autism. She is nonverbal, has a history of challenging behaviours, including kicking, biting, screaming, tantrums, bolting, SIBs, pica, etc. Despite these considerable obstacles she has worked full-time at union scale for over 21 years with the assistance of a full-time job coach/behaviour support specialist that she mostly pays for with her take-home earnings. She is a two-time national award winner, having received awards for Outstanding Personal Achievement from the Association for Persons in Supported Employment (APSE) and the Outstanding Individual with Autism from the Autism Society of America (ASA).

Nancy started while in high school on a work experience scheme, collecting and reshelfing books at a library and delivering inter-office mail at a College of Education building at a local university. She then transitioned seamlessly into a job with local county government, first delivering inter-office appointment messages and later inter- and intra-office mail delivery and mail catch. She has always had good work habits when the carved jobs matched her desires to have movement in her job and variation to her tasks, but still needs the help of a job coach because of her low impulse control and the periodic changes in job duties. The remaining portion of her job coach cost is paid by a comprehensive Medicaid Waiver, as are her residential service cost and the transportation costs she has by having her own car. She is valued at work, as evidenced by her excellent performance reviews, well known and well liked by her co-workers and peers in the community. She has an excellent quality of integrated community life that has been presented by her parents in 32 US states and Canada.

(With thanks to Joe and Marilyn Henn – contactable at hennpen@aol.com – for providing this account of their daughter, and for their permission to publish it)

Living arrangements

A substantial proportion of adults with autism continue to live with their parent(s) (Anderson et al., 2014). Of those who no longer live with parents, the small minority of highly able individuals who find salaried employment generally live independently in their own homes. For those less able to live independently, the preferred option is to establish **supported living** arrangements, enabling individuals to live in their own homes, whether as tenants or owner-occupiers, whether alone or with others, and whether requiring 24-hour support or merely weekly visits (National Autistic Society UK website). Residential homes offering on-site 24-hour support for large groups of adults with autism are now rare – at least in the UK. However, for those autistic adults with the most complex needs, residential care homes catering for small groups may be provided either by local support groups or by commercial organisations (see Box 13.5). At best, these offer 24-hour care and support, with personalised learning programmes and activities. Occasional reports of abuse in commercially run homes underline the need for regulation and oversight of this type of living arrangement.

Relationships

Life partnerships Very few individuals with ASD (about 4 per cent) enter into life partnerships, and an even smaller number enter into life partnerships that last. Relationships between a person with high-functioning autism and some-one who is not autistic are likely to break down because the partner who is not autistic finds the relationship too difficult to sustain. However, this is not always the case, given persistence and patience on both sides. Personal accounts by, for example, Maxine Aston (2001), Christopher and Ghisela Slater-Walker (2002) and Ashley Stanford (2014) are illuminating concerning the difficulties that may be encountered – and sometimes overcome. Relationships between two individuals both of whom are autistic appear to have a better chance of lasting. A couple described by Sacks (1995: 263–264), for example, both of whom had a diagnosis of Asperger syndrome, reported how they met at college and recognised each other's autism with a sense of 'affinity and delight'. This had kept them together, living out their autism with their two autistic children in the privacy of their home, and 'acting normal' in their public lives.

Life without a long-term partner, and effective celibacy, may reflect social inadequacy rather than a lack of interest in sexual relationships, especially in males (Mehzabin & Stokes, 2011). Masturbation is common, and is supported in appropriate circumstances for those for whom a sexual relationship is not a realistic possibility. For a small proportion of individuals the lack of a 'girlfriend' or 'boyfriend', and sometimes specifically the lack of a sexual partner, is a source of distress and obsessive concern that can lead to inappropriate or even criminal behaviour, though this is rare (Stokes & Kaur, 2005).

Friendships Many people with ASD become interested in having friends of their own age as they mature (Bauminger & Shulman, 2003). However, fewer than a quarter of adults with autism are reported to have friendships that have been made by the individuals themselves as opposed to, for example, '**befriending**' relationships (Orsmond et al., 2004). The nature and quality of the friendships made are also somewhat limited, being typically based on a shared interest or hobby rather than on personal intimacy. Sometimes friendships are made with someone who has a disability of a different nature, where there can be mutual support. One such friendship that has lasted many years is described in Box 5.2.

Box 5.2   Friendships that endure

'David' is now in his 40s, living in his own flat, and working, as he has done for several years, in a university library, where his job is to fetch old books or documents from storage in the basement when these are requested by readers. Although a superficially outgoing person, David is self-preoccupied and finds relationships difficult. He likes to stick to routines, and has obsessive and often anxious thoughts that dominate his conversation. He has never been diagnosed as having ASD, though he knows that he is sometimes described as autistic; and it is doubtful whether a diagnosis would now have positive or negative effects on his life (it might be just one more thing to worry about).

David has a friend whom he has known for many years. This friend has well-controlled schizophrenia and lives locally. The pair generally meet twice a week, once at the friend's home and once at a local café for a drink and a snack. Occasionally they have a meal together or visit relations for a day out. David's practical competencies enable him to organise these trips, and to ensure his friend's wellbeing (e.g. reminding him to take his medication). Equally, the young man with schizophrenia is socially undemanding and good-humouredly tolerant of David's obsessive behaviours and anxieties. They understand each other, and are understanding of each other's idiosyncrasies, as friends should be.

Social media have greatly increased possibilities for forming relationships 'at a distance', and many able individuals with ASD write blogs or have Twitter accounts, or share problems and solutions through sites such as Facebook. There are, in addition, numerous dating sites catering specifically for people with the 'Asperger syndrome' diagnosis, and a few offering 'friendship or dating' to people with ASD more generally. There are clearly some risks attached, especially to less able individuals. Overall, however, communication via keyboard and screen, where nonverbal communication signals play a vestigial role, offers the ideal medium for people with ASD, bringing with it a massive increase in socialising possibilities. The longer-term effects on individuals remain to be seen, but are likely to prove positive.

Other relationships   Lower-functioning individuals with ASD are likely to depend for their social relationships on family or other carers. These relationships are often close and central to the individual's sense of security and quality of life. However, such relationships are dependent in nature, and reliant on the skills and commitment of the close carer. Looser relationships may also be formed within residential groups or within groups associated with work or leisure activities, as outlined next.

Leisure activities

Leisure activities tend to be predictable for any one individual with ASD, and often solitary – or at least of a kind that can be enjoyed with or without the company of others. The most able, usually those who live and work without support, enjoy computer-related activities, listening to music, travelling, photography, reading (though novels are almost never on the list), while finding informal socialising difficult and stressful.

In their study of social activities in a large group of mixed ability adolescents and adults with autism, Orsmond et al. (2004) found that three-quarters of the group spent time walking or taking some other form of exercise each week; nearly half spent at least some time on a particular hobby; a third took part in some group recreational activity, often organised for them by others. A third attended church on a weekly basis. This latter statistic may reflect the fact that the study was carried out in the US where church attendance is high. However, churches in the UK are also often involved in informal support. For example David, described in Box 5.2 above, regularly attends his local church and church-organised events.

The least able individuals, who may show little initiative in filling their own time, nevertheless usually have some preferred activity (e.g. leafing through a mail-order catalogue) and a preferred place to be (their own bedroom or a quiet corner of a sitting room or garden away from others). These times of 'doing their own thing' offer respite from the stresses of conforming to the expectations and directions of others, and deserve recognition as legitimate forms of leisure activity.

Hazards

Criminality   The risk of an individual with autism committing a punishable offence is very low (Howlin, 2000). Nevertheless, a study of individuals in three secure hospitals in the UK found a slightly higher than expected prevalence of individuals on the autism spectrum (Hare et al., 1999). The majority of these individuals had additional problems, including severe intellectual disability or a mental health condition. The crimes for which they were imprisoned involved violence against people or property, with an unusually high rate of arson. Several of the individuals studied had obsessive interests in violence of one kind or another, including wars, weaponry or Nazism. Hare et al. reported a low rate of sexual violence in these individuals. However, Attwood (1998) noted that higher ability males with ASD who access pornography websites may inadvertently offend because they take the behaviours depicted on such websites to be the norm. Recent studies highlight the need for training prison staff to recognise and cater appropriately for the needs of offenders with ASD (see the Special Issue of the *Journal of Intellectual Disabilities and Offending Behaviour*, 2013, Volume 4, Issue 1/2; also Murphy and McMorrow, 2015).

Addiction and antisocial behaviour   There is no evidence to suggest that individuals with ASD are more likely than others to become addicted to drugs, alcohol or gambling. However, as Howlin (2000) remarks, given the rigidity of behaviour patterns in autism, such behaviours are likely to be difficult to modify, once established. Other antisocial behaviours are also rare, although inadvertent offence may be given by inappropriate behaviours (e.g. spitting, or masturbating in public), and challenging behaviours may be misinterpreted as intentionally offensive when in fact resulting from stress or frustration. Acts that cause injury are more likely to be self-directed than other-directed, although this is not invariably the case.

Accidents and illness   These are more common in people with ASD than in the general population, especially in the less able (Shavelle et al., 2001). Occasional cases of attempted suicide are reported in children with autism, regardless of IQ, in whom suicidal thoughts are unusually common (Mayes et al., 2013). Teasing and bullying were identified as significant factors putting autistic children at risk of suicidal thoughts and/or attempts. In high-ability adolescents and adults with ASD, rates of suicide and attempted suicide are also unusually high, as noted in Chapter 4, and often associated with feelings of social inadequacy, anxiety and depression (Shtayermman, 2008; Kato et al., 2013).

Life expectancy

Life expectancy is lower in people with ASD than in the general population. Three major studies (reviewed by Mouridsen, 2013) have shown that death rates are three times higher in young or middle-aged adults with ASD than in the general population. Lowered life expectancy does not appear to be associated with premature ageing or other deterioration, but rather with learning disability and vulnerability to accidents, often in association with seizures (Bilder et al., 2013). The studies reviewed by Mouridsen also found an association with gender, females being more vulnerable than males, for reasons not understood.

Judging Long-term Outcomes

The kinds of hopes and expectations of parents of typically developing children outlined at the beginning of the section on adult outcomes are, of course, those that parents of children with ASD might have had for their children in advance of discovering that their child is autistic. Judged by these criteria, outcomes for people with ASD may indeed be rated as 'poor' or 'very poor' in 58 per cent of cases (Howlin et al., 2004).

Judged by different criteria, for example 'the best possible outcome for that individual', outcomes might still be judged to fall far short of 'very good' or 'good' for many individuals, with large cultural differences associated with available services and social attitudes. However, the real-life cases of Nancy and David, outlined in Boxes 5.1 and 5.2, illustrate how a reasonably good quality of life can be enjoyed by individuals with autism, including those who are quite low-functioning. This suggests that adult outcomes may be more meaningfully judged in terms of maximising the quality of life for individuals, rather than in terms of how 'normal' or 'successful' they are. Issues relating to appropriate goals of intervention, education and care for people with ASD are discussed further in Chapters 12 and 13.

SUMMARY

The frequency of occurrence of autism is usually estimated in terms of prevalence: that is, the proportion of individuals within a total population sample who have a diagnosis of autism at a particular point in time. Estimates of the prevalence of autism have risen since the 1980s, and continue to rise. If autism really has become more common, it will be of vital importance to search for the environmental factors underlying this increase. However, there are several reasons why increased prevalence may be more apparent than real: definitions of autism have broadened, especially at the 'borderline normal' end of the spectrum; public awareness of autism has increased; and diagnostic services are more available now than in the past.

Males outnumber females across the spectrum, to a greater extent at the top end of the ability range than at the lower end. However, it is increasingly suggested that ASD is under-diagnosed in more able girls and women. If this is true, and can be corrected, the ratio at the top end of the spectrum may change. No reliable geographical or racial differences in the distribution and prevalence of ASD have been reported, but evidence on this point is lacking. The early claim that autism occurred more often in families of middle or high socio-economic status has been largely disproved. However, some very slight doubt remains relating to this issue, and here again further research is needed.

Regarding age of onset, a clear-cut distinction between 'early onset autism' and 'regressive autism' is increasingly questioned. However, it remains true to say that in a majority of cases, autism-related behaviours emerge within the first two years of life, after apparently normal early development. In a minority of cases, normal development may continue into the third year prior to a loss of skills and onset of autism-related behaviours. It is unclear as to whether or not these 'regressive' cases are triggered by some event (e.g. illness or trauma) in the child's life. Occasional cases of 'acquired autism' have been reported in older children or adults, associated with diseases that damage certain parts of the brain. In such cases, the autistic symptoms do not generally persist.

In some ways, people with ASD do not change with development. In particular, autism-related behaviours rarely completely disappear, however much improvement is achieved through appropriate care and intervention. In addition, the individual's innate capacities for language and learning remain more or less constant, as they do in people without ASD, significantly influencing life-long development. However, many positive changes do occur. In the majority of individuals, the severity of the abnormalities and impairments associated with autism reduces, and behaviour becomes more 'normal' over the years. Exceptions to this can occur, however, particularly during adolescence when some – usually temporary – regression is not uncommon. Behaviour can also regress at times of stress, but such regression is usually transient if the sources of stress can be minimised. There is a very slightly raised risk of being detained in a secure institution for a criminal offence (often related to a particular obsession); and a significantly reduced life expectancy, largely explicable in terms of comorbid epilepsy and learning disability, increasing vulnerability to accidents.

Adult outcomes have been judged in various studies to be 'very good' in a small minority of cases, and 'poor' or 'very poor' in the majority, based on measures of academic success, employment, independent living, life relationships, friendships and leisure activities. However, if adult outcomes are judged in terms of maximising the quality of life for individuals, rather than in terms of how 'normal' or 'successful' an individual is, a more positive picture emerges, given appropriate care and support.

PART II

WHAT CAUSES AUTISM?

A FRAMEWORK FOR EXPLAINING AUTISM

WHY EXPLAINING AUTISM IS IMPORTANT

COMPLICATIONS AND SIMPLIFICATIONS
Identifying a Realistic Agenda
Keeping the Explanatory Levels Apart and Putting Them Together
Simplifying the Search for Causes

ASSESSING THE MERITS OF CAUSAL THEORIES
Some Points to Bear in Mind
Criteria for Judging the Strength of Theories

SUMMARY

AIMS

The main aim of this chapter is to establish a framework for thinking about causal explanations of autism, to be used in subsequent chapters in Part II. Additional aims are to stress the importance of understanding the causes of autism, and to foster a critical approach to theoretical explanations of autism.

WHY EXPLAINING AUTISM IS IMPORTANT

It is of considerable practical importance to understand the causes of autism. Better understanding is needed to reduce the prevalence and symptom severity of debilitating forms of ASD that are associated with low learning and language ability and multiple medical and behavioural problems. The desirability of preventing or curing 'pure' autism in high-functioning individuals is questionable (see the opening section of Chapter 12). However, helping such people to achieve their potential, and also treating the distress that has warranted a diagnosis in the first place, is clearly desirable. To do this effectively it is necessary to understand the causes of the problems they face.

Although far from complete, the process of unravelling the **proximal**[1] (nearest: most immediate) **neuropsychological** causes of autism has already contributed to establishing rationales for **psychosocial**, **behavioural** and educational intervention (see Chapter 12). When the intermediate **neurobiological** causes – i.e. abnormalities of brain structure, chemistry and function – in autism are better understood, it is certain that pharmacological and possibly other physical treatments will be developed that effectively target specific aspects of behaviour, possibly in specific subgroups of individuals. Identification of **etiological** causes of autism is important for prevention. The identification of environmental factors that may be involved is particularly urgent and potentially important, because environmental factors may be modifiable, offering the prospect of reducing the incidence of ASD and associated problem behaviours. Understanding the genetic abnormalities that can cause, or make an individual vulnerable to, autism may also contribute to prevention in the future.

There are also theoretical spin-offs from investigations into the causes of ASD. In particular, such research should contribute to what is known about the links between brain and behaviour in typical development, and to understanding links between the functions of particular genes in shaping normal brain development. These advances in knowledge should have practical applications for the health and wellbeing of many groups of children.

---

[1]Words or phrases in bold type on first occurrence can be found in the Glossary.

COMPLICATIONS AND SIMPLIFICATIONS

Identifying the causes of autism is an exceedingly complicated and difficult undertaking, for the following reasons.

- Autism is a complex condition affecting very many aspects of behaviour. It is also very variable in the ways in which it is manifested in different individuals and at different stages of development, as emphasised in earlier chapters.
- There are three broad levels at which accounts of the causes of autism-related behaviour may be pitched, as identified in the second paragraph of this chapter. Not only must the causes of manifest behaviours associated with ASD be understood at each of these levels separately; in addition, ways in which the different levels of explanation relate to each other must also be identified, as shown by the arrows in Figure 6.1.
- There is no simple explanation of autism: the causes of autism-related behaviours are complex, cumulative and interactive.

In the next three subsections more will be said about each of these sources of difficulty in turn, with an explanation of the strategies to be used to simplify the material to be presented in subsequent chapters in Part II.

Identifying a Realistic Agenda

In the long term it may be possible to explain all the myriad bits of the puzzle which is autism: why age of onset varies; why young children with autism often have larger-than-usual heads; why they are often fussy eaters; why they so commonly

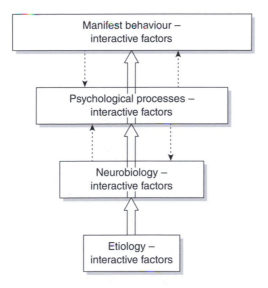

Figure 6.1 *Causal links that must be established*

develop epilepsy; the relationship between autism and exceptional achievement; why autism has not been removed from the gene pool by natural selection; and so on and so forth – an impossible agenda given the limitations of current knowledge. In the shorter term, therefore, the priority is to understand the causes of the diagnostic behavioural characteristics:

- Socio-emotional-communicative impairments and anomalies (SEC impairments).
- Restricted and repetitive behaviours, including sensory-perceptual anomalies (RRBs).

It is also important to understand the causes of the two most common and jointly debilitating specifiers:

- Learning disability.
- Language impairment.

Subsequent chapters in Part II will focus on this simplified agenda.

Keeping the Explanatory Levels Apart and Putting Them Together

In subsequent chapters in Part II, theories and evidence relating to causes of ASD-related behaviours will be considered at each explanatory level separately. Specifically, Chapter 7 considers what is known about the *etiology* (**distal** or 'root' causes) of the four sets of ASD-related behaviours listed under the bullet points above. Chapter 8 considers the *neurobiology* ('brain bases') of these ASD-related behaviours. Chapters 9 and 10 summarise current theory and evidence relating to the *neuropsychology* (proximal or 'immediate') causes of SEC impairments and RRBs, and of learning disability and language impairment. Links between explanatory factors at different levels of explanation are referred to where these have been reliably demonstrated.

Most space is given to explanation at the neuropsychological level for various reasons. First, more is known about the neuropsychology of ASD-related behaviours than about either the etiology or neurobiology underlying these behaviours. In the second place, educational, psychosocial and behavioural treatment methods should ideally be based on a detailed understanding of the neuropsychological processes underlying the patterns of ability and disability that typically occur in people with ASD. In this connection, it might be argued that understanding the neurobiology and especially the etiology of ASD could lead to prevention or cure, and that these aims should take priority over improvements to educational or behavioural treatments. However, the desirability of eliminating autism from the population may be questioned (see Chapter 12), whereas interventions that increase day-to-day competencies and decrease maladaptive behaviours are unarguably desirable. A third, purely pragmatic reason for the imbalance between space given to neuropsychology as opposed to other levels of explanation is that etiology and neurobiology both involve specialised knowledge too detailed to include in this book. Only the most basic information about these subjects is therefore covered in Chapters 7 and 8, with references cited where fuller accounts can be found.

Simplifying the Search for Causes

A diagram representing the causal links that may be implicated in any complete explanation of autism, let alone of autistic behaviours in any one individual, would show a dense tangle of cause–effect links. Major sources of this complexity are outlined below, before ways of simplifying the search for causes are suggested.

Sources of complexity

No single causal pathway   Early attempts to explain autism focused on explanations implicating a single causal factor, or 'single **common pathway**', at one or another level of explanation. Some of these early theories were mentioned in Chapter 1. These, and other examples of single common pathway theories, are shown in Box 6.1.

Box 6.1   Some single common pathway theories

At the etiological level

Genetically determined oversensitivity to oxygen (as administered at birth) (Rimland, 1964).

At the neurobiological level

Abnormal function of the reticular activating system in the brain (Hutt et al.,1964).
Abnormal function of the vestibular system in the brain (Ornitz & Ritvo, 1968).
Basal ganglia and mesial frontal abnormalities (Damasio & Maurer, 1978).

At the neuropsychological level

Lack of innate capacity for emotional relatedness (Kanner, 1943).
Faulty conditioning (Ferster, 1961).
Cold or neglectful parenting, especially by the mother (Bettelheim, 1967).
Severe language disorder (Churchill, 1972).
Defective understanding and use of symbols (Ricks & Wing, 1975).
Defective sequencing ability (Tanguay, 1984).
Impaired theory of mind (Baron-Cohen, 1989).

Single common pathway explanations of autism are attractive because they are parsimonious. However, **single factor theories** of ASD are undermined by evidence relating to what has been called the **broader autism phenotype (BAP)** or **lesser**

variant autism (Pickles et al., 2000; Wilcox et al., 2003; Dawson et al., 2002). This evidence shows that it is quite common for relatives of individuals with ASD to show signs of one or another kind of autism-related behaviour, in isolation from any other signs. A sibling, for example, may be something of a loner, but is not obsessive or routine-bound, and has good language. A father may be an avid collector of something, but at the same time sociable and articulate. An aunt may have had speech and language therapy as a child, and was slow to learn to read, but she has no problems with personal relationships and is not one-track minded or routine-bound. Evidence that gave rise to the concept of a broader autism phenotype, or lesser variant autism, shows that the SEC impairments and RRBs that define ASD – also vulnerability to language/learning impairments – are dissociable: any one of them can occur without the others. It follows that they must have at least partly different causes (Happé et al., 2006).

Many-to-one and one-to-many Life would be easier for those seeking to understand the causes of autism if each facet of autism-related behaviour had a single, clear-cut explanation at each level – etiological linking to neurobiological linking to neuropsychological. Unfortunately this is not the case. For example, impaired **mentalising** may be a critical cause of SEC impairments, as is suggested in Chapter 9. However, obsessive interests, abnormal sensory perception, and poor language comprehension, if present, may also contribute. Similarly, RRBs (including sensory-perceptual anomalies) may possibly result mainly from poor control of **arousal** levels, as is also discussed in Chapter 9. That said, anxiety, maladaptive learning or comorbid obsessive-compulsive disorder may also contribute. The phrase 'many-to-one' (coined, I think, by Uta Frith) neatly captures the fact that each facet of autism-associated behaviour has many contributory causes (see Figure 6.2a).

At the same time, a single causal factor can have multiple effects. For example (and again considering only the neuropsychological level of explanation), impaired mentalising is not only a critical cause of SEC impairments, but also an important cause of impaired sense of self and a cause of certain anomalies of language. Hence the phrase (also Frith's) 'one-to-many' (see Figure 6.2b).

Multi-directional causal links It might be assumed that links in the chain of causes and effects always travel 'upwards', as suggested by the central arrows in Figure 6.1: that is to say, from root causes to brain bases to the immediate neuropsychological causes of manifest behaviour. Unfortunately, yet again, the reality is not in fact so simple: as well as 'forwards' cause–effect links, there are also 'sideways' causal links. For example, at the neuropsychological level, impaired ability to recognise faces aggravates a pre-existing lack of interest in, and lack of attention to, faces, which then feeds backwards into the original recognition impairment, making it worse than it originally was. Similarly, at the neurobiological level, a congenital abnormality in a **subcortical** structure that normally sends information to certain **cortical** structures will affect the development and function of those cortical structures. At the etiological level it is likely that genes underlying vulnerability to autism are interactive as well as cumulative.

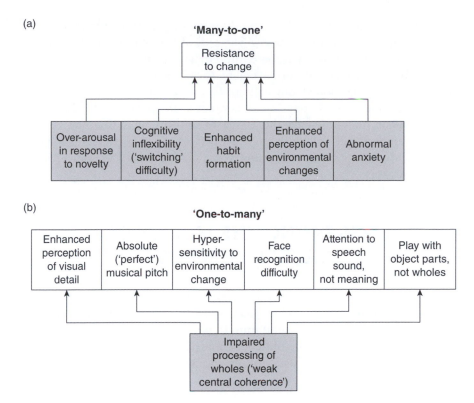

(a)

'Many-to-one'

Resistance to change

Over-arousal in response to novelty

Cognitive inflexibility ('switching' difficulty)

Enhanced habit formation

Enhanced perception of environmental changes

Abnormal anxiety

(b)

'One-to-many'

Enhanced perception of visual detail

Absolute ('perfect') musical pitch

Hyper-sensitivity to environmental change

Face recognition difficulty

Attention to speech sound, not meaning

Play with object parts, not wholes

Impaired processing of wholes ('weak central coherence')

Figure 6.2 *Examples of (a) 'many-to-one' and (b) 'one-to-many'*

Individual differences   Many of the causal factors mentioned above as possibly contributing to autistic behaviour do not apply to everyone with autism. The whole complex of interactive causal factors contributing to autism-related behaviours in any one individual will therefore be unique.

Simplifying the search for causal factors

In view of the complexity and diversity of causal pathways to autism in its various forms, let alone in unique individuals, the following simplifying strategy will be used in subsequent chapters in Part II.

Only the most important causal factors at each level of explanation will be considered. These will be referred to as 'critical causes' or 'critical causal factors'. Such critical factors are those that may be **necessary** and/or **sufficient** to cause a certain set of autism-related behaviours to develop. By 'necessary' is meant that a particular causal factor must be present for a particular effect to occur. For example, the AIDS virus is a necessary cause of AIDS: people do not develop AIDS unless exposed to the virus. It is also a 'sufficient' cause, because nothing else is needed for AIDS to occur. By contrast, there is no necessary cause of an ailment such as toothache. Rather, toothache can occur for a number of reasons such as an abcess, caries or breaking a tooth, any of which can be sufficient for it to occur, but none of which is a necessary cause – because there are alternatives.

It is safe to assume that there are certain necessary and/or sufficient causes of each of the defining impairments in ASD, and of the major specifiers. In what follows, these critical causes will be explored. The contributory role of factors which are neither necessary nor sufficient to explain facets of autism-related behaviour may be mentioned, but will not be discussed in detail. Parents, teachers, therapists and others in day-to-day contact with specific individuals on the spectrum do not, of course, have the luxury of simplifying in this way. For them, in order to understand and respond appropriately to a particular behavioural difficulty or stumbling block to learning, it may be necessary to unravel a whole complex of causes.

ASSESSING THE MERITS OF CAUSAL THEORIES

At present no one knows for certain what causes autism, whether in terms of root causes, brain bases or neuropsychological anomalies. It is essential, therefore, to keep an open mind, but at the same time to be critical, in the best sense of that word, when considering theories of the possible causes of autism. In what follows, some points to bear in mind when critically appraising the merits of any particular theory are suggested.

Some Points to Bear in Mind

Recent does not necessarily mean right

The list of 'single common pathway' explanations of ASD, outlined in Box 6.1, shows that explanatory theories come and then usually go, to be superseded by other theories, which are superseded in their turn. Each of the early theories was among the most recent when first presented, but most were subsequently rejected. There is no reason to suppose that this process has entirely ceased, although with the benefit of 50–60 years of research, recent theories are more securely evidence-based than earlier theories.

Old does not necessarily mean wrong

That said, old theories should not be entirely discounted. Sometimes a theory is largely ignored when first proposed, but is recognised years later as having been ahead of its time. For example, in 1943 Kanner proposed that autism derives from 'an innate inability to form the usual biologically provided affective contact with people'. This theory was ignored for several decades because, first, psychoanalytic explanations of autism dominated the literature; then **behaviourist** explanations; then explanations based on thinking of the brain as if it were a computer – 'information processing' models. Fifty years after it was first proposed, Kanner's theory that ASD is an innate, brain-based condition was revived (by Hobson, 1993, in particular) and is now seen as consistent with mainstream contemporary theories, as will become clear in Chapter 9. Similarly, the theory that dysregulation of arousal levels may explain RRBs in ASD, also discussed in Chapter 9, was first proposed by Hutt et al. in 1964. Consider also one of the earliest attempts to establish a set of diagnostic criteria for ASD, namely 'Creak's Nine Points' (see Box 1.2). These included 'abnormal response to perceptual stimuli', now reinstated within diagnostic criteria after many years of absence; and 'apparent unawareness of personal identity', a characteristic confirmed by recent research, but little commented on in the intervening period.

It is also important to appreciate that theories receiving even temporary recognition are not plucked out of thin air: they are all based at the very least on observation and experience, and usually also on evidence from research. So, for example, Bettelheim's psychoanalytic theory was based on evidence that mothers' relationships with their young autistic children are abnormal. It was later realised that this is not because these mothers are by nature cold and uncaring, as originally suggested, but because it is difficult, often unrewarding and sometimes distressing to try to establish a loving, interactive relationship with a young child with autism, especially if the nature of the child's problem is not at first understood. It is now widely recognised that parents and other main carers of young children with ASD may need support and advice as to how best to establish a loving relationship with their difficult child, and perhaps how to cope with their own feelings of disappointment and frustration.

Who says?

The people who know about autism in vivid detail are people who are themselves autistic, their families, carers, and others in day-to-day contact with them. Any theory that is not informed by, and consistent with, the experience of the majority of those closely involved with autism is not likely to be correct. Research findings generally confirm what parents, teachers and high-functioning people themselves know. Research may clarify or extend what 'insiders' know, while rarely conflicting with it (and when it does, it is generally the research that needs to be looked at again). Equally, anecdotes or observations from insiders' accounts are often the seed corn for a particular theoretical hypothesis. For example, the first study of pretend play with which I was involved, carried out at a time when it was commonly said that children with autism cannot pretend, was motivated by a teacher telling me that a not very able girl with autism had returned from a visit to a stately home and trailed a coloured scarf behind her, saying 'bird': she had seen peacocks on her day out!

People with ASD and those who care for and work with them may not, however, be in a good position to see the bigger picture: they see one, or a few, of the trees in vivid detail, but not the whole wood made up of many and diverse trees. Researchers and theoreticians have their eyes on the wood as a whole. Reliable evidence about autism *in general* must therefore come from research studies, and these must be properly conducted and properly interpreted. Well-conducted, appropriately interpreted research studies are most likely to be found in journals that use the vetting process of **peer review**. Research reports that are published without peer review constitute what is known as the **grey**

literature. It is wise to be aware of the theories and evidence being discussed in the grey literature: there is rarely smoke without fire, and much of the grey literature is written by parents or clinicians who have detailed experience of autism. However, the more reliable source of evidence and theories concerning the causes of autism is the peer-reviewed journals. All the research studies referred to in subsequent chapters are published in journals with a high standard of peer review.

Criteria for Judging the Strength of Theories

When judging the **explanatory power** of theories relating to autism, the following criteria should be borne in mind.

Specificity criterion   According to this criterion, if a theory proposes that critical factor x is *necessary and sufficient* to cause a particular facet of autism, then factor x (whether at the etiological, neurobiological or neuropsychological level of explanation) must be specific to, that is to say, unique to, people with ASD. If factor x is *not* specific to individuals with ASD there is a problem of explaining why other individuals, to whom factor x also applies, do not show autistic behaviours. For example, it was proposed for a time that an impairment of explicit theory of mind (see Chapter 3) is the critical cause of the socio-emotional-communicative impairments diagnostic of autism. However, typically developing children below the age of 3 years 6 months, as well as many learning disabled individuals, also fail tests of explicit ToM, but are not autistic. This impairment cannot, therefore, be the necessary and sufficient cause of SEC impairments in ASD.

Universality criterion   This criterion states that if a theory proposes that critical factor x is a *necessary* (even if not sufficient) cause of one of the defining or additional shared features of autistic behaviour, then factor x must be shown to occur universally in all individuals with ASD. If not universally present, then factor x cannot logically be a *necessary* cause of that facet of autism-related behaviour. For example, if it is proposed that impaired mindreading is a necessary cause of SEC impairments in autism, then it must be shown that *all* individuals with ASD have impaired mindreading.

Primacy criterion   The primacy, or 'causal precedence', criterion requires that factor x must occur at an earlier developmental stage than the abnormality that factor x is supposed to explain. This is because it is a law of nature that causes precede effects. The original much-hyped 1980s/1990s 'impaired theory of mind' explanation of socio-emotional-communicative impairments in ASD failed on this criterion, because SEC impairments occur in infants with ASD usually within the first 30 months of life. Because the ability to pass explicit ToM tests does not mature in typically developing children until much later than this, lack of an explicit ToM cannot explain the early signs of SEC impairments in autism.

SUMMARY

It is important to understand the causes of autism in order to progress towards better treatments and possible prevention of debilitating forms of ASD at some future time. Understanding the causes of autism will also contribute to understanding brain development and brain–behaviour relations in typically developing children.

However, explaining autism is difficult, for numerous reasons. These include the fact that autism is a complex condition affecting very many aspects of behaviour. It is also very variable in the ways in which it is manifested in different individuals and at different stages of development. In addition, there are three broad levels at which accounts of the causes of autism may be pitched: the etiological or 'first causes' level; the neurobiological or 'brain bases' level; and the neuropsychological or 'immediate causes' level. Not only must the causes of autism be understood at each of these levels separately; the ways in which etiological factors give rise to neurobiological abnormalities and anomalies, which in turn cause neuropsychological abnormalities, must also be identified. Moreover, there is no single critical cause, no 'single common pathway', at any of the three levels of explanation. Instead, it is certain that the causes of autism-related behaviours are complex, cumulative, interactive and to some extent individualistic.

Some ways of simplifying the explanatory task are outlined, to be used in subsequent chapters of Part II of this book. These include the following: focusing only on the universal or most common behavioural characteristics; focusing on the identification of causal factors at each level of explanation separately; and seeking to identify only the main, or most critical, cause(s) of each of the universal or very common behavioural impairments, ignoring more minor contributory causes.

Finally, it is important to maintain a critical attitude when considering the relative merits of particular theories of the causes of autism. The most recent theory is unlikely at this stage of knowledge to be completely correct; equally, older theories should not be automatically discounted. The research evidence cited in support of a particular theory should be carefully considered before being accepted, and the explanatory adequacy of each theory judged on the criteria of specificity, universality and primacy.

ROOT CAUSES

> # AIMS
>
> The main aim of this chapter is to provide a brief account of what is currently known about the etiology, or root causes, of autism. Secondary aims of the chapter are: (1) to supply some basic information and terminology relating to genetics, focusing in particular on those facets of genetics that have particular relevance for the etiology of ASD; (2) to ensure a broad understanding of what is meant by 'environmental factors'; (3) to stress the likelihood that almost all cases of ASD result from unique combinations of several genetic and/or environmental factors, single-cause cases being unlikely to occur; (4) to link the cumulative and heterogeneous nature of causal factors involved in individual cases to heterogeneity among outcomes. A final aim is to stress that knowledge in this field is incomplete, with many issues in need of further investigation.

INTRODUCTION

Idiopathic and Syndromic Forms of ASD

The root causes of 85–90 per cent of cases of ASD are poorly understood. The medical term for conditions that arise from within an individual for unclear reasons is idiopathic. This chapter is mainly concerned with what is known about the root causes of idiopathic ASD.

However, as indicated in the set of possible 'specifiers' in DSM-5 diagnostic criteria, ASD occasionally co-occurs with some other developmental syndrome – for example, Down syndrome – the cause of which is known. Such cases may be referred to as **syndromic autism/ASD**.[1] There are many forms of syndromic autism (Freitag et al., 2010; Miles, 2011) which can provide clues as to the causes of idiopathic ASD. Some forms of syndromic autism will therefore be mentioned below where relevant for understanding the causes of idiopathic autism. It is important to note, however, that cases of syndromic ASD cannot be fully explained in terms of the known cause, or causes, of any accompanying medical syndrome. If the genetic anomaly underlying, for example, Down syndrome were sufficient to cause ASD, then all individuals with Down syndrome would also have ASD – which is clearly not the case.

The Concept of Risk Factors

There is no single cause of autism, as pointed out in the previous chapter. Rather, it is likely that there are many 'risk factors', none of which is by itself either necessary or sufficient to cause ASD, but which, if occurring together in certain combinations, become sufficient.

---

[1]Words or phrases in bold type on first occurrence can be found in the Glossary.

Possible risk factors for developing ASD fall into two groups: genetic and environmental. These are not mutually exclusive. It is likely, for example, that cases of late-onset ASD result from an environmental 'trigger' impinging post-natally on an individual with a genetic vulnerability to the development of ASD. An example of where this may have happened is described in Box 7.3 later in the chapter. It is also likely that a range of environmental factors originating in the mother's mental and physical health, and her exposure to or ingestion of certain substances during pregnancy interact with genetic risk factors prenatally to cause early-onset ASD.

'Risk factors' for ASD, whether solely genetic, solely environmental, or a combination of the two, contribute to the development of a unique individual. This unique individual outcome can be described as a **phenotype**. However, the term 'phenotype' can also refer to outcomes characteristic of a particular group. Thus reference is sometimes made to an 'autism phenotype', which describes people with typical autism, or to the 'broader autism phenotype' (BAP), which refers to people with mild autism-related behavioural traits, as described in Chapter 6.

Genetic and environmental risk factors are considered separately below. In each case, an explanation of what constitutes a genetic (or environmental) risk factor is given first. Evidence showing that genetic (or environmental) risk factors are involved in the etiology of ASD is outlined next. The current state of knowledge concerning genetic (or environmental) risk factors follows. Finally, there is a brief section outlining how the risk factors that have been identified may contribute to abnormal brain development and function.

GENETIC RISK FACTORS

What are 'Genetic Risk Factors'?

Genetic risk factors may be associated with the *chromosomes* inherited from biological parents, the *genes* that make up the chromosomes, the *constituents of genes and gene products*, and the *DNA between genes* that may influence gene expression. An individual's complete genetic inheritance is referred to as their **genome**. However, when selective aspects of genetic inheritance are being discussed, usually in relation to particular traits – for example height, hair colour, or vulnerability to particular diseases – the word **genotype** is more commonly used. Every individual's genome is unique except in the case of identical (or **monozygotic (MZ)**) twins, who develop from the same fertilised egg. Twins who develop from different fertilised eggs do not share identical genomes, and are referred to as **dizygotic (DZ)** twins. The genomes of dizygotic twins are no more and no less alike than those of non-twin siblings.

Unlike the genomes for very simple organisms, human genomes do not provide a blueprint for development. Instead, they set constraints on development ensuring that a human baby develops (and not something quite different), and that lifetime changes involving growth, maturation and ageing occur in species-predictable ways. Within these constraints the genes and their products generally have regulatory and mutually interactive roles rather than prescriptive roles. This allows for environmental factors to interact with gene products and influence development.

Evidence for the Involvement of Genetic Factors

Cases of syndromic ASD

The fact that full or partial forms of ASD co-occur with certain genetically-determined conditions more often than can be explained by chance, albeit rarely, shows that a range of genetic anomalies can predispose an individual to the development of autism-related behaviour. Some examples are outlinedin Box 7.1.

Box 7.1   Genetic risk factors for syndromic ASD: Some representative examples

Chromosomal disorders

Individuals with *Turner syndrome* are females who have only one sex-linked X- chromosome, instead of the normal pair – (X X in females; X Y in males).

Individuals with *Down syndrome* have three copies of chromosome 21 in all or most cells, instead of the normal pair of copies. This is why another term for Down syndrome is 'Trisomy 21'.

Prader-Willi syndrome is most commonly caused by structural and functional abnormalities of genes on the paternal copy of chromosome 15. However, in approximately 25 per cent of cases the affected person has two copies of chromosome 15 inherited from his or her mother instead of one copy from each parent.

Single gene disorders

In *Fragile-X syndrome* a single gene on the X-chromosome – the 'FMR1' gene – is affected. 'FMR' stands for 'Fragile-X Mental Retardation'. Obviously this gene was named after the link with this particular syndrome had been established.

In *Tuberous Sclerosis Complex*, a single gene – either the TSC1 gene on chromosome 9 or the TSC2 gene on chromosome 16 – is affected. 'TSC' stands for 'Tuberose Sclerosis Complex', the name having been given after the link with the syndrome had been established.

In *Phenylketonuria (PKU)*, a single gene on chromosome 12 – the PAH gene – is affected. 'PAH' stands for phenyl-alanine hydroxylase, which is an enzyme needed to extract certain protein-building nutrients from food. The PAH gene provides the instructions for making this enzyme. (NB: If detected early, PKU is treatable.)

Twin studies

Studies of twin pairs (reviewed by Ronald & Hoekstra, 2011) show that in monozygotic (MZ) twins, one of whom has ASD, the second twin is highly likely to have ASD also. Moreover, of those second twins who do not have the full set of behaviours diagnostic of ASD, many show some facets of autism in their behaviour, i.e. they can be described as falling within the broader autism phenotype (BAP). In dizygotic (DZ) twins, on the other hand, far fewer second twins either have ASD or fall within the BAP. The differences between typical outcomes for second twins from MZ twin pairs as opposed to DZ twin pairs are shown in Figure 7.1. The precise percentages of second twins who have ASD, or fall within the BAP, vary slightly across the various studies reviewed by Ronald and Hoekstra. However, the percentages illustrated, taken from Bailey et al. (1995), are representative. The high rate of **concordance** in MZ twins, contrasted with the high rate of **discordance** in DZ twins, provides irrefutable evidence that genetic factors strongly predispose individuals towards developing full or partial forms of ASD.

Family studies

Studies of **first-degree relatives** (i.e. biological parents and siblings) of ASD **probands** (individuals with ASD) show that the chance of an individual with ASD having a brother or sister who is also autistic, or who has one or another autism-related behavioural trait, is far higher than can be explained in terms of chance (Constantino et al., 2010; Geschwind, 2011). The parents of an individual with ASD are also unusually likely to have some slight behaviour anomaly, either past

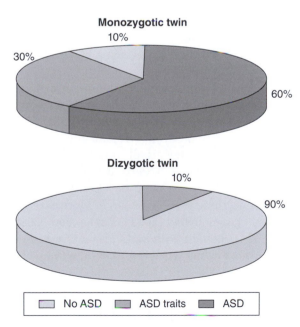

Figure 7.1 *Typical outcomes for second twins from monozygotic and dizygotic twin pairs in which one twin has ASD*

or present, which places them within the BAP (Bernier et al., 2012). Families in which more than one person has ASD, and/or close relatives fall within the BAP, are referred to as **multiplex families**. The common occurrence of multiplex families not only provides evidence of the role of genetic factors in the etiology of autism, but also shows that these factors are often **familial**.

Less frequently, ASD occurs in an individual who has no relatives with either ASD or autistic-like behaviour traits. Such individuals are sometimes referred to as having **sporadic** ASD, as opposed to familial ASD; and families in which an isolated, or sporadic, case of ASD has occurred are referred to as **simplex families**.

Because they are not familial, it might be thought that all cases of sporadic ASD must be caused solely by environmental factors. This would be a false inference, however, for the following reasons. First, many developmental syndromes (Williams syndrome, Down syndrome, for example) are not familial, but are nevertheless caused by genetic abnormalities. Such syndromes result from damage or deterioration of genetic material within the egg or sperm, occurring during the lifetime of one or other parent and commonly associated with parental ageing. Similarly, it has been shown that a significant proportion of cases of sporadic ASD are associated with submicroscopic anomalies of genetic material, especially in the offspring of older fathers (Hultman et al., 2011; Frans et al., 2013). If – as may be the case in Western societies in which lifelong partnerships are decreasingly the norm – more older men than previously are fathering children, this could be one factor contributing to increased prevalence of ASD.

Current Knowledge of Genetic Risk Factors for ASD

A great deal is known about genetic risk factors for ASD. This knowledge comes from studies using a range of methodologies, some of which are briefly described in Box 7.2.

Despite the sheer quantity of studies and findings relating to genetic risk factors for ASD, this knowledge is incomplete, confusing, and often controversial. In addition, it is developing and changing all the time as more becomes known about the functions of individual genes in typically developing individuals, and as methods of genetic assessment become increasingly sophisticated. Because of the uncertainties and rapid rate of change relating to knowledge of genetic risk factors for ASD, only a brief review of what is known more or less for certain is presented here, plus some indications concerning ongoing research. More extended reviews can be found in Betancur (2011), Geschwind (2011), Persico and Napolioni (2013), and Rutter and Thapar (2014). Readers with particular interest in genetic risk factors should look for later reviews as and when these become available and publications cited here become outdated.

Many genetic risk factors

ASD is **polygenic** in origin: individually, none of the possible or likely genetic risk factors for ASD, technically known as **genetic variants**, causes ASD. Cumulatively, however, and in certain combinations, genetic variants can cause or significantly

> ## Box 7.2   Methods used in research into the genetic bases of autism
>
> **Genetic screening** involves the analysis of DNA samples. The genetic material is analysed using various strategies, including the following:
>
> **Genome-wide association screening (GWAS)** may be carried out in a search for genetic anomalies in a particular population.
>
> **Candidate genes** may be specifically investigated. For example, it is known that certain neurochemical system abnormalities are frequently found in people with ASD, and the genes involved in the normal development of these systems constitute candidate genes.
>
> **Linkage studies** involve analysing genetic samples from two or more affected relatives in the same family to see whether there are genetic anomalies held in common. Genome-wide screening or candidate gene assessment may be used in linkage studies.
>
> **Association studies** involve analysing genetic samples from individuals with a clear diagnosis of ASD and comparing the results with samples from individuals who are not autistic. Genome-wide screening or candidate gene assessment may be used in association studies.
>
> **Quantitative trait loci (QTL)** studies are similar to association studies but more precise in that, instead of looking for gene abnormalities that are associated with autism as a whole, they look for gene abnormalities that may be associated with specific behaviours that occur in autism, such as 'desire for sameness' or 'age of speech onset'.
>
> **Cytogenetics** is used in the study of chromosomal abnormalities. Techniques used include the following:
>
> **Fluorescence in situ hybridization (FISH test)** is used to detect and localise the presence or absence of specific DNA sequences on chromosomes.
>
> **Array comparative genomic hybridization (aCGH)** is used to detect chromosomal copy number variations (CNVs – see below).
>
> **Animal models** are used to study the behavioural consequences of eliminating or 'knocking out' a particular gene post-conception. Rodents are the animals most commonly used. For example, the gene responsible for establishing a neurochemical mediator of social reward is known, and it has been claimed that 'knockout mice' lacking this gene also lack the kinds of social behaviour that might be dependent on social reward.

contribute to the development of ASD. There may in fact be 'tens or perhaps hundreds' of genetic risk factors for ASD (Betancur, 2011). Betancur's challenging statement implies that the genetic factors that may contribute to ASD are not just diverse, but probably unique in individual cases (cf. the case made in the book by Waterhouse (2013), referred to in Chapter 4).

Shared risk factors

Many of the common genetic variants that have been identified in people with ASD are **pleiotropic**, referring to the fact that they also occur in individuals with other mental health conditions (e.g. schizophrenia) and **neurodevelopmental disorders** (e.g. developmental dyslexia, **specific language impairment (SLI)**, attention deficit with hyperactivity disorder (ADHD)) (Cross-Disorder Group of the Psychiatric Genomics Consortium, 2013; Rutter and Thapar, 2014). Findings of pleiotropy help to explain why, for example, some facets of schizophrenia overlap with those of ASD; and why certain neurodevelopmental disorders co-occur with ASD more frequently than can be explained by chance.

Kinds of genetic variant

There are several different kinds of genetic variants. Some affect whole chromosomes, some affect individual genes, and some affect the DNA between genes.

Chromosomal variants A whole chromosome may be missing or re-duplicated, or have so many missing or structurally abnormal genes that the whole chromosome is compromised. Some of the developmental syndromes that are present in various forms of syndromic ASD are chromosomal disorders, including Down syndrome, Turner syndrome, Fragile-X syndrome, and Prader-Willi syndrome. Certain chromosomal abnormalities therefore constitute risk factors for the development of ASD, although being neither necessary nor sufficient by themselves to cause ASD.

Gene variants Individual genes may be either missing or re-duplicated (as in chromosomal variants), or there may be variations in the sequencing of DNA molecules within a gene. **Copy number variations (CNVs)** of individual genes (involving the deletion or duplication of a gene) are in most instances common. They are therefore sometimes referred to as **copy number polymorphisms (CNPs)**, where 'polymorphism' refers to the fact that a particular genetic variation occurs in more than 1 per cent of the general population. CNPs, or **common variants** as they are sometimes called, are 'normal' in that they contribute to making every individual genome unique (except in the case of MZ twins), thereby contributing to individual differences in physique, temperament, cognitive abilities, and so forth. The effect on development of any individual instance of copy number variation is tiny. However, there is evidence to suggest that an accumulation of common variants in certain combinations may underlie vulnerability to many common diseases and mental health conditions. In the case of ASD there is evidence that over 50 per cent of liability, or vulnerability, to developing ASD results from the additive effects of inherited common variants (Klei et al., 2012). This finding helps to explain why certain ASD-related behavioural traits tend to run in families, often manifesting in mild forms – presumably where there is some accumulation of certain common variants, but not a sufficient accumulation to produce full ASD.

Not all CNVs are common: some are in fact rare. These rare variants usually consist of mutations arising *de novo* in an individual, as opposed to being inherited. Rare mutations have been shown to constitute significant risk factors for the development of ASD, although of less significance than common variants (CNPs) (see the review by De Rubeis & Buxbaum, 2015; also chapters in Section 2 of the book edited by Buxbaum & Hof, 2012).

Genes that are missing, re-duplicated, or structurally abnormal in some other way, and that have been shown to predispose an individual to the development of ASD, are referred to as **susceptibility genes** (for ASD), or **candidate genes**, where the link is likely, but not fully established. Some susceptibility genes can be identified from forms of syndromic ASD that result from disruption of function of a single gene. Single-gene disorders that can co-occur with ASD include tuberous sclerosis and Williams syndrome. Candidate genes include those known to be implicated in conditions such as intellectual disability and language impairment, which are the major specifiers in DSM-5 diagnostic criteria. The process of identifying those genes most likely to be affected in ASD is ongoing. Given that there are thought to be approximately 20,000 genes in the human genome, and given that this figure is itself a matter of controversy, progress towards identifying all susceptibility genes for ASD is certain to be slow.

Between-gene DNA variants   Variations in the sequences of molecules in DNA situated between genes are common in the general population, frequently involving a reversal of the order in which two molecules occur in a sequence. Such variations are referred to as **single-nucleotide polymorphisms** (**SNPs**, usually pronounced 'SNiPS'). SNPs influence how individual genes are expressed: they have what are sometimes called **epigenetic** effects. Like other common genetic variants, they are 'normal' in that they help to produce phenotypic diversity and individuality. There is no strong evidence to date to suggest that any specific SNPs constitute risk factors for the development of ASD. Nevertheless, given that so little is known, relatively speaking, about how genes are expressed, research into SNPs as possible risk factors for ASD will continue.

Genetic Risk Factors and Abnormal Brain Development

Someone reading the above summary of what is known about genetic risk factors for ASD might reasonably ask how such numerous and diverse factors, possibly in numerous and diverse combinations, might all cause or contribute to ASD. Although there is no clear answer to this question at present, genetic risk factors for ASD must all, in some way or another, contribute to whatever anomalies of brain structure and function underlie ASD-related behaviour (Rutter & Thapar, 2014).

Belmonte, Cook et al. (2004) described the multiplicity of risk factors for ASD, whether genetic or environmental, as 'fanning in' to produce whatever brain anomalies underlie autism-related behaviour. In Chapter 8, where the brain bases of ASD are considered, it will be seen that these anomalies are widely considered to involve reduced **connectivity** within and between certain **neural networks/ circuits/systems**. Guilmatre et al. (2009) noted that the CNVs most likely to constitute risk factors for ASD all occur within genes that contribute to establishing and maintaining neural **synapses**. Similarly, Zoghbi and Bear (2012) have argued that the genetic anomalies known to be involved in forms of syndromic autism would be likely to interfere with synaptic formation and functioning.

Research aimed at establishing links between known risk factors for ASD and known brain anomalies associated with ASD is a certain growth area for research over the next decade, not least because establishing such links is a necessary step towards developing effective physical treatments (Zoghbi & Bear, 2012).

ENVIRONMENTAL RISK FACTORS

What are 'Environmental Risk Factors'?

Environmental risk factors may include those operating *prenatally* with effects on the developing **embryo** and **fetus**; factors operating *perinatally*, i.e. around the time of birth; and factors operating *postnatally*. They may involve *internal bodily states*, as well as *external factors*, i.e. those impinging on the individual from the outside.

Examples of environmental factors associated with internal bodily states include the fact that each gene operates in an environment created by the activities of other genes; similarly, each neurochemical involved in brain function operates in the environment created by other neurochemicals; moreover, brain function and behaviour are affected by an individual's physiological state more generally, including their nutritional and health status. Examples of environmental factors impinging 'from the outside' include those associated with the mother's bodily state during pregnancy; obstetric and other perinatal interventions; as well as factors such as illnesses, deprivation, and exposure to toxic chemicals that may affect development postnatally. It is important, therefore, not to look for environmental risk factors only among external factors affecting a child postnatally: environmental factors are much broader than this.

Environmental factors operating from the moment of conception interact with the given genome, or genotype, to produce a phenotype. There is an increasing amount of research into ways in which genetic and environmental risk factors combine and influence each other to produce full or partial forms of ASD: it is no longer a case of '*either* genetic factors *or* environmental factors cause ASD'. Instead it seems likely that ASD-related behaviours most frequently result from interactions between genetic and environmental factors (Chaste & Leboyer, 2012; Tordjman et al., 2014; Kim et al., 2015).

Evidence for the Involvement of Environmental Risk Factors in ASD

Twin studies   The findings from twin studies summarised in Figure 7.1 provide powerful evidence for the role of environmental factors in the etiology of ASD, as well as for the role of genetic factors. This is because the following facts need to be explained:

- In approximately 10 per cent of MZ twin pairs, one has ASD and one does not have ASD in any form, whether full or partial.
- In the 60 per cent of cases in which both MZ twins have ASD, learning ability and the severity and pattern of autism-related behaviours varies considerably, and to no lesser extent than in DZ twin pairs both of whom have autism (Le Couteur et al., 1996).
- In 30 per cent of MZ twin pairs, one has ASD in its full form but the other has only some features of autism-related behaviour. Moreover, this is reflected in differences in brain structure and function (Kates et al., 2004; Belmonte & Carper, 2006).

Shared genes cannot explain these differences, which must be explained by environmental factors, broadly interpreted.

Sporadic ASD As stated above, some cases of sporadic (non-familial) ASD can be explained, or partially explained, in terms of genetic abnormalities associated with damage or deterioration to the egg or sperm during the lifetime of one or the other parent, or shortly after conception. However, only a small percentage of sporadic ASD cases can be explained in this way – 10 per cent in a study by Sebat et al. (2007). It is possible that the percentage of cases of sporadic ASD that can be wholly or partly explained by genetic anomalies may increase as a result of further research. However, it is unlikely that genetic anomalies by themselves will ever provide an adequate explanation of all cases of sporadic ASD. The majority must therefore be explained wholly or in part by environmental factors. This conclusion is reinforced by the fact that cases of sporadic ASD are known to occur in association with certain environmental factors, as detailed later.

Regressive ASD 'Regressive ASD' was defined in Chapter 5 as a mode of onset in which development is normal until the second half of the second year of life or into the third year, but then autism-related behaviours appear, sometimes gradually, sometimes quite suddenly. This mode of onset could suggest that some environmental factor is causally involved, either acting alone or in combination with genetic vulnerability to ASD.

Rising incidence of ASD The dramatic rise in the incidence of ASD over the last couple of decades could plausibly be explained or partly explained by environmental factors of relatively recent origin. This has not been proven to be the case. However, this possibility has intensified the search for environmental factors of recent origin, not least because if such factors can be identified and counteracted, the incidence of ASD might be reduced.

Current Knowledge of Environmental Risk Factors for ASD

Many 'candidate' environmental factors

As in the case of genetic variants, there are a great many potentially relevant environmental risk factors for ASD. Also as with genetic variants, many possibly relevant environmental factors have not yet been investigated. In particular, very few of the many thousands of chemical compounds that are present in our homes (in furnishings, cleaning aids, food additives, children's toys, cosmetics, fragrances, pest control products), in our places of work (especially in agricultural or industrial settings), and in the air we breathe (especially in towns and close to busy roads) have been assessed for possible adverse effects on fetal development (Grandjean & Landigran, 2014; Kalkbrenner et al., 2014; Lyall et al., 2014).

This statement should, however, be counterbalanced by the fact that if many such chemical compounds were highly significant risk factors for ASD, then the incidence of ASD would be even higher than it is. It is more likely that several – possibly many – chemicals in the man-made environment will eventually be identified as constituting weak risk factors for full or partial forms of ASD, only playing a contributory role when present in combination with an accumulation of other genetic and/or environmental risk factors.

Shared risk factors

Several of the possible environmental risk factors for ASD identified in the next subsection are, like genetic risk factors, pleiotropic. That is to say, they are risk factors not only for ASD, but also for other mental health or behavioural disorders, including schizophrenia, ADHD and intellectual disability. As in the case of genetic risk factors, this helps to explain why ASD so often co-occurs with, or has unclear boundaries with, other disorders.

Known or suspected environmental risk factors

Known or suspected environmental risk factors for ASD are listed below under the headings prenatal factors, perinatal factors and postnatal factors. Some factors in the environment that have been investigated but which are (almost) certainly *not* contributory causes of ASD are also identified. Evidence relating to candidate environmental risk factors generally can be found in reviews by Scott et al. (2013), Lyall et al. (2014) and Kalkbrenner et al. (2014). Reports of research studies relating to specific risk factors are cited below, where available.

Prenatal factors affecting fetal development via the mother

- Exposure to valproic acid/sodium sulphate medication, commonly prescribed as an anticonvulsant but also for migraine and some psychiatric disorders (Christensen et al., 2013). Exposure to this medication during the early months of pregnancy appears capable of causing ASD-related behaviour in the absence of any other risk factors (Arndt et al., 2005).
- Exposure to traffic-related air pollutants, especially those from diesel (Yoshimasu et al., 2014; Lam et al., 2016).
- Exposure to certain pesticides, for example organophosphates, organochlorines (Shelton et al., 2014).
- Infections with fever (e.g. rubella, flu) (Zerbo et al., 2013).
- Cytomegalovirus infection (Sakamoto et al., 2015).
- Immune system abnormalities (Easson & Woodbury-Smith, 2014) (possibly associated with infections).
- Diabetes (Xu et al., 2014).
- Obesity (Surén et al., 2014).
- Stress (Roberts et al., 2014).
- Migrant status (possibly associated with maternal stress and/or Vitamin D deficiency) (Bolton et al., 2014).

- Vitamin D deficiency during pregnancy (possibly associated with season of birth and/or with immigrant status) (Fernell et al., 2015).
- Certain antidepressants (Rai et al., 2013).
- Short interpregnancy interval and multiple births (possibly associated with nutrient depletion) (Gunnes et al., 2013).
- Pregnancy complications, for example bleeding, pregnancy-related hypertension or pre-eclampsia; also a maternal history of abortion(s), miscarriages(s) or stillbirth(s) (Lyall et al., 2012).

Several of the candidate risk factors listed above, some of which fall into the category of **teratogens**, are most likely to be associated with ASD if they occur during the first three months of pregnancy. This generalisation does not, however, hold true for all the risk factors listed – see Figure 7.2.

The following have been proposed as possible environmental risk factors for ASD, but investigations to date have produced conflicting results. More research is needed either to rule them in, or to rule them out:

- Maternal exposure to chemicals known as endocrine disruptor chemicals (EDCs) in, for example, flame retardants in home furnishings, vinyl flooring, and some cosmetics (Getso & Ibrahim, 2014).
- Abnormally high levels of **testosterone** (male hormone) in the mother (Lombardo et al., 2012; but see also Farrant et al., 2013).
- Maternal fatty acid supplements (omega-3) (Lyall et al., 2013).
- Maternal folic acid supplements during pregnancy (DeSoto & Hitlan, 2012) (but NB: supplements taken *prior* to conception reduce the risk for ASD – see Surén et al., 2013).

Environmental factors impinging on the unborn child prenatally that have been investigated but shown *not* to constitute significant risk factors for ASD (although they are in some cases risk factors for other mental health or neurodevelopmental disorders) include maternal vaccinations containing the mercury-based preservative **thimerosol** (Makris et al., 2012), maternal alcohol intake or smoking, infertility treatments, and antenatal ultrasound scans (Scott et al., 2013; Lyall et al., 2014).

Perinatal factors Perinatal risk factors are sometimes discussed under the heading of 'obstetric complications', and can include the following (for relevant research findings, see the reviews by Scott et al. (2013) and by Lyall et al. (2014), previously cited):

- Maternal age.
- Pre-term delivery and/or low birthweight.
- Abnormal fetal presentation and/or umbilical cord complications.
- Birth injury or trauma, including fetal distress (associated with, for example, birth asphyxia).
- Caesarian section.
- Neonatal jaundice (variously caused).
- Prolonged or otherwise difficult birth.
- Low neonatal APGAR score.[2]

---

[2]The APGAR test is done by a doctor, midwife or nurse, who examines the newborn's breathing, heartrate, muscle tone, reflexes and skin colour. Maximum score is 10. A score of 7 or less is treated as a matter of concern.

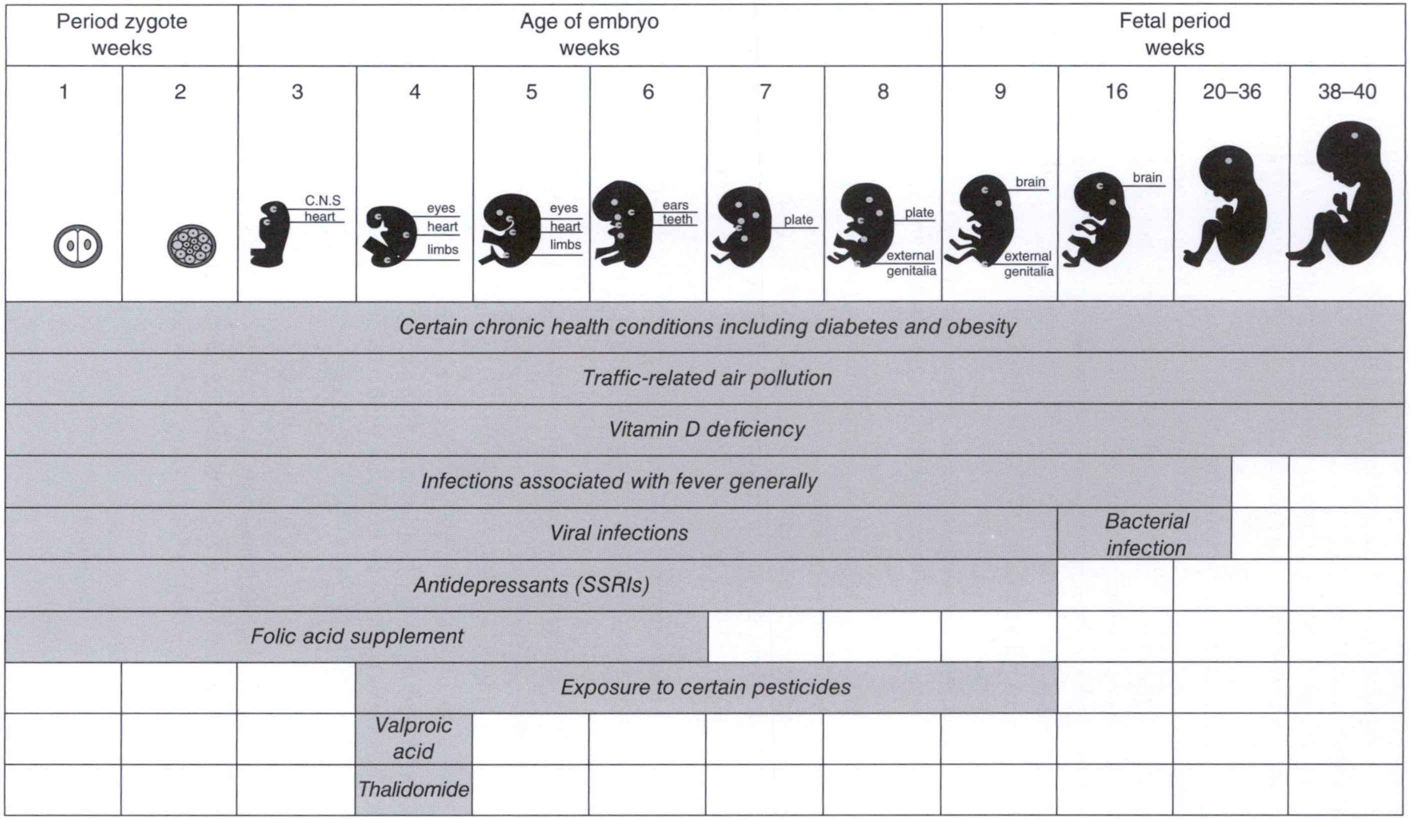

Figure 7.2 *Time points during gestation when the developing fetus may be affected by environmental risk factors for ASD*

The above factors rarely occur singly. So, for example, a breech presentation or umbilical cord complication may justify delivering the baby by Caesarian section; similarly, pre-term or low birthweight babies are unlikely to achieve high APGAR scores. In addition, maternal health problems, including some of those listed as prenatal risk factors for ASD (e.g. pregnancy-related hypertension, pre-eclampsia, diabetes) may contribute to obstetric complications. Finally, abnormal embryonic and foetal development, however caused, may also predispose towards obstetric complications. It is unlikely, therefore, that ASD ever results from a single birth complication in isolation from other prenatal and perinatal factors.

Postnatal risk factors As noted above, cases of regressive, i.e. late-onset, autism suggest that something in the environment within which the infant's brain is developing either halts or reverses normal brain development. For a time, it was suspected that the MMR (measles, mumps, rubella) vaccination might cause or trigger late-onset ASD. It was suggested that either the vaccine preservative thimerosal (mentioned above) was to blame, or that a component of the measles vaccine caused a gut disorder introducing harmful chemicals into the brain. However, evidence from numerous large and rigorous studies carried out in several different countries showed indisputably that MMR vaccination is not significantly implicated as a causal factor in autism (for reviews, see Klein & Diehl, 2004; Doja & Roberts, 2006; see also Uchiyama et al., 2007).

Nevertheless, as many reviews of the evidence point out, the lack of a *statistically significant* relation between the MMR vaccination and regressive autism does not rule out the possibility that in *very rare cases* the MMR is, figuratively speaking, the straw that breaks the camel's back. For example, in a child with a strong genetic susceptibility to autism it might be that the addition of just one further risk factor, conceivably fever following MMR vaccination, could precipitate brain changes leading to the onset of ASD. Families who have seen their child deteriorate following vaccination may be very rare indeed but they have, most understandably, wanted to make their voices heard. One family I knew a while back had this experience, as described in Box 7.3.

Postnatal factors which, unlike the MMR vaccination, carry *statistically significant* risk for ASD include:

- Exposure to traffic-related air pollution (Roberts et al., 2013).
- Exposure to certain pesticides (Quaak et al., 2013; but see also González-Alzaga et al., 2014).
- Infections of various kinds, including cytomegalovirus infection (Sakamoto et al., 2015), gut infections (Theije et al., 2011), and viral infections associated with high fever/encephalitis (Shoffner et al., 2010).
- Immune system abnormalities associated with vulnerability to infections (Abdallah et al., 2013), but also possibly familial, i.e. genetic in origin (McDougle et al., 2015).
- Severe material and social deprivation in early infancy (Kumsta et al., 2015; see also Box 7.4).

Box 7.3 'Sarah': One in a million?

Sarah was a normally developing baby for the first 14 months of her life: healthy, sociable, playful and communicative. She was a second child, so her parents knew what to expect in terms of normal development, and they had no concerns about her during this first year. Following the MMR vaccination at 14 months, however, Sarah became extremely ill, running a high temperature and falling into what her parents describe as a coma for 24 hours or more. When she came round she was drowsy for several days and 'very poorly', as if recovering from a bad bout of flu. She was unresponsive, and did not seem to recognise her parents or her older brother.

As she recovered physically Sarah remained much more passive than she had been before, and although she clearly knew members of the close family, she did not approach them or solicit their attention as she had done previously. She seemed content to sit and play repetitively with a spinning top which she bent down to listen to, or a favourite musical box which she held close to her ear. Most distressingly for the family, she no longer attempted to speak, and only communicated with them when she wanted to be fed or picked up or have some other need provided for. She was diagnosed with ASD before she entered school, and attended special schools throughout her childhood.

Sarah has in fact done remarkably well with the help of her family, speech and language therapists, teachers and others. Now an adult, she has useful language and good self-help skills. She uses social media and has established some 'at a distance' friendships. However, she remains moderately autistic, and will never achieve full independence.

Of critical importance in Sarah's case is the fact that several members on both sides of the family have, or have had, autism-related traits in their behaviour, such as late talking, marked social reserve, or a preference for routines and dislike of change. This has not stopped any of them from living full and successful lives. However, Sarah was almost certainly genetically vulnerable to developing autism.

(With thanks to 'Sarah's' parents for permission to publish this description, details of which have been changed to ensure anonymity)

The effects of the above risk factors may be cumulative. For example, there is some evidence to suggest that repeated hospitalisation for viral infections (as opposed to a single hospitalisation) is associated with ASD (Abdallah et al., 2013). Similarly, it is plausible to suggest that the effects of exposure to toxic substances in exhaust fumes, or to certain pesticides, builds up over time during the infant's first year or two of life, causing or contributing to the form of late-onset autism in which development is normal for the first couple of years, then plateaus with autism-related behaviours appearing.

Several of the above postnatal risk factors for ASD overlap with known prenatal risk factors, and the effects of such risk factors may also be cumulative. For example, if the mother's pregnancy as well as the child's earliest weeks and months are spent living near busy roads, the effects of toxic traffic fumes will be cumulative. Similarly, if the mother passes cytomegalovirus infection to her unborn child, who then continues to carry it, the risks posed by that infection are present both before and after birth.

Box 7.4   The 'Romanian orphans' study

Evidence for the fact that severe deprivation in very early childhood is a risk factor for ASD comes from studies of children whose earliest months and years were spent in orphanages in Romania where they suffered severe material and social neglect before being adopted into families in the UK, the US, Canada and elsewhere.

In the UK, a cohort of these children has been studied from the time they were adopted, through early childhood, into adolescence and approaching adulthood, with reports on development being published at intervals throughout this period. The most recent account of the group now referred to as 'English Romanian Adoptees' is that by Kumsta et al. (2015), cited above. In this account, the persistent psychological effects of early deprivation are summarised as being characterised by deficits in social cognition and behaviour, plus some other quasi-autistic features, often accompanied by cognitive impairment and symptoms of ADHD. However, not all the adoptees are so affected, and it is suggested that differences in outcome may be explained, at least in part, by genetic differences.

Environmental Risk Factors and Abnormal Brain Development

As with genetic risk factors, the diverse environmental risk factors for ASD identified above must all have the potential to contribute in some way or another to the anomalies of brain structure and function underlying ASD-related behaviour (Belmonte, Cook et al., 2004; Rutter & Thapar, 2014). So, for example, experiments on rats and mice show that the anticonvulsant drug valproic acid taken during pregnancy interferes with **synaptogenesis** (Chomiak & Hu, 2013). Immune system responses to infections include the production of substances called **cytokines**, which are important for the formation and function of neural networks in the brain (Goines & Ashwood, 2013). Similarly, the chemicals in certain pesticides interfere with the formation and function of neural networks (Stamou et al., 2013). Certain particles in vehicle exhaust fumes are described as 'neurotoxic' (Costa et al., 2014), and it is thought that other chemicals present in the environment, not as yet investigated, may also be neurotoxic.

Future research into the root causes of ASD will no doubt include attempts to identify the specific roles of diverse environmental risk factors as contributory causes of full and partial forms of ASD, as well as heterogeneity within ASD. Interactions between specific genetic and environmental risk factors will also constitute a focus of future research.

SUMMARY

In approximately 10–15 per cent of cases, ASD co-occurs with a developmental syndrome of known genetic origin. These cases are referred to 'syndromic autism'/ 'syndromic ASD'. From these cases it can be inferred that whatever causes the other developmental condition can also be a risk factor for autism. Most cases of ASD are, however, 'idiopathic', meaning that the root causes of the condition are unknown.

The etiology of idiopathic autism is discussed in terms of genetic and environmental risk factors. What is meant by 'genetic' and 'environmental' factors is outlined, and evidence for the role of both types of risk factor as potential contributory causes of ASD is presented. Summaries of the current state of knowledge concerning genetic and environmental risk factors are then given. It is stressed that most if not all the risk factors discussed have individually quite weak effects on development, but cumulatively and in certain combinations become sufficient for ASD-related behaviours to develop. Combinations of genetic and environmental risk factors are likely to be common. It is also stressed that combinations of risk factors are unlikely to be precisely the same in any two cases of ASD, contributing to individual differences in the severity and complexity of resulting developmental anomalies. However, all risk factors, whether genetic or environmental, have the potential capacity to influence brain development and function, from conception through to adulthood, in ways that underlie autism-typical patterns of development and behaviour.

BRAIN BASES

> ## AIMS
>
> The main aim of this chapter is to provide a summary of what is known concerning the neurobiology, or brain bases, of autism, and to indicate likely growth areas of research. However, to understand the material presented it is necessary to have some minimal understanding of the neurotypical brain. A secondary aim of the chapter is therefore to provide this basic information for readers with no prior specialist knowledge.

THE NEUROTYPICAL BRAIN

In this introductory section some basic facts concerning the structure, the chemical constituents and the overall mode of function of the neurotypical brain will be presented, followed by a section on normal brain development. The material is highly selective, covering only information most relevant to the account of brain bases of autism that follows. However, some basic terms are defined at the outset. A full account of neurotypical brain structure, function and development can be found in Carlson (2014), with simpler accounts in primers of child development such as those by Bee and Boyd (2012) or by Berk and Meyers (2015).

Neurotypical Brain Structure

The main part of the human brain, the **cerebrum**,[1] is divided into two **cerebral hemispheres**, referred to as the left and right cerebral hemispheres, corresponding to the left and right sides of the body. The hemispheres are symmetrical in as far as they both consist of a **frontal**, **temporal**, **occipital** and **parietal lobe** similarly positioned in each hemisphere. The hemispheres are joined together by thick bundles of fibres which make up the **corpus callosum**. The surfaces of the cerebral hemispheres are enfolded into numerous convolutions (**gyri**), and crevices (**sulci**), providing a much greater surface area than would otherwise be the case. The enfolded brain surface constitutes the **cerebral cortex**, made up of **grey matter** (see below). The cerebral cortex is approximately 2.5 mm thick in humans and is responsible for most of the major functions of which we are aware, including many facets of sensation and motor activity, perception and memory, social ability, language, thought and reasoning.

The bulk of the cerebral hemispheres is subcortical, subserving functions of which we are less aware and over which we exert less conscious control. These include emotional reactions and behaviours, subserved by structures making up the **limbic system**; also implicit or unconscious learning of the kinds on which

---

[1]Words or phrases in bold type on first occurrence can be found in the Glossary.

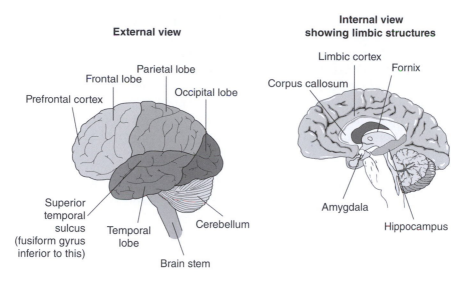

External view

Parietal lobe
Frontal lobe
Occipital lobe
Prefrontal cortex

Superior
temporal
sulcus
(fusiform gyrus
inferior to this)
Temporal
lobe
Cerebellum
Brain stem

**Internal view
showing limbic structures**

Limbic cortex
Fornix
Corpus callosum

Amygdala
Hippocampus

Figure 8.1 *Major structural divisions of the brain*

animals and human babies are reliant; also **vegetative functions**, including sleep and wakefulness, appetite, temperature control and some sexual behaviours.

At the back of brain, positioned below the cerebral hemispheres, is the **cerebellum**, or 'little brain', with its own left and right sides and cortical surfaces. The cerebellum was until relatively recently thought to be involved solely in motor activity. It is now thought to be involved also in various cognitive and social functions, though its precise roles are not well understood.

The whole brain is joined to the spinal cord by the **brain stem**, which carries the spinal nerves subserving sensation and movement in the head and face. The brain stem also has the essential function of integrating the spinal and cerebral components of the **central nervous system (CNS)**. The major structural divisions of the brain are shown in Figure 8.1.

Some distinctions at more detailed levels of description are as follows.

- **Neurons** are cells involved in transmitting information in the form of electrical impulses. Clusters of neurons, all of which are involved in transmitting and receiving the same information, are called **nuclei** (singular: **nucleus**). The cell bodies of neurons are greyish-brown in colour, and constitute grey matter in the brain. The cerebral cortex is composed of grey matter, as is much of the cerebellum; there are also clumps of grey matter within subcortical regions.
- **Axons** are nerve fibres that carry information from one neuron to another, whereas **dendrites** are nerve fibres that act like antennae, receiving the information carried by axons from neighbouring cells. The point at which an axon from one neuron junctions with the dendrites of another is called a synapse.
- **Glial cells** protect, support and maintain neurons, including forming the **myelin sheaths** around axons. Glial cells are whiteish in colour, and constitute **white matter** in the brain.

Neurotypical Brain Chemistry

Neurochemicals in the brain fall into various – sometimes overlapping – categories according to their major function, or functions. Three important groups of brain chemicals are **neurotransmitters**, **neuromodulators** and **neurotrophins**.

Neurotransmitters are chemical substances released by one neuron to stimulate or inhibit activity in other neurons. Neurotransmitters act as 'messengers' carrying 'information' from one neuron to other neurons equipped with specialised **neuroreceptors** selectively responsive to the transmitter substance. Over 100 neurotransmitters have been identified within the human body. Some operate solely within the **peripheral nervous system (PNS)** with highly specialised functions to do with, for example, digestion or circulation. Other neurotransmitters operate in both the peripheral and the central nervous system (CNS) with a broad range of functions.

Neuromodulators are substances that stimulate or depress the chemical output from neurons (comparable to volume control on a TV set). All of the neurotransmitters listed above also act as neuromodulators. **Serotonin, dopamine, acetylcholine (A.CH)** and **noradrenaline** modulate neural activity within their own specialised **brain circuits** (referred to as the 'serotoninergic', 'dopinergic', 'cholinergic' and 'adrenergic' systems respectively). **Glutamate** and **gamma-amino butyric acid (GABA)**, on the other hand, are active throughout the brain, with major roles in the excitation and inhibition of neural activity. Certain other neuromodulators are classified as hormones rather than as neurotransmitters. These hormonal neuromodulators include **cortisol, oxytocin** and **vasopressin**, and testosterone.

Neurotrophins are involved in brain growth and maintenance. The most important neurotrophin is **brain derived neurotropic factor (BDNF)**, which is active in the brain from conception onwards. Both serotonin and GABA also act as neurotrophins prenatally, as does **reelin**.

Box 8.1 provides brief descriptions of the major functions of the neurochemicals identified above.

Neurotypical Brain Function

The whole brain functions as a hierarchy of nested systems referred to as neural circuits, systems or networks. Each network consists of interconnected nuclei that operate together to subserve a particular function. Those circuits that involve relatively few nuclei situated close together in the brain are referred to as **local networks**. These carry out highly specific functions, such as registering the colour or the shape of an object. To register all salient aspects of an object simultaneously and as a whole (e.g. the colour, shape, size and movement of a bird), activity in several local networks must be co-ordinated in a **global network**. Some global networks are very widely distributed within the brain, involving both cerebral hemispheres. For example, hearing is mediated by the auditory nerves that connect mechanisms in the left and right inner ears to nuclei in the brain stem, which

Box 8.1 Functions of some major neurochemicals in the brain

Serotonin plays a role in the development of brain cells and their connections, and in the organisation of brain growth prenatally. (It is for this reason that it is considered inadvisable for pregnant women to be prescribed medications designed to reduce serotoninergic activity – see Chapter 7.) Serotonin subsequently has both excitatory and inhibitory functions, and plays a major role in digestion, as well as contributing to the regulation of blood pressure, body temperature, pain thresholds, appetite, mood and sleep. Serotonin also contributes to cognitive functions, including memory and learning.

Dopamine is involved in motor functions (people with Parkinson's disease have dopamine abnormality) and also in the mediation of reward value, or 'feel good' factors (most recreational drugs act via dopaminergic reward systems), and thus is also important for attention and learning.

Noradrenalin (norepinephrine) is involved in **autonomic nervous system (ANS)** functions, including the neurochemical correlates of fear and anxiety, such as sweating and increased heart rate. In the central nervous system it has a role in the maintenance of sustained attention and in this way contributes to learning.

Acetylcholine (A.CH) is also mainly involved in ANS functions, initiating involuntary muscle activity (e.g. in digestion) in particular, and stimulating the excretion of certain hormones. In the CNS it contributes to wakefulness and arousal, mood (including aggression), sexuality and thirst.

Gamma-amino butyric acid (GABA) exerts inhibitory control on neural activity throughout the brain, acting in synergy with **glutamate**, which exerts excitatory control. A balance between the activities of GABA and glutamate is required to achieve adaptive control of muscle tone and movement, as well as many cortical functions including vision and arousal.

BDNF is critically involved in the production, differentiation and positioning of neurons in the brain (and elsewhere in the body) prenatally. Thereafter it supports the survival of existing neurons, and stimulates the growth of new neurons and synaptic connections in the brain, having a critical role in neural plasticity and memory.

Reelin, in combination with BDNF and serotonin (see above), contributes to prenatal brain development.

Oxytocin modulates activity within brain circuits mediating pain perception, emotion, appetite, sexual behaviour and social bonding. It also has a major role in mediating bodily functions associated with pregnancy, childbirth and breast feeding.

Vasopressin has important roles in certain autonomic functions, including water retention. It has sometimes been suggested that it may have some role in mediating social engagement and reward, but this is not proven.

Cortisol produces bodily changes in response to stress ('fight or flight' readiness), and variations in cortisol levels are associated with the sleep–wake cycle. Cortisol also has an anti-inflammatory role within the immune system.

Testosterone is mainly associated with male sexuality, but may also be associated with certain cognitive abilities, including spatial sense and some facets of memory/learning.

connect to the primary hearing centres in the left and right temporal lobes, and thereon to adjacent auditory association areas in each temporal lobe.

To function efficiently, the components of any network, whether local or global, must be connected with each other. The necessary connectivity is dependent on the availability and integrity of grey and white brain matter (see the section on brain anatomy, above), and on the neurochemicals that transmit and modulate 'information' within a network (see the section on brain chemistry, above). In addition, the coherence of activity within any local or global network is dependent on the synchronisation of the firing of groups of neurons within the network. The synchronised activity of large groups of neurons gives rise to rhythmic **oscillations**, or 'brain waves', of various frequencies named with letters of the Greek alphabet – for example the 'alpha' and 'gamma' brain rhythms.

Neurotypical Brain Development

Prenatal development

The brain starts to develop within the first month after conception, with the formation of the neural tube within which the central nervous system will grow. Within the first four months of gestation, the neural tube has differentiated into a recognisable brain shape within the head, on a long stalk within which is what will become the spinal column. Most of the brain neurons an individual will have over a lifetime develop during these first four months. These neurons develop in the base of the brain and then migrate to other sections of the brain to form specialised structures and systems. Among the earliest neurons to develop are the clusters of cells forming nuclei in the brain stem; also a particular type of cell called **Purkinje cells** that are found in the **cerebellar vermis**. The first axons and dendrites begin to develop in the last two months before birth.

Postnatal development

At birth the most developed parts of the brain are the evolutionarily old parts that regulate vital functions, such as respiration, sleeping, eating and eliminating waste products. The least developed part of the brain is the evolutionarily new cerebral cortex, which subserves higher-order functions.

During the first 18 months of life, multiple new connections are established between neurons in the process of synaptogenesis. Synaptogenesis involves the growth of axons and dendrites that connect with each other creating new synapses. This process is mainly driven by the infant's experiences, and occurs throughout the brain but especially in the previously underdeveloped cerebral cortex. The proliferation of new nerve fibres (grey matter) is accompanied by increases in protective and supportive glial cells (white matter), and as a result of these combined growth processes the weight of the brain normally doubles between birth and 18 months.

Thereafter, a process of **synaptic pruning** occurs, in which the less-used axonal pathways are eliminated and only the most-used pathways are retained. In addition, space for the proliferating axons and dendrites is made by the **programmed** cell death, or **apoptosis**, of some of the surrounding neurons (the prenatally formed neuron 'bank' allows for this). The combination of synaptogenesis followed by synaptic pruning and programmed cell death is sometimes referred to as a process of 'sculpting' the brain into a functionally efficient form.

Spurts in brain growth, with ensuing processes of synaptic pruning and cell death, occur at roughly predictable ages from infancy through childhood and adolescence. These growth spurts are selective, building and sculpting specific brain systems in turn. The earliest spurt in brain growth occurs within the first few months of life, when the cortical components of the auditory and visual systems are developed. Another growth spurt occurs at around age 2;0, accompanied by gains in language development. A further growth spurt occurs at around age 4;0, accompanied by a step change in the ability to think about one's own thoughts and those of other people, an ability that is impaired in autism (see Chapter 3). Further spurts of brain growth, mainly involving increased connectivity between neurons in the frontal lobes and neurons in relatively distant parts of the brain, continue through middle childhood to the late teenage years, each accompanied by stepwise improvements in increasingly sophisticated and human-specific abilities such as abstract reasoning and mathematical ability. Further growth may occur during adulthood if new skills or knowledge are acquired, providing evidence of **plasticity**. From middle age onwards, however, there is a gradual loss of grey matter in specific brain regions, associated with a decline in cognitive abilities (Cowell et al., 2007). This decline may be exacerbated by age-related diseases such as dementia.

An important aspect of brain development that begins prenatally and continues from infancy is **lateralisation**. As noted above, the cerebrum, also the cerebellum, are divided into left and right sections. Subcortical structures are also bilaterally paired. The left and right members of a pair of structures often subserve different but complementary functions. So, for example, the auditory cortex in the right cerebral hemisphere receives sound coming predominantly from the left ear, whereas the auditory cortex in the left hemisphere receives sound coming predominantly from the right ear. Similarly, speech production is generally carried out in the left hemisphere, whereas prosody (the emotion-bearing patterns of pitch and intonation) is generally carried out in the right hemisphere. Rather confusingly, paired structures are often referred to using singular rather than plural terms, for example 'the temporal lobe', the **amygdala**', 'the **hippocampus**'. Unless otherwise stated, the singular terms should be taken to refer to paired structures.

What drives neurotypical brain development

Brain development is ultimately controlled by the activities of *genes* and their products, including many of the neurochemicals mentioned in a previous section. However, *environmental factors* are also important. As noted in the previous chapter, certain neurotoxins to which a developing child may be exposed pre- or postnatally have adverse effects on brain development. More importantly, and on the positive side, synaptogenesis is driven by sensory, motor, social and emotional experiences that stimulate the growth of axons and dendrites, increasing brain connectivity and building the brain circuits that will subserve an increasingly wide repertoire of abilities and behaviours. The chemical processes involved in synaptogenesis are, however, mediated by *gene* products. Moreover, the processes of pruning and programmed cell death are also *genetically* controlled. However, because experience determines which neuronal connections are well established (and hence not pruned) as opposed to those that are poorly established (and hence pruned), *environmental factors* also have a role in brain sculpting. This kind of interplay between genetic and environmental factors is typical of the processes of brain development and change throughout the lifespan, ensuring that every individual is unique.

There is, however, some disagreement concerning the balance between the contributions of nature (as dictated by genes) and nurture (involving experience), particularly concerning the extent to which the genes control exactly what circuits are built, and in which parts of the brain. During the 1980s and 1990s, so-called **modularists** (Fodor, 1983; Pinker, 1994, 1997) argued for an innately specified set of learning mechanisms subserved by innately specified circuits, or 'modules', in the brain, allowing only limited scope for environmental inputs to alter the brain's basic architecture. This view was questioned by **constructivists** such as Elman et al. (1996), who – while fully accepting that there are certain innate (i.e. genetic) constraints on brain development – emphasised instead the plasticity of the brain. Debate concerning the extent to which brain development is or is not genetically determined continues, and is relevant to explanatory theories of ASD (see Chapter 9); also to discussion of the extent to which ASD may or may not be ameliorated or even 'cured' (see Chapter 12).

THE AUTISTIC BRAIN

Brain Structure in ASD

Introduction

Brain structure can be studied at numerous levels. These range from the identification of clearly defined component parts such as those identified in Figure 8.1 above, through the identification of functional networks, to the identification of individual cell groups ('nuclei') and **nerve tracts**, to the analysis of the molecular structure of individual cells or cell types. There are correspondingly many different methods of studying brain structure, some of which are listed in Box 8.2. Studies of brain function, summarised in Box 8.4 later in the chapter, may also be informative concerning anomalous brain structure in ASD, because structure and function are inseparably related.

Many of the methods described in Box 8.2 have been used to study brain structure in autism from the 1970s onwards. However, few firm conclusions could be drawn from early research because findings were inconsistent across studies. These inconsistencies arose because of differences in the study methods used, and the fact that group sizes were small as well as varying in age, ability and sometimes

---

Box 8.2 Methods of research into brain structure in people with ASD

Autopsies/post-mortem studies Useful for detailed examination at both macro and micro levels of analysis, and has the advantage that examination can be extended over time. Disadvantages: small numbers of cases available, tending to be older individuals or individuals with multiple disorders that may have affected the brain.

Computerised (axial) tomography (CT/CAT scan) Uses X-rays; useful for examining bony tissue, but undesirable because of radiation risks.

Structural magnetic resonance imaging (sMRI/MRIs) Uses a machine-generated magnetic field that resonates in ways that can be used to build up a detailed three-dimensional image of brain structure. There are no known risks involved, which gives **sMRI** its main advantage over CAT scanning. However, the scanning machine is claustrophobic and noisy, and the individual being examined has to keep still for significant periods of time; also use of the machines is expensive. For all these reasons, studies of people with ASD tend to include small numbers of participants, and few studies include very young or low-functioning individuals unless sedated.

Diffusion tensor imaging (DTI) is a method of brain imaging particularly suited for examining brain tissue at a more microscopic level than can be achieved with the standard form of sMRI.

Animal models involve **lesioning** specific brain areas in animals, usually rats or mice, and assessing subsequent effects on the animal's behaviour (compare the use of animal models in genetic research, Box 7.2).

Insights from forms of syndromic ASD can indicate abnormalities of likely relevance to ASD. For example, autistic traits in people with tuberous sclerosis are associated with malformations of temporal lobe cortex. Fragile-X and Turner syndrome both involve structural abnormalities within the limbic system.

---

gender across studies. Given the small group sizes, heterogeneity would also undoubtedly have contributed to difficulties in drawing any firm conclusions (Hahamy et al., 2015). There was also a focus on individual structures or subregions in the brain, rather than on widely distributed brain circuits subserving related sets of behavioural functions. Targeting isolated structures as possible brain correlates of anomalous behaviour in ASD is a bit like focusing exclusively on Oxford Circus to explain gridlocked traffic throughout central London.

However, progress is now gathering pace, for three main reasons. First, research groups are now working co-operatively, sharing methodologies and pooling data, rather than working in isolation from each other (see Di Martino et al., 2014, for an account of these changes). This means that comparable data sets can be assembled from participant groups numbering in the hundreds. From these large-scale studies, certain commonalities can be discerned across groups and subgroups, despite individual differences. Secondly, age-related changes are now better understood and taken into account (Greimel et al., 2013; Itahashi et al., 2015). Thirdly, the early focus on individual structures or subregions within the brain has largely given way to studying brain networks, or circuits, subserving ASD-related behavioural functions (see, for example, Zielinski et al., 2012; Itahashi et al., 2015). Related to this, it is recognised that certain broad characteristics of brain growth and structure may apply generally to people with ASD, irrespective of heterogeneity at more detailed levels of analysis (Boucher, 2011; Casanova, 2012).

A brief summary of what can be said with reasonable certainty concerning structural brain anomalies in ASD is included below under the heading 'What is known'. Detailed expositions of current knowledge can be found in chapters in the book edited by Buxbaum and Hof (2012). However, because this is a rapidly developing area of research, interested readers should look for later reviews when these become available.

What is known

It is now generally recognised that the set of behaviours that define or are commonly present in autism are associated with abnormal brain connectivity. Anomalous brain connectivity was first argued to be of central importance for an understanding of the brain bases of autism in the early years of this century (Belmonte, Allen et al., 2004; Courchesne & Pierce, 2005). In the decade following publication of these seminal papers there were steep year-on-year increases in studies demonstrating anomalous connectivity in autism, and its role as the major structural anomaly in the brains of people with ASD is not now disputed.

Atypical patterns of connectivity in ASD derive from abnormalities in the density, distribution and cellular construction of grey and white matter in the brain. Where these abnormalities consist of unusually dense growth of neurons and their projections, 'hyper-connectivity' occurs. Where the abnormalities consist of unusually sparse growth of neurons, their projections and/or their supporting glial cells, 'hypo-connectivity' occurs. Both hyper- and hypo-connectivity have critical effects on brain function. Together they can account for the combination of circumscribed areas of high ability and splinter skills (associated with hyper-connectivity), as well as the behavioural impairments (associated with hypo-connectivity) in autism.

There remain many uncertainties, however, as to where in the brain hyper- and hypo-connectivity reliably occur; also concerning the nature of the abnormalities – whether associated with increases or decreases of grey or of white matter, or both. Findings from research studies designed to answer these questions are copious, often confusing, and incomplete. Some of the better-established findings are outlined below.

Abnormalities of cerebral cortex   There is clear evidence implicating atypicalities in the density of grey and white matter in the cerebral cortex in people with ASD. This evidence comes partly from studies of the exterior surfaces of the brain and partly from studies of the cellular structure of cortical regions.

Studies using measures of the exterior surfaces of the brain have shown that the *thickness* of the cortex at various sites, the total *surface area* of the cortex, and the *gyrification* (i.e. degree of folding) of the cortical surfaces all vary from neurotypical norms at some or other stage of development (Wallace et al., 2010, 2013;

Hazlett et al., 2011; Ecker et al., 2013; Libero et al., 2014). However, the precise anomalies of cortical thickness, surface area and gyrification that have been reported are numerous and varied, almost certainly because the groups studied have differed in age, if not ability and gender. To date, most such studies have focused on high-functioning adolescent or adult males with ASD, and there is a clear need not only to clarify and confirm age-related changes in such participants, but also to extend the use of these measures to lower-functioning groups and to females.

Studies of the cellular structure of the **minicolumns** of grey and white matter in the **cortex** of people with ASD also reliably show abnormalities. The precise nature of these abnormalities is unclear, probably because of age-related changes. However, it is generally agreed that minicolumns are more numerous but smaller and narrower than normal in people with ASD, at least at certain stages of life. In addition, the boundaries between grey and white matter within minicolumns and their projections are less well differentiated than normal, reducing the efficiency of communication between minicolumns in different cortical regions (Casanova, 2012). Cortical minicolumns have been likened to microprocessors which – in the typically functioning brain – co-ordinate and regulate activity within the cortex. It has been argued that minicolumnar abnormalities in ASD are associated with enhanced processing of detail (associated with hyper-connectivity) but impaired executive control (associated with hypo-connectivity) (Opris & Casanova, 2014).

Cerebellar abnormalities   Post-mortem and sMRI studies show that grey matter in the cerebellum is decreased relative to the neurotypical brain. Reduced numbers of Purkinje cells in the cerebellum was first demonstrated by Ritvo et al. (1986), and this finding has stood the test of time (Fatemi et al., 2012). The cerebellum is a structure of interest because of the role of Purkinje cells in the inhibitory control of neural activity (see the section on GABA, below). Reduced inhibition deriving from cerebellar abnormality has disruptive effects not only on motor behaviour (as was once thought), but also on cognitive, affective and sensory behaviours (Fatemi et al., 2012).

Abnormal circuitry   Those regions of the cortex, also those subcortical structures within which, or between which, abnormalities of grey and white matter are most consistently found, are – unsurprisingly – those that are constituents of widely distributed brain circuits subserving behaviours that are aberrant in people with ASD. Circuits with likely or possible relevance to autism include what are termed:

- The **social brain** (Adolphs, 2009).
- The **default mode network (DMN)** (involved in retrospection, introspection, theory of mind and thinking about the future – Buckner et al., 2008).
- The **salience network** (involved in attention switching and goal setting – Menon & Uddin, 2010)

Detailed information relating to these brain circuits in people with autism can be found in Pelphrey et al. (2011) on the social brain, Zielinski et al. (2012) on the social brain and the salience network, and Washington et al. (2014) on the default mode network. Atypical connectivity has also been found with the network of structures involved in language processing (see, for example, Kimura et al., 2013; Li, Xue et al., 2014). Language processing in people with ASD is, in addition, characterised by atypical lateralisation, with the normal predominance of left hemisphere involvement being either reduced or reversed (Lindell & Hudry, 2013).

Extended reviews of the evidence and implications of the impaired connectivity model of the brain bases of ASD can be found in Maximo et al. (2014), Kana et al. (2014) and McPartland and Jeste (2015). The latter authors not only review the evidence, but also link it back to genetic variants known to disrupt synaptic growth and function. The importance of building bridges across from etiological factors to brain anomalies in ASD was stressed in papers by Belmonte, Cook et al. (2004), Guilmatre et al. (2009) and Zoghbi and Bear (2012), cited towards the end of Chapter 7. The paper by McPartland and Jeste is important because it reaches back towards etiological factors, contributing towards the essential work of linking the different levels of causal analysis.

Brain Chemistry in ASD

Introduction

Understanding the **neurochemistry** of autism is vitally important for the development of effective physical treatments. This has been recognised for very many years, and the search for neurochemical abnormalities in autism, such as might be treatable by medication or dietary changes, began soon after autism was identified as a distinct developmental disorder. Early research was, however, limited by the methods available, which consisted of post-mortem studies, the analysis of various bodily fluids, or using a medication experimentally and assessing the outcome. As more direct methods of study have become available (see Box 8.3), studies of the neurochemistry of autism have proliferated, and this is now a growth area in research.

What is known

There is as yet no consensus concerning the precise nature of neurochemical abnormalities in people with ASD. However, there is ample evidence that several of the major neurotransmitters, neuromodulators and neurotrophins identified earlier in this chapter are affected in someway or another. Evidence relating to each of these substances in ASD is summarised below, in approximate order of established significance from best to least well established.

Serotonin Serotonin (5-hydroxytryptamine, or 5-HT) is conveyed from one neuron to another by a **serotonin transporter** (**SERT** or **5-HTT**) substance. This substance carries serotonin generated within one synapse to specialised receptor cells on target neurons. Abnormalities of the serotinergic neurotransmission system could therefore arise in at least three ways. First, there could be over- or under-production of serotonin (5-HT) itself. Secondly, there could be a problem with the transporter substance, 5-HTT/SERT. Thirdly, there could be abnormalities in the provision and action of serotoninergic receptor cells.

Box 8.3   Methods of assessing brain chemistry

Post-mortem studies Examination of post-mortem brain tissue can show whether, for example, the specialised nerve tracts and receptor cells involved in any one neurochemical system are intact. However, this method presents similar problems of interpretation to those outlined in Box 8.2, above.

Lumbar puncture may be used to draw off a sample of cerebro-spinal fluid for analysis. However, this is an invasive procedure and its use for non-clinical purposes is controversial.

Blood or urine samples can be informative about the by-products of brain metabolism.

Efficacy studies Studies of the effects of medications known to have their effects on particular neurotransmitters or neuromodulators provide an indirect method of assessing brain neurochemistry.

Insights from forms of syndromic ASD can indicate abnormalities of likely relevance to ASD. For example, **phenylketonuria** (PKU) is associated with abnormalities within the serotoninergic system.

Magnetic resonance spectroscopy imaging (MRSI/MRS) This noninvasive procedure (similar to sMRI as described in Box 8.2) provides information about the chemical constituents of specific brain regions.

Positron emission tomography (PET scan) uses a radioactive 'tracer' injected into the bloodstream, the progress of which can be monitored by the scanner. This measures changes in blood flow, indicating levels of activity in specific neurochemical systems. It is used clinically, but is undesirable for research because of radiation risks.

Animal models Medications of potential usefulness to treat undesired behaviours associated with ASD are generally first tested on animals, usually rats or mice.

There is some evidence that all three abnormalities occur more often in people with ASD than in neurotypical individuals. However, none of the three types of abnormality occurs in every autistic individual, or even in a majority of people with ASD. For evidence of abnormal levels of serotonin, see Oblak et al. (2013) and Gabriele et al. (2014). For evidence of lowered amounts of 5-HTT/SERT, see Wiggins et al. (2013). For evidence of reduced numbers of serotonin receptor cells, see Oblak et al. (2013) (as above). The likely effects of serotonin-related abnormalities in autism are wide-ranging, given that serotonin acts not only as a neurotransmitter, but also as a neuromodulator and – prenatally – as a neurotrophin.

Glutamate and GABA   Glutamate is normally the most abundant excitatory neurotransmitter, and GABA (gamma-butyric-amino-acid) the most abundant inhibitory neurotransmitter, operating throughout the brain. As noted in Box 8.1, the normal production, transportation and reception of both these substances is essential to maintain a balance between hyper- (too much) and hypo- (too little) neural activity. Any abnormality associated with either of these neurotransmitters may upset this balance in one or the other direction.

The theory that autism might result (at the level of the brain) from an imbalance between the major excitatory and inhibitory neurotransmitters, glutamate and GABA was first articulated by Hussman in 2001 (see also Rubenstein & Merzenich, 2003). The subsequently named 'EI theory' aroused considerable interest among autism researchers, and reduced levels of GABA have now been demonstrated in the brains of people with ASD in numerous studies (see Blatt, 2012, and Rojas et al., 2014, for reviews). There is some evidence to suggest an excess of glutamate in the brains of people with ASD. However, this evidence is less secure than evidence relating to reduced levels of GABA. Nevertheless, even if the production, transportation and reception of glutamate is within normal limits in ASD, reduced inhibitory control would by itself lead to higher than normal levels of excitation, and 'noise' in the neural transmission system.

Dopamine   As with serotonin, there are well-established abnormalities, possibly of various kinds, in the dopaminergic system in people with ASD (Hosenbocus & Chahal, 2012; Nguyen et al., 2014). It has long been suggested that malfunctioning of the dopaminergic system contributes to motor abnormalities in autism (Damasio & Maurer, 1978). More recently, abnormalities of dopamine production, transmission and reception have been linked with emotion dysregulation and anomalies of attention (Gadow et al., 2014) and with executive dysfunction and repetitive behaviour (Kriette & Noelle, 2015).

Acetylcholine   Unlike the serotinergic and dopinergic systems, the cholinergic system was not intensively studied in people with ASD until the beginning of the present century. A post-mortem study by Perry et al. (2001), however, showed reduced numbers of acetycholine receptors – so-called **nicotinic receptors** – in the parietal lobes of people with ASD. Reduced numbers of nicotinic receptor cells have since been found to be widespread in the brains of people with ASD, with likely implications for understanding impairments of attention, memory and learning, and also possibly the imbalance between inhibitory and excitatory brain activity in ASD (Deutsch et al., 2014). In view of this evidence, the case for developing treatments targeting nicotinic receptor cells has been strongly argued by Deutsch and colleagues, as well as by Mukaetova and Perry (2015).

Oxytocin   The role of oxytocin in sexual behaviours and childbirth was known nearly a century ago. However, it was not until a study of prairie voles was published in the late 1980s that the broader role of oxytocin in mediating pair bonding and maternal behaviour was established. The possible relevance for understanding the brain bases of autism, and for the treatment of autism, was argued for soon afterwards (Modahl et al., 1992). Since the possible relevance of oxytocin for understanding autistic social impairments was appreciated, numerous treatment trials and studies of oxytocin levels have been reported (see Preti et al., 2014, and Young & Barrett, 2015, for reviews). Other studies have focused on the genetic foundations of a putative abnormality associated with oxytocin in ASD (LoParo & Waldman, 2014). Findings from this spate of research studies are, however, quite mixed. So the jury is still out as to the role of reduced oxytocin production/transportation/reception as a contributory cause of ASD; also as to the usefulness of oxytocin-based treatments (see Chapters 12).

Vasopressin Vasopressin is another hormone that has been shown in animal studies to have some role in the regulation of social behaviour. On this basis it has been hypothesised to play a role in causing autism, and studies of oxytocin and vasopressin are often undertaken together. However, the argument for the involvement of vasopressin is less strong than is the case for the involvement of abnormalities associated with oxytocin (Heinrichs & Domes, 2008).

BDNF (brain-derived neurotrophic factor) and reelin In the early years of this century researchers began to question whether the abnormalities of brain anatomy that had been established (see above) might result from neurotrophic abnormalities – i.e. abnormalities in those neurochemicals that are significantly involved in constructing and positioning nerve cells in the developing embryo and fetus, and thereafter renewing and maintaining them. As already mentioned, over the last couple of decades GABA (which is a neurotrophin as well as a major neuromodulator) has been shown to be depleted in the brains of people with ASD. Serotonin, which is also actively involved in brain-building pre- and postnatally, is also known to occur in abnormal quantities in the autistic brain, as noted above. However, investigations of BDNF, also of reelin, over the same period have failed to produced consistent findings (see Halepoto, Bashir, & AL-Ayadhi, 2014, and Kasarpalka et al., 2014, for reviews of studies of BDNF; and Wang et al., 2014, for a meta-analysis of studies of the reelin gene). Uncertainty remains, therefore, regarding the possible roles of both BDNF and reelin in the genetic and brain bases of autism.

Noradrenalin (norepinephrine) Noradrenalin appears to have little explanatory value for ASD when considered alone. However, the adrenal glands form part of the **hypothalamic-pituitary-adrenal axis (HPA)**, a major component of the neuroendocrine system that controls reactions to stress and regulates many body processes.

Cortisol Cortisol is secreted by the adrenal glands in response to stress. Levels of cortisol also show normal variation associated with the sleep–wake cycle (see Box 8.1). Observations of vulnerability to anxiety, also sleep difficulties in children with autism, led to some early studies of cortisol levels (e.g. Hill et al., 1977; Richdale & Prior, 1992). Studies have continued somewhat intermittently, and with mixed findings (see Spratt et al., 2011, and Taylor & Corbett, 2014, for summaries).

Testosterone The '**extreme male brain**' theory, first argued for by Baron-Cohen and Hammer in 1997, postulates that exposure to abnormally high levels of testosterone *in utero* leads to excessively masculinised brain development in people subsequently diagnosed with ASD. However, support for the theory is slight, and has come almost exclusively from the group proposing the theory. This does not necessarily invalidate the findings reported, but replication by independent research groups would be necessary to strengthen the case for the involvement of fetal testosterone. Moreover, there are both arguments (e.g. Falter et al., 2008) and evidence (Whitehouse et al., 2012) against the theory.

Comment

There is no doubt that certain neurochemicals are critically involved in the brain bases of autism. In particular, it is probable that abnormalities affecting the neurotrophic activities of serotonin and GABA pre- and postnatally contribute significantly to the atypicalities of brain growth and structure described in the previous section. In their neurotransmitter and neuromodulator roles, abnormalities in the production and/or transportation and/or reception of serotonin and GABA almost certainly exert further lifelong effects on brain function and hence on behaviour in people with ASD. The dopaminergic system is also almost certainly affected in people with ASD. Furthermore, reduced production of GABA would allow the excitatory activities of glutamate to become unusually dominant in the brains of people with autism.

The roles that the other neurochemicals identified above may play in the causal chains leading to autism-associated behaviour are less clear. The lack of clarity regarding whether to rule in or to rule out roles for some or all of these substances in some or all cases of ASD almost certainly results from the fact that research studies into the neurochemistry of autism are not as yet benefitting from the inter-research-group co-operation that has so significantly benefitted the study of brain structure (Di Martino et al., 2014). Inconsistencies in the findings from research studies of oxytocin or BDNF, for example, could well result from small group sizes and differences in age, gender and overall ability of groups studied. Because a secure understanding of the neurochemistry of autism (or of subgroups within the spectrum) would provide a sound basis for the development and testing of drug and dietary treatments for autism, it is to be hoped that research in this field will be prioritised over the next decade.

Brain Function in ASD

Introduction

Given the clear evidence of atypical brain structure and neurochemistry in people with ASD, brain function could not be anything other than atypical. Indeed, much of the evidence of structural anomalies in the brains of people with ASD (summarised above) comes from studies of brain function. So, for example, if the emotion-registering areas of the brain are found to be inactive when someone is watching a video clip of a car crash or a bare-knuckle fight, then it can be inferred that these brain areas are either structurally abnormal or disconnected from those parts of the brain registering the visual and auditory detail of the events depicted. Conversely, investigations of structural anomalies help to identify functional anomalies, and this reciprocal relationship should be borne in mind when considering the more direct methods of assessing brain function outlined in Box 8.4.

Box 8.4   Methods of assessing brain function

Positron emission tomography (PET scan) (see Box 8.3) Can be used to measure levels of activity in specific brain regions during specific activities (but contraindicated for research as opposed to clinical purposes because it uses radioactive material as a 'tracer').

Single photon emission computed tomography (SPECT) Similar to PET scan method: assesses blood flow using a radioactive 'tracer', from which to infer relations between brain activity and specific behavioural functions.

Functional magnetic resonance imaging (fMRI) Similar to sMRI (see Box 8.2), but measures levels of ongoing brain activity rather than brain structure. The person being scanned is generally asked to undertake a particular task designed to involve a particular function, such as reading aloud, or counting, or watching an emotion-arousing video.

Electroencephalography (EEG) Involves placing electrodes on the skull and measuring brain electrical activity in response to certain stimuli (evoked response potentials, or ERPs) or in resting situations. Somewhat invasive, but – given careful preparation – can be used with very young or vulnerable individuals, as well as with older children or adults.

Magnetoencephalography (MEG) Measures magnetic fields produced by electrical activity in the brain to assess the brain's response to particular stimuli. For technical reasons it is more sensitive than **electroencephalography (EEG)**. It is also less invasive than EEG: the person being assessed sits in a comfortable chair with their head in what looks like a hair dryer of the kind used in hairdressing salons.

Computational modelling can be used to simulate ways in which neural networks operate in the brain, and is generally used to study processes involved in learning.

What is known

Findings from studies of brain function in ASD supplement and reinforce what is known about anomalous brain structure and neurochemistry. Studies using **functional magnetic resonance imagery (fMRI)** and electroencephalography (EEG), in particular, have done much to establish patterns of hyper- and hypo-connectivity within brain circuits with particular relevance for ASD. For example, both fMRI (Di Martino et al., 2009) and EEG (Tavares et al., 2013) have been used to investigate brain structures involved in face processing – a key component of the *social brain* – in people with ASD. fMRI was used in a study by Assaf et al. (2010) to investigate whether or not the typical neural correlates of the *default mode network* are active in people with ASD when asked to carry out DMN-related tasks. fMRI was used to investigate disconnectivity within the dopaminergic reward system, or *salience network*, in a study by Abrams et al. (2013). Reviews of evidence from studies of brain function in people with ASD can be found in Philip et al. (2012) and in Coben et al. (2014).

Brain Development in ASD

Compared with neurotypical brain development and decline, as outlined earlier in the chapter, what is known about brain changes over the lifespan in people with ASD suggests an atypical trajectory.

One of the best-established findings concerns over-rapid brain growth in early infancy (Courchesne, 2004). Specifically, although brain size, as indexed by head size, is normal (or slightly smaller than normal) in newborns who later develop ASD, the circumference of the head increases abnormally rapidly during the first 18 months of life, reflecting abnormally rapid brain growth. For many years it was assumed that over-rapid growth in the earliest months of life was specific to the brain. However, more recent studies have shown that increases in body height and weight are also abnormally rapid in infants who will develop ASD (Chawarska et al., 2011; McKeague et al., 2015).

At age 2;0 years, head circumference, and by inference the volume of the brain, in these infants is significantly larger than average (Courchesne, 2004). This reflects the fact that in infants who will develop ASD, grey matter (neurons) and white matter (glial cells) proliferate unusually rapidly during the first 18 months of life. In addition, during the second half of the second year the normal processes of synaptic pruning and cell loss do not occur (Tang et al., 2014).

Abnormally rapid brain growth does not continue, however. Between the ages of 2;0 and 5;0 years, rate of brain growth is normal, although total brain volume remains enlarged relative to that of typically developing children (Hazlett et al., 2011).

Moreover, from adolescence into late middle age, sMRI scans show abnormal *decreases* in total brain volume in most people with ASD, relative to neurotypical comparison groups (Courchesne et al., 2011; see also Greimel et al., 2013; Itahashi et al., 2015), although rare cases of persistent **macrocephaly** have been reported (Barnard-Brak et al., 2011). Reduced brain volume during adolescence may result from the fact that the spurt of brain growth that occurs in neurotypical teenagers may not occur in autistic teenagers. On the other hand, abnormally large decreases in brain volume during adulthood are more likely to result from greater than normal loss of grey and white matter as the brain ages.

COMMENT

It is important to remember that most individuals with ASD are much more 'normal' (neurotypical) than 'abnormal', and some are highly able. Moreover, nearly all individuals with ASD have some 'splinter' skills – things they can do significantly better than most other things. Sometimes these spared abilities achieve savant levels, as described in Chapter 3.

The challenge for explanations of autism at the level of brain bases is therefore to be consistent with the fact that the brains of many people with an ASD diagnosis are in most respects operating effectively though probably differently from the brains of people without autism. Even in less able individuals, where brain function is clearly more compromised, facets of brain function (and by inference structure and neurochemistry) can be relatively spared, and in cases of savant ability developed to underpin super-normal levels of function.

It is important, therefore, not to jump to a conclusion from the evidence presented above regarding abnormalities of brain structure and neurochemistry, that the brains of people with ASD are predominantly 'abnormal' and 'malfunctioning'. In the first place, studies reporting negative findings (no abnormalities) are somewhat less likely to be published than studies reporting positive findings (significant differences from the norm). Similarly, the negative findings in published studies that produced a mixed set of results are often overlooked in favour of stressing the positive findings.

It is also important not to underestimate the benefits, in terms of behavioural abilities, that 'abnormalities' of brain structure may bring. Local network hyper-connectivity, associated with superior perception of visual detail, is one such example already referred to.

Finally, the capacity of the brain to compensate must not be underestimated, especially in individuals with conditions present from infancy, as in autism. Compensation can be achieved by extending the role of intact brain systems to subserve functions more usually subserved by compromised brain systems. Moreover, neural plasticity ensures capacities for brain growth and development that are advantageous to the individual, even if atypical (consider how efficiently individuals born without hands use the feet for many skilled 'manual' tasks).

A final point to make is that it is important to bear in mind that the terms 'atypical' or 'anomalous' imply difference, but carry no necessary implication of 'inferior' or 'worse' (after all, Mozart's brain must have been 'atypical', but none the worse for that).

All these considerations suggest that an important goal of future research into the brain bases of ASD should be to understand how this efficiency is achieved. This will entail focusing attention on the abilities of people with autism across the spectrum, in addition to focusing attention on the brain bases of behavioural impairments.

SUMMARY

Some basic information about the structure, neurochemistry, function and development of the brain in neurotypical people was outlined at the outset of the chapter. This opening section concentrated on providing information of likely relevance to understanding brain anomalies in ASD, and on introducing and defining some of the key terms to be used later in the chapter. Commonly used methods of assessing brain structure, the neurochemistry of the brain, and brain function were also listed and defined at points within the chapter.

Regarding what is known about the brain correlates of autism-related abilities and disabilities, the evidence is copious, sometimes conflicting, and generally difficult to interpret with any certainty. However, it is widely accepted that there is abnormal connectivity within and between various brain regions and structures. Both hyper- and hypo-connectivity occur, and it is generally thought that hyper-connectivity within local networks is associated with isolated peaks of ability, whereas hypo-connectivity between more widely distributed regions or structures is associated with autism-related behavioural anomalies or impairments. Stated crudely, the autistic brain is – to a lesser or greater extent, varying with the complexity of each individual's problems – not wired up normally. In the case of language, this 'abnormal wiring' extends to the abnormal lateralisation of some language-related processes.

Anomalous connectivity in the brains of people with ASD probably results from abnormalities in the density of grey matter and/or white matter in specific brain regions or structures – sometimes too much, sometimes too little. Abnormalities may vary with age, gender, and also with the complexity of an individual's autism-related problems. Abnormal densities of grey matter have been found in the cerebral cortex, the cerebellum, and in subcortical structures that are key components of the neural circuits identified in bullet points earlier in the chapter. Sometimes nerve tracts are under-developed, with a loss of co-ordinated activity between structures. At the cellular level, the generator, transmitter and/or receptor cells of certain neurochemical systems have been found to be sparse or malfunctioning. Neurochemical systems that are probably most affected in ASD are the serotoninergic and dopaminergic systems, with the balance between excitatory and inhibitory substances (GABA and glutamate), as well as the 'social bonding' hormones oxytocin and vasopressin, also affected.

It is important *not* to infer from the above that the brains of autistic people do not function effectively in many respects – indeed, in most respects in the case of people with high-functioning ASD. The human brain is relatively 'plastic', i.e. capable of finding different ways of working if the 'normal' route is not available. It is also important to give full weight to the fact that the brain anomalies in ASD may sometimes produce individuals with superior talents. The challenge for explanations of autism at the level of brain bases is therefore to be consistent with the fact that the brains of many people with ASD are in most respects operating effectively, though probably differently from the brains of people without autism.

PROXIMAL CAUSES 1: DIAGNOSTIC BEHAVIOURS

AIMS

The main aim of this chapter is to provide an account of theories and evidence relating to the immediate, or proximal, causes of the socio-emotional-communicative impairments and restricted and repetitive behaviours that constitute diagnostic criteria for ASD. An underlying aim is to emphasise the multiplicity of factors that may significantly contribute to any one facet of autism-related behaviour – sometimes affecting only a relatively small subset of individuals, but always contributing to heterogeneity in individual outcomes.

INTRODUCTION

Until recently, psychological[1] theories predominated in the literature concerning the causes of autism. Theories concerning the etiology and brain bases of autism were certainly proposed from the earliest years following publication of Kanner's seminal paper in 1943. However, the methods available for studying genetics, or for studying brain structure, function and neurochemistry, were quite limited until the last decade or so of the twentieth century. Because of this, relatively little was known about human genetics as a whole, or about the fine detail of typical brain development, structure and function – let alone about the genetics or neurobiology of autism.

Understandably, therefore, attempts to understand the causes of autism-related behaviours were mainly pitched at the level of psychological processes and systems. Theories and evidence at this level of explanation proliferated over the years: theories have come and gone; some came and went only to be revived decades later. In this chapter, most space is given to the most recent and/or best supported theories. However, some indications of older theories, or the stages of development of a particular theory, are sometimes included to emphasise the fact that there is as yet no definitive and universally accepted account of 'The Psychology of Autism'.

The chapter is in two major sections, one on neuropsychological explanations of socio-emotional-communicative (SEC) impairments and one on neuropsychological explanations of restricted and repetitive behaviours (RRBs). Each of these major sections opens with a short subsection headed 'What Has to be Explained', where reference will be made to the detailed descriptions of the diagnostic behaviours provided in Chapters 2 and 3. In each major section there is then an extended subsection covering 'Explanatory Theories'. The chapter ends with the usual Summary.

---

[1]As the brain correlates of major psychological processes are increasingly understood, 'psychological' explanations are increasingly expected to be 'neuropsychological'. In what follows, 'neuropsychological' will generally be used where the brain correlates of a particular psychological process are known. 'Psychological' will be used elsewhere.

SOCIO-EMOTIONAL-COMMUNICATIVE IMPAIRMENTS

What Has to be Explained

Neuropsychological accounts of the proximal causes of ASD must be capable of explaining the diagnostic SEC impairments as detailed in DSM-5. Descriptions and examples of diagnostic SEC impairments according to DSM-5 can be found in Box 2.1.

Any account of the proximal causes of SEC impairments in people with a diagnosis of ASD must also be capable of explaining SEC impairments that are present before a diagnosis is made, namely impairments of dyadic and triadic interaction (see Chapter 3). In addition, much more is known about the detailed characteristics of SEC impairments than can be compressed into a set of diagnostic criteria, and some expansion of these criteria can be found in Chapter 3 in the subsections relating to 'Impaired mindreading', 'Impaired emotion processing' and 'Communication impairments'.

Explanatory Theories

In this section, potential explanations of dyadic interaction impairments are considered first on the principle that early-occurring anomalies will help to explain later-manifesting anomalies (consistent with the primacy criterion identified in Chapter 6). Possible explanations of impaired mindreading, emotion processing and communication are then considered in turn.

Explaining impaired dyadic interaction

Candidate theories   Various explanations of impaired dyadic interaction in ASD have been proposed, based on what is known about the innate social, emotional, communicative and cognitive capacities of typically developing infants and toddlers. It is important to note that 'innate' does not necessarily imply 'congenital'/'manifest from birth'. Rather, it indicates that some facet of physical or behavioural development is genetically programmed to come on-stream at a certain life stage (which is not to say that genes are the sole determinants of these developments). The capacity for language acquisition, the onset of puberty, and the processes associated with normal ageing are examples of such developments. All the innate capacities and propensities listed below – and the list is not exhaustive – have some role in establishing and maintaining reciprocal bonds between babies and their primary caregivers, with obvious survival value for the infant; hence they have been 'written into' the genes. Several, but not all, are congenital, i.e. are present in typically developing neonates; the remainder are observable within the first three months of life (for supporting references, see primers of child development, for example Bee and Boyd, 2012; Berk and Meyers, 2015).

- *Social orienting.* This term refers to typically developing neonates' preferential attention to social stimuli (such as faces, voices, and movements of the mouth, eyes or hands), as opposed to non-social stimuli.
- *Eye salience and gaze following.* Other people's eyes capture and hold the attention of typically developing neonates, and they can discriminate whether another person's eyes are directed towards them or averted. When the other person's eyes are averted, the infant's eyes tend to move in the direction of whatever the other person is looking at. This is the response known as gaze following, which is a precursor of joint attention.
- *Social learning.* Typically developing neonates recognise their mother's voice, having heard it *in utero*. By the third week of life, neurotypical infants recognise the faces of primary caregivers and spend more time looking at them than at unfamiliar faces. These rather amazing attainments indicate that certain perceptual and memory/learning capacities are present even before birth.
- *Imitation.* The propensity to imitate others' facial postures (e.g. tongue protrusion) occurs in typically developing neonates. They may also spontaneously imitate certain hand movements. By the end of the third month typically developing infants imitate others' facial expressions of emotion.
- *Social motivation* refers to the intrinsic reward-value of social stimuli, as indicated by typically developing neonates' spontaneous initiation of eye contact and their expressions of pleasure (social smiling, vocalisations) during social engagement within the first three months of life.
- Synchronisation of vocalisations and movements in dyadic interactions is observable in typically developing infants by the age of three months. This indicates the existence of capacities for fine-grained *timing* in both the perception and production of movements and sounds.

Critical assessment of the theories All the above propensities and capacities are at least partially impaired in people with ASD. This could suggest that one or more of them underlie impaired dyadic interaction, as has been argued by various researchers. Thus it has been argued that a *social orienting* deficit might underlie SEC impairments in ASD (Dawson et al., 2004; Leekam & Ramsden, 2006). Similarly, it has been suggested that problems of *eye salience and gaze following* may contribute to SEC impairments in incipient autism as well as in established autism (Baron-Cohen, 1995; Jones et al., 2008). Impaired *imitation* was for a time argued to be an important cause of the social impairments in ASD (Williams et al., 2001; Ramachandran & Oberman, 2006), although it is now clear that imitation impairments in ASD are selective rather than pervasive (Vivanti & Hamilton, 2014). Persistent face and voice recognition problems (Boucher et al., 2000; Weigelt et al., 2013) might suggest that a *social learning/memory* deficit contributes to SEC impairments from the start.

These four hypotheses are, however, weakened by the fact that they all critically involve the ability to see people's faces and body movements, and to hear their voices, but people who are congenitally blind or deaf are not generally autistic (Hobson & Lee, 2010; Szymanski et al., 2012). Nor do individual accounts of people born deaf-blind suggest that even this most debilitating form of sensory impairment is reliably or frequently accompanied by autism (see websites of relevant support organisations). People born with severe sensory impairments can, of course, compensate through their intact sensory channels, and may exercise their intact **social orienting**,[2] imitation and social learning capacities utilising these channels. It is difficult to argue, however, that babies born blind can compensate for loss of eye direction detection and gaze following by using hearing or touch.

Another difficulty with the above four hypotheses is that dyadic relating is not usually reported to have been abnormal in the first year of life. Instead, parents commonly report a *decline* in their child's sociability usually some time in the second year. Impaired social orienting, failure to make and maintain eye contact, failure to imitate facial expressions (especially smiling), failure to respond differentially to the faces and voices of familiar carers as opposed to those of strangers would, if present, surely all have been noticed within the first year of life.

For both the above reasons, impaired *social motivation* is a stronger candidate for explaining the decline in dyadic interaction in incipient autism. The case for a fundamental deficit in the innate reward value of social stimuli (being fed, cuddled, looked at, smiled at, played with, cooed at or talked to) has been made over many years (e.g. Mundy, 1995, 2003; Sigman & Capps, 1997), and most recently by Chevallier et al. (2012). Awareness of social interaction with familiar others, and associated experiences of comfort, safety and pleasure, can be experienced through any of the senses, including touch taste and smell: it is not reliant on either vision or hearing. Moreover, failure to experience reward from social interactions would gradually undermine the innate tendencies to make eye contact, to imitate the movements and facial expressions of others, to respond preferentially to the faces and voices of familiar carers. The impaired social reward hypothesis is therefore consistent with the fact that dyadic interaction is unimpaired during the first year of life but then declines.

Impaired *timing* as a cause of social, linguistic and motor abnormalities in ASD was first argued for by Newson (1984) and later by Boucher (2001), Wimpory et al. (2002), and most recently by Allman (2011). One of the strengths of this hypothesis is that fine-grained timing is involved in almost every kind of active behaviour as well as in the integration of neural activity within the brain (Brock et al., 2002). Feldman (2007) has spelled out the role of timing for the normal development of reciprocal social interaction, and it could be argued that the failure to co-ordinate and synchronise social interactions during the first year of life undermines those facets of dyadic relating that operated normally at first. This hypothesis, although plausible, has not been intensively investigated.

There may in fact be no single initial behavioural deficit from which all other dyadic interaction impairments accrue: in any one individual there may be more than one initial deficit, leading to a cascade of knock-on effects. In addition, the initial neuropsychological deficits that can lead to impaired dyadic relating may differ across individuals. Given the multiplicity and heterogeneity of etiological factors (genetic and environmental) that may contribute to autism, and given also the range of ages, from six months to the beginning of the third year, at which signs of incipient autism are first detectable, it seems

---

[2]Words or phrases in bold type on first occurance can be found in the Glossary.

quite likely that the earliest-occurring neuropsychological deficits underlying impaired dyadic relating, and thereafter contributing to the broad range of SEC impairments in ASD, are also heterogeneous.

What can also be said with reasonable certainty is that disturbances of synaptic development associated with known risk factors for ASD (see Chapter 7), and which are manifested in the early overgrowth of brain matter in infants with incipient autism (see Chapter 8), are in some way implicated. In cases of regressive autism, this may be the result of neurodegeneration, as suggested by Kern et al. (2013), rather than early overgrowth. However, the net effect would be the same in terms of maldevelopment and subsequent malfunction of key regions of the social brain.

Explaining impaired mindreading

There are two distinct approaches to explaining how human beings develop mindreading abilities: the modularist and constructivist approaches. As noted in the previous chapter, the modularist approach is rooted in the view that certain uniquely human, highly specialised capacities have arisen via genetic mutations which – as a result of their significant survival value – became written into the genes as innate capacities. These **domain-specific** capacities are conceptualised as brain-based **modules** that are pre-set to mature at specific ages or stages of development.

The constructivist approach argues that uniquely human, specialised capacities, such as those for mindreading, language and numeracy, are built up over time from one or more of the very early manifesting capacities listed in the previous section, combined with **domain-general** learning abilities (Karmiloff-Smith, 1992, 2006).

These competing accounts of the origins of mindreading ability still figure in explanations of impaired mindreading in ASD, as outlined next.

Explaining impaired mindreading in terms of modular deficits   When an impairment of explicit theory of mind (ToM) in children with autism was first demonstrated in a seminal study by Baron-Cohen and colleagues (1985), the authors explained the impairment as resulting from a lack of an innate modular capacity for **metarepresentation**. The definition of 'metarepresentation' and its relation to various forms of mindreading became controversial topics in philosophy as well as in psychology over the next three decades, and controversies remain (see Carruthers, 2009, and commentaries on this article). Stated simply, however, metarepresentation may be defined as 'the ability to form a **representation** of a representation', making it possible to think about thinking – to reflect on and reason about one's own and other people's perceptions, knowledge, motivations, memories, etc.

Shortly after publication of the 1985 paper, however, one of the authors of the paper, Frith, distanced herself from the suggestion that impaired performance on false belief tasks (see Chapter 3) derives from impaired metarepresentation (Frith, 1989). Frith proposed instead that failure to pass these tests results from impaired ability to form in one's own mind any representation ('idea') of what may be in someone else's mind in the first place – let alone form a metarepresentation. Frith introduced the term 'mentalising' to refer to the ability to represent in one's own mind the content of someone else's mind – their 'mental state'. She noted that mentalising is necessary not only for explicit ToM, but also for many early-occurring forms of mind-sharing in typically developing children, including the triadic interaction behaviours that manifest in typically developing infants towards the end of their first year. Implicit ToM had not at this time been demonstrated in typically developing babies. However, implicit ToM, like explicit ToM and triadic interaction, clearly involves mentalising.

Frith (1989; see also Frith et al., 1991) initially proposed that mentalising is an innate, pre-programmed capacity primed to 'switch on' in typically developing babies at a specific stage in development. This proposal was based on the model of the acquisition of normal mindreading proposed by Leslie (1987), one of the other authors of the seminal 1985 paper. Leslie has continued to argue that it is necessary to posit innate modular mechanisms to explain not only success on mindreading tasks, but also to explain the emergence of pretend play in typically developing children, noting that pretence, like mindreading, is impaired in children with autism (Leslie, 1987; German & Leslie, 2004). However, Frith and her collaborators later abandoned the modularist explanation of the origin of mentalising ability in favour of a constructivist explanation, as outlined below.

The first-named author of the 1985 paper, Baron-Cohen, also started out in the modularist camp. His mindreading model (Baron-Cohen, 1995) and his later empathising system model (Baron-Cohen, 2005) posited a set of innate capacities corresponding to some of the congenital or very early manifesting capacities underpinning dyadic social interaction. These were somewhat coyly named: the Intention Detector (ID), the Eye Direction Detector (EDD), the Shared Attention Mechanism (SAM), the Theory of Mind Mechanism (ToMM) and, when his empathising system model took over from the original mindreading model, The Empathising SyStem (TESS) was added to the set. Baron-Cohen's 'SAM' and 'ToMM' equate with mentalising ability and metarepresentation, respectively. Thus Baron-Cohen's model incorporated Frith's concept of an innate, domain-specific mechanism for mentalising (typically available from the end of the first year of life), as well as Leslie's concept of an innate mechanism for metarepresentation (typically available around the end of the fourth year of life). When Baron-Cohen first propounded his mindreading and empathising system models he placed considerable emphasis on this bank of innate modular mechanisms, arguing that SAM and ToMM are defective in autism. Subsequently, however, he has focused almost exclusively on the problems that people with ASD have in 'reading the mind in the eyes', arguing that this underlies the mentalising deficit. This brings Baron-Cohen into the constructivist camp, as described below.

Latterly, it has been largely left to philosophers to argue the case for the existence of innate domain-specific modular abilities to explain the development of mindreading in typically developing infants and impaired mindreading in ASD (Adams, 2013; Carruthers, 2013; but see also Gerrans & Stone, 2008).

Explaining impaired mindreading in terms of a constructivist model   In a semi-nal book entitled *Autism and the Development of Mind*, Hobson (1993) argued the constructivist view that our specifically human capacities for understanding other minds are rooted in infants' and toddlers' experiences of inter-relatedness with other people. He further argued that autistic children's fundamental disor-der should be conceptualised as 'a disruption in the usual interpersonally coordi-nated patterns of intersubjective *relatedness*' (Hobson, 1993: 79 – his italics), thus missing out on the foundational stage of internally representing others' mental states. In making this argument, Hobson was explicitly returning to Kanner's early hypothesis that autism stems from lack of 'the innate ability to form the usual biologically provided affective contact with people'. Hobson referred to this as **affective agnosia**, or 'emotion blindness'.

'Emotion blindness' would, he argued, diminish the very young infant's desire for social interaction because there would be no shared pleasure in it, only a self-centred pleasure from the sensations provided by, for example, being rocked or tickled. More importantly, the lack of co-experience of emotion would impair the ability to realise (unconsciously, of course) that other people have emotions like the child's own: that 'Daddy can feel happy or sad, like me'. Thus the infant misses out on the first stage of understanding about others' – and their own – mental states. A little later in development, when the typically developing infant understands that Daddy wants (and I want) the cake, the infant with ASD will have no understanding of the shared 'wanting', and the shared attention to, the cake. Protodeclarative communication, such as bringing and showing or pointing at something interesting, will not occur because the child has no awareness of the possibility of sharing emotions or mental states.

Influenced perhaps by Hobson's arguments, or by the cogent and detailed case made for constructivism by writers such as Karmiloff-Smith (1992, 2006), Frith abandoned a modularist explanation of impaired mentalising in autism in favour of a constructivist interpretation (Frith & Frith, 2003; Frith, 2013; Happé & Frith, 2014). Frith (2013) notes, for example, that *eye gaze processing* and the *detection of biological motion* are impaired in people with ASD, and considers whether one of these early manifesting but persistent impairments might underlie impaired mentalising in autism.

Gallagher (2004) and Tager-Flusberg (2005) have argued that typically devel-oping babies' innate preference for attending to human faces, voices and body movements (*social orienting*) ensures a wealth of perceptual information from which 'immediate and intuitive' representations of others' mental states are formed. Both these authors have proposed that because infants with incipient autism lack innate social orienting propensities, and actually avoid interacting with other people, they lack the perceptual experiences from which mental states of others are intuitively inferred.

Similarly, it has been hypothesised that impaired mentalising could result from impaired experience of *social reward* (Chevallier et al., 2012) or impaired *timing* (Feldman, 2007).

In sum, although constructivists may disagree as to which of the innate capac-ities underlying dyadic interaction in typically developing babies are absent or impaired in infants with incipient ASD, they are united in arguing that babies' bodily and perceptual experiences of themselves and of other people during the earliest weeks and months of life provide the essential building blocks of mentalising. Moreover, there is widespread agreement that mentalising ability is initially manifested in implicit ToM and impaired triadic relating – i.e. by the end of the typically developing infant's first year.

Regarding the capacity for metarepresentation, all of the authors in the constructivist camp argue that when mentalising ability is supplemented by certain domain-general abilities that become available to the typically developing 3;0–4;0 year old, 'thinking about thinking' becomes possible. Frith (2013) argues for the critical role of language. Tager-Flusberg (2005) argues that both language and certain **executive functions** are required to pass false belief tasks. Gallagher suggests that **central coherence** may be important. All these claims are supported by research: see, for example, Fisher et al. (2005) or Tager-Flusberg and Joseph (2005) on the link between explicit ToM and language; Pellicano (2007) or Kimhi et al. (2014) on the link with executive function; and Jarrold et al. (2000) or Pellicano (2010) on the link with central coherence. General intelligence also clearly helps to determine whether an individual can solve false belief tasks and this may be why many non-autistic learning disabled individuals fail tests of explicit ToM. In the case of autism, central coherence and certain executive functions are probably always impaired (see below), and language and learning ability are sometimes impaired. According to the constructivists, therefore, it is not hard to see why people with ASD fail on tests of explicit ToM.

Explaining impaired emotion processing

Most suggested explanations of impaired emotion processing in autism invoke impairments of integration. These theories revolve around the fact that normal experience, whether social or not, almost always involves affective (emotion-related) as well as perceptual and cognitive content, and these components are experienced as integrally related.

Hermelin and O'Connor (1985) were the first to suggest that in autism there is a problem in the integration of the affective and cognitive components of experience. This problem would lead to questions such as 'Did I like it when I went on the bouncy castle?' (see the section on empathy in Chapter 3).

Ben Shalom (2000; Faran & Ben Shalom, 2008) has proposed the more specific hypothesis that people with ASD experience the physiological components of emotion but fail to associate this experience with whatever stimulated the emotion. Thus someone with ASD might see a snake and experience a cold sweat and other physiological correlates of fear, without automatically connecting their bodily sensations with the snake. Equally, an infant with incipient autism would experience the physical pleasure of being stroked or tickled, but they would not associate the pleasurable feelings with the person stroking or tickling (compare the 'impaired experience of social reward' theory, outlined earlier in the chapter). Ben Shalom's hypothesis fits well with the observation that, while emotion contagion and the experience of the physiological components basic emotions is intact in people with ASD, understanding of what other people's or one's own emotion *is about* (that is to say, the cognitive as opposed to the affective component of any experience) is not integrated with the physiological components. The hypothesis is also consistent with theoretical models of emotion processing in mainstream psychology. In mainstream pyschology a distinction is commonly made between 'emotions' defined as raw physiological sensations, and 'feelings' defined as the conscious identification of what the emotion is about – what provoked it, and what kind it is: is it 'fear' or 'amusement' or 'surprise', for example (LeDoux, 1998)?

Failure to experience 'feelings', in this special sense, is compatible with the 'emotion blindness' theory, as argued for first by Kanner and later by Hobson. If one has no idea what another person's emotion is about, one is not in a position either to share it (except in terms of physiological arousal) or to respond appropriately. Impaired appreciation of what another person's emotion is about is also a cornerstone of Baron-Cohen's 'impaired empathising system' theory. According to this theory, the inability to appreciate the content of another person's emotion results from impaired mentalising (referred to as 'theory of mind') (Baron-Cohen et al., 1997; Wheelwright & Baron-Cohen, 2011).

In an extended review of the literature on emotion processing in autism, Gaigg (2012) argues for there being a disconnect between experienced emotion and the experiences giving rise to an emotion, regardless of whether the experiences are social or non-social – i.e. regardless of whether or not mentalising is involved. This argument gives much greater weight than previously to the role of impaired emotion processing as disruptive to all sorts of learning. It will be of considerable importance to see how this argument develops, because the reward-value of experience – whether positive or negative – is absolutely central to how we learn and what we learn. Explanatory theories centring on impaired integration are, in addition, clearly compatible with evidence on anomalous structural and functional brain connectivity in people with ASD.

Explaining impaired communication

In the section on impaired communication in Chapter 3 it was pointed out that both the means of interpersonal communication (language and nonverbal communication signals) and also the rules and conventions governing the use of language and nonverbal signals in interpersonal communication (pragmatics) are impaired in people with ASD.

Explanatory theories relating to *impaired language* are reviewed in the next chapter. Regarding *impaired comprehension and use of nonverbal signals*, impaired comprehension of facial expressions of emotion (Uljarevic & Hamilton, 2013; Golan et al., 2015) might be explained in terms of one or another of the theories outlined in the section on impaired emotion processing, above. Recent demonstrations of impaired use of gesture (Sowden et al., 2013; Watson et al., 2013), and of impaired integration of gesture and speech (Silverman et al., 2010; Hubbard et al., 2012), have yet to be explained. However, the latter problem is consistent with an impairment of cross-modal processing, which was an early contender for an explanation of impaired ability to match familiar faces with the voices of the people pictured (Boucher et al., 1998). A cross-modal processing impairment constitutes a form of impaired integration of sensory stimuli, and is consistent with anomalous neural connectivity in the brain. Defective timing might also offer an explanation of impaired integration of speech and gesture.

Impaired pragmatics can largely be explained in terms of impaired mindreading and emotion processing. Impaired mindreading causes the person with ASD to communicate without consideration of the other person's mental states: their knowledge, beliefs, feelings, etc. (Cummings, 2013; Fernández, 2013). Because people with ASD have no intuitive appreciation of 'where the other person is coming from', their communication is self-centred not just in topics that may be pursued, but also in poor turn-taking, poor listening, and failure to use the appropriate conversational and grammatical devices that help to clarify meaning.

Brain correlates of SEC impairments

The brain correlates of each of the innate abilities underlying dyadic interaction are well known, and generally form part of 'the social brain'. As noted in Chapter 8, brain scans and EEG studies of children and adults with ASD reliably show that key structures and connectivity within the social brain are dysfunctional and/or structurally abnormal. It may be assumed that – even if present and intact at birth, as the evidence relating to the gradual onset of autism suggests – one or more of these capacities is irrecoverably disrupted by abnormalities of brain development during the first two years of life. For a detailed exposition of the development of the social brain, and the disruption of normal development in people with ASD, see Frith and Frith (2010). Also as noted in Chapter 8, structures and connectivity within the default mode network (DNM) which subserves mentalising and mindreading have also been shown to be dysfunctional and/or structurually abnormal (Li, Mai et al., 2014).

RESTRICTED AND REPETITIVE BEHAVIOURS

What Has to be Explained

Descriptions of the restricted and repetitive behaviours, including sensory-perceptual anomalies, that constitute diagnostic criteria for ASD according to DSM-5 were reproduced in Box 2.1. Expanded descriptions of repetitive and restricted behaviours, sensory-perceptual anomalies, and also the links between these contrasting forms of RRBs can be found in Chapter 3. The lack of creativity and imagination which constitutes the flip side of repetitive and restricted behaviour was also described and discussed in Chapter 3.

Explanatory Theories

There are a considerable number of explanatory theories to cover in this section, some of which are overlapping, none of which can by themselves offer a complete explanation of all forms of RRBs, and none of which is proven. To clarify the emerging picture, differentiable theories are presented individually, whereas over-lapping or related theories are presented as groups, under the following headings.

- The impaired control of arousal theory.
- The impaired executive function theory.
- Six sensory-perceptual imbalance theories.
- Two anomalous learning theories.
- Non-specific aggravating factors.

The impaired control of arousal theory

This theory revives a hypothesis first proposed half a century ago by Hutt et al. (1964). These authors proposed that levels of physiological arousal are poorly controlled in people with autism. Arousal levels determine levels of wakefulness and sleep, including levels of alertness, attention and readiness to respond in awake states. The physiological correlates of arousal include variations in heart rate and blood pressure. At the level of the central nervous system, arousal is regulated by the **reticular activating system**, which runs from the brain stem to the cerebral cortex, mediated by the activity of specific neurotransmitters.

Hutt et al. (1964) hypothesised that abnormalities within the reticular activat-ing system in autism limit the degree of control that people with autism are able to exert over their own arousal levels, leaving them vulnerable to both hyper- and hypo-sensitivity to sensory stimuli in all modalities. They further hypothesised that repetitive behaviours occur both as a means of reducing sensory stimulation to counteract over-arousal (anticipating the concept of 'sensory soothing'), and as a means of increasing sensory experience to counteract under-arousal (anticipating the concept of 'sensory seeking').

The Hutts and their colleagues were not the only researchers of that period to argue for an impaired arousal explanation of repetitive and restricted behaviours in autism. Ornitz (1976), for example, proposed that a failure of homeostatic regulation of sensory input leading to impaired **sensory modulation** could explain these behaviours. The impaired arousal theory was not, however, pursued until the work of researchers such as O'Neill and Jones (1997) and Gal et al. (2002), mentioned above, once again focused researchers' attention on the relationship between sensory anomalies and repetitive behaviours in ASD.

In 2006, Liss and colleagues (see also Orekhova & Stroganova, 2014) argued that abnormalities of arousal levels could explain not only hyper- and hypo-sensitivity to sensory stimuli, but also certain attentional abnormalities, such as **over-focused attention** and difficulty in detaching attention from a particular stimulus. In a detailed and authoritative review of research into RRBs in autism, Leekam et al. (2011) also argue that the 'impaired arousal' theory has potential explanatory value for RRBs.

The impaired arousal theory does, however, face some conceptual difficulties. In particular, although dysregulation of arousal levels is consistent with problems of sensory modulation, it can less easily explain the more widespread problems of sensory processing that are commonly, possibly universally, present in people with ASD (summarised in Chapter 3 – for a fuller account, see Baranek et al., 2014). Moreover, sensory processing impairments occur in a clinically recognised group of individuals who are not autistic. The differentiation or overlap between 'sensory processing disorder' and sensory processing anomalies in ASD has only begun to be investigated (Schoen et al., 2009).

In sum, the impaired arousal theory is a major contender as an explanation, or part explanation, of RRBs in ASD but is currently in need of further theoretical development and testing.

The impaired executive function theory

Definition   The notion of an executive system in the brain derives from an analogy with computers in which a master program controls and directs all the software programs on the machine. Based on this analogy, the term 'executive functions', as used in psychology, generally covers the set of cognitive processes that are involved in the organisation and control of mental and physical activity. At the minimum, executive functions enable an individual to:

> STOP doing one thing: this involves *inhibitory control* and the ability to *disengage attention* from a current stimulus, ongoing thought process or action;
>
> SWITCH to something else: this involves *mental flexibility*; not just stopping doing one thing, but shifting attention to a new stimulus or shifting **mental set**;
>
> START on something else (e.g. a new topic of thought or a different physical action): this involves *generating* a new focus of attention such as a topic or goal, *planning* how to achieve the goal, and *initiating* the selected behaviour.

Executive functions are also involved in:

> ORGANISING ongoing behaviour;
>
> MONITORING ongoing behaviour;
>
> TROUBLESHOOTING or MAKING CORRECTIONS, if required.

These additional components may involve *strategy generation*, *decision making*, **self-monitoring** and **action–outcome monitoring**, and **working memory**. All the terms in upper case, italic or in bold type above appear in accounts of executive functions, plus others not included here. Not surprisingly, 'executive function' is often described as an umbrella term, covering multiple processes.[3]

History   Evidence suggestive of executive dysfunctions (EDFs) was first demonstrated in people with ASD by Rumsey (1985), although anticipated in an influential paper by Damasio and Maurer, published in 1978. Rumsey's finding of

---

[3]A narrower meaning of 'executive function' occurs in Baddeley and Hitch's model of working memory (Baddeley, 1986, 2000), but the term is used only in its broad sense here.

perseverative, or 'stuck-in-set', behaviour in autistic adults was quickly confirmed in other studies, including one by Russell et al. (1991) with particularly striking findings, as summarised in Box 9.1.

Box 9.1   The 'windows task'

The original task devised by Russell and his colleagues consisted of placing a chocolate, or other desired treat, in one or the other of two boxes placed side by side on a table directly in front of the child being tested, and between the child and the Tester sitting opposite. Three sides of each container were opaque, but the sides facing the child had 'windows' enabling them to see what, if anything, was in each box. The child's task was to point to one of the boxes which the Tester would then have to open, leaving the other box for the child to open. In order to win the treat, the child must therefore point to the empty box, so that the box with the treat in it is left for them to open.

In the original experiment, children with Down syndrome and typically developing 4;0 year olds quickly learned to point to the empty box. Astonishingly, the majority of the children with autism were completely unable to succeed on the windows task, making the wrong response as many as 20 times in succession.

This striking finding could suggest that children with ASD have impaired response inhibition: they simply cannot stop themselves from pointing to the container in which they can see the chocolate. Or possibly they have difficulty in disengaging their attention from the treat, so point to where their attention is held. However, numerous alternative explanations have been explored over the years, with Russell and various colleagues painstakingly investigating and attempting to rule out alternative explanations.

The experiments reported by Rumsey and by Russell and colleagues, amongst others, showed that people with autism have problems in *stopping* doing one thing, *disengaging* their attention from an ongoing response pattern, and *switching* attention so as to start doing something different. At around the same time, various reports of impaired *generativity* in autistic children were published (for references, see the section on 'Imagination and Creativity: Strengths and Weaknesses' in Chapter 3).

Following publication of these early papers, and armed with the concept of an executive system with top-down control of lower-order processing, hypothetical links between EDFs and various facets of autistic behaviour were intensively investigated and discussed (see Hill, 2004, and Russo et al., 2007, for reviews). Findings on tests of various executive functions were, however, very mixed, tending to vary according to the age and ability of those being tested, and the specific tests used (Prior & Ozonoff, 2007).

Moreover, regarding suggestions that impaired executive control could explain RRBs, it became increasingly evident that this explanation did not satisfy either the primacy criterion (that proposed causes must precede their proposed effects) or the specificity criterion (that proposed causes of autism-specific behaviours must not occur in non-autistic groups) (see Chapter 6). Regarding the primacy criterion:

whereas motor stereotypies and resistance to change are present in infants and toddlers with ASD (Kim & Lord, 2010; Wolff et al., 2014), most aspects of executive control develop over an extended period of childhood into late adolescence. Moreover, very early developing executive functions are not impaired in preschool children with ASD (Griffith et al., 1999). Regarding the specificity criterion, executive dysfunctions are common in learning disabled individuals without autism (Hill, 2004). There is, in addition, something of a chicken–egg problem concerning the relationship between EDFs and repetitive and restricted behaviours. This is because the most reliably-occurring EDFs in people with autism are associated with perseveration – which is by definition a form of repetitive behaviour.

In their extended review of research and theory relating to RRBs cited above, Leekam et al. (2011) make these arguments, among others, as evidence against impaired executive function as the major, or critical, cause of RRBs. Davis and Plaisted-Grant (2015), however, move the discussion on by arguing that their 'low endogenous noise' hypothesis (see below) can explain the mixed findings on EDFs in autism, as well as explaining other manifestations of repetitive behaviour. Pellicano (2012a) makes the additional important point that regardless of the fact that EDFs are unlikely to be able to explain RRBs in autism, the intactness or otherwise of executive functions have real-life consequences for people with ASD.

Six sensory-perceptual imbalance theories

(i) The weak central coherence theory   In 1983, Shah and Frith showed that children with ASD have superior ability to pick out a particular detail of a picture representing a whole object or scene. The test they used resembled the kind of puzzle sometimes found in books bought for children to pass the time on a journey, as illustrated in Figure 9.1.

In 1989, Frith suggested that people with autism have a 'weak drive for central coherence', basing her notion of 'coherence' on work in psychology showing that neurotypical people have a strong tendency to look for meaning in sensory experience. Frith argued that a weak drive for meaning, or what she termed **weak central coherence (WCC)**, could explain not only the results of her study with Shah, but also early reports that children with autism solve jigsaw puzzles by attending to the shape of the pieces rather than to the pictures; and that they recall sentences or lists of related words no better than they recall lists of unrelated words (Hermelin & O'Connor, 1970).

Frith (1989) further suggested that superior ability to process detail resulted from impaired ability to integrate parts into wholes. In neuropsychological terminology, superior **local processing** was hypothesised to result from defective **global processing**. An explanation in terms of impaired global processing fits well with first-hand accounts such as that of John van Dalen, quoted in Box 3.4, who describes the effortful route he must take to assemble in his mind the parts of an object (such as a hammer) and the name of the object, and his knowledge of the properties and functions of the object. The suggestion that superior local processing results from impaired global processing is also intuitively plausible: if we are poor at doing one thing, we may compensate by becoming unusually good at doing the next best thing. The combination of enhanced local processing with

Figure 9.1 *A test of the ability to pick out a detail, in this instance a face, concealed within a larger picture*

impaired global processing is also consistent with what is now known about anomalous brain connectivity in people with ASD.

Following the introduction of the WCC theory, there was a spate of reports of phenomena consistent with the suggestion that enhanced local processing is typical in people with ASD (see Box 9.2 for some examples).

However, there was less support for the suggestion that global processing ability is impaired in autism. Specifically, several studies showed that people with ASD are able to perceive wholes rather than parts, and to attend to meaning rather than to surface appearances or sounds, if directed towards doing so. For example, if shown a large capital letter 'A' made up of many smaller-sized letter 'Hs' and specifically directed to name the large letter, individuals with ASD are as fast and as accurate as comparison groups (Plaisted et al., 1999). However, if asked simply what letter they see, they show a bias towards naming the smaller letter in the design (Ozonoff et al., 1994).

Evidence against impaired global processing led Frith, now working with Happé, to modify the WCC theory. They relinquished the suggestion of a deficit in global processing, and suggested instead that the findings on sensory-perceptual processing in autism could be interpreted in terms of a preference, or bias, towards processing parts rather than wholes (Happé & Frith, 2006). They based this suggestion on the assumption that biases towards global as opposed to local processing are distributed as a continuum within the general population. Thus 'while the person with weak coherence may be poor at seeing the bigger picture, the person with

---

Box 9.2 Evidence relating to the weak central coherence theory

Superior recognition of inverted faces Participants are shown several passport-type photographs of unknown faces. A short while later each face is shown to the participant again, paired with a face the participant has not seen before, both faces being presented upside down. The participant is asked: which of these did you see just now? People with ASD perform better than people without ASD. Conclusion: because it is known that it is the ability to process upright faces as wholes that makes processing inverted faces difficult for most people, it may be concluded that people with ASD do not process faces as wholes.

Superior (faster than average) performance on the block design test High-functioning people with ASD are faster than people without ASD on this test (described in Box 4.1). Conclusion: people with ASD, unlike others, are not slowed down by seeing the goal pattern as an unsegmented whole: the 'bits' of the pattern are immediately obvious to them.

Detail-focused and fragmented drawings Participants are shown line drawings and asked to copy them. People with ASD are, unusually, likely to start by drawing a detail, and to draw fragments of the original picture rather than indicating the whole.

Inferior ability to assemble a given set of sentences to tell a coherent story This suggests impaired ability to integrate parts into meaningful wholes.

(Examples are taken from the review by Happé and Frith, 2006, where relevant references can be found.)

---

strong coherence may be a terrible proof reader' (Happé & Frith, 2006: 15). The new suggestion was that people with ASD have a cognitive style that places them among those who are particularly poor at seeing the bigger picture. In colloquial terms, they 'can't see the wood for the trees'.

(ii) The enhanced perceptual function theory The **enhanced perceptual function (EPF)** theory was proposed by Mottron and Burack (2001; see also Mottron et al., 2006) in response to evidence of enhanced local processing in the absence of any absolute impairment of global processing in people with ASD. Mottron and Burack use the term 'perceptual' quite broadly to include the detection of what they term 'surface properties' of stimuli, such as the pitch and loudness of auditory stimuli, and the contours and proportions of visual stimuli.

Mottron and Burack were particularly influenced by their investigations of savant abilities in two individuals, one with outstanding musical abilities (Mottron et al., 1999), the other with outstanding drawing ability (Mottron & Belleville, 1993). The young woman with savant musical abilities has **absolute pitch** (sometimes referred to as perfect pitch) and superior ability to identify single notes played within a chord, indicating exceptional perception of auditory detail. These exceptional auditory abilities are not confined to savants, as they are shared by many individuals on the spectrum (Heaton, 2003). The savant draftsman studied

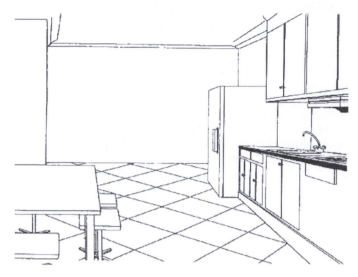

Figure 9.2 *A spontaneous drawing by the savant artist E. C. (kindly provided by Laurent Mottron, Professor of Psychiatry and Marcel and Rolande Gosselin Research Chair in Neuroscience of Autism, University of Montreal)*

by Mottron and Belleville can draw perfect circles and ellipses, and his spontaneous drawings demonstrate exceptionally accurate reproduction of contours, proportions and perspective, as illustrated in Figure 9.2, demonstrating superior perception of visual detail. The exceptional local processing abilities of these savants led Mottron and his colleagues to hypothesise that enhanced processing of the surface properties of visual or auditory stimuli could explain anomalous sensory-perceptual processing in people with ASD without invoking a deficit in global processing.

Subsequent studies by this group have confirmed enhanced perception of stimuli, whether visual or auditory, that are processed in primary sensory cortical areas of the brain (Bertone et al., 2005; Bonnel et al., 2010). However, contrary to the original version of the EPF theory, Bonnel et al. also reported impaired processing of complex stimuli, but only in lower-functioning individuals.

(iii) The enhanced discrimination–reduced generalisation theory Plaisted et al. (1998) reported a study in which children with ASD and age- and ability-matched typically developing children were given two visual search tests. In one test children were shown a display of letters and instructed to find, for example, a green 'S' from among some red or green 'Ts' or 'Xs'. In this 'single-feature' task, children had only to look for the 'S' shape, ignoring colour. In the second test children were instructed to find, for example, a green 'X' from among some green 'Ts' and red 'Xs'. In this **conjunctive search** task, children had to look for the unique combination of colour and shape distinguishing the target

letter from surrounding distractors. Children with ASD performed as well as the typically developing children on the single-feature task, and outperformed them on the conjunctive search task.

From this experiment (and other related experiments that followed) Plaisted and her colleagues concluded that people with ASD have *enhanced* ability to extract the unique elements of a stimulus such as are utilised in *discriminating* between stimuli, i.e. telling them apart; combined with *reduced* ability to process the similarities between individual items such as are utilised in *generalising* across stimuli, i.e. responding to a novel stimulus on the basis that it resembles previously experienced stimuli. So, for example, a child with an ASD might be exceptionally sensitive to the differences between one make of cornflakes and another, but insensitive to the similarities and therefore reluctant to eat cornflakes of an unfamiliar brand.

(iv) The hypo-priors theory   In an extended critique of earlier theories in this group, Pellicano (2012b) concluded that neither the weak central coherence theory nor the enhanced perceptual function theory is fully compatible with available evidence. She suggested instead that reduced generalisation, as argued for by Plaisted and her colleagues, might be critical for understanding sensory-perceptual anomalies in ASD.

Generalisation underlies the formation of **prototypes**, or what Pellicano refers to as **priors**, which are stored in long-term memory and against which new exemplars may be compared. In the example used above, most of us could describe what we consider to be 'prototypical cornflakes' and we don't quibble if the make offered to us when away isn't quite the same as what we have for breakfast at home. For a child with no prototype – instead only an image of the cornflakes she eats at home – even small differences in colour, shape, texture, taste will be unexpected and responded to with suspicion and frustration. Reduced generalisation is, therefore, and as suggested by Plaisted and colleagues, likely to be accompanied by enhanced discrimination: differences become more important than similarities.

Pellicano and Burr (2012) used mathematical modelling to support their argument that the existence of **hypo-priors** (poorly defined or narrowed prototypes) in people with autism leads to greater than usual reliance on incoming sensory signals. They go on to argue that this can explain both hyper-sensitivity and hypo-sensitivity to sensory stimuli, sensory soothing as well as sensory seeking, RSMs as well as forms of IS, and also the phenomenon of sensory overload. These claims, although intuitively plausible, clearly need to be fleshed out and tested.

(v) The aberrant precision of predictive coding theory and (vi) the low endogenous noise theory   These two theories extend, respectively, Pellicano and Burr's hypo-priors theory and Plaisted et al.'s **enhanced discrimination-reduced generalisation** theory.

The aberrant precision theory was proposed by Friston et al. (2013) in a commentary on the Pellicano and Burr (2012) paper, and an extended account of the theory can be found in Lawson et al. (2014). These authors link the role of 'priors', as defined by Pellicano and Burr, to probabilistic predictive coding in the brain.

They argue that weak establishment of priors would lead to an over-reliance on sensory evidence in anticipating, or predicting, perceptual experiences. This in turn, they argue, would lead to prediction errors – misperceptions – which the autistic person attempts to minimise by self-generated repetitive actions.

The low endogenous noise theory was proposed by Davis and Plaisted-Grant (2015). This theory builds on the literature relating to the effects of 'neural noise' in the brain, possibly resulting from brain stem abnormalities (cf. the 'impaired control of arousal' theory). Whereas others, such as Rubenstein and Merzenich (2003) and Simmons et al. (2007), had hypothesised that *excessive* neural noise could explain sensory-perceptual anomalies in ASD, Davis and Plaisted-Grant argue that *reduced* neural noise would increase acuity at sensory levels at the same time as reducing spontaneous shifts of attention.

Comment All six theories considered in this section focus on an imbalance between the processing of raw sensory data and the higher-order processes that select, organise and utilise these data in the form of complex percepts – an imbalance between bottom-up processing and top-down control. The exact nature and source(s) of this imbalance remain in dispute. It is worth noting, however, that theories within this group are increasingly driven by what is known about neural functioning. This increases the complexity of the theories, but in ways that are necessary for a detailed understanding of the peculiarities of sensation and perception that are part of autism. Further developments in this field are likely, and interested readers should look out for new research reports.

Similarly, all six theories outlined above are claimed by their proponents to be capable of explaining at least some of the repetitive and restricted behaviours characteristic of people with ASD. However, these claims remain to be substantiated, and studies investigating hypothetical links are likely to be reported over the next few years.

Two anomalous learning style theories

The hypersystemising theory As noted in Chapter 8, Baron-Cohen et al. (2005) hypothesised that exposure to abnormally high levels of testosterone *in utero* leads to excessively masculinised brain development in people subsequently diagnosed with ASD. According to the extreme male brain theory, the behavioural results of this over-exposure are a combination of impaired empathising (discussed above) and **hypersystemising** tendencies (Baron-Cohen et al., 2005; Baron-Cohen, 2009).

Systemising is defined by Baron-Cohen in terms of a drive to analyse and build rule-based systems that can predict 'non-agentive events'. 'Hypersystemisers', as identified by their high scores on the 'Systemising Questionnaire' (SQ) (Baron-Cohen et al., 2003), tend to be interested in how machines or technical devices work; in how objects – whether buildings or pieces of furniture – are constructed; in computer programming; maps, routes and travel networks; weather forecasting; and numerical systems of all kinds from betting systems to higher maths.

Unusually strong systemising tendencies in people with low-functioning autism are argued to cause repetitive behaviours and inability to cope with change. However, in higher-functioning individuals hypersystemising tendencies can be harnessed to achieve academic and professional success, contributing to outstanding achievements in fields such as maths, physics and computer programming.

There is some evidence of stronger systemising tendencies in neurotypical males than in neurotypical females; and some evidence that systemising tendencies are more dominant in people with ASD (both males and females) than in the general population (Lawson et al., 2004). However, it has yet to be shown that hypersystemising is specific to people with ASD. Nor has it yet been shown that hypersystemising is universal in people with those forms of ASD that include repetitive and restricted behaviours of the kinds hypersystemising is said to explain.

A further criticism of the hypersystemising theory is that 'systemising' is not a concept widely used by psychologists or neuropsychologists other than Baron-Cohen and his collaborators. Phrases such as 'pattern perception' and 'rule extraction' are more commonly used to refer to the kinds of functions ascribed to 'systemising'. And personality traits such as 'persistence' and 'conscientiousness' are used to refer to the kind of 'drive' ascribed to 'hypersystemisers'. Novel concepts in psychology and neuropsychology are welcomed and quickly utilised if judged to have validity and practical usefulness – the speed with which the concept of 'mentalising' was adopted illustrates this. The concept of 'systemising' has not been widely adopted, although it is used in a handful of studies on gender differences in neurotypical populations. This may be because the functions ascribed to systemising are those more generally ascribed to **procedural memory**, as noted below.

The uneven memory/learning abilities theory   Memory and learning are inseparable, although the words have some different connotations and uses. Whatever we learn is in some sense remembered. And whatever is remembered has in some sense been learned. This is why the study of memory is important when considering the 'what' and 'how' of learning.

Following Tulving (1995), human memory is widely considered to consist of several partially independent systems, as shown in Box 9.3.

It is well established (Bowler et al., 2011; Gaigg et al., 2014) that even very high-functioning people with ASD have impaired **episodic memory**: they do not 're-experience' events in which they have participated, such as 'your first day at school', although they may compensate by learning relevant facts, such as 'the Reception Class teacher was Miss Brown'; 'the peg for my coat had a picture of a rabbit beside it'. Less able people with ASD almost certainly have, in addition, some degree of impairment of **semantic memory**, resulting in difficulty in acquiring facts and also word meanings. By contrast, individuals with any measurable abilities across the spectrum generally have intact or relatively intact **perceptual memory** and **immediate memory**, additional to their intact procedural learning abilities (see Boucher et al., 2012, for a review of relevant evidence).

The more widespread and severe an individual's memory impairments, the more that individual will be reliant on their intact memory/learning systems (Ullman, 2004), a phenomenon which Ullman refers to as the **see-saw effect**. As in the example above, high-functioning individuals will compensate for impaired episodic memory by capitalising on their unimpaired semantic memory. They may

---

Box 9.3 Definitions and descriptions of human memory systems

System	Definition and description
Perceptual	Briefly retains 'snapshot' records of single items (e.g. a flower, a musical note, a whiff of scent), providing the option of further processing. Perceptual memories are not accessible to consciousness and are described as *implicit*. They cannot be reflected on or reported verbally, and are also described as *non-declarative*. They do, however, influence behaviour.
Procedural	Used for the acquisition of associations, habits, skills and the extraction of regularities from experience. What is learned is *implicit* and *non-declarative* (see above). Learning in most animals is procedural, as is early learning in human babies.
Semantic	Stores factual information, including word meanings. What is learned is available to consciousness and described as *explicit*. Because semantic knowledge can be reflected on and reported verbally, it is also described as *declarative*.
Episodic	Stores complex information about personally experienced events (e.g. what happened, where, when, how did I feel, who else was there, etc. etc.) Sometimes referred to as *relational memory*, because the different elements of this kind of memory belong together. What is remembered is *explicit* and *declarative* (see above).
Working	Holds the contents of *immediate memory* (see below) or recently retrieved information in short term stores referred to as the *visuo-spatial scratchpad* and the *phonological loop*. Information in these stores is consciously modified, reorganized or otherwise manipulated.
Immediate	A component of *working memory* (see above) which holds recently perceived visual-spatial or verbal information in unmodified form for a limited time. The unmodified information held in immediate memory is available to consciousness and can be rehearsed, resulting in rote-learning. Sometimes referred to as *short-term memory (STM)*.

also rely to an unusual extent on their unimpaired perceptual, procedural and immediate memory abilities. Lower-functioning individuals, who lack the ability to compensate effectively using semantic memory, will be forced to rely heavily on the latter three forms of memory.

An unusual degree of reliance on a limited set of intact memory/learning systems may help to explain at least some facets of repetitive and restricted behaviour across the spectrum, as originally suggested by Bachevalier (1994, 2008) and Kemper and Bauman (1998), and more recently in my own publications (Boucher et al., 2005, 2008). Specifically, enhanced *perceptual learning* is consistent with Mottron and colleagues' 'enhanced perceptual function' theory, outlined above, and may help to explain some savant abilities (Bókkon et al., 2013; Mottron et al., 2013). An unusual degree of reliance on *immediate memory* can help to explain echolalia and rote learning. Enhanced reliance on *procedural memory* in the absence of episodic memory can help to explain why autistic people frequently acquire associations that are resistant to change in the light of multiple differing experiences (e.g. that dogs/balloons/swimming pools are frightening). It can also help to explain the dominance of habits and routines (always heading towards the same seat in the bus; always taking the same route to school/work/the shops) in place of varying behaviour in ways involving the kinds of **future thinking** that is linked to episodic memory (Lind & Bowler, 2010). Compensatory reliance on procedural learning is also consistent with the unconscious extraction of regularities from experience referred to as 'enhanced pattern perception' by Mottron et al. (2013), and as posited in Baron-Cohen's hypersystematising theory.

Non-specific aggravating factors

Chapter 6 included a section headed 'Many-to-one' in which it was stated that for any set of autism-related behaviours there are numerous potential contributory causes or aggravating factors. RRBs were used to illustrate this point precisely because so many different factors may be involved. The majority of 'aggravating factors' are, however, neither specific to, nor universally present in, people with ASD: that is to say, they commonly cause forms of repetitive behaviours and behavioural rigidity in people who are not autistic, as well as contributing to this set of behaviours in some (but not all) people who are autistic. Some known aggravating factors are considered below.

Anxiety/stress   At times of stress many people will pace or rock; and when particularly anxious about something, most of us take comfort from those things that feel familiar and 'safe'. High levels of anxiety are so common in people with autism, and anxiety is such a likely contributor to behavioural inflexibility in autism, that for many years RRBs were generally explained *only* in terms of an attempt to create and maintain predictability in an otherwise confusing and anxiety-provoking environment.

Maladaptive learning   This is most likely to occur in those individuals least able to express themselves linguistically or to exercise control over events in more overt and conscious ways. For example, an individual who finds the close proximity of other people stressful and unpleasant may learn (unconsciously) that spitting tends to make people move away, so spitting becomes for that individual a habit that is reinforced because gaining space lowers the individual's anxiety. Some socially 'active but odd' individuals discover that enquiring what someone's name is or the make of car they drive almost always achieves a friendly response. This is reinforcing, so the question becomes that individual's habitual way of opening up an interaction; and because they cannot sustain a conversation, the same question may be repeated, sometimes over and over again, to the same person.

Comorbid conditions associated with repetitive behaviours   Brain-based disorders such as Tourette's syndrome, Lesch-Nyan syndrome and OCD are all associated with repetitive behaviours of certain kinds. All three of these conditions are known to co-occur with autism, albeit rarely, and some of the most intractable repetitive behaviours in a small percentage of individuals with ASD probably reflect such comorbidity.

SUMMARY

Theoretical explanations of key facets of SEC impairments are considered in the first major section of this chapter, followed by an account of theoretical explanations of RRBs.

Candidates for the immediate, neuropsychological cause or causes of *impaired dyadic interaction* are outlined and discussed. It is concluded that a decline in dyadic interaction over the first year or so of life is most readily explained in terms of the 'impaired experience of social reward' theory (Chevallier et al., 2012). The effects of such an impairment would be gradual, building up over the first year of life, consistent with data relating to onset of ASD. Another possible explanation for the decline and subsequent significant and persistent impairment of dyadic interaction is impaired timing. Although a strong theoretical case might be made for it, this hypothesis has not been investigated. It is important to bear in mind that the origins of impaired dyadic interaction may differ across individuals, with one initial problem leading to or exacerbating another.

Regarding the immediate causes of *impaired mentalising and mindreading capacities*, it was initially proposed that an impairment of explicit ToM results from a genetically determined failure to develop a 'theory of mind module' in the brain. When it became clear that this could not explain impaired implicit ToM and impaired triadic relating, some modularists – including philosophers as well as psychologists– argued for a genetically-determined failure to develop an 'implicit ToM module', or 'mentalising mechanism'. Meantime, the argument that specialist mindreading modules are not programmed into brain development but are instead constructed over time on the basis of innate abilities such as those involved in dyadic relating, plus the operation of domain-general learning abilities, became current in mainstream developmental psychology. Constructivist explanations of impaired mentalising/implicitToM and impaired explicit ToM in autism are now widely argued for. However, the details of processes which may be involved are not agreed on.

Regarding the *impairment of emotion processing*, lack of emotional reciprocity in people with autism is generally agreed to result from failure to integrate the physiological experience of emotion with a conscious understanding of what the emotion is about – what precipitated it and whether it constitutes, for example, fear as opposed to anger. Failure to appreciate what one's own, or another person's, emotion is about is commonly ascribed to impaired mentalising. However, it has recently been suggested (by Gaigg, 2012) that there may be a wide-ranging impairment of the integration of emotion with experience, such as would disrupt many sorts of learning, non-social as well as social. This novel hypothesis remains to be tested.

Impaired communication across the spectrum is closely associated with the impairments of mindreading and emotion processing. Specifically, because people with ASD lack intuitive appreciation of others' mental states (their knowledge, beliefs, feelings, desires, etc.), communication tends to be egocentric not just in topics that may be pursued, but also in poor turn-taking, poor listening, and failure to use the appropriate conversational and grammatical devices that help to clarify meaning. Comprehension of others' nonverbal communication signals is impaired by difficulties in 'reading' other people's emotional expressions, with nonverbal expressivity sometimes marred by problems of integration and timing. When language impairment is also present, communication is further significantly compromised.

Attempts to explain the repetitive and restricted nature of autistic behaviour have a long history. In the 1960s and 1970s, it was commonly suggested that the preference for routines and insistence on sameness represented attempts to make a confusing world more predictable and less anxiety-provoking. There is no doubt that anxiety and some other non-specific factors, including maladaptive learning, and in some cases the presence of certain comorbid conditions, contribute to stereotyped behaviours and resistance to change.

However, as early as the 1960s and 1970s, some clinician-researchers suggested that impaired control of physiological arousal levels might explain the odd sensory reactions of children with autism, their stereotypic movements and utterances, and resistance to change. This theory lay dormant for three decades, but has recently been strongly argued for by Leekam et al. (2011).

The dominating view during the 1980s and 1990s was that repetitive and restricted behaviours in autism result from executive dysfunctions (EDFs). After intensive investigation, however, it was concluded that EDFs are unlikely to be able to explain RRBs in autism because this explanation fails to meet the required criteria of primacy, specificity and universality (as detailed in Chapter 6).

In 1989, Frith introduced the concept of weak central coherence (WCC), sparking a debate concerning the locus of problems associated with an imbalance between bottom-up and top-down sensory-perceptual processing in people with ASD, such as could explain the various forms of repetitive and restricted behaviour. Mottron and colleagues' 'enhanced perceptual function' (EPF) theory, and Plaisted's **'enhanced discrimination – reduced generalisation' theory** were more concerned with sensory-perceptual abnormalities themselves, as opposed to their possible roles as causes of repetitive behaviours. However, the most recent three theories within this group – Pellicano and Burr's 'hypo-priors' theory, Lawson and colleagues' 'aberrant precision' theory, and Davis and Plaisted-Grant's 'low endogenous noise' theory – all argue for causal links between the sensory-perceptual abnormalities that they see as critical and RRBs in ASD. These links remain to be empirically demonstrated. However, the convergence of interest in abnormalities affecting the way sensory information is utilised in higher-order processing and the increasing sophistication of theories in this field is encouraging.

   Two theories focusing on anomalous learning strategies as explanations of RRBs are Baron-Cohen's 'hypersystemising' theory, associated with the 'extreme male brain' hypothesis, and my own 'uneven memory/learning abilities' theory. Neither of these theories has been taken up by the wider autism research community, and the paired notions of 'empathising' and 'systemising' have proved more fruitful for the study of gender differences in the normal population than for the study of autism. If the 'uneven memory/learning abilities' theory were to gain support in the longer term, I would expect it to prove compatible with theories envisaging higher-level processing abnormalities of the kinds that enforce reliance on lower-level processing and forms of learning – in particular, excessive reliance on perceptual, immediate and procedural forms of memory.

   A final caveat is in order, of a kind made repeatedly throughout this book. Behaviours falling under the DSM-5 descriptions of RRBs are extremely varied, both within and across individuals and at different ages and stages of development. Moreover, the developmental trajectories of RRBs in ASD are heterogeneous (Richler et al., 2010). This suggests that there may be no single common factor underlying RRBs as currently defined, but instead a number of contributory and interacting factors, the mix being different in different individuals.

PROXIMAL CAUSES 2: ADDITIONAL SHARED CHARACTERISTICS AND MAJOR SPECIFIERS

> ## AIMS
>
> The first part of this chapter follows on directly from the previous chapter in that it aims to provide an account of the immediate, or 'proximal', causes of those 'shared characteristics' described in Chapter 3 but which are not included in the diagnostic criteria. The second part of the chapter moves away from explanations of shared characteristics to consider possible causes of the two major sources of diversity among people with ASD. These are the 'major specifiers' described in Chapter 4, namely learning disability and language impairment.

ADDITIONAL SHARED CHARACTERISTICS

Imagination and Creativity: Strengths and Weaknesses

What has to be explained

A lack of imagination and creativity in people with ASD was referred to earlier as the flip side of repetitive and restrictive behaviours: if you can't think of new things to do, say, think about, draw, cook, etc., you will inevitably get stuck in a rut doing 'the usual' things, perhaps just repeating and repeating them. Studies of facets of imagination and creativity in people with ASD have, however, produced confusingly mixed results (see Chapter 3). Specifically, it seems that people with ASD *can* pretend and reason imaginatively, and they *can* generate a whole string of different words or ideas for pictures, but only in certain circumstances. If prompted to use some junk materials in pretend play, for example, or if asked to generate as many animal names as possible within a minute, even lower-functioning people with autism perform relatively well; whereas they do not use the junk play materials spontaneously, and if asked to generate 'as many words as possible' (with their eyes shut) they perform poorly. Attempts to explain uneven imaginative abilities in ASD must also take into account the fact that a small minority of exceptionally able people with ASD make innovative contributions to, for example, computer programming, theoretical physics or philosophy – possibly also to musical composition.

Explanatory theories

In the early 2000s it would have been confidently proposed that executive dysfunctions (EDFs) could explain not only RRBs in autism, but also the lack of creativity and imagination. However, the role of EDFs as a cause of RRBs has since then been widely questioned (see Chapter 9). This makes it less easy to argue that lack of creativity is caused by EDFs.

Nevertheless, there *is* a problem in *generating* novel ideas, words, drawings – unless some cue is provided. This suggests a memory retrieval problem, such as would not apply if an individual were running through a closely related subset of ideas, where one response cues another: for example, 'pig' cues 'cow' cues 'horse' cues 'dog', etc.; or '(round) sun' cues 'moon' cues 'face' cues 'apple', etc.

Similarly, there *is* a problem of *planning*, if conceptualised as 'future thinking' (Lind & Bowler, 2010; see Chapter 9). Future thinking involves the projection of 'self' into an imagined future experience or activity. It also involves bringing together the components of a plan, such as where, when, with whom, with what preparations. Impaired planning might therefore relate more to anomalies of sense of self or to impaired integrative capacities than to executive dysfunction (Lind et al., 2014).

There may also be a problem of *initiating*, or getting started on, a non-routine activity, or a different activity from that in which one is currently engaged. An anecdote from my own experience, recounted on Box 10.1, illustrates this kind of 'behavioural inertia'.

Box 10.1   An illustration of behavioural inertia contrasting with purposeful activity

On arrival at a residential centre for lower-functioning young adults with ASD, I went to the dining room where a dozen or so of the residents were having tea, seated round a table. All were appropriately occupied spreading jam onto bread, stretching out for biscuits, going to the trolley for a second cup of tea. There was little interaction and the room was oddly silent, but in other respects the level of purposeful and appropriate activity gave no clue as to the young people's autism. When the eating and drinking were finished, however, and each individual had cleared away their own plates, mugs, etc., no doubt following a well-learned routine, the majority returned to their seats at the table and relapsed into inactivity, not interacting, not looking around, with one or two rocking or engaged in some other stereotopic activity. The contrast between the normality of the routinised behaviour and the lack of self-initiated purposeful activity at the end of the meal was very striking.

An inability to voluntarily initiate an action or activity might be ascribed to **psychic akinesia**.[1] Whereas **akinesia** refers to a neuromuscular condition involving impairment or loss of voluntary movement (as in Parkinsons's disease, for example), psychic akinesia is defined as 'an absence of voluntary motion without any apparent motor deficit'. When it occurs in non-autistic individuals, it is described as being accompanied by reduced affect, and by compulsions and repetitive actions. A prompt, however, such as a direct command or physical support, enables the person to carry out complex physical and mental tasks fully efficiently. The potential relevance of psychic akinesia for understanding some facets of autism, or some individuals with autism, is inescapable. And the

---

[1]Words or phrases in bold type on first occurrence can be found in the Glossary.

potential relevance for day-to-day care and intervention is even more striking and important. However, there are no reports of research investigating possible links between autism and psychic akinesia. Therefore the suggestion made here that this condition might help to explain the mixed findings on creativity and imagination in ASD must be seen as speculative.

Islets of Ability

What has to be explained

As in the case of imaginative and creative abilities, it is mainly the unevenness – the mixture of 'can' and 'can't' do – that has to be explained. In Chapter 3, the concept of 'fine cuts' was introduced, referring to the phenomenon – which is particularly striking in autism – of two closely-related facets of behaviour, one of which is impaired, the other unimpaired. In what follows, each of the 'fine cuts' outlined in Chapter 3 will be briefly discussed. Possible explanations of the even more striking phenomenon of savant abilities will also be considered.

Explaining some 'fine cuts'

Spared social interaction ability: Attachment   'Attachment' is demonstrated by an infant's or young child's preference for maintaining contact with or physical closeness to primary caregivers, by showing distress if left with strangers, and relief and comfort-seeking on reunion with the familiar caregiver. At times of stress or distress, infants and young children will preferentially seek out an attachment figure and go to them for security and comfort. Attachment has clear survival value and is evolutionarily old, occurring in primates and most other mammals in some form or other. It can therefore be safely assumed that attachment behaviours are genetically programmed to occur from an early age, and will manifest themselves so long as primary caregiving is normally nurturant and responsive to the infant's and young child's needs.

Relatively normal attachment in most children with ASD can therefore be explained in terms of the intactness of the genetically determined predisposition to form attachments. However, secure attachment is also dependent on the sensitivity of primary caregivers to the child's needs, and in the case of infants with incipient ASD, the expression of needs may be idiosyncratic. In addition, as their child's 'autistic-ness' emerges, primary caregivers (usually parents) have to come to terms with the fact that their baby has stopped developing entirely normally. This may disturb their interactions with the child and help to explain why attachment is only 'relatively' normal in children with ASD (Oppenheim et al., 2009; Kahane & El-Tahir, 2015).

Spared communicative ability: Protoimperatives   The fine cut between intact use of protoimperatives and impaired use of protodeclaratives is readily explained in terms of whether or not mentalising/mindreading is involved. Protoimperative behaviours merely involve indicating in some way a wanted object or action, whereas protodeclarative behaviours involve the ability to represent in one's own mind 'that Daddy will like to see my picture', 'that Granny will see what I am pointing to'.

Spared cognitive abilities: Rote memory, fitting and assembly tasks, mechanical reading Unusually good rote memory may result indirectly from an impairment of key memory systems such as would leave affected individuals no option but to compensate as far as possible by using spared forms of learning (the 'see-saw effect' noted in the previous chapter). Spared forms include immediate memory, which underpins rote learning. An unusual degree of reliance on this kind of memory/learning would tend to maximise an individual's potential in this area, producing a relative peak of ability.

The sparing of fitting and assembly skills even in moderately or severely learning disabled individuals with ASD is consistent with the enhanced perceptual function argued for by Mottron and his colleagues, and discussed in Chapter 9. Mottron's research group has shown that less able individuals with ASD tend to process incoming sensory information solely in the primary sensory regions, leading to enhanced perception of simple stimuli, but impaired perception of more complex or meaningful stimuli such as would normally involve associative cortical regions (Bonnel et al., 2010). Enhanced perception of visual detail, in the absence of meaningful associations, can explain the peaks of ability in fitting and assembly tasks that are most striking in lower-functioning individuals with autism.

Enhanced perception of visual detail in the absence of meaningful associations can also explain the kind of mechanical reading ability that sometimes occurs in less able autistic individuals. However, in this case it has to be assumed in addition that associations have been implicitly acquired, linking letter shapes and letter combinations to spoken sounds.

Explaining savant abilities

Savant abilities occurring in learning disabled individuals, often those with autism, is most commonly explained in terms of enhanced perceptual and/or procedural learning abilities, coupled with extensive spontaneous practice. For representative summaries of the evidence and arguments supporting the component parts of this explanation, see Dawson et al. (2008), Pring (2008) and Snyder (2010).

Uneven Motor Skills

What has to be explained

In Chapter 3 it was stated that impairments of motor skills are almost certainly a universal feature of autism, but that some skills are conspicuously spared in at least some individuals, for example in skilled pianists or agile climbers. Moreover, the patterns of strengths and weaknesses are quite varied, and may be different in higher-functioning as opposed to lower-functioning individuals.

While bearing in mind the spared abilities in this domain, the following forms of motor impairments are commonly observed, as identified in Chapter 3:

- Abnormalities of gait and posture.
- Clumsiness and slower than average movement repetition.
- Co-ordination problems ('dyspraxia').
- Impaired imitation of others' self-directed body movements.

Motor stereotypies – RSMs – could be included under the heading of motor impairments. However, their possible causes were considered in the section on 'Explaining RRBs' in Chapter 9, and are not further discussed here.

Explaining motor impairments

The immediate, or proximal, causes of motor impairments and anomalies in people with ASD are part-physical and part-neuropsychological.

Physical factors   Physical causes of impaired motor skills in at least some people with ASD include reduced muscle tone – hypotonia – which may be associated with **joint laxity** (Shetreat-Klein et al., 2014). These physical anomalies explain, or help to explain, the abnormalities of posture and gait that are commonly observed in people with ASD across the spectrum. Hypotonia and loosely articulated joints can also help to explain why both gross and fine movement are often described as clumsy and/or slow. This combination of physical anomalies is common in a number of neurodevelopmental disorders of known genetic origin, especially but not exclusively those associated with learning disability. Such disorders include Down syndrome, Williams syndrome and Prader-Willi syndrome, all of which occasionally co-occur with ASD, with possible implications for understanding genetic variations that may predispose to autism.

Persistent toe-walking when it occurs in people with ASD occasionally results from a physical anomaly known as 'tight heel cords', in which the Achilles tendons are either **hypertonic** or congenitally short (Barrow et al., 2011). However, it may in some cases be neurological in origin (Accardo & Barrow, 2015), which could be consistent with a currently unexplained (and controversial) association between toe-walking and language impairment. Other cases of persistent toe-walking appear to result simply from habit: if asked to walk normally the individual is capable of complying, but once their attention shifts from the way in which they walk, the tip-toe pattern returns. Toe-walking resulting from habit can be corrected (Marcus et al., 2010). Toe-walking of physical or neurological origin is more difficult to treat.

Neuropsychological causes   Poor co-ordination may affect both gross and fine movements, and although likely to be due in part to neuromuscular anomalies, the major cause is neuropsychological, involving impaired motor planning and control. Planning and control of fine movement can be assessed using 'reach and grasp' tasks, as illustrated in Figure 10.1 (the apparatus is shown as though the reader were sitting opposite the person being tested).

The apparatus illustrated in Figure 10.1 is taken from a paper by Hughes (1996). In Hughes' study, the child's task was to lift the bar using one hand and place it end-up in one of the rings, following an instruction. The instructions were varied according to whether the bar should be picked up at the black or the white end, and whether it should be placed in the blue or the red ring. Some of the placements are awkward to carry out unless the grip used is varied from 'overhand'

Figure 10.1 *Starting off with an overhand grip (top picture) results in a comfortable positioning of the hand when placing the black end of the bar into a ring (lower picture, left). However, it results in an awkward positioning when placing the white end of the bar into the ring (lower picture, right) (from Hughes, 1996: 103)*

(as in the figure) to 'underhand'. Use of the underhand grip requires the ability to plan and control a goal-directed movement, and the lower-functioning autistic children in Hughes' experiment were less able to do this than either typically developing preschool children or intellectually disabled children without autism. Subsequent studies have demonstrated that impairments of motor planning and control also occur in people with higher-functioning ASD (van Swieten et al., 2010; Forti et al., 2011; Stoit et al., 2013). There is some dispute as to the precise nature of the neuropsychological impairments underlying findings such as that of Hughes. Do people with ASD lack the ability to envisage (at an unconscious level) the end-point or goal of the movement? Or do they not (unconsciously) plan the sequence of muscular activities required? Do people with ASD have problems of action preparation and initiation, as suggested earlier in this chapter, rather than problems of action execution? Is there a problem to do with timing, affecting the smooth synchronisation of movement components? Do people with ASD lack some kind of checking, or error-correction, ability? Do they lack a detailed body schema such as might direct their movements accurately? It might have been suggested that executive dysfunction was involved, but this was ruled out in studies by Rinehart et al. (2006) and van Swieten et al. (2010).

Naming poor co-ordination in ASD 'dyspraxia' or 'developmental co-ordination disorder' is not helpful, because the precise nature and neuropsychological origins of these disorders has not been established. Readers who have an interest in more detailed discussion of these impairments as they occur in ASD might start by looking at the work of Mostofsky and colleagues over recent years, covering the nature of the difficulties, their brain bases, and also treatment options (see Mostofsky & Ewen, 2011, as a starting point, but interested readers should search for recent publications by Mostofsky's group).

Finally, impaired imitation of others' body movements probably results from problems of self–other equivalence mapping (as mentioned in Chapter 3), rather than from impaired motor abilities *per se*. However, the problem was at one time thought to be associated with dysfunctional **mirror neurons** (Williams et al., 2001; Oberman & Ramchandran, 2007), and this theory is still discussed (see, for example, Gallese et al., 2013), although supportive evidence is lacking (Hamilton, 2013). Mirror neurons are cells that are activated in motor areas of the brain when we see another person carrying out an action. Thus these cells 'mirror' the neural activity in the brain of the individual carrying out the action. The **broken mirror theory**, as it came to be called, generated considerable excitement for a time, because it was claimed to help explain not only impaired imitation in people with ASD, but also the impairments of empathy and mindreading.

Explaining spared motor abilities

The sparing of some motor abilities, even in quite low-functioning individuals (see Chapter 3), reflects the fact that well-practised, highly automated movements are performed well, whereas the acquisition of new skills, or responding to a novel motor task that requires conscious control, pose greater difficulty. This pattern of findings is consistent with the autism-specific pattern of memory/learning strengths and weaknesses which has been commented on in various sections of this chapter and the previous one. Specifically, procedural memory is strikingly unaffected in people with ASD, as demonstrated not only in the relative ease with which they acquire associations, habits and routines, but also in stringent tests used in research studies (Brown et al., 2010; Nemeth et al., 2010; Foti et al., 2015). Intact procedural memory is consistent with unimpaired implicit – unconscious – acquisition and performance of motor skills. By contrast, any kind of new learning that involves remembering instructions, or consciously learning from past mistakes, will be affected by the kinds of problems of explicit – conscious or 'declarative' – memory and learning known to occur in people with ASD.

Impaired Sense of Self

What has to be explained

A varied range of evidence shows that self-concept in people with autism is limited in certain specific ways. Despite having good factual knowledge about who they are ('a boy', 'age 15', 'my name is Darren', 'I go to school at X college', 'I am good at maths', 'I enjoy swimming'), they lack the kind of autobiographical memories that enliven our sense of who we are ('that time I scored the winning goal', 'when I had to go to hospital', 'the arguments I get into …'). They also lack understanding of their own emotions and the ability to name them, and they have poor understanding of how they may be seen by other people.

Explaining poor sense of self

Impaired mentalising Frith, who first argued that impaired mindreading in autism results from an inability to represent in one's own mind the mental states of others, went on to suggest that impaired mentalising would also affect knowledge and understanding of one's own mind (Frith & Happé, 1999; Happé, 2003). So, for example, someone with autism might have the physical feelings that go with being happy but not be able to represent in their own mind – to know – that 'I am happy', any more than a smiling gurgling baby *knows* – is consciously aware – that she is happy.

Impaired mentalising would impoverish not only knowledge of one's own emotional states, but also knowledge of one's own psychological states and predispositions, for example, 'I tend to get depressed', 'I'm not that interested in other people'. It would also reduce the ability to see oneself as others might see us, for example, 'I probably come across as a bit of a swot', 'I'm popular because I can make people laugh'.

Impaired episodic memory Impaired episodic memory would impoverish the autistic person's sense of self in terms of a personalised, as opposed to a purely factual, autobiography. However, there is a potential 'chicken–egg' problem here, in that the essence of an episodic memory is that one retains a sense of having experienced certain events *oneself* – of having been there at the time, of having either participated actively in the event, or of having reacted in some memorable way to some seen or heard event. Episodic memories always involve the 'I' in some way, what Jordan and Powell (1995) termed 'the experiencing self'. Theoretically, therefore, episodic/autobiographical memory might be impaired as result of an impoverished self-concept, rather than vice versa.

However, another key characteristic of episodic memory is that it involves binding together the disparate elements of an experience. For this reason, episodic memory is sometimes referred to as **relational memory**. Studies by Bowler and colleagues (2014), Lind et al. (2014) and Gaigg et al. (2015) do in fact show that the major problem underlying impaired episodic memory is one of binding together the elements of a complex experience rather than an impaired sense of self. It is therefore safe to conclude that an impairment of episodic/relational memory underlies impaired autobiographical memory and thereby self-concept, rather than cause and effect occurring the other way around.

MAJOR SPECIFIERS

In this section, proximal causes of the two most common and debilitating specifiers identified in DSM-5, namely learning disability and language impairment, are considered. Proximal causes of other listed specifiers will not be considered here:

some are medical conditions that are more readily explained at the etiological and/or neurobiological level (e.g. Fragile-X syndrome, tuberous sclerosis); some are rare (e.g. catatonia); and accounts of the proximal causes of relatively common comorbid neurodevelopmental and mental conditions such as ADHD, anxiety and depression can be found in the relevant specialist literatures.

Learning Disability

What has to be explained

In Chapter 4 it was reported that the results of intelligence tests such as the Wechsler scales (Wechsler, 1999, 2004) show that nonverbal intelligence quotients (NVQs) are generally higher than verbal quotients (VQs) in learning-disabled people with ASD. NVQs mainly reflect fluid intelligence, or 'g' (general reasoning capacity, largely but not wholly genetically determined). VQs, on the other hand, mainly reflect crystallised intelligence, or 'knowledge' such as is acquired from day-to-day experience and from education. This knowledge includes factual information, such as that Paris is the capital city of France. It also includes words and word meanings, for example that 'dog' refers to an animal with four legs, which barks, wags its tail, etc. Explanations of learning disability in ASD must be capable of explaining why crystallised intelligence is generally more impaired than fluid intelligence.

Explanatory theories

There has been remarkably little research into the causes of learning disability in ASD, despite the fact that it is extremely common, and – in combination with autism and language impairment – extremely handicapping. There appears to be a widespread assumption that learning disability is simply another comorbid condition, probably associated with generalised brain abnormality, and of no great theoretical interest. However, if this were true, fluid intelligence should be as least as much affected as crystallised intelligence, which is not the case.

Four likely causes of learning disability in lower-functioning people with ASD are considered below, bearing in mind the need to explain the VQ < NVQ discrepancy. They are: impaired language; socio-cultural deprivation; an impairment of semantic memory/learning ability; and subaverage fluid intelligence. These four causal factors are likely to be cumulative and interactive.

Impaired language Factual knowledge of the kind assessed in tests of crystallised intelligence (and many school exams) is acquired mainly via language, whether from parents, peers or teachers, or from books or the internet. Impaired language, and especially impaired language comprehension, will reduce a child's ability to acquire this kind of knowledge. In addition, vocabulary and the ability to explain word meanings is directly assessed in tests of crystallised intelligence, and any form of language impairment that affects vocabulary acquisition will lower scores on these tests.

Socio-cultural deprivation Socio-cultural deprivation involving lack of environmental stimulation can contribute to learning disability. However, deprivation originating in the child's home circumstances is not often a factor in the case of autism – at least in countries where ASD is recognised and support services are available. On the other hand, the autistic child's avoidance of social interaction and communication, their dislike of novelty or change, effectively reduces the range of their experiences and learning opportunities, as noted in the previous chapter. This kind of self-originating deprivation would tend to impact on crystallised intelligence.

Impaired semantic memory/learning ability   As noted in the previous chapter, neuropsychologists have identified five memory systems that enable people to learn (see Box 9.3). These are the perceptual, procedural, semantic, and episodic memory systems, and the immediate memory component of working memory. As also noted previously, people with ASD across the spectrum have uneven memory abilities. In particular, episodic memory is always impaired (Bowler et al., 2011), impacting on autobiographical memory in particular. In lower-functioning individuals with ASD, semantic memory is also almost certainly impaired. Impaired semantic memory would directly reduce the ability to acquire a store of factual knowledge. It would also reduce the ability to acquire a mental dictionary of word meanings, and the resulting language impairment would further impact on the ability to acquire the kinds of information essential for academic success and for scoring well on tests of crystallised intelligence.

Unfortunately, there have been few recent studies of semantic memory in lower-functioning autism, almost all recent work on memory in ASD having been carried out with high-functioning groups. The results of tests of semantic memory in lower-functioning ASD, as summarised in Boucher et al. (2012), are suggestive of impairment. However, more research is needed to confirm or disconfirm the 'semantic memory impairment' explanation of learning disability when it co-occurs with autism.

Subaverage fluid intelligence   Because general reasoning ability, possibly associated with speed of processing, is involved in most kinds of learning, subaverage fluid intelligence, if present, will invariably constitute a contributory cause of generalised learning disability, whether in people with ASD or in individuals with learning disability without autism. In learning disabled people with ASD, fluid intelligence, as assessed by tests of nonverbal IQ, is generally below average – sometimes significantly so. This undoubtedly helps to explain their learning disability. However, subaverage fluid intelligence cannot by itself explain the VQ < NVQ discrepancy, which is more readily explained by one or more of the other factors considered above.

Language Impairment

What has to be explained

Key points from the description in Chapter 4 of language abilities across the spectrum are summarised in Table 10.1. In this table, four subgroups are profiled under the headings high-functioning language-normal (HF-LN), high-functioning language impaired (HF-LI), lower-functioning language impaired (LF-LI) and

Table 10.1 Linguistic anomalies and impairments across the spectrum

HF-LN	Somewhat delayed language onset and slowed development in some but not all individuals.
	Idiosyncratic usage of words or phrases.
	Narrow or literal understanding of word/phrase meaning.
	Reduced use of 'mental state' words.
	Early difficulties with deictic terms.
	Subtle differences in the content and organization of the conceptual networks underlying linguistic meaning.
	Tendency to formulaicity, i.e. repetitive use of certain phrases or expressions.
	Despite these minor abnormalities, language and speech are – clinically speaking – 'normal'.
HF-LI	Minor anomalies as for HF-LN, +
	Clinically significant phonological/articulatory impairments.
LF-LI	Significantly delayed language onset and slowed development, plateauing at 'clinically impaired' level.
	Moderate to severe impairment of word/phrase meaning.
	Mild to moderate (MA-appropriate) impairments of grammar and of phonology/articulation.
	Apparent superiority of expressive language as compared to comprehension, resulting from the tendency to reproduce echoed or rote-learned chunks of language verbatim.
	Persistent problems with mental state terms and deixis.
LF-NV*	Very limited comprehension of spoken language.
	Some habitual phrases, acquired via echolalia, may be used, sometimes meaninglessly, sometimes with idiosyncratic meaning, rarely with conventional meaning.

*Excluding cases of mutism

lower-functioning non-verbal (LF-NV). Subgrouping in this way obscures the fact that in reality language abilities form a continuum across the spectrum. However, it facilitates consideration of the set of causes that may be contributing to variations in language profiles.

In the following sections, the underlying causes of linguistic anomalies and impairments summarised in Table 10.1 are considered. However, the effects on language and speech of comorbidities such as hearing loss, epilepsy, cerebral palsy, cleft palate or other medical conditions are not considered here, although clearly they are of critical importance when considering the intervention and support needs of individuals.

Explaining linguistic anomalies common to all individuals with ASD

Those linguistic anomalies that are shared by all individuals on the autism spectrum, including individuals in the HF-LN group, must be caused by factors that are associated with autism itself. These shared factors include the impaired dyadic interaction and impaired mindreading ability underlying SEC impairments, and the sensory-perceptual anomalies associated with RRBs. One further factor may be involved, though its involvement is not widely recognised. This is the impairment of episodic memory (referred to in the section on learning disability, above). Each of these causal factors, and their likely effects on language, is considered below.

Impaired dyadic interaction   This would effectively deprive infants and toddlers of much of the raw material of spoken language acquisition, from the earliest protoconversations in which babies and carers exchange vocalisations, to carers', siblings' and others' ongoing use of language. More specifically, it has been shown that infants with incipient autism are less likely than typically developing infants to look at the mouth of someone who is speaking, and that reduced looking predicts future language impairment (Young et al., 2009). These anomalies of one-to-one interaction would tend to delay language onset and slow the acquisition of both receptive and expressive language.

Defective mindreading   In arguing for the role of defective mindreading as a cause of impaired language in autism, Bloom (2000: 55) noted:

> Learning a word is a social act. When children learn that ... 'rabbit' refers to rabbits, they are learning an arbitrary convention shared by a community of speakers, an implicitly agreed-upon way of communicating. When children learn the meaning of a word, they are – whether they know it or not – learning something about the thoughts of other people.

Early word learning is normally based in part on the apprehension of social cues such as the speaker's direction of gaze. Young children with ASD are less likely than other children to utilise such cues (Baron-Cohen et al., 1997; Parish-Morris et al., 2007), leading to a bias towards the acquisition of unshared, idiosyncratic word meanings. Consistent with this, joint attention impairments in children with ASD have been shown to be associated with language delay, and predict later language competence generally (e.g. Siller & Sigman, 2008).

Impaired mindreading can also explain the problems that young or less able individuals have in understanding and using person-centred (deictic) terms, such as 'you'/'me', 'here'/'there', 'now'/'then' (Hobson et al., 2010). Diminished use of mental state words such as 'think' or 'know' (Tager-Flusberg, 2000), and impaired comprehension of words referring to emotions (Hobson et al., 1989), may also be explained by defective mindreading.

Finally, impaired mindreading helps to explain why language comprehension has consistently been shown to be more affected than expression, in that individuals with ASD fail to take account of other people's knowledge, thoughts and feelings in interpreting others' speech (Surian et al., 1996). However, the apparent superiority of expressive as opposed to receptive language ability also owes something to spared, or relatively spared, immediate memory and rote learning.

Sensory-perceptual anomalies   Anomalies of the kinds described in Chapter 4, and discussed in the section on RRBs in the previous chapter, would have certain predictable effects on language acquisition and processing across the spectrum. In particular, anomalous speech perception may contribute to delayed language onset (Eigsti & Fein, 2013). It could also underlie the abnormalities of pre-speech vocalisation detected in most children with ASD (Oller et al., 2010), and the many minor anomalies of speech–sound production noted in a study of HF-LN adults (Shriberg et al., 2001).

Abnormalities of sensory-perceptual processing conceptualised in terms of weak central coherence (Happé & Frith, 2006) or enhanced perceptual processing (Mottron et al., 2006) would predispose towards encoding the acoustic characteristics of heard speech in place of meaning, as demonstrated in early studies by Hermelin and O'Connor (1970) and more recently by Järvinen-Pasley et al. (2008). This, combined with good immediate memory and rote learning, may help to explain the **formulaicity** so heavily relied on in expressive language, even by individuals with clinically normal language (Perkins et al., 2006). Rote memorisation of phrases or sentences will also contribute to the 'little professor' effect noted by Asperger.

If, as suggested in the most recent theories concerning abnormal sensory-perceptual processing in ASD, generalisation and the formation of categories and concepts ('priors') are impaired, semantic knowledge would be correspondingly affected (see references to the work of Plaisted and colleagues, also Pellicano and colleagues, in the previous chapter).

Working memory impairment   There is some evidence to suggest that the component of working memory (WM) known as the **phonological loop** functions somewhat less efficiently than in typically developing individuals (Schuh & Eigsti, 2012). This may well be a knock-on effect of the sensory-perceptual anomalies considered above, and would have similar repercussions for language.

Impaired episodic memory   All individuals with ASD, including the most able, have impaired episodic memory, as noted in the section on learning disability above. Episodic memory, aka relational memory, underlies the ability to spontaneously recall contextual detail relating to personally experienced events. Contextual information could include where and when the event occurred, who one was with, how one felt at the time, what the weather was like, what happened just before or just after the event, and so on. Episodic/relational memory impairment would reduce the range of information on which word meanings are based. High-functioning children with ASD are likely to compensate by using their preserved memory abilities for facts, associations and rote learned sequences (Tyson et al., 2014). For example, to most typically developing 6;0 –7;0 year olds, 'party' has a rich set of connotations, gleaned from the varied experiences of many different parties. For the young HF-LN child with autism, the meaning of 'party' is, at best, likely to be made up of a set of facts, such as 'there is cake', 'there are a lot of people', 'it is noisy'. It follows that although a large vocabulary may be acquired using semantic (fact) memory, word meanings will be relatively narrow and idiosyncratic.

Explaining language impairments in the HF-LI group

Possible causes of the phonological/articulatory impairments that have been noted in about 10 per cent of high-functioning individuals have not been investigated.

As noted in Chapter 4 (Box 4.2), this kind of linguistic impairment can result from impaired knowledge of the phonology of spoken language, which can in turn result from abnormal speech perception, or even inattention to others' speech, as has been suggested by Cleland et al. (2010). Clinically significant phonological impairments commonly occur in children with specific language impairment (SLI), and it is also plausible to suggest that a subset of people with ASD, including those in the HF-LI group, have comorbid SLI (see below). Strictly 'articulatory' as opposed to 'phonological' impairments, on the other hand, would most probably result from verbal dyspraxia, a motor disorder (Donnellan et al., 2015). Systematic investigation of the potential explanations of LI when it occurs in high-functioning individuals is needed.

Explaining language impairments in the LF-LI group

The autism-specific profile of language impairments in the LF-LI group (summarised in Table 10.1, above) is partly caused by those factors that underlie subtle anomalies in the language acquired by people in the HF-LN group, as detailed above.

However, to explain the differences in language attainment between most high-functioning individuals with ASD as compared to all lower-functioning individuals, some other causal factor – or factors – must be involved. The most obvious of these additional factors is subaverage fluid intelligence, and this is considered first, below. However, it has also been suggested that comorbid SLI may be a major factor, and this possibility is also discussed. Finally, the role of a pervasive impairment of **declarative memory** affecting semantic as well as episodic memory is discussed.

Subaverage fluid intelligence   Fluid intelligence, defined in terms of general reasoning ability and/or speed of processing underpins most kinds of human learning and behaviour. Unsuprisingly, therefore, subaverage fluid intelligence has been shown to correlate with delayed and limited language acquisition in middle- and lower-functioning people with ASD (Stevens et al., 2000). This kind of generalised learning difficulty cannot, however, easily explain the autism-specific profile of language impairment in which some facets of language are more impaired than others. Some other factor or factors must be involved, as considered next.

Comorbid SLI   In the early days of autism research it was suggested that the language impairments associated with autism were caused by comorbid 'developmental dysphasia' (Rutter et al., 1971; Churchill, 1972), now referred to as specific language impairment or SLI. SLI is defined as persistent language impairment in the absence of other known disorders. It is an umbrella term, covering early manifesting impairments in any aspect of language comprehension or expression, whether to do with the spoken language sound system (phonology and phonotactics), linguistic meaning (lexical semantics), grammar (syntax and morphosyntax) or the use of language in communication (pragmatics). Most commonly, however, expression is more affected than comprehension; and phonology and syntax are more affected than semantics or pragmatics (Leonard, 2000; Loucas et al., 2008).

The early hypothesis that language impairment in autism results from comorbid SLI was tested by Bartak and colleagues (1975, 1977) and found to be unsubstantiated.

However, a small group of children with 'mixed autism-SLI' was identified. When language impairment (as opposed to communication) was no longer seen as an essential accompaniment to autism, interest in the 'comorbid SLI' theory declined.

However, in 2001, Kjelgaard and Tager-Flusberg revived the hypothesis. There was at that time considerable interest in certain genes thought to be risk factors for both ASD and SLI, and also in certain similarities in the brain regions affected. Kjelgaard and Tager-Flusberg argued that the profiles of language impairment in ASD and SLI were also similar. None of these claims has been clearly supported in subsequent research (see reviews by Williams et al., 2008; Bishop, 2010; Luyster et al., 2011). All these reviews conclude that although there is some evidence of links between the two conditions genetically, neurobiologically and in terms of clinical profiles, differences outweigh similarities.

In particular, the most common profile of impairments in SLI differs in key respects from the 'autism-specific language profile' that emerges from large-scale studies of older children and adults with LF-LI. Indeed, the relative rarity in these groups of phonological and syntactic impairments (other than those commensurate with mental age) argues strongly against comorbid SLI as a major contributor to language impairments in ASD. The superiority of syntactic processing in LF-LI groups compared with groups with SLI (Botting & Conti-Ramsden, 2003; Shulman & Guberman, 2007; Riches et al., 2010) strengthens this conclusion. These arguments do not, however, preclude comorbid SLI as a contributory cause in a minority of cases – perhaps between 10 and 20 per cent of available evidence (Bartak et al., 1975; Rapin et al., 2009; Cleland et al., 2010). On the assumption that this percentage is stable across the spectrum, the effects of comorbid SLI should be most apparent in high-functioning individuals, and could explain phonological impairment in the HF-LI group. Within the LF-LI group, comorbid SLI would constitute one of numerous minor factors contributing to heterogeneity within this group.

Pervasive impairment of declarative memory   I and my research colleagues have hypothesised that impaired semantic memory, additional to the impairment of episodic memory that occurs across the spectrum, not only contributes significantly to learning disability when it occurs in people with ASD, as argued above, but also to language impairment in this group (Boucher et al., 2008, 2012; Bigham et al., 2010).

This hypothesis is based on a model of normal language acquisition proposed by Ullman (2001, 2004) in which phonology and syntax are relatively effortlessly acquired by young typically developing children using procedural memory; whereas linguistic meaning is acquired at a more conscious – 'declarative' – level, using the episodic and – most importantly – semantic memory systems (for definitions of the different memory systems, see Box 9.3). Utilising Ullman's model, we have hypothesised that individuals in the LF-LI group have a pervasive impairment of declarative memory affecting their ability to acquire word meanings, as well as affecting their ability to acquire factual knowledge (and hence crystallised intelligence, as argued in the preceding section). In the absence of fully functioning declarative memory/learning systems, lower-functioning children with

ASD would compensate by using their intact procedural memory to acquire mental-age-appropriate phonology and grammar, and their intact rote learning abilities to acquire at least some words and phrases. Unusual reliance on rote memory is consistent with echolalic speech, contributing to the observation that expressive language in people with LF-LI is superior to comprehension. Unusual reliance on associative learning, such that A triggers a memory of B, C triggers a memory of D, is consistent with the observation that words or phrases used by people with LF-LI are often triggered by some specific situation or cue. Fay and Schuler (1980) memorably described these first associations as being 'tenaciously stored and recycled as if they were cast in concrete'. They also noted that new words or phrases acquired by single-trial associative learning have one specific **referent**, comparable to the limited meaning of proper names (such as 'Emily Smith', 'Everest' or 'Berlin'). By contrast, words and phrases acquired over time by hearing them used in numerous and varied contexts have broad and generalisable referents.

Explaining lack of language in the LF-NV group

Despite the fact that even very low-functioning people with ASD have some islets of ability and may achieve some degree of independence in everyday living, language (whether spoken or signed) seems to be beyond their capacity to acquire. This inability extends to language comprehension as much as linguistic expression, except in rare cases of pervasive mutism. Pervasive mutism is most likely caused by **verbal apraxia**, involving difficulty in co-ordinating the movements involved in speech (Rapin, 1996), or possibly psychic akinesia, in which there is a difficulty in the voluntary initiation of actions, rather than in carrying them out (Donnellan et al., 2015). The much more common near-complete inability either to understand or to use language seems likely to result from a combination of severe impairments of mindreading, fluid intelligence and the kinds of learning subserved by declarative memory systems. However, none of the above suggested that causes of lack of language in autism is proven.

SUMMARY

There are a number of potential explanations of the *uneven patterns of spared and impaired creativity and imagination* in ASD – patterns that may differ across the spectrum. Factors that might contribute to impaired creativity and imagination include a memory retrieval impairment, an anomalous sense of self, a problem in assembling and integrating the components of a plan, or a difficulty in the spontaneous initiation of novel actions or activities. The message here is that more research is needed, such as might unlock the creative capacities of more individuals for whom repetition is the default behaviour.

Regarding *islets of ability*, it was stated in Chapter 3 that 'fine cuts' are theoretically important because they are informative about the causes of specific impairments in autism: if skill A is impaired but closely related skill B is unimpaired, this narrows down possibilities concerning the cause of the impairment of skill A. In the case of spared, or relatively spared, attachment in children who are by definition socially impaired, it can be inferred that the defining social impairments do not result from a lack of genetically determined attachment drives and behaviours. In the case of spared protoimperative or 'demand' pointing as compared to protodeclarative 'sharing' gestures, the key difference concerns whether or not mentalising is involved.

It is argued here that other things that people with ASD do well – sometimes astonishingly well by any standard, sometimes just better than their overall levels of ability might predict – result from exceptionally well-developed compensatory use of spared abilities. This is analogous to the ways in which people with physical disabilities compensate, developing skills that other people can't begin to emulate, such as painting with feet (in the absence of hands), or operating a computer using a device mounted on the head (in cases of quadriplegia). Because less able people with ASD have reduced ability to extract meaning from sensory inputs, together with problems of memory and learning and also difficulties in initiating novel activities, they engage *faute de mieux* in repetitive 'practice' of tasks and activities in which they can achieve. This, it is suggested by various authors who have studied savant abilities in ASD, enables such individuals to develop to an exceptional degree those sensory-perceptual and learning capacities that are available to them.

Diverse factors contribute to *uneven motor abilities* in autism. Some of these factors, such as hypotonia and joint laxity, are physical and relative easy to assess and to understand, although difficult to treat. Others are more subtle, involving the planning, execution and control of voluntary movements. Strikingly spared abilities may be those that have been acquired unconsciously via the procedural memory system, and which can be executed automatically, with little if any conscious control.

Impaired sense of self in people with ASD can almost certainly be explained by the difficulties they have in two major neuropsychological systems: mentalising and episodic memory. Impaired mentalising affects the ability to represent in one's own mind one's own emotional experiences and psychological characteristics and dispositions. It also affects the ability to appreciate other people's thoughts, feelings, knowledge, etc. as they may relate to one's self – a failure to see oneself as others may see us. Impaired episodic – 'relational' – memory causes a narrowing of autobiographical knowledge which, by default, consists mainly of factual knowledge in people with ASD.

The causes of *learning disability* when this occurs in people with ASD include below-average fluid (nonverbal) intelligence and also some degree of what is termed here 'self-originating socio-cultural deprivation'. However, neither of these two contributory factors can explain the VQ < NVQ discrepancy that characterises the performance of most lower-functioning individuals with ASD on intelligence tests. It is argued here that this discrepancy is more readily explained by a combination of impaired semantic memory and, inextricably related to this, impaired language (see below). Impaired semantic memory would impact on the acquisition and retention of factual information such as is assessed in some

VQ-subtests (and many school tests and exams). Impaired language would reduce scores on tests of crystallised intelligence partly because language is the medium through which most factual information is acquired, and partly because some VQ subtests probe the individual's knowledge of language directly.

The causes of *language impairment* (as opposed to communication impairment) in autism have been under-researched since the diagnostic criteria for autism changed in the late 1980s to include people with normal intelligence and clinically acceptable language. Before that time, it was thought that language impairment was an essential, perhaps critical, facet of autism, and in the early 1970s some influential clinician-researchers hypothesised that autism itself results from an extremely severe form of SLI. It now seems likely that comorbid SLI occurs only in a minority of individuals with ASD – perhaps between 10 and 20 per cent. Comorbid SLI may therefore explain the phonological/articulatory impairments observed in a subset of high-functioning individuals. It may also help to explain some of the heterogeneity in language profiles in lower-functioning groups. However, it cannot explain the pervasive impairment of language in lower-functioning ASD.

Below-average fluid (nonverbal) intelligence and some degree of 'self-originating socio-cultural deprivation' would contribute to delays and limitations in the acquisition of language. However, neither of these contributory factors has the power to explain the profile of language impairment that most commonly occurs in people with lower-functioning ASD, nor the tight linkage between learning disability and language impairment in this group. It is argued here that these can be explained by a pervasive impairment of declarative memory, affecting the semantic as well as the episodic memory system. This hypothesis is currently being investigated.

PART III

PRACTICAL ISSUES

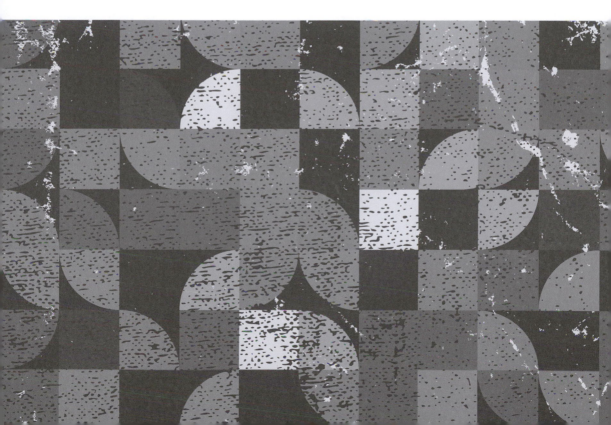

ASSESSMENT, DIAGNOSIS AND SCREENING

AIMS

The aims of this chapter are: (1) to clarify the different but overlapping functions of assessment, diagnosis and screening; (2) to consider some of the pros and cons of diagnosis before outlining processes involved and methods that may be used to diagnose ASD; and (3) to provide basic information concerning different functions and methods of screening for ASD.

ASSESSMENT

Assessments in the field of autism are carried out for a variety of different purposes. The most obvious of these is to make a diagnosis. There are, in addition, many assessment procedures designed to estimate the probability that an individual has ASD, but which fall short of yielding a reliable diagnosis. These are generally referred to as screening tests. In addition to diagnosis and screening, assessment may be carried out for numerous other purposes: for example, to help determine educational placement or progress, to monitor response to an exclusion diet, or to make a case for awarding disability allowance.

Diagnostic assessments are designed to determine whether or not an individual belongs to a particular diagnostic group, in this case the group of individuals with autism spectrum disorder as defined in DSM-5. Screening assessments are designed to identify those who may be at significant risk for a particular disease or disorder, either warranting immediate diagnostic assessment or future monitoring. Assessments relating to intervention, education and care are, by contrast, designed to evaluate the abilities, problems, needs, etc. of individuals. The contrasting aims of assigning individuals to groups as opposed to focusing on individuals echo the contrast made earlier in the book between the generalised descriptions of autism-related behaviours in the diagnostic manuals and the particular or manifest behaviour of different individuals at different life stages and in different contexts. Assessments for diagnosis or screening gather information relevant to generalised descriptions of autistic behaviour, whereas assessments for intervention, etc. gather detailed and particular information about individuals. There should be no conflict or sense of competition between the two types of assessment: they serve different functions, both of which are important.

However, this chapter focuses exclusively on diagnosis and screening. Assessments used in specialist fields of intervention, education and care are too numerous and varied for even summary coverage to be attempted here. Information on the assessments used in specialist fields can be found in the relevant literature; for example, concerning neurological assessment, speech and language assessment, assessments of educational progress, employment potential, or the assessment of capacities for independent living.

DIAGNOSIS

Why Diagnose?

Diagnosis is a tool, not an end in itself. It has a number of uses, the most important of which are indicated below.

Uses of diagnosis

To help people with ASD themselves and their families   The main purpose of diagnosis is to achieve useful ends for people with ASD themselves, their families and other carers. So, for example, in the case of a young child, a diagnosis of an ASD can do all of the following:

- Give parents a lever with which to obtain appropriate education or other intervention for their child.
- Help parents to make sense of their child's problems ('So that's why she never looks at me'; 'That's why he has a tantrum if I try to get him to wear new shoes').
- Guide parents' hopes and expectations for their child.
- Help parents and others to share their problems and learn from others (by joining a parents' group, reading, attending conferences, workshops or discussion groups).
- Protect parents from negative reactions from others ('Some people with autism have a very sensitive sense of smell – I'm afraid she doesn't like your perfume', 'He doesn't mean to be rude – he's autistic and doesn't like being touched').

Similarly, a diagnosis of an older child or adult can help to explain why an individual is different from most others in certain ways, alleviating the frustration and distress resulting from misunderstanding or misinterpreting the individual's behaviour. For example, it may be frustrating and upsetting to parents that their teenage son does not want to go out with friends in the evenings and is bullied and labelled a swot by his peers, until they know why their son prefers to be alone and to study his special interest subjects. A husband's undemonstrative behaviour and lack of emotional warmth may be misinterpreted as lack of love and commitment, until the reason for it is understood. Diagnosis of an able teenager or adult can also enable them to understand themselves better and to feel more comfortable with 'who they are'. Finally, a formal diagnosis may be necessary to access practical assistance such as a place in a specialised educational unit, **respite care**, financial support, or assistance in obtaining supported accommodation.

To facilitate communication between practitioners   Diagnosis is also useful as an aid to communication among practitioners and professionals. For example, a family doctor writing a referral for a child for a hearing test may write 'Joe has mild autism' in place of a more detailed description of Joe's autism-related behaviours that may be relevant to the audiologist's administration and interpretation of data from the hearing test. Similarly, mention of a diagnosis of 'ASD' on documents preceding a child's enrollment at a new school instantly conveys important preliminary information to teaching staff. Use of a diagnostic label for communication between practitioners is, of course, only as good as their shared understanding of the terms used (Preece & Jordan, 2007). It also conveys a limited amount of information, not specific to the individual, which may be enough for some purposes but not for others.

To provide information needed for the provision and financing of services   Statisticians, policy makers and administrators concerned with the provision and financing of health, educational and social services need information concerning the incidence and prevalence of ASD based on authoritative diagnoses. If diagnoses are not made, then provision will not be made. Of course, even when good diagnostic services are available and operating well, it may not ensure that the best possible provision will be made because there are always limiting factors. At least, however, the information is there on which to base claims. The anecdotes recounted in Box 11.1 illustrate how critical a diagnosis is for the allocation of scarce resources at local level.

Box 11.1   Tales of two cities: The use and abuse of diagnostic labels for obtaining appropriate educational provision

In *City A* there was for a time a strong lobby among educationalists against diagnosing children, on the grounds that 'labelling' was stigmatising, and that it would lower teachers' expectations of children or create prejudice against them. These are reasoned arguments based on legitimate fears. However, the net effect of *not* using the 'label' was that children with ASD were described instead as having 'communication difficulties' (and sent to special units for language-impaired children) or as having emotional or social difficulties (and sent to schools for children with emotional and behaviour problems) or as simply learning-disabled (and sent to schools for 'slow learners'). No special educational provision for children with autism was made until, eventually, parent pressure and government legislation forced the city's Local Education Authority to recognise that there is a group of children for whom a diagnosis of ASD signals a very particular set of educational needs that should be provided for.

City B, by contrast, had long recognised that an autism-related diagnosis provides an indicator of a child's special needs, and excellent educational provision was made for children on the autism spectrum from infancy to post-16. In this city, however, somewhat less good provision was made for children with certain other kinds of special educational needs. As a result there was pressure from some parents of children who were not autistic but who had some social, emotional, communicative or learning difficulty, for their child to be diagnosed as autistic. These parents hoped that the 'ASD' label might qualify their child for the special teaching and support available to children with autism – even if not entirely appropriate for their own child.

To ensure comparability between participants assessed in different research studies Suppose that for the purposes of increasing group size, two research centres want to combine their results of fMRI investigations of brain activity in adults with ASD.

This will potentially strengthen findings only if the groups studied in each research centre are similar in terms of their detailed diagnostic profiles as well as being similar in age, gender distribution and other possibly relevant factors. If the two centres have recruited participants whose diagnostic profiles differ – perhaps in severity levels or the presence/absence of significant specifiers – combining data will make significant findings less rather than more likely to emerge.

To take a more extreme example, suppose that two studies of a particular method of preparing young learning disabled adults for job interviews produce radically different results, Study A showing the method to be very useful, Study B suggesting that it makes no difference to interviewees' success. A likely explanation of the discrepant results is that participants in the two studies differed in terms of their diagnosis, Study A assessing individuals with learning disability without ASD, and Study B assessing learning disabled individuals who were also autistic. To ensure comparability, diagnosis of ASD would have been necessary.

Given that one of the aims of scientific research is to build up a body of findings replicating an effect across many comparable studies, failure to ensure that groups taking part in autism research have been diagnosed according to agreed criteria undermines the usefulness of research.

Arguments against diagnosis

Despite the many uses of diagnosis, there are some arguments against diagnosing, as well as occasional misuses or abuses, as considered below.

Adverse effects for individuals and families   In Box 11.1 it was mentioned that a diagnosis can have stigmatising effects that might include lowering teachers' expectations of particular children or creating prejudice against them. Stigmatising effects are in fact more likely to be experienced in the wider world where knowledge and understanding are more limited than in most schools. The words 'autism' or 'autistic' conjure up for many people ideas of incomprehensible difference that they find personally threatening, and they may react accordingly. So a child with an ASD diagnosis may be omitted from the class-wide invitation to a birthday party; a family that is open about their child's autism may be refused a booking for an activities holiday; an adult with 'autism' on their CV may not be considered for a job interview, however strongly recommended as suitable.

The extent and severity of the stigmatising effects of what is sometimes pejoratively called 'labelling' are related to the degree of ignorance that exists and the scope for stereotyping that ignorance provides. One of the arguments for educational **inclusion**[1] is to help to reduce ignorance within the general population (see Chapter 13). National and local autistic societies also work hard to dispel the ignorance, prejudice and stereotyping that underlie stigma. In this they are sometimes helped, but sometimes hindered, by the media. Most importantly, individuals themselves and families face down stigma by speaking openly about their experiences, writing about them and, above all, being able to laugh about them. Martin Ives and Nell Munro, who are parents of a child with ASD, write:

---

[1]Words or phrases in bold type on first occurrence can be found in the Glossary

> Sooner or later most parents reach a point where they feel less sensitive about what other people might think or say. It is this tougher skin combined with a liberal sense of humour that sees most parents through. (Ives & Munro, 2002: 70)

Ironically, use of diagnostic labels is essential for dispelling ignorance and stigma: it is not possible to demystify autism and take the fright out of it without using the term. In addition, *not* using diagnostic labels does not make people's perceived differences go away, nor does it prevent other people from reacting negatively. Claire Sainsbury, who has a diagnosis of Asperger syndrome using DSM-IV criteria, writes:

> When I didn't have an official diagnostic label my teachers unofficially labelled me as 'emotionally disturbed', 'rude' and so on, and my classmates unofficially labelled me 'nerd', 'weirdo' and 'freak'; frankly I prefer the official label. It's the stigma attached to being different that's the problem, not the label. (Sainsbury, 2000: 31, quoted in Ives & Munro, 2002)

Fortunately, the truth of Claire Sainsbury's last statement is more widely recognised now than it was some years ago when arguments against diagnostic 'labelling' were being strongly aired. Unfortunately, however, prejudice and stigma remain.

Overuse or misuse of diagnosis   In the section in Chapter 5 dealing with the apparent rise in the prevalence of ASD it was noted that this might be explained by a loosening of the diagnostic criteria, or a loosening of the interpretation of these criteria, to include individuals on the borderline between 'normality' and 'non-normality'. Whether or not this greater inclusiveness of individuals at the 'top' end of the spectrum constitutes overuse/misuse depends on whether or not the diagnosis is beneficial to the individual and those close to him or her. Baron-Cohen and colleagues (2001) noted that many individuals who score highly on their widely used screening test, the Autism-Spectrum Quotient (see below), do not warrant a diagnosis because their autistic traits and tendencies, even if marked, are causing them no significant distress or difficulty – at least at the present time. Of course this situation may change, as in the individual mentioned in Chapter 2, who had lived at ease with his autistic traits until the threatened break-up of his second marriage brought him to the attention of a psychiatrist at the age of 60. An example of the outright abuse of diagnosis can be found in the story of City B in Box 11.1, where parents may sometimes have persuaded clinicians to describe their language-impaired, emotionally disturbed or intellectually disabled child as being on the autism spectrum to obtain specialist education for their child within the excellent autism teaching units in that city.

In sum, some objections to diagnosis can be made, and occasionally diagnosis is overused or misused. However, the legitimate and important uses of diagnosis far outweigh any arguments against so-called 'labelling'.

The Diagnostic Pathway

The currently recommended **diagnostic pathway** for individuals with suspected autism in the UK can be found on the website of the National Institute for Clinical Excellence (NICE). Unfortunately, what happens in reality is often rather different,

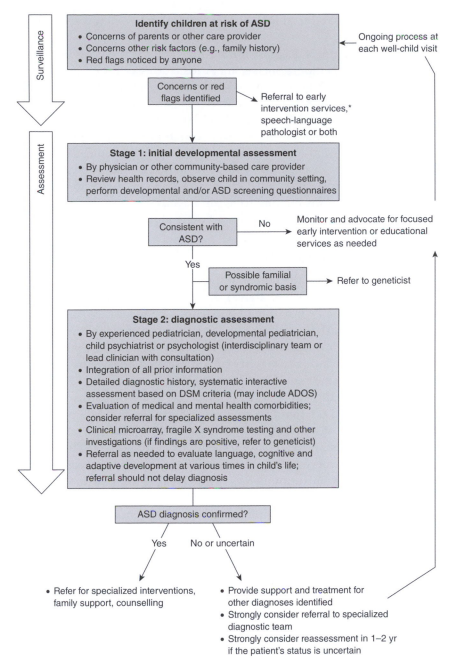

Figure 11.1 *A recommended diagnostic pathway (from Anagnostou et al., 2014)*

according to surveys of parents' and adult autistics' experiences of diagnosis in the UK (Jones et al., 2014; Crane et al., 2015; but see also Braiden et al., 2010).

In a concise but highly informative review of 'evidence-based practice' written for Health Care professionals working in Canada, Anagnostou et al. (2014)

include the figure reproduced here as Figure 11.1, concerning a recommended diagnostic pathway.

The route to obtaining a diagnosis for a young child in the US is less idealised, and advice from the National Society for Autism stresses the responsibilities of parents in initiating, organising and co-ordinating appropriate assessment and provision. Unsuprisingly, socio-economic status (SES) is strongly related to the age of diagnosis in the US (Mandell et al., 2010; Fountain et al., 2011). Regional variations in age of diagnosis have also been reported to occur in Canada (Frenette et al., 2013) and Australia (Bent et al., 2015), reflecting the availability of expert services. For discussions of national and regional differences in diagnostic practice, see Freeth et al. (2014). In what follows, routes to diagnosis are discussed in general terms relating to *when* diagnosis is desirable, and *by whom* and *where*, with separate consideration of young children as compared to older children and adults.

When should a diagnosis be made?

Young children   In view of the potential usefulness of a diagnosis for the parents of a young child with ASD (see above), it might be assumed that the obvious answer to the question 'When should a diagnosis be made?' is 'As soon as possible' (Braiden et al., 2010). In clear-cut cases this is unarguably the appropriate answer, most available evidence suggesting that early diagnosis and intensive forms of intervention can reduce the severity of ASD-related behaviours and improve prognosis in at least some cases (see Chapter 12).

There are dangers, however, in assuming that early diagnosis is invariably best for the child and the family. Some research suggests that a proportion of children who appear to warrant a diagnosis of ASD at two years old no longer warrant the diagnosis at age four years (Sutera et al., 2007). This is consistent with large-scale surveys that show the diagnosis of very young children with social and communication delays is not 100 per cent accurate, given the methods currently available. The diagnosis of ASD in their child, even if it comes as some kind of relief from doubt and frustration, is always painful and sometimes traumatic for parents, requiring many adjustments of relationships and expectations within the family. If the diagnosis is overturned a year or two later, the family's anxieties and attempts at adjustment may have been needless. Safer answers to the question 'When?' in the case of young children might therefore be 'As early as it can be done with reasonable certainty', or 'As soon as the benefits of diagnosis for the child and family outweigh any adverse effects of possible misdiagnosis'.

In practice, each clinician or clinical team has to make a judgement on each individual case. A strategy recommended by a government-led working party in the UK is to proceed towards diagnosis in stages, with the initial stage focusing on the child's and the family's immediate needs rather than on giving a name to the child's problems (Le Couteur et al., 2003). Focusing on and responding to needs at the outset and then taking the diagnostic process slowly should decrease the chances of error while not depriving the child and their family of support.

Older children and adults   Older children and adults who have not previously been diagnosed with an ASD are often at the more extreme ends of the spectrum. In very low-functioning individuals, the predominance of needs relating to physical and intellectual disabilities may lead to signs of autism being overlooked until, as sometimes happens, behavioural signs of autism become prominent and need to be addressed. In the case of Craig, for example (described in Box 4.3), notably poor social and communication skills were not easily explained by his diagnosis of Williams syndrome. The additional diagnosis of autism helped his parents and teachers to understand him better, and to work with him more effectively. The answer to the 'When?' question in the case of low-functioning individuals is therefore: 'Never too late if the autism diagnosis achieves better provision for their needs' (Bennett et al., 2005).

In high-functioning individuals, autism-related behaviours may be well compensated for or masked by superior academic achievement. The structure provided by home and primary school may also help high-functioning children to cope without excessive stress. Coping mechanisms may, however, break down in the more demanding and less structured environments of secondary school, college, and independent adulthood, with relationship failure and stress-related depression or anxiety bringing high-functioning older children or adults to the attention of educational or clinical psychologists or psychiatrists (see, for example, the case of Mr A. described in Box 4.4). There is a slight risk that high-functioning adults are misdiagnosed with a mental health problem, the chronic problems associated with the individual's autism being overlooked, and inappropriate treatment prescribed. Careful **differential diagnosis** (e.g. from schizoid personality disorder, anxiety disorder or OCD) is therefore particularly important for these people.

For highly able older children or adults, the answer to the 'When?' question is therefore again pragmatic: 'When a diagnosis helps them to understand themselves, or to be better understood by those around them, or to receive needed intervention or support'. An example of how positive it can be for an individual to obtain a diagnosis, albeit belatedly, is wonderfully described by 'PJ' in Box 11.2.

By whom and where should a diagnosis be made?

Infants and young children   Once concerns have been raised about a young child's development, the first professional to be consulted is generally the family doctor. What happens next is dependent on a range of factors, including the degree of delay and difference in any particular child's development, the knowledge and experience of autism of the doctor first seen, and the availability of specialist facilities in the country or region of the country in which the family lives.

At best, the child will be immediately referred to a multidisciplinary child development clinic for assessment. The professionals who may be involved in this assessment will probably include a paediatrician or paediatric neurologist, a clinical or educational psychologist, a speech and language therapist/pathologist, and a preschool education or family liaison specialist. An example of good practice in the diagnostic assessment of young children is described in Box 11.3.

Box 11.2 From 'Peter' to 'PJ': Reflections on late diagnosis

Some 15 years ago I was asked to see a young man (introduced to me as 'Peter') who despite having a degree in a very marketable subject, and despite frequently being shortlisted for appropriate posts in his field, nevertheless repeatedly failed on interview. He was becoming depressed, and thought that the problem might be something to do with his speech. I thought that Peter's speech was generally clear, but that what he told me about himself suggested that he might have 'Asperger syndrome'. Because I am not qualified to diagnose, I referred Peter to a colleague specialising in the diagnosis and treatment of high-functioning people with ASD. My suspicions that Peter was on the autism spectrum were confirmed, and the effect of receiving a diagnosis was described by Peter in the following words:

> It felt like I had woken up from a walking coma after 30 years. Up to the time I got a diagnosis, I felt I was living as somebody else. I felt a sense of relief because I had felt before that there was something there, but I did not know what it was; getting a diagnosis answered a lot of questions. It also felt as if my life had eventually turned the right way up. . . . it helped me find who I truly was. Because not only did it answer many questions and turn my life the right way up, but it also gives me a chance to 'rebuild myself'. Since my diagnosis, my name is PJ because this is my new identity and, as such, Peter died the day I got diagnosed.

(From PJ Hughes, 2007)

In the intervening years since he obtained a diagnosis, PJ has done an amazing amount to publicise and explain ASD to other people, as well as playing an active role within his local Autism Support Group and at national level. He writes and gives talks about autism from his own personal perspective. He was a Trustee for the National Autistic Society (UK) for four years, and was entertained at 10 Downing Street when the NAS celebrated its Golden Anniversary in 2012. PJ is currently on the NAS's National Forum of experts and advisors.

(With thanks to PJ for providing the above information and agreeing to its publication)

Child development clinics offering multidisciplinary assessments are not, however, available in all countries or regions. Children may then be referred for diagnostic assessment by a child psychiatrist or paediatrician, or by a clinical or educational psychologist specialising in autism-related problems. However, it would be unusual for a diagnosis to be made by a single professional without reference to information from others, and reports from other specialists would probably be requested before making a diagnosis. It is particularly important for more than one professional to be involved in the process of making a diagnosis, because it has been shown that collaborative assessment leads to more reliable

---

Box 11.3   An example of good practice in the diagnostic assessment of a young child

The Lorna Wing Centre is run by the National Autistic Society (UK) and situated in a tree-lined residential road in a London suburb. Staff who may be involved in assessing a particular individual, whether child or adult, include a psychiatrist, clinical and educational psychologists, and speech and language therapists, plus dedicated administrative staff. Key points of procedures used when assessing a young child include the following.

Prior to an appointment, information about the child is obtained by letter or phone from the child's doctor, and from responsible people at the child's playgroup or school, as appropriate and with parents' permission.

The child's parent(s)/major carer(s) are contacted by telephone to tell them what to expect when they visit, and to ask them to explain to the child that the visit should be fun, and that it will help them 'and Mummy and Daddy' (as appropriate). They are asked about the child's interests, and what they might like for lunch (which is provided at the Centre); and it is suggested that the child should bring a favourite toy, book or DVD – even a pet, if practicable!

Photographs of rooms and of staff at the Centre may be sent to the family in advance, to mitigate the unfamiliarity of the place and the people the child will meet.

The diagnostic visit lasts from 10.00 am until 4.00 pm. This allows time for a leisurely settling-in phase, often centred on the kitchen where there are drinks and snacks, with time to explore other rooms in the Centre, and for the child to become familiarised with staff. Only one assessment is carried out on any one day, so the number of strange faces is small.

Once the child has settled in, an extended interview is carried out with the child's parent(s)/carer(s) by a member of the team, including administration of the DISCO (see below). As and when the child is willing to separate, they are invited to go with another member of the team to the playroom (or back to the kitchen), where their behaviour, learning and language abilities are assessed.

After lunch there is an extended feedback/question-and-answer session with the parents, which includes advice about future intervention, management, educational placement and likely prognosis.

After the visit the professionals who have carried out assessments meet and draw up a report to be sent to the parents and, with the parents' permission, to heads of local services.

(With thanks to the Manager of the Lorna Wing Centre, who supplied this information)

and earlier diagnosis than diagnosis by a single person, however experienced (Risi et al., 2006).

Prompt referral to a multidisciplinary centre or other diagnostic clinic is, unfortunately, not what reliably happens as a result of an initial visit to the family doctor. Doctors who are in genuine doubt as to whether they are looking at a child who might have a significant developmental problem, as opposed to a child who is just a little on the slow side developmentally, may refer the child for assessments that might help to clarify the nature and cause of the child's behavioural anomalies but which are not designed to assess the child for possible autism. For example, the child might be referred to an audiologist for hearing assessment, a speech and language therapist for assessment of communicative development, an educational psychologist for assessment of developmental level or intelligence, a neurologist for investigation of motor abnormalities, or the preschool clinical psychology service or family therapy clinic if the GP suspected emotional problems related to difficulties within the family (which could, of course, result from stresses centred on the child). Referrals such as these may be useful in helping to rule in or rule out some possible causes of the child's developmental differences, and thus contribute to differential diagnosis. However, none of these assessments by themselves is sufficient for an authoritative diagnosis of ASD, and referring the child for a succession of specialist assessments can introduce undesirable delay. At worst, the family doctor will give unwarranted, if well-meant, reassurance of the kind 'She's fine; you've nothing to worry about', or a temporising response such as 'He's probably just a slow starter – let's see how he's doing in six months'.

Older children and adults   Older children and adults are most likely to be referred or to self-refer to a psychiatrist, clinical psychologist or counsellor on account of relationship problems or mental health problems, especially anxiety and depression. Occasionally (inadvertent) criminality brings an older child or adult to the attention of medical practitioners as in, for example, the case of Gary McKinnon, the young man belatedly diagnosed with Asperger syndrome after hacking into the Pentagon's computer files.

Guidelines set out by the National Institute for Clinical Excellence (NICE) in the UK advise that the diagnosis of adults with suspected ASD should:

- be undertaken by professionals who are trained and competent;
- be team-based and draw on a range of professions and skills;
- where possible involve a family member, partner, carer or other informant, or use documentary evidence (such as school reports) of current and past behaviour and early development.

Methods for Diagnosing ASD

There are currently no methods for diagnosing ASD using physical tests, although arguments for one or another potential **biomarker** have proliferated over recent years (for reviews, see Goldani et al., 2014; Ruggeri et al., 2014). Given the heterogeneity of risk factors for ASD (see Chapter 7) and the heterogeneity of brain correlates of ASD (see Chapter 8), it may be the case that no single biomarker will be found which reliably indicates autism in all cases (Anderson, 2014). Neither can ASD be diagnosed on the basis of physical appearance, such as provides an initial diagnostic indicator of numerous congenital medical conditions; nor on the basis of the kinds of behavioural tests that produce clear-cut evidence of, for example, visual impairment or cerebral palsy. Instead, diagnosis must be made by assessing an individual's developmental history and current patterns of behaviour, and comparing the results of these assessments with the diagnostic criteria for ASD as detailed in DSM-5 or ICD-10.

In the next subsections, some well-authenticated methods of collecting information about the individual in the past and present are described. By 'well-authenticated' is meant that the methods have been shown to be both **reliable** and **valid**. By validity is meant that the test has a high level of **sensitivity** (defined as producing a low proportion of **false negatives**) and a high level of **specificity** (defined as producing a low proportion of **false positives**). For discussion of the concepts of reliability and validity in relation to diagnostic tests for ASD, see Lord and Costello (2005).

The 'gold-standard' procedures

Autism Diagnostic Interview-Revised (ADI-R) The ADI-R (Rutter, Le Couteur, & Lord, 2003) was frequently described as constituting the 'gold standard' for diagnosis of an ASD-related disorder as defined in DSM-IV. It was not designed to differentiate between putative subtypes of ASD, and seems likely to retain its position as the most widely used interview schedule post-publication of DSM-5. The ADI-R consists of a lengthy semi-structured interview in which a parent or primary caregiver is questioned by a trained clinician using a set of questions designed to obtain the information summarised in Box 11.4.

Box 11.4   Topics on which information is elicited in the ADI-R

- The family background, education, previous diagnoses (if any) and medications (if any) of the child or adult who is being assessed.
- Their behaviour, in general terms.
- Early development and developmental milestones.
- Language acquisition and any loss of language or other skills.
- Current functioning with regard to language and communication.
- Social development and play.
- Interests and behaviours.
- Other clinically relevant behaviours, such as hearing impairment, self-injury or epilepsy.

The interviewer records and codes responses in a standardised way that provides both an overall score and scores on key domains of autism-related behaviour. If scores in each of these domains reach certain levels, then a diagnosis of ASD based on DSM-5 criteria can be made. The severity of an individual's autism, in terms of problematic behaviours within each domain, is also rated, as required in DSM-5.

A long-recognised weakness of the ADI-R, however, has been a lack of sensitivity to signs of ASD in toddlers and very young children (Risi et al., 2006; Wiggins and Robbins, 2008). Modifications of the ADI-R for use with children aged 12–47 months have been developed (Kim & Lord, 2012a) but appear to remain unsatisfactory (de Bildt et al., 2015). Specifically, this interview schedule lacks sensitivity to signs of ASD in more able children in this age group. No doubt attempts to correct this weakness will continue, and interested readers should look out for developments.

Autism Diagnostic Observation Schedule (ADOS)   In a 'best practice' diagnostic assessment, the ADI-R has for many years been supplemented by information from the Autism Diagnostic Observation Schedule (ADOS) (Lord et al., 1999). The original ADOS consisted of four sets of specified activities, to be carried out using a kit of materials supplied with the test. Sets of activities are referred to as 'modules', each module being designed for use with individuals within a particular age or ability range, from preschoolers with little or no language to adults with fluent language. Activities specified within each module are initiated by the clinician, who both interacts with and observes the child or adult being assessed. A series of 'presses' are written into the instructions for testing, designed to elicit certain initiations and responses by the individual being tested. However, no direct instruction is involved. The activities used for assessing children with 'flexible phrase speech' are listed below, in the order in which they are introduced:

A construction task.......make believe play......joint interactive play...

free play...snack... response to name...response to joint attention cue...

birthday party.....bubble play ....anticipation of a routine with objects...

demonstration task ('Show and tell me how...').......conversation.....

description of a picture.....looking at a book

The observer, who must be trained in the procedures and scoring methods to be used, takes notes during the assessment and codes the individual's behaviour according to listed items immediately after administration of the session. From this information a score is obtained and a specified calculation, or **algorithm**, is applied to determine whether or not a diagnosis of ASD is appropriate.

In response to the increasingly appreciated need for early diagnosis, a second edition of ADOS was published in 2012. ADOS-2 consists of five instead of four modules, an additional 'toddler' module having been added, designed to assess communication, social interaction, play, and restricted and repetitive behaviours in children from 12 months of age. The toddler module appears to have good diagnostic validity (Luyster et al., 2009), and is consistent with DSM-5 criteria (Guthrie et al., 2013). When ADOS-2 is used together with the modified scoring and interpretation of the ADI-R, described above, diagnostic validity for the assessment of very young children is high (Kim & Lord, 2012b)

Interview schedules with a broader focus

Although the combined use of the ADI-R and ADOS-2 is widely considered to offer a highly reliable method of diagnosing ASD, these assessment procedures focus exclusively on the detection of autism. This tight focus ignores the fact that 'ASD' is not a clear-cut condition: it sometime occurs in partial forms, or in combination with other conditions such as ADHD, specific language impairment, learning disability or dyspraxia. Two diagnostic procedures are outlined next which aim not only to detect autism, if present, but to build up an individual's profile of abilities and disabilities so that appropriate advice can be offered regardless of whether or not an autism diagnosis is made. Both these procedures consist of extended interview schedules to be carried out by a trained interviewer in a face-to-face session. When a child or low-functioning individual is being assessed, the interview is carried out with a parent or other primary carer. In the case of high-functioning adults, interviews are carried out with the person being assessed plus a family member who has known them from childhood. In all cases, the interviewee's responses are scored according to a prescribed protocol and analysed using prescribed algorithms.

Two well-authenticated methods of identifying whether or not an individual warrants a diagnosis of ASD, but at the same time building up an extended profile of the individual's strengths and weaknesses and therefore their intervention and support needs, are outlined below.

The Diagnostic Interview for Social and Communication Disorders (DISCO) The DISCO (Wing et al., 2002) is considered first because it is a well-tried and -tested, highly respected procedure. Topics covered during the interview fall under the headings listed in Box 11.5.

Box 11.5 Topics on which information is elicited in the DISCO

- Infancy history.
- Age of any setback in development.
- Gross motor skills.
- Self-care, e.g. feeding, dressing, domestic skills, independence.
- Communication.
- Social interaction with adults and with age peers, including social play.
- Imitation.
- Imagination.
- Skills, e.g. reading and writing, number, money, dates and time, special abilities.
- Motor and vocal stereotypies.
- Responses to sensory stimuli.
- Repetitive routines and resistance to change.
- Emotions.
- Activity pattern.
- Maladaptive behaviour.
- Sleep pattern.
- Catatonic features.
- Quality of social interaction.
- Any history of psychiatric conditions or sexual problems.

The DISCO was developed in accordance with the concept of autism as a spectrum of related conditions, consistently argued for by Lorna Wing, and it has proved an accurate tool for diagnosing autism spectrum disorder as defined in DSM-5 (Kent et al., 2013).

The Developmental, Dimensional, and Diagnostic Interview (3Di) The 3Di (Skuse et al., 2004) is an extended interview schedule predicated on the concept of ASD as a dimensional condition in the sense that very many distinct dimensions of behaviour may (or may not) be affected to a greater or lesser extent. As in the DISCO, the behavioural dimensions assessed are not exclusively those associated with strengths and weaknesses diagnostic of ASD. The major innovation associated with this procedure is that the trained interviewer enters responses onto a computer which analyses the data and produces an immediate report.

The 3Di is a well-validated screening tool, and the latest version of this interview schedule, the 3Di-5, produces results consistent with DSM-5 symptomatology (Skuse, 2013).

Other diagnostic instruments

Numerous other diagnostic checklists, rating scales and observation schedules have been developed over the years, each designed to identify individuals with autism according to whatever diagnostic criteria were current. Some of these have been updated as diagnostic criteria have been modified. None of these instruments, however, can be relied on as safely as the ADI-R (especially in combination with the ADOS-2) or the DISCO – possibly also the 3Di, although this procedure has been less exhaustively validated – in making a diagnosis. This does not imply that the currently recommended methods of diagnosis are 100 per cent reliable and will not themselves be modified or superseded in the future: they are just the most reliable diagnostic tools available at the time of writing.

SCREENING

Why Screen?

Screening in the field of medicine is used to identify those who may be at significant risk for a particular disease or disorder. It may be carried out across a whole population, for example screening all women within a certain age range for early signs of breast cancer. Alternatively, screening may be carried out with a selected group of individuals thought to be at increased risk of developing a disease, for example women with a family history of breast cancer.[2] Those identified as likely to have the disease, or to be at significant risk of developing it at a later date, may

---

[2]In the US, the terms *primary or Level 1* screening and *secondary or Level 2* screening are used to differentiate between whole population screening and selected population screening, respectively.

be referred for fuller diagnostic assessment, for precautionary treatment or advice and/or for future monitoring. Screening tests are also widely used by researchers to check (a) that the participants in the group targeted in a study do, in fact, have the condition under investigation and (b) that the participants in any comparison group do *not* have the condition, even in very mild form.

To be useful and also economically justifiable when used in population-wide clinical assessment, screening tests must have been shown to have high levels of sensitivity and specificity (see above). A 'well-validated' or 'well-authenticated' screening test also has high **predictive value**. The predictive value of a screening test reflects how accurately that test predicts the proportion of individuals in the population screened who have – or who may have – a particular disease or disorder, as compared to the proportion who need no further investigation or treatment.

In view of evidence that early intensive intervention improves outcomes in individuals with ASD, universal screening of toddlers and very young children has been called for in the US and is under discussion in many other countries. Given that there is to date no reliable biomarker for ASD, the development of effective behavioural methods of screening for ASD in very young children is now seen as urgent (Camarata, 2014).

Methods of Screening for ASD

Toddlers and very young children

There is a proliferation of methods on offer, some focusing on whole population screening and some directed towards screening groups considered to be 'at risk' (usually because there is a sibling or other close family member with ASD). Eighteen different methods of screening for incipient ASD in toddlers and young children are reviewed by García-Primo et al. (2014). In addition, some widely used screens for general developmental progress have sections that relate specifically to the detection of possible autism. For example, the widely used 'Ages and Stages Questionnaire' (Brookes Publishing Co.) has an optional section on 'social-emotional development'.

The most extensively tested and refined screening tool for the early detection of autism is the *Checklist for Autism in Toddlers (CHAT)* (Baird et al., 2000). The CHAT was designed for use by doctors and nurses during routine check-ups, and consisted of certain structured observations of the child's behaviour as well as nine 'yes/no' questions to be answered by a parent or other primary caregiver. Two of the questions were considered to be critical probes for autism-related behaviour. These questions were:

> Does your child ever PRETEND, for example, to make a cup of tea using a toy cup and teapot, or pretend other things?
>
> Does your child ever use his/her index finger to point, to indicate INTEREST in something?

The CHAT proved to have good specificity, but relatively weak sensitivity, i.e. it produced few false positives but an undesirable number of false negatives.

With the permission of the original authors, the *Modified Checklist for Autism in Toddlers (M-CHAT)* was developed in the US by Robins et al. (2001). The M-CHAT consists of 23 questions presented as a written checklist, to be answered by a parent or other primary caregiver. The first nine questions come from the CHAT, and the additional questions are designed to obviate the need for behaviour observation. The M-CHAT is, moreover, designed to cater for infants within a wider age range than the original, namely from 16 to 30 months. High rates of sensitivity, specificity and predictive power were reported following a large-scale study of the validity and usefulness of this screening procedure (Dumont-Matthieu & Fein, 2005).

Most recently, a follow-up questionnaire has been introduced as a check on children identified as possible cases of ASD, this two-stage procedure being referred to as *M-CHAT-Revised with Follow-up (M-CHAT-R/F)*. Tests of this latest revision look promising as a method of universal screening for ASD (Robins et al., 2014). Being in the form of questionnaires to be completed by parents using 'yes/no' responses, it is quick and cheap to carry out, is not dependent on specially trained clinicians, and ensures that only those toddlers highly likely to have ASD and/or a related condition of significant concern go through to full-scale clinical evaluation. This test was originally available only in English but is now available in translation in several non-English-speaking countries.

Adults

The *Autism-Spectrum Quotient*, sometimes referred to as the ASQ but more usually referred to as the AQ (Baron-Cohen et al., 2001; Woodbury-Smith et al., 2005), is currently recommended by the UK's National Institute for Clinical Excellence (NICE) as one of the sources of information that may contribute to diagnosis in adults. An outline of test content and scoring is shown in Box 11.6.

Versions of the ASQ/AQ using parental report have been developed for use with adolescents (Baron-Cohen et al., 2006) or with primary school-age children (Auyeung et al., 2008), but are less well validated and less commonly used than the well-authenticated adult version.

Across the age range: Toddlers to adults

Three well-validated screening instruments suitable for use with children and adults have been derived from the diagnostic instruments outlined in the previous main section of this chapter.

The Social Communication Questionnaire (SCQ)   The SCQ (Rutter, Bailey, & Lord, 2003) consists of 40 questions selected from the ADI-R (see above). Questions are designed to elicit 'yes/no' responses, and to be completed by a parent, primary carer or (in the case of a high-functioning adult) the individual themselves with assistance from a close family member. The advantage of the SCQ is the speed with which it can be completed and then scored by a clinician. For example, it can be completed on arrival at a clinic prior to a consultation, providing the clinician with critical guidance as to how best to proceed during the consultation.

Box 11.6   The Autism-Spectrum Quotient (AQ) – Adult version

Content: The AQ is a self-report questionnaire consisting of 50 items made up of ten questions assessing five different areas:

- Social skills.
- Attention switching.
- Attention to detail.
- Communication.
- Imagination.

Items relating to the five different areas are randomly distributed across the questionnaire. Following each question, four responses are listed, one of which the respondent must circle/underline. Options for responding are:

definitely agree; slightly agree; slightly disagree; definitely disagree

Scoring: Each question is specifically designed to elicit *either* an 'Agree' *or* a 'Disagree' response from individuals with ASD or ASD-related traits. Two points are scored for ASD-predictive 'definitely agree'/'definitively disagree' responses; one point for ASD-predictive 'agree'/'disagree' responses; and no points are scored for non-ASD-predictive responses. A total score of 32 or more is indicative of a significant level of ASD-related behavioural traits.

The DISCO Signposting Set   The DISCO Signposting Set (Carrington et al., 2014) is a 14-item questionnaire using questions selected from the DISCO. Like the DISCO, the Signposting Set is an interview schedule to be carried out and scored by a clinician, who questions a parent/primary caregiver or the adult being assessed. The specified aim of the DISCO Signposting Set is to provide clinicians with a reliable guide as to whether or not they should proceed with a full clinical evaluation. Initial tests of this procedure have reported high levels of sensitivity and specificity and good alignment with DSM-5 criteria (Carrington et al., 2015).

The Developmental, Dimensional, and Diagnostic Interview – short version (3Di-sv)   The 3Di-sv (Santosh et al., 2009) is an interview schedule designed to be administered by a trained clinician or researcher. It consists of 112 questions (fewer than half the number of questions in the full-form 3Di) and is reported to take 45 minutes to administer, with responses being entered into a computer programme. As in the full-form 3Di, a report is instantly available. Santosh et al. report good levels of sensitivity and specificity, and consistency with outcomes from the full-form of the 3Di and also from the ADI-R. Although a powerful screening test, its usefulness to a broad range of clinicians or researchers is reduced by the time taken to administer this test, and the need for a specially trained interviewer.

The Social Responsiveness Scale (SRS)   The SRS (Constantino et al., 2003) is 65-item questionnaire designed to be answered by a parent, teacher, or other person who is currently familiar with the individual being investigated. For each item, one of four given responses ranging from 'not true' (which scores '1') to 'almost always true' (which scores '4') must be circled or underlined. As its name suggests, this questionnaire probes social reciprocity in particular, and is well suited for the detection of autism-related traits or tendencies in individuals – including adults – who may, or may not, have the full form of ASD.

As with methods of diagnosis, numerous other methods of screening for ASD or for ASD-related traits or risk factors have been developed over the years. These include a variety of checklists, rating scales and observation schedules, some of which are language and/or culture specific (see the review of screening methods for toddlers by García-Primo et al., 2014, mentioned above). Some of the older, English-language tests, such as the *Autism Behaviour Checklist (ABC)* (Krug et al., 1978) and the *Childhood Autism Rating Scale (CARS)* (Schopler et al., 2002), have stood the test of time and may still be used as quick-and-easy spot checks for signs of autism.

SUMMARY

Assessment in the field of autism is used for a variety of purposes, most notably for diagnosis and screening, but also for assessing individuals' strengths, needs and progress with regard to intervention, education and care. Assessments for diagnosis and screening (the topic of the present chapter) are designed to determine group membership, or the likelihood of group membership, whereas assessments associated with intervention, education and care focus on individuals' strengths, needs, progress, suitability for support, etc.

Diagnosis is a tool with certain functions. Major functions include: enabling more able individuals with ASD to understand themselves; helping families and carers to better understand the nature of the problems they and the cared-for person may be experiencing; accessing services and other forms of support; and planning for the future. However, diagnosis also facilitates communication between practitioners, in that diagnostic terms act as shorthand to convey information that would otherwise have to be detailed. Diagnosis is also necessary for estimating prevalence and thus for estimating the need for provision of educational, health care and other services. Finally, diagnosis is needed to ensure comparability between participants assessed in different research studies.

It has sometimes been argued that 'labelling' individuals with a diagnosis is stigmatising, creating prejudice and lowering expectations of that individual. In response it has been argued that it is the condition itself, and the fact that individuals with ASD are perceived as 'different', that creates stigma, not the labelling process.

The appropriate time for a diagnosis to be made is as soon as the gains to be made for the individual and their family outweigh the disadvantages of possible misdiagnosis (which can occur in the case of infants and very young children). The processes of obtaining a diagnosis vary from country to country and regionally within any country. For infants and young children, the process at best starts with the family medical advisor and moves quickly to a specialist diagnostic centre offering multidisciplinary diagnostic assessments. Another reasonably satisfactory route to diagnosis involves referral from the family doctor to a specialist practitioner, who then obtains information from other specialists such as may be needed to arrive at a secure diagnostic decision. Unfortunately, many families, even in developed countries, encounter delay and difficulty in having their young child fully and efficiently assessed. High-functioning adults with undiagnosed ASD, who have coped well during their school years and possibly into middle or older age, may benefit from diagnosis if life stresses increase to the extent that the person's autism causes significant distress or difficulty. Such individuals generally come to the attention of clinical psychologists or psychiatrists for diagnostic evaluation.

The most authoritative diagnostic instruments now available are the Autism Diagnostic Interview-Revised (ADI-R) and the Autism Diagnostic Observation Schedule – 2 (ADOS-2) used in combination. The Diagnostic Interview for Social and Communication Disorders (DISCO), also the 3Di, provide a broad picture of an individual's strengths and needs, which may include an ASD diagnosis.

Screening in the autism field is used to identify individuals at significant risk of having ASD, rather than to produce a reliable diagnosis. An effective screening method has high specificity, sensitivity and predictive value. Screening whole populations, or selected populations, of very young children for ASD is important because of evidence suggesting that early intervention is more effective than later intervention (Webb et al., 2014). The Modified Checklist for Autism in Toddlers (M-CHAT), now revised to include selective follow-up screening, is the best authenticated of a large number of infant screening procedures. For adults, the self-report Autism-Spectrum Questionnaire (AQ) is widely used. For use across a wide age range, typically from about 4;0 years upwards, the Social Communication Questionnaire (SCQ) and the Social Responsivity Questionnaire (SRS) are quite widely used, with the DISCO-Signposting Set and short-form of the 3Di promising well for use by clinicians.

INTERVENTION

THE AIMS OF INTERVENTION

PROS AND CONS OF INTERVENTION
Prevention and Cure
Treatment

POSSIBILITIES FOR PREVENTION AND CURE
Prevention
Cure

TREATMENT METHODS
Discriminating Between the Options
Evidence-based versus Non-evidence-based Treatments
Evidence-based Non-physical Treatments
Borderline Evidence-based Non-physical Treatments
Evidence-based Physical Treatments
Borderline Evidence-based Physical Treatments
Non-evidence-based Physical Treatments
Unproven Does Not Necessarily Mean Useless

FUTURE DIRECTIONS

SUMMARY

AIMS

The main aim of this chapter is to provide information about a representative sample of currently available interventions, broadly interpreted to include possibilities for prevention and cure as well as treatments designed to promote development and learning or to reduce unwanted behaviours. A secondary aim is to stimulate a critical approach to issues relating to intervention, in particular by: (1) outlining the arguments of the 'neurodiversity' movement, which queries the appropriateness of intervening; and (2) establishing a framework for evaluating the efficacy of treatment methods.

THE AIMS OF INTERVENTION

Intervention is interpreted here as including prevention, cure and treatment. Interventions for idiopathic autism only will be considered. Forms of syndromic autism are many and varied, with some forms theoretically amenable to prevention in particular, if the genetic basis of the particular syndrome is known and relatively simple. However, whether lowering the incidence of, for example, tuberous sclerosis or Prader-Willi syndrome would have any significant impact on the incidence of ASD is questionable. We do not know why autism occurs in some cases of certain syndromes but not in other cases. So preventing or curing the co-existing syndrome might well be insufficient to prevent the occurrence of autism. This is not, of course, to question the desirability of reducing population frequencies of those debilitating medical conditions involved in syndromic ASD.

The aim of *prevention* is to eliminate autism from the population or at least to reduce the incidence of autism. Prevention would achieve this by ensuring that people with ASD are not conceived; or, if conceived, not born; or, if conceived and born with prodromal autism, then not exposed to whatever environmental experiences might convert incipient autism to a diagnosable condition.

The aim of *curing* autism is to reduce the prevalence of ASD in the population. This could be achieved by 'correcting' underlying brain abnormalities and thereby 'normalising' behaviour; and/or targeting behaviour directly with the aim of modifying it to meet standards of 'normality' or 'typicality', with or without associated changes of brain structure and/or function.

The major aims of most forms of *treatment* of people with ASD are to facilitate development and to increase an individual's competencies and control over their own lives. Other treatments aim to eliminate or ameliorate behaviours or comorbid conditions that are patently distressing or disadvantageous to the individual with ASD; and/or those that impact significantly negatively on others, whether carers, classmates, workmates, or people in the street; and/or those that place especially heavy financial burdens on society or may rank as antisocial or criminal.

The aims of preventing, curing or treating autism might at first glance seem unquestionably desirable. However, this is not the case, especially where prevention or cure are concerned. Before considering methods of intervention, therefore, some of the pros and cons of intervening are outlined, first in the case of prevention or cure, then in the case of treatment.

PROS AND CONS OF INTERVENTION

Prevention and Cure

Arguments in favour

Preventing or curing autism might be assumed to be desirable from the point of view of individuals, even the unborn whose predictable suffering, it might be argued, can be prevented. It might also be assumed to be desirable for families who would be spared the sacrifices, stresses and strains associated with living with and caring for a person with ASD. It might well be considered desirable for society in general, given the huge financial costs associated with providing for the health, educational, social and care needs of people with ASD, especially those who are less able. Prevention or cure might, in sum, be judged to have positive outcomes for individuals, families, and society in general. There are, however, counter-arguments, as considered next.

Arguments against

Counter-arguments relating to individuals It would be wrong to assume that all people with ASD would have preferred not to have existed or would want to be 'cured'. Indeed, many individuals at the high end of the spectrum have vociferously argued of late that people with ASD are simply *different* from 'neurotypical people': they are not 'disordered', let alone 'sick', medically speaking. They argue instead that autism is the product of the normal distribution of behavioural traits such as 'sociability', 'persistence', 'attentional focus', entailing that a small proportion of the population is born with poor socialising potential but powerful capacities for sustained attention on the minutiae of a particular topic of interest. The 'Aspies' who argue in this way are aligned to what is called the **neurodiversity**[1] movement. This movement extends well beyond ASD in arguing that many, if not all, people who in the past might have been considered to be 'disabled' in some way or another should now be considered to be simply 'different'. For those highly able people with ASD making this case, questions relating to prevention or cure simply don't arise – and are, in fact, understandably objectionable.

However, when the neurodiversity concept of ASD is used to argue against seeking to prevent or cure autism when it occurs in severe form accompanied by multiple additional problems, it is much more questionable. We cannot ask people with autism plus severe learning difficulties and minimal language plus, perhaps, tuberous sclerosis, epilepsy, phobias, compulsions and sleeping

---

[1] Words and phrases in bold type on first occurrence can be found in the Glossary.

difficulties whether they might have preferred to have been born without these problems, or whether they might like to be 'cured'. We can, however, consider their vulnerability to frustration and distress, and the limitations of what gives them pleasure, and cautiously conclude that their quality of life is significantly compromised by their conditions. For discussion and further references relating to the neurodiversity argument, see Krcek (2013) and Kapp et al. (2013); also a balanced and humane blog by John Elder Robison posted on the Autism Speaks website in 2013.

Counter-arguments relating to families It would also be wrong to assume that all families and other close carers experience living with and caring for a person with ASD as a predominantly negative experience. In the long term, many parents report positively about the experience of bringing up a child with autism, saying that it had enriched their lives and provided challenges leading them to develop an inner strength and acceptance of life's setbacks they might not otherwise have developed (Krauss & Seltzer, 2000; Park, 2001).

Counter-arguments relating to society Finally, it would be wrong to assume that autistic people do not make contributions to society. Many of the world's top scientists, mathematicians, computer programmers, philosophers and others appear to have (or to have had, in the case of historical figures) autism-related traits and tendencies that contribute directly to their academic prowess. It would do the human species no good at all, in fact it would be a retrograde step for the species, to eliminate the set of behaviour traits that combine to produce so many of the world's highest achievers.

It is harder to argue, however, that lower-functioning people on the spectrum make significant contributions to society. Some savant artists have produced work that has been shown around the world; and savant calculators or estimators have astonished live and TV audiences with their amazing abilities. Other contributions are more subtle, to do with what might be termed 'lessons in life' – about how we view ourselves and how we come to appreciate individuals for themselves, seeing past their disabilities and learning to love them (Isanon, 2001). But our own 'lessons in life' should not come at the expense of people whose lives are so curtailed by their disabilities.

In sum, it should not be assumed that ridding the world of people with ASD would constitute an unquestionably positive outcome. At the same time the real suffering of many people with ASD, the strains on families and other carers, and the huge financial burdens borne by society must be recognised. The challenge is, therefore, to work towards the prevention or cure of complex, disabling forms of ASD, while not undermining the persistence in the gene pool of those variations that predispose an individual towards analytic thinking and the pursuance of complex ideas and projects with a degree of persistence and tolerance of solitude that is rare. For individuals with 'pure' autism, life can be good; strains and costs to families are neither excessive nor lifelong, and society gains rather than loses from their existence. Most importantly, they themselves proclaim their right to exist and to be accepted and valued for who they are.

Treatment

Arguments in favour

It is important to stress again that those individuals who have some SEC impairments as well as restricted interests but who are living reasonably contented lives do not warrant a diagnosis of ASD (Baron-Cohen et al., 2001). 'Treatment', therefore, is irrelevant to such people.

Treatment is only relevant to those whose SEC impairments and RRBs, combined in many cases with additional physical and mental health problems, neurodevelopmental disorders and learning difficulties, warrant a diagnosis such as will enable them to access a range of relevant services.

Treatment for such people must surely be desirable from all points of view. For example, interventions that decrease the severity of core symptoms and increase an individual's competencies and control over their own lives empower the individual and increase self-esteem. Such interventions reduce demands on carers, and can make the carer–cared for relationship more reciprocal. Reducing an individual's dependence on others can also reduce costs to the State. For instance, if a 20-year-old borderline achiever still living at home can be taught how to read and to understand money, how to cross roads safely and use public transport, then they can do some of the household shopping and travel to their place of work or to leisure activities. This may postpone the time when the individual will need to move into a bedsit or flat, supported by the State. Similarly, supporting a 20-year-old high-achieving but obsessive and anxious individual to satisfy the demands of a university degree course will increase the likelihood of their finding salaried employment and achieving financial independence in adulthood.

Arguments against

Despite the obvious arguments in favour of treatment, some counter-arguments have been proposed. In particular, the assumption that being like the majority, being 'normal'/'typical', is inherently desirable may be questioned. As is increasingly argued by the large and varied population of people with disabilities, being 'different' can have its own advantages and does not necessarily imply a need to be made less different (see the references relating to 'neurodiversity', above). It might also be argued that, especially for individuals with severe and multiple difficulties, enhancing quality of life (aiming for happiness, wellbeing) rather than straining towards unattainable goals of normality/typicality should be the pre-eminent aim of intervention (Florian et al., 2000).

These caveats should be borne in mind when evaluating justifications for treatments that aim to increase an individual's competencies. They raise questions such as 'When is difference advantageous or at least acceptable to the individual first and foremost, but also to those associated with the individual, and those providing for them?' 'When, on the other hand, is difference a source of unhappiness, frustration or difficulty to the individual?' 'When may treatment be counter-productive to an individual's happiness and wellbeing?'

Treatments that aim to eliminate or reduce maladaptive behaviours must also be undertaken cautiously. In the first place, the likely benefits of any such treatment must outweigh the risks of negative side-effects. This is particularly important where treatments are invasive, involving, for example, medications, dietary supplements or electrical brain stimulation. In the second place, judgements as to what constitutes 'maladaptive' or 'unwanted' behaviour are not always straightforward. For example, an obsession with firearms could lead to antisocial behaviour, but might equally well provide a focus of interest and pleasurable activities (reading specialist magazines, visiting museums). Similarly, behaviour that is 'unwanted' in some contexts may be acceptable in other contexts. For instance, some form of stereotypic movement or vocalisation may release tension and be perfectly acceptable at home, but not in church or in the classroom.

POSSIBILITIES FOR PREVENTION AND CURE

Prevention

The incidence of people with ASD may be reduced by genetic counselling. In particular, couples who have relatives with ASD, or relatives who fall within the broader autism phenotype (BAP), or who are themselves autistic or who fall within the BAP, can be advised of their increased chance of having a child on the spectrum. This, however, re-introduces the question as to whether or not it is desirable to manipulate population frequencies of normally distributed traits that can facilitate high academic achievement.

The incidence of ASDs might also, theoretically, be reduced by detection *in utero* and subsequent abortion. However, there is at present no way of identifying a fetus with the potential for later development of ASD. And if there were, abortion would be highly controversial for numerous reasons.

If it were ever proved that autism can result solely from some environmental factor or set of factors operating *in utero* or very early childhood in the absence of any evidence of a familial disposition to autism-related behavioural traits, eliminating exposure to such environmental factors could lower the incidence of ASD without interfering with the gene pool. To date, no such factor has been identified.

For infants born into multiplex families, and therefore at heightened risk for the development of ASD, it may be possible to reduce this risk by intervening in the first year of life. A study by Green et al. (2015) reported some encouraging results using 'Video Interaction to Promote Positive Parenting' with very young high-risk infants. However, a great deal more research would be needed to demonstrate whether or not 'pre-emptive' intervention may be effective.

Cure

Most parents of a child with ASD are – at least in the years following diagnosis – desperate to find a cure for their child. The ideal of 'different, not disabled' propounded by the neurodiversity movement must ring hollow to parents of a 6;0 year old who compulsively eats grass and doesn't speak, or of a clever 10;0 year old who clings to the car door screaming every morning when taken to school. Not only do parents of any young autistic child bear extra burdens, they also suffer the disappointment of not having an 'ordinary child' who has friends, plays football or goes to ballet class, who will pass the usual exams, even if not brilliantly, have boy/girlfriends, settle down with a secure future, and be there for them in their old age. Parents of a child with ASD are therefore easy prey for purveyors of miracle cures. However, of the dozens of interventions claiming to cure autism, few have been rigorously evaluated for either effectiveness or safety.

Many untested 'cures' for autism are made in entirely good faith, perhaps by parents who have seen their own child's autism radically diminish and who want to share their experience with other parents. Other treatments (whether to cure, or to relieve the severity of, an individual's autism) are proposed by behavioural practitioners such as special needs teachers, psychologists or occupational therapists who sincerely believe they have found a method 'that works' but who have not had their method evaluated objectively by disinterested others. Many proclaimed 'cures' are, however, offered by charlatans who stand to profit by selling something to desperate parents. As noted in an article by Shute:

> Snake-oil salesmen litter the Web. One site tells parents they can 'defeat the autism in your child' by buying a $299 book; another touts a video of 'an autistic girl improving after receiving [expensive and possibly dangerous] stem cell injections'. (Shute, 2010: 82)

Among the more bizarre interventions anecdotally claimed to offer a cure are swimming with dolphins, getting a large friendly dog as a pet, and dosing the child with a substance similar to bleach.

More encouragingly, reports of individuals diagnosed with ASD in early childhood who no longer warrant ASD diagnosis in later childhood or early adulthood (see Chapter 2) suggest that for some individuals at least, an 'optimal outcome' – i.e. essentially a 'cure' – is possible, given intensive psychosocial or behavioural treatment from very early childhood (Orinstein et al., 2014; but see also Bölte, 2014). Optimal outcome (OO) individuals retain traces of the significant SEC impairments and RRBs that characterised them at the time of diagnosis. But having few close friends and somewhat restricted interests does not constitute a mental health disorder. Unless the individual is anxious or depressed for reasons related to their residual autism, the diagnostic label has no further usefulness. Treatments that may contribute to optimal outcomes are considered in the next main section.

TREATMENT METHODS

Discriminating Between the Options

For the overwhelming majority of individuals with ASD for whom a cure is not achievable, there is a host of treatments on offer. For parents the choice must be bewildering. For practitioners prescribing medications or advising on other kinds of interventions, balancing the pros and cons of available treatments must also be daunting.

There are, however, ways of discriminating between treatment options. Three important distinctions will be used to structure the discussion in this subsection. These are distinctions between the following:

- *Evidence-based* as opposed to *non-evidence-based* treatments. This distinction is critical. As noted by Matson and colleagues:

  > The number of interventions used in the field of autism is astronomical. Unfortunately, while there are effective and well-researched methods, many of the techniques that parents use have no empirical support. These interventions are expensive, take up valuable time, and in some cases are dangerous. (Matson et al., 2013: 466)

  The distinction between 'effective and well-researched methods' and methods for which there is no acceptable empirical support is considered in some detail below.

- *Comprehensive treatment models (CTMs)* that target the set of behaviours that defines ASD, as opposed to *focused intervention practices (FIPs)* which target one particular facet of ASD-associated behaviour. This could be one facet of the defining impairments, for example poor eye contact, or repetitive utterances. Or one of the problems occurring in association with autism might be targeted, for instance pica or sleep problems.
- *Non-physical treatments* such as behavioural and psychosocial interventions and educational practices as opposed to *physical treatments* such as medications, dietary supplements, exclusionary diets, sensory or sensory-motor stimulation (with putative effects on the brain), or direct stimulation of brain activity.

Treatments also differ in a number of other ways which will not be systematically noted in what follows, but which may be important when considering treatment options in individual cases. These include:

- The age-group for which they are suitable.
- Where, by whom, and how the treatment is carried out, whether at home, in school or clinic; whether by parents/carers, or by one or more of a range of professionals or paid assistants; whether the intervention is self-delivered (e.g. using e-learning packages) or delivered one-to-one, or in formal or informal groups.
- The cost of the treatment.

Evidence-based versus Non-evidence-based Treatments

Evidence-based treatments

By 'evidence-based' is meant that the efficacy, safety and cost-effectiveness of the treatment have been assessed in methodologically rigorous **efficacy studies** (plural) and consistently found to be effective, acceptably safe even if there are some side-effects, and cost-effective. All medicines and other treatments approved by national authorities such as the Federal Drugs Administration (FDA) in the US or the National Institute for Clinical Excellence (NICE) in the UK are evidence-based in this sense. Some commonly used efficacy study designs are outlined in Box 12.1.

Box 12.1 Efficacy study designs

Open label studies monitor the progress made by participants having a previously untested treatment. The participants (and/or their families or carers) know that they are having the treatment and they know the effects the treatment should have if successful.

Crossover designs used to evaluate the effectiveness of physical interventions consist of a period when participants are on treatment and a period during which they receive a **placebo**. Behaviour at the beginning and end of each period is compared to assess behavioural change, and the behavioural change on treatment and on placebo is compared to test the prediction that more improvement will be seen over the treatment period than the placebo period. Half the group will start with a treatment phase and half on placebo, and allocation to these subgroups should be randomised using an approved procedure. If neither the actively involved researchers nor the participants and their families know which individual is in which subgroup, this is a **double blind trial**. If the researchers know about subgroup membership but the participants and their families do not, this is a **single blind trial**.

Crossover designs used for the evaluation of non-physical interventions compare progress during periods of treatment with progress during periods of no treatment (making blind trials impossible) or alternative treatment (in which case blind trials are possible, but difficult to ensure).

Parallel designs are commonly used in the evaluation of both physical and non-physical interventions. In this type of design the progress of two groups of participants is compared, one of which receives the intervention that is being evaluated while the control or comparison group receives either a placebo (in studies of physical interventions) or no treatment/a contrasting intervention (in studies of non-physical interventions). Participants are randomly allocated to groups. This type of design is referred to as a **randomised control trial (RCT)**. Double blind trials should be used when evaluating physical interventions, but are less easy to achieve in studies evaluating non-physical interventions.

Single subject experimental designs (SSEDs) assess a single-measure outcome in a single participant who acts as their own control in an 'off-on' or 'off-on-off' treatment paradigm.

The **open label design** constitutes an appropriate starting point for evaluating an intervention, in that it can produce suggestive evidence such as might be needed before embarking on a large-scale controlled study. However, open label studies cannot prove that any positive effects result from the intervention as opposed to **non-specific factors**. **Crossover designs** can produce clearly interpretable and reliable findings when used to evaluate physical treatment methods, but are less satisfactory for the evaluation of non-physical interventions, because there is no exact equivalent to a placebo. **Parallel designs** may therefore be preferred in efficacy studies of non-physical interventions for people with ASD, although using no treatment control groups is ethically questionable. **Single subject experimental designs (SSEDs)** are particularly useful for assessing treatment effects in conditions such as ASD where it may be difficult to carry out group-based efficacy studies. And although findings from isolated studies using this design carry very little weight, consistent findings from a set of related SSEDs can provide useful preliminary evidence concerning a particular treatment.

More detailed points of method with particular relevance for efficacy studies of interventions for autism are outlined in Box 12.2. Fuller accounts of issues relating to design and methodology in the evaluation of interventions for autism can be found in Smith et al. (2007).

As is clear from the above, acceptance as an evidence-based treatment involves passing very stringent tests of both effectiveness and safety. But if these tests are passed, the treatment can be used with confidence. For a particularly clear summary of the processes involved in licensing a treatment for use see McClure (2014).

Non-evidence-based treatments

Non-evidence-based treatments include all those where:

- Efficacy tests have not been carried out.
- Efficacy tests have been carried out, but have not been methodologically rigorous.
- Methodologically rigorous efficacy tests have produced negative or mixed findings.

Borderline treatments

The distinction between evidence-based and non-evidence-based treatments is not always clear-cut. New treatments have to be tried out, cautiously at first, perhaps using an open label study design (see Box 12.1 above). The first one or two large-scale efficacy studies may produce promising results – for example, findings that are mixed but predominantly positive; or findings that suggest that a particular subset of people with ASD can be helped in this way. In such cases, further investigation is needed.

Evidence-based Non-physical Treatments

This section outlines nine psychosocial or educational programmes which have been shown in methodologically acceptable studies to produce at least some significant behavioural gains when used with people with ASD. There is considerable overlap in the kinds of methods used in most of these programmes. However, they also differ in a number of ways, for example in the age range targeted, in the goals of intervention and in the settings in which they may be delivered.

Box 12.2   Points of method in efficacy studies of interventions for autism

Participant groups should be:

- Large enough to have **statistical power**.
- Fully representative of the group targeted by the treatment, avoiding sampling bias.
- Reasonably homogeneous in terms of diagnosis, sex, age and ability; and, in the case of studies using parallel designs, groups should be matched on factors that might influence outcomes.

Interventions should be:

- Delivered in the same way to all participants, for example in terms of drug dosage or the precise methods used in non-physical interventions (this is particularly important when several different people are involved in delivering a psychosocial or educational intervention, perhaps across several different schools or research centres: training may be required).
- Delivered by more than one teacher/therapist working with different individuals (in non-physical interventions); and, in studies using a parallel design, the commitment of those delivering the intervention under study should be no greater than commitment to the comparison intervention.

Measures used to assess behaviour before and after intervention should:

- Relate clearly to the behaviours targeted.
- Be clearly defined and operationalised, so that different assessors all work to the same standard.

Assessors (those evaluating behaviour before and after treatment) should:

- Not be involved in delivering the intervention.
- Be trained in rating behaviour on the outcome measures and in the coding system used to enter ratings into a database; and assessor reliability should be systematically checked by having more than one assessor rating a proportion of the assessment sessions.

Applied Behaviour Analysis (ABA)   ABA as a treatment for autism is based on the principles of behaviourist **learning theory** as exemplified in the 'Lovaas model' (Lovaas et al., 1989). Key features of this model are: (1) accurate and objective observation and data-recording of an individual's behaviour; (2) an understanding of the immediate cause(s) of the behaviour – what precipitates it and what maintains it; and (3) a step-by-step cumulative process to replace maladaptive behaviour with adaptive behaviour by manipulation of the precipitating and sustaining factors. Rewards such as verbal approval or small treats are given for desired responses or approximations to such responses, with rewards withheld in other circumstances.

ABA has for many years been used relatively successfully (short of a cure) with young children with ASD (Herbert & Brandsma, 2002; Granpeesheh et al., 2009). Although focusing at any one time on highly specific behaviours (e.g. increased tolerance of eye contact; using a spoon to eat, instead of fingers), when used with infants or young children over an extended period the treatment may be considered to constitute a **comprehensive treatment model (CTM)**. However, ABA is most successful when used in **focused intervention practices (FIPs)** with older individuals, for example to ameliorate challenging behaviours or to increase the use of verbal requests (Matson et al., 2011; Bishop-Fitzpatrick et al., 2014).

When used intensively with young children with autism, ABA is delivered one-to-one by a trained therapist (or team of therapists) working in the child's home. This has some disadvantages. In particular, family life must be organised around treatment sessions. In addition, the intensive use of trained professionals over an extended period is expensive. Although many countries will now fund ABA or other ABA-based treatments (see below), funds allocated may not be sufficient, or not forthcoming (perhaps because a child has not yet been authoritatively diagnosed) and families may have to bear some or all of the costs. Intrusiveness and expense are not issues for all families. I have seen ABA-based treatment carried out effectively with children in families where both parents are in full-time well-paid work, and the employment of a therapist is actually less disruptive to family life than a treatment requiring intensive input from one or more parent.

A more cogent objection to ABA when used in unmodified form with young children with ASD is that it is essentially adult-led and imposed on a child. Moreover, in the past, certain practices associated with ABA were strongly criticised on ethical grounds. These practices were discontinued long ago, and ABA therapist training now stresses the importance of establishing a positive relationship with the child being treated. Nevertheless, ABA remains essentially an adult-led, controlling intervention.

Early Intensive Behavioural Intervention (EIBI)   As its name indicates, EIBI is an intensive form of ABA which, to be maximally effective, must be used early in the child's life (Klintwall & Eikeseth, 2014). It is delivered by trained therapists usually working in the child's home for at least 20 hours per week.

EIBI suffers from the same potential disadvantages as ABA (when used as a comprehensive treatment for young children with autism). In particular, it is expensive and risks being intrusive. However, descriptions of current practices in the delivery of EIBI go a long way towards mitigating the essentially controlling nature of ABA (see, for example, www.childautism.org.uk/ABA). EIBI is widely available and the treatment of choice for many funding authorities as well as families.

It is important to note that EIBI (and by association ABA) is evidence-based in so far as a small number of group-based efficacy studies have produced mainly positive findings. However, two comprehensive reviews of available evidence have concluded that results from these studies should be considered with caution (Warren et al., 2011; Reichow et al., 2012). Moreover, claims that ABA/EIBI can cure autism have not been substantiated (Bölte, 2014).

Functional Communication Training (FCT)   FCT is a widely used behaviourally-based focused intervention practice (FIP) for problem behaviours in nonverbal individuals with or without ASD. The treatment, first described by Carr and Durand in 1985, involves identifying situations in which a particular problem behaviour occurs and analysing why the behaviour occurs – what the individual achieves by, for example, hitting out, throwing a tantrum or biting their hand. The individual is then provided with and trained to use a more acceptable way of non-verbally communicating what they do not have the words to express, for instance 'I've had enough'/'I can't do this'/'Leave me alone'. There is ample evidence that FCT is effective (see Kurtz et al., 2011, for a review of evaluative studies). It is also ethical and safe, whereas some other ways of dealing with problem behaviours, for example by physical restraint, are vulnerable to abuse.

Early Start Denver Model (ESDM)   This CTM is designed for use with infants and toddlers aged from 12 to 48 months. It uses a very systematic approach involving specific individualised objectives agreed with the family, and specified activities using structured teaching strategies broadly based on principles from ABA. Progress is measured through ongoing data collection on each targeted objective. As with EIBI, intervention using ESDM is only effective if carried out intensively (a minimum of 15 hours per week and preferably more than 20 hours).

However, ESDM treatment differs from ABA/EIBI in certain critical respects. Most importantly it is play-based, utilising the individual child's interests and preferences. Treatment is also relationship-based, in that it is delivered through shared activities and interpersonal exchange, with an emphasis on positive affect. It is generally carried out one-to-one, partly by a trained therapist working in a clinic setting and/or in the child's home, and partly by family members working under the guidance of a therapist. ESDM treatment may also be delivered in small group sessions, reducing costs.

The stated aims of ESDM treatment are to increase the child's rate of normal development in all domains, while simultaneously decreasing the symptoms of autism. The rationale behind the intervention is that early intensive behavioural stimulation can lead not only to behavioural change in a child with ASD, but also to changes in brain growth and activity (Sullivan et al., 2014). ESDM treatment has been shown to be behaviourally effective in one well-controlled group efficacy study (Dawson et al., 2010) and in several methodologically acceptable single-subject efficacy studies. Preliminary evidence of normalised brain activity was reported by Dawson et al. (2012).

ESDM training manuals and training courses are now available in many languages all over the world, with therapist training, ESDM treatment and parent support often being offered under the auspices of a university department which also carries out research into ASD. There are numerous such departments in the

US (e.g. Duke University's Center for Autism and Brain Development, where ESDM treatment and associated brain research are carried out); also in Canada and in Australia (see Box 12.3). Research and practice in the autism field are less well integrated in the UK, which is regrettable.

Box 12.3 An example of the integration of applied research with services to individuals with ASD and their families within a university setting

The Victorian Autism Specific Early Learning and Care Centre (V-ASELCC) was established at LaTrobe University in Melbourne as a collaboration between the university's Autism Research Centre in the School of Psychology and Public Health, its Community Children's Centre (providing day-long care for young children) and the Royal Children's Hospital. V-ASELCC is funded by the Australian Federal Government, and is involved in all of the following:

Early intervention using the ESDM (see main text). Treatment is delivered by ESDM-trained professionals to small groups of very young children with ASD in a specially designated wing of the Children's Centre.

Parent support A key component of the ESDM is parent understanding and collaboration, and training workshops and information sessions for parents are held regularly at the Centre. Treatment targets for their child are agreed with parents and progress is monitored jointly by parents and therapists.

Staff training Training courses for ESDM therapists are offered under the auspices of the V-ASELCC. Training in the early detection of possible cases of ASD is also offered to Maternal and Child Health nurses working in the community, using the results of research carried out in the Autism Research Centre. Training on the ADOS is also offered to community practitioners and researchers.

Applied research undertaken in the Autism Research Centre has not only included studies contributing to methods of early identification (Barbaro et al., 2013), but also studies evaluating methods of delivering ESDM treatment to toddlers and preschoolers with ASD (Vivanti et al., 2014). Studies of ASD characteristics and causes are also ongoing within the Autism Research Centre.

(With thanks to Professor Cheryl Dissanayake for her assistance in drafting this account)

Pivotal Response Treatment/Training (PRT)   PRT, like ESDM treatment, utilises some of the principles of behaviourist learning theory as in ABA but in naturalistic settings and using naturalistic forms of reward. When used as a Comprehensive Treatment Model, the stated aims of PRT are also broader than those of either EIBI or ESDM treatment in that the 'pivotal' areas targeted are those that are implicated in a wide range of day-to-day behaviours. These include motivation and the self-initiation of behaviour, responsiveness to multiple environmental cues, and the **self-regulation** of emotional state (Koegel et al., 2006; Koegel & Koegel, 2012). These pivotal areas of function are targeted with the aim of facilitating the child's development overall, but with particular reference to social, emotional and communication abilities.

PRT also differs from the previously described treatments in that it is specifically designed to be used consistently across a range of settings, promoting the **generalisation** of gains in target behaviours. Thus, although PRT when used with young children with ASD is described as first and foremost 'family centred', other healthcare providers such as occupational therapists or speech therapists working with the child are also involved in delivering the treatment, as are staff in any daycare or preschool attended by the child.

Although the delivery of PRT involves training a broad range of individuals, it has been shown that this can be done effectively and economically using a video feedback training package (Robinson, 2011).

PRT has also been developed for use with older children with ASD in classroom settings (Stahmer et al., 2010, 2012). It may also be used as an FIP, for example, to improve joint attention skills (Vismara & Lyons, 2007).

Efficacy studies of PRT have produced generally positive findings (see the review and critique by Cadogan & McCrimmon, 2015). However, most of these studies were carried out with school-age children. PRT has not been widely used with infants and toddlers (but see Steiner et al., 2013).

Learning Experiences: An Alternative Programme for Preschoolers and Parents (LEAP) A key component of this programme, developed by Strain and Bovey (2008), is that it is delivered in inclusive preschool settings, with children with ASD learning in classrooms alongside typically developing preschoolers. Children attend for 15 hours per week of classroom instruction provided by a trained teacher and an assistant working with approximately 10 typically developing children and 3 to 4 children with ASD. A speech and language therapist, and sometimes an occupational therapist or physiotherapist, is commonly available to work with the children in specially arranged classrooms designed to support child-directed play. The primary goals of the curriculum are to expose children with autism to typical preschool activities and to adapt the typical curriculum for the children with autism only when necessary. Social interaction with typically developing peers, peer modelling and peer-mediated instruction are central to the programme, which does not include one-to-one intervention. However, opportunities for systematic instruction are part of the curriculum, and ABA-related teaching–learning strategies are used systematically, for example to prompt and reinforce targeted behaviours. Parent involvement and parent training are included in the programme, with a view to generalising behavioural gains from school to home.

There is a body of evidence supporting the effectiveness of LEAP. Most of the positive evidence comes from single-case studies, although two group-based efficacy studies also demonstrated effectiveness (Strain & Bovey, 2011; Boyd et al., 2014). The demands on teachers and assistants delivering the programme are, however, considerable, and there is some risk of loss of **fidelity** and teacher burnout (Coman et al., 2013).

Treatment and Education of Autistic and related Communication handicapped Children (TEACCH) – Structured Teaching 'Division TEACCH' is an organisation centred at the University of North Carolina, which offers a broad range of resources and services to individuals with ASD or related problems, their families, and others involved in the treatment, education and care of people with ASD throughout their lives. The intervention known as Structured Teaching was the first of these services to be developed many decades ago, and the principles of Structured Teaching are now used in homes, schools, clinics and adult residential settings world-wide.

Structured Teaching utilises some of the principles of behaviourist learning theory, as do other evidence-based treatments described above. However, the TEACCH method differs from those previously described in that it is designed to capitalise on two notable characteristics of people with ASD: first, their tendency to develop and adhere to routines; and secondly, their relatively good ability to use visual information as compared to difficulties in utilising auditory information. Utilising rather than combating the autistic person's preference for the familiar, Structured Teaching is undertaken as far as possible in the same surroundings and in the same manner following a familiar schedule. Tasks are as far as possible based on the use of materials to be handled, and pictures are used to convey or support instructions as to what is involved in any particular task. Visual supports are also used to indicate sequences and schedules in daily life, for instance the timetable to be followed on a particular day at school, or the sequence of actions involved in making a cup of coffee. Visual prompts are used to support the development of adaptive habits and routines, such as washing hands before a meal.

When used with young children in the home, tasks are generally designed to increase daily-living skills following a developmental schedule. However, the TEACCH Structured Teaching method is most widely used in educational settings and in speech-language therapy or occupational therapy clinics, where very specific competences, such as number concepts, matching written labels to pictures or tieing shoelaces, are targeted. This treatment method therefore comes into the category of a multi-purpose FIP, and evidence confirming the effectiveness of Structured Teaching methods comes from studies with narrowly focused targets (see, for example, Carson et al., 2008). A meta-analysis by Virues-Ortega et al. (2013) showed that Structured Teaching should not, however, be considered an evidence-based CTM. In Chapter 13 more is said about the broad TEACCH approach to supporting individuals and families.

Augmentative and Alternative Communication systems (AACs) The best known and, at the time of writing, the most widely used AAC is the *Picture Exchange Communication System (PECS)* (Bondy & Frost, 2001; Frost & Bondy, 2011). PECS was developed for use with nonverbal children or adults, including those with autism (see Box 4.3 for an example of the successful use of PECS by a nonverbal child with complex problems).

As its name suggests, the major aim of PECS is to promote and facilitate communication. This is done using pictures, such as those illustrated in Figure 12.1.

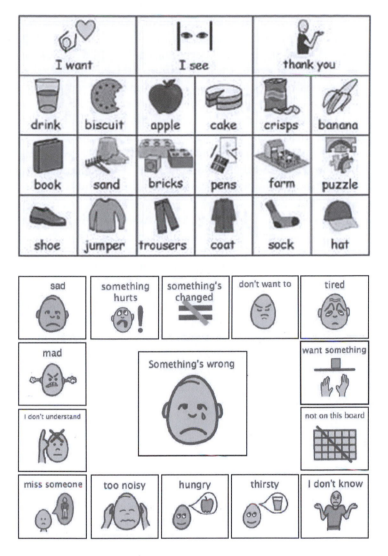

Figure 12.1 *Examples of picture cards used in some augmentative and alternative communication systems*

In the first phase of treatment the link between a picture and what it stands for may have to be established. Once this has been done, the individual is prompted to pass the picture of a desired object, for example a juice drink, to a 'communication partner', who immediately supplies the desired object. This is the first and most critical step towards intentional communication. The 'vocabulary' of pictured items is then gradually increased according to the individual's major wants and needs, and communicative use of pictures is generalised by being used with different communicative partners and in different situations. For learners who progress beyond the use of single pictures, phrases such as 'I want' are first introduced, and minimal 'sentences' such as 'I want juice drink' are amplified or varied as additional verbs, prepositions and adjectives are introduced (see Figure 12.1). The ability to respond to requests or questions from a communication partner represents the most advanced stage of communication therapy covered by PECS. Once communication using pictures has been established, a further aim of PECS is to promote the individual's use of speech. However, although PECS may be considered an evidence-based treatment for communication impairments, whether related to autism or in individuals with other conditions such as learning disability or verbal apraxia without autism, it has proved less successful in promoting speech (Flippin et al., 2010; Lerna et al., 2014).

Most other forms of AAC are designed mainly to overcome problems of speech production, rather than impaired communication *per se*. However, a simplified signing system such as *Makaton* may be used initially to promote and facilitate communication (see, for example, Scattone & Billhofer, 2008). Makaton clearly has an advantage over PECS in so far as it does not involve a physical set of symbols. However, individuals with verbal dyspraxia or related forms of motor co-ordination problems may find signing difficult (Gernsbacher et al., 2008). In addition, sign-based communication requires that communication partners are conversant with the system being used.

The use of *computers* and *keyboards* using pictograms is a relatively long-established form of AAC for people with major physical disabilities.[2] Most computer-based systems now incorporate a speech generation device (SGD) of the kind used by the cosmologist Stephen Hawking, and are available in hand-held form (tablets). There is a burgeoning array of apps designed to promote communication using electronically generated speech (Mirenda, 2014). No doubt developments in this area will continue, including practitioner and user reports of the usefulness of individual apps.

At the time of writing, one study comparing the usefulness of PECS, signing and a speech generation device to promote and facilitate communication in children with ASD has been reported (Van der Meer, Sutherland et al., 2012). The most interesting finding from this preliminary study was that the children taking part had different preferences for the AACs offered them, and all made gains in communication when treated using their preferred option. (For a discussion of the need to determine what treatment works best for each individual, see Stahmer, Schreibman, & Cunningham, 2011).

Cognitive behavioural therapy (CBT)   CBT is a highly structured, focused intervention practice (FIP) widely used for the treatment of mental health disorders

---

[2]In the mid-1980s I shared an office with a psychologist who was working with a man with a very severe form of cerebral palsy that made speech or signing impossible. This man was thought to be moderately or even severely learning disabled until supplied with a computer and a set of icons as a keyboard which he instantly mastered, proving himself to be of entirely normal intelligence. I can't recall how he was enabled to operate this AAC, but I do remember the mixture of elation (at having enabled this man to communicate) and horror (in imagining his previous 'locked in' state) felt by my colleague.

in the general population, that has been used successfully to treat some specific problems in high-functioning adolescents with ASD (Danial & Wood, 2013). Problems for which there is evidence of effectiveness are anxiety (Sukhodolsky et al., 2013; Ung et al., 2015) and – provisionally – obsessive behaviours (Vause et al., 2014). A meta-analysis of studies using CBT with autistic adults showed that this form of treatment can be used successfully to reduce mental health problems, but is not effective in increasing social or communicative behaviours (Binnie & Blainey, 2013).

Borderline Evidence-based Non-physical Treatments

Non-physical CTMs falling into the 'borderline evidence-based' category, as defined above, include several long-established treatment methods for which there is some limited evidence of effectiveness when used with toddlers and young children with ASD.

One such intervention is the *Walden Toddler Program* (McGee et al., 1994). This programme was developed as one component of services offered by Emory University's Autism Center, which provides information, resources and support to families of children with ASD aged 0–5 years. The Walden Toddler Program uses a modified form of ABA called 'incidental teaching', which capitalises on the learner's personal interests and preferences across a range of settings. When used in childcare settings, treatment is delivered within an inclusive group of children with and without autism (cf. LEAP, described above). Parents are trained in delivery of the programme at home, ensuring that the treatment is maintained across settings and is intensive. The Walden Toddler Program aims to promote verbal language, social development and independent daily living skills, and an efficacy study by McGee et al. (1999) suggested that these aims were unambiguously achieved. However, the methodology used in this study has been criticised (Stahmer & Ingersoll, 2004).

Other borderline evidence-based treatments include several that focus on treatment through child-led play and positive interactions between the child and the therapist, parent(s), teachers and peers who may be involved in delivering the treatment. Examples of treatments falling within this broad category include the following.

Developmental Individual-difference Relationship-based (DIR)-Floortime approach (Greenspan & Weider, 1999, 2009; see also Hess, 2013). A handful of efficacy studies of this treatment have been carried out, with some positive findings. However, a review of these studies found them to be methodologically weak (Mercer, 2015).

The *Early Social Interaction (ESI)* method (Wetherby & Woods, 2006) was developed in response to the National Research Council's (US) (2001) recommendation that 'intensive' treatment for infants and very young children with ASD should be interpreted as involving at least 25 hours of programmed teaching/learning every week and, by implication, a collaboration between community-based services and parents/carers. The way in which this collaboration is established and delivered is critical, as interestingly discussed and demonstrated in an efficacy study of ESI (Wetherby et al., 2014).

The *Social Communication, Emotional Regulation, Transactional Supports (SCERTS)* intervention (Prizant et al., 2006) has been assessed in one evaluative study (Molteni et al., 2013) which reported some provisional evidence of effectiveness.

Similarly, the *Relationship Development Intervention (RDI)* programme (Gutstein, 2000) has only been evaluated in one study (Gutstein et al., 2007) reporting provisional evidence of effectiveness.

The *Son-Rise Programme*, sometimes known as the *Option Method* (Kaufman & Kaufman, 1976), has proved a survivor. This intensive, home-based treatment has generally had a bad press, mainly because of its claim to have achieved a cure (of the originators' son),[3] but also because of the excessive demands it puts on families (Williams & Wishart, 2003). However, one well-designed but small-scale efficacy study demonstrated positive effects, leading the authors to conclude that further evaluation is indicated (Houghton et al., 2013).

The *Children's Toddler School (CTS)* intervention is entirely community-based using an inclusive childcare setting with a teacher–child ratio of 1:3 (Stahmer & Ingersoll, 2004). Treatment methods are eclectic, comprising a mix of incidental teaching, pivotal response training (PRT), structured teaching (TEACCH), the picture exchange communication system (PECS), and DIR/Floortime. A recent quite large-scale efficacy study by Stahmer, Akshoomoff, & Cunningham (2011) produced evidence of gains in language, adaptive behaviour and overall developmental level in children who had attended the CTS for at least eight months.

The *Hanen More Than Words Programme* (Sussman, 1999; Weitzman, 2013), like several of the intervention programmes mentioned above, was developed within a university department offering a range of services to children with ASD and their families. Although well known and quite widely used, this parent-skilling intervention has not been well researched (but see Carter et al., 2011). The Hanen Centre's more recently developed *Takes Two to Talk* programme suffers from the same lack of supportive evidence.

The *Early Bird* treatment programme (Shields, 2001) is designed to support parents with a child aged 4;0–8;0 years to develop their child's social and communication abilities. The programme is run under the auspices of the National Autistic Society in the UK which organises training and workshops for professionals and parents, as well as providing written and video support materials. The programme utilises methods and materials from TEACCH and from PECS, and is based on the ethical principles articulated by the Society as 'SPELL' (standing for Structure, Positive, Empathy, Low arousal, Links). Early Bird is widely used by speech-language therapists and preschool special needs teachers in the UK working collaboratively with parents. Unfortunately, no studies of its effectiveness have been published in the peer-reviewed literature.

---

[3]A relative of mine who was involved in the treatment of the Kaufmans' son confirms the claim of what would now be referred to as an optimal outcome rather than a cure.

The *Preschool Autism Communication Trial (PACT)* is a parent-skilling intervention developed by a multidisciplinary team of professionals working with young children with autism in the UK. In contrast to the untested Early Bird programme, PACT has been rigorously evaluated at various stages. Some early gains were reported (Green et al., 2010), and despite doubts concerning its cost effectiveness (Byford et al., 2015), PACT has recently been shown to have significant positive effects on longer-term outcomes (Pickles et al., 2016). Although placed here under the heading of 'Borderline Evidence-based Treatments', therefore, it may well be the case that PACT, once more widely used and tested, moves into the group of 'Evidence-based Treatments'.

Various forms of *psychotherapy* may be used with the aims of improving socio-emotional interaction and communication or treating mental health disorders and problem behaviours across the age range of individuals with ASD (El-Ghoroury & Krackow, 2011). Psychoanalytic understandings of autistic behaviour did not die with Bettelheim (1967; see Chapter 1), but have continued to be argued for by, in particular, Tustin (1981/1995; see also Alvarez, 1996; Alvarez & Reid, 1999), and psychotherapeutic treatment models remain dominant in France. Play therapy is the treatment of choice when working with young children (see, for example, Josefi & Ryan, 2004). 'Acting out' through drawings (Rhode, 2009) or fantasy play (Gould, 2011) may be used with school-age children (see Figure 12.2). A variety of 'talking therapies' may be used in the treatment of high-functioning adolescents and adults (see the special issues of the *Journal of Contemporary Psychoanalysis* and *Psychoanalytic Inquiry*, both published in 2011). Unequivocal evidence of the efficacy of psychotherapeutic approaches to treating people with ASD is not available. Cumulatively, however, individual case reports published over very many years suggest that this approach to treatment does have positive outcomes for certain individuals at various life stages.

Comment

Many of the treatments mentioned in the above subsection are marketed vigorously (and in good faith) by their proponents, despite the fact that there is only fragile evidence, or no evidence, to support claims made for their effectiveness. All the treatment methods in this borderline category *may* be effective, safe and cost-effective, either as CTMs or as FIPs. They *may* work well for subsets of individuals with ASD. There *may* be successful outcomes on some key measures but not others. But these are unknowns (except possibly in the case of PACT).

It is worrying that several of the above methods are widely used despite (at the time of writing) not being securely evidence-based. There are, in addition, numerous other psychosocial, behavioural and educational methods that are not mentioned here. Some of these might fall into the 'borderline evidence-based' category, though space precludes their mention. Others, however, could be described as 'fad' treatments with no clear theoretical basis and no likelihood of effectiveness (Foxx & Mulick, 2015).

Figure 12.2 *An illustration of how drawing may be used to externalise and understand feelings as a means of increasing behavioural self-control (with thanks to Lizzie and family)*

Evidence-based Physical Treatments

There are, at the time of writing, no securely evidence-based physical Comprehensive Treatment Models for autism. As suggested by LeClerc and Easley (2015: 393), this may be because:

> ... pharmaceutical companies have generally shied away from investing in treatments for autism ... In particular, the pharmaceutical industry has shown risk aversion with regard to conducting research in autism, a disorder with a hazy pathophysiology, a high level of heterogeneity, few clear biomarkers, and poorly developed outcome measures for clinical studies.

However, a number of medications targeting specific problem behaviours in ASD have been approved for cautious use by several of the national advisory/licensing authorities (see McClure, 2014, and LeClerc & Easley, 2015, for reviews). These include the following:

> *Melatonin* has been found to be effective for the treatment of sleep problems in children with ASD, preferably to be used only if behavioural interventions have failed, and then preferably in combination with a behavioural programme.

> *Risperidone* and *aripiprazole* (both antipsychotics) have been approved by the FDA for the treatment and management of irritability, challenging behaviour and self-harm. Caveats concerning the use of these drugs include advice against using them for children; the need to ensure short-term use only; and the need to monitor individuals taking these drugs to ensure that adverse side-effects (of which several are common) do not outweigh behavioural benefits.

> *Methylphenidate* (a stimulant drug marketed under the brand name *Ritalin*) is cautiously approved by some but not all national agencies for the treatment of comorbid ADHD. Caveats here are that this drug is effective only for some individuals; also that there is a considerable risk of a range of adverse side-effects (McClure, 2014).

> *Anticonvulsants* and *antidepressants* (including *fluoxetine*) are recommended strictly for use to control, respectively, any epileptic or mood disorders (including anxiety and obsessive behaviours) that may co-occur with ASD.

Borderline Evidence-based Physical Treatments

Two forms of treatment targeting ASD-specific behaviours are currently under fairly intensive investigation with some promising, but as yet inconclusive, results. These treatments are as follows:

> *Oxytocin* medication may prove useful to enhance social engagement (Liu et al., 2012; Gordon et al., 2013; but see also Dadds et al., 2014). This treatment has not as yet been approved by any of the national vetting agencies (McClure, 2014).

> *Transmagnetic stimulation (TMS)* involves direct stimulation of the brain designed to correct a postulated imbalance between excitatory and inhibitory neural activity (as described in Chapter 8) and to correct 'aberrant synaptic plasticity'. In a review of available studies, Oberman et al. (2015) concluded that there is not yet enough evidence to support the use of TMS as a treatment for ASD, stressing the need for further research.

Non-evidence-based Physical Treatments

Untested or inadequately tested treatment methods

Some argued-for treatments are based on purely anecdotal evidence. More often, claims for a treatment are made on the basis of efficacy studies that are methodologically inadequate. Many such treatments might be described as falling within the group of **complementary and alternative medicines (CAMs)**, sometimes referred to as **alternative and allied healthcare (AAH)**.

It is important to stress that if any currently untested, or inadequately tested, interventions for ASD, or for specific facets of ASD-related behaviour, were rigorously evaluated and found to be safe, effective and cost-effective, that treatment method would be recommended by the relevant advisory and licensing authorities. To give just one example: acupuncture, which is widely used in China as an intervention for autism, has been subjected to a small number of properly conducted efficacy studies, with some evidence of effectiveness (Cheuk et al., 2011; Lee et al., 2012). Although at the time of writing this evidence is inconclusive, if further well-controlled efficacy studies were to strengthen the already promising evidence, acupuncture as a treatment for certain facets of ASD-related behaviour would be accepted as evidence-based and almost certainly licensed for use.

Treatments that have been evaluated with negative outcomes

There are, in addition, some treatments that have been assessed in methodologically rigorous studies and shown to be ineffective and/or unsafe. Some of these treatments are listed in Table 12.1.

Table 12.1 Physical treatments that have been reliably shown to be ineffective and/or unsafe

Treatment	Effectiveness and safety
Chelation	Ineffective (Davis et al., 2013). Unsafe (Brent, 2013; NICE, 2013)
Gluten or casein-free diet	Ineffective. Many undesirable side effects (Mulloy et al., 2010)
Hyperbaric oxygen therapy	Effectiveness unproven (Ghanizadeh, 2012; Halepoto et al., 2014). Unsafe (NICE, 2013)
Holding therapy	No objective evidence of effectiveness; ethically dubious and possibly unsafe (Chaffin et al., 2006; Mercer, 2013)
Vitamin and mineral supplements – various	Probably unjustified and may lead to excess intake (Lundin & Dwyer, 2014; Stewart et al., 2015)
Secretin injections	Ineffective (Williams et al., 2012)
Sensory integration therapy	Ineffective (Lang et al., 2012)
Auditory integration therapy	Ineffective (Sinha et al., 2011; see also NICE, 2013)

Unproven Does Not Necessarily Mean Useless

Despite the lack of evidence, or predominantly negative evidence, concerning the effectiveness of many widely publicised treatments for autism, both non-physical and physical, it may be that some such interventions are useful for some but not all individuals with ASD. Given the enormous diversity among individuals with ASD, this would not be surprising (Herbert & Weintraub, 2013; Stahmer, Schreibman, & Cunningham, 2011). However, more research is needed to identify which subsets of individuals either do or don't benefit from a particular form of treatment.

In addition, some interventions claiming to moderate autism-related behaviours may not achieve their stated aim, but do have demonstrably positive effects on parents' interactions with their child (Green et al., 2010; Carter et al., 2011). This is likely to be of benefit to the child in the longer term.

Placebo effects are also likely to be common (Masi et al., 2015). All of us are susceptible to placebo effects, especially when it is particularly important to us to feel that we are doing *something* to ameliorate a major health problem (our own cancer, our child's autism). We need to feel in control, as far as possible, and feeling at least partially in control can make us feel better, psychologically and sometimes physically. The way that parents feel about their child has consequences for the child – any child, not just a child with ASD. Reducing the feelings of helplessness and desperation that some parents feel in the early years of caring for an autistic child can have indirect beneficial effects for the child. If an unproven treatment method is harmless and believed by parents/carers to be efficacious, and especially if no evidence-based treatment is readily available or affordable for that family, then it could be counter-productive to argue against use of that treatment.

Making these points is not intended to legitimise the continued use of non-evidence-based treatments, let alone any that have been shown to be unsafe or to have significant undesirable side-effects, or to be ethically questionable. There are, now, evidence-based interventions for most facets of ASD that are effective, safe, ethically acceptable and cost-effective. These forms of intervention should be preferred unless or until any currently unproven treatment has been reliably shown to meet these criteria.

FUTURE DIRECTIONS

It is an exciting time to be writing about interventions for people with ASD, in that some treatment methods can at last be properly described as effective, safe and 'evidence-based'. In particular, although optimal outcomes are rare, there is evidence that very young children with an early diagnosis of ASD can benefit from certain well-specified treatment programmes delivered intensively. Perhaps most exciting is the possibility that early intensive treatment can capitalise on brain plasticity and reverse or compensate for abnormalities of brain growth and function that originate in the infant and toddler years. It is also encouraging that there are now various evidence-based interventions, some physical, some non-physical, that are effective and safe for treating many of the problem behaviours and mental health disorders that frequently co-occur with ASD, usually in older children or adults. Despite this exciting progress, there are notable gaps in the interventions literature, as identified below.

It has not to date been demonstrated that the positive effects of early intensive non-physical treatments are sustained and correlate with long-term outcomes.

The claim that early intensive treatment can reverse or compensate for abnormalities of brain growth and function has yet to be proved, and the theoretical bases for linking specific treatments (including potential physical treatments) with brain changes have not been clearly established.

There are no securely evidence-based physical treatments for the SEC impairments and RRBs that are diagnostic of ASD, although two such interventions (oxytocin and transmagnetic stimulation) show some promise.

Neither of the two major specifiers, learning disability and language impairment, have received much attention in the literature on ASD: Why do they so commonly co-occur with idiopathic ASD? Why are they so closely linked? And how might they be prevented, cured or treated? Preventing the co-occurrence of these major specifiers could help to meet the challenge of keeping autism-related genetic variations in the gene pool, while alleviating the distress suffered by individuals with low-functioning forms of ASD and their families, and mitigating the heavy demands that low-functioning autism in particular makes on State support and provision.

It is to be hoped that future research in the field will extend to answering the above questions.

SUMMARY

'Intervention' is defined here as including methods of prevention, cure or treatment of autism. Prevention and cure aim to reduce the incidence and prevalence, respectively, of autism in the population. Treatment of ASD-related behaviours and associated conditions aims to improve quality of life for affected individuals and to reduce demands on families, local services and the State.

Arguments for and against attempting to prevent or to cure autism are outlined, including arguments made by members of the neurodiversity movement. It is concluded that these arguments hold in so far as it would be disadvantageous to the species to lose from the gene pool those genetic variations that underlie facets of autism predisposing individuals to high achievement in certain fields. However, the argument made by some of the more extreme members of the neurodiversity movement against treating those facets of ASD-related behaviour and comorbidities that compromise quality of life is not accepted. The challenge is, therefore, to ensure the persistence in the gene pool of those variations predisposing individuals to certain kinds of academic success while alleviating the distress and difficulty affecting the large majority of individuals with ASD.

Potential methods of prevention are outlined and briefly discussed, including genetic counselling (which could impoverish the gene pool); abortion of identified prodromal ASD (which would be highly controversial if indeed feasible; and would also risk impoverishing the gene pool); and the identification and removal of environmental factors causing or significantly contributing to the development of ASD.

Regarding methods of cure, it is generally agreed by experts in the field (including major organisations representing parents) that there is currently no 100 per cent successful cure for autism. The desperation of many parents to find a cure for their child's autism is recognised as the main factor creating a profitable market for charlatans selling untested and sometimes potentially dangerous 'cures' on the web or in popular media. Encouragingly, however, there are now some authoritative reports that 'optimal outcomes' can be achieved in at least some individuals given intensive behavioural/psychosocial/educational treatment from very early childhood. Such individuals have some residual autistic traits, but these do not cause any unusual distress or difficulty such as would warrant a diagnosis.

With regard to treatments short of a cure, there have over the past 50 years been dozens, if not hundreds, of suggested treatments for autism, or for facets of autism, or for comorbid conditions associated with autism, few of which are evidence-based in the proper sense of the phrase. To be recognised as 'evidence-based', a treatment – whether for autism or any other disease or mental health disorder – must have been reliably shown to be effective, safe and cost-effective in methodologically stringent efficacy studies. Some frequently used efficacy study designs and points of method of particular relevance in efficacy studies of autism are outlined.

Using distinctions between Comprehensive Treatment Models (CTMs) and Focused Intervention Practices (FIPs), and between non-physical and physical treatments, the best-established evidence-based CTMs and FIPs for autism-related problems are then individually described. The most effective of these treatments are non-physical intervention programmes used from as early as 12 months of age and delivered intensively under the auspices of specifically trained practitioners. All use some of the principles exemplified in Applied Behavioral Analysis (ABA). However, the majority go beyond ABA in specifying the use of child-led activities, the active involvement of parents/carers, and systematic collaborative delivery across different settings, including inclusive settings. Elements of these effective treatment methods can be maintained through school into adulthood, where appropriate.

Some 'borderline-evidence-based' treatments are then more briefly described. Finally, treatments that have been evaluated for effectiveness, safety and cost-effectiveness but found to fail on one or more of these criteria are identified. Emphasis is placed on the importance of knowing which interventions are authoritatively described as unsafe, so that use of these treatments can be avoided. Treatments that are safe but which have been authoritatively judged to be ineffective should not, however, be dismissed out of hand. This is because they may be useful for some but not all individuals with ASD, and/or they may have useful effects other than those predicted in efficacy studies. In particular, they may have useful placebo effects directly or indirectly benefitting the autistic individual being treated.

In the short section headed 'Future Directions' it is recognised that there are still major gaps in our knowledge of how to treat, cure or selectively prevent ASD, and that these major limitations need to be addressed in future research.

CARE

AIMS

The aims of this chapter are to provide an introduction to the large and complex topic of care for people with ASD in the context of the principle of inclusion, and to demonstrate that, while examples of good practice can be cited, the ideals of inclusion are not often realised in practice.

INCLUSION

The Principle of Inclusion

Inclusion is used in this chapter in the broad sense of the moral right of every person to be included as a valued member of their society and not discriminated against because of difference (Renzaglia et al., 2003). According to the principles of **normalisation** (Nirje, 1969), from which the concept of inclusion developed, people with disabilities should be enabled to have lives as similar as possible to those of people without disabilities; they should be enabled to achieve good quality of life; and they should have the same human rights as people without disabilities. The concepts of both inclusion and normalisation take as their starting point that diversity is to be welcomed as enriching to communities, and provision should be made for this diversity in schools, workplaces and elsewhere. The more recently evolved 'neurodiversity movement', referred to in the previous chapter, reasserts these principles.

In this chapter the principle of inclusion sets the standard for identifying the care needs and rights of people with ASD, and for judging the quality of the provision made. According to current ideals in most developed countries, all members of society, including those with disabilities, should be provided with, or have access to, the following:

- Food, shelter, warmth, protection from harm.
- Emotional and social stimulation and support.
- Opportunities for physical, mental and social activity fostering the development and maintenance of capacities and skills.
- Health care, education, and employment or financial support as of right, and access to social services, financial and legal advice and representation as needed.

In addition, there should be recognition of the following rights:

- The right to self-determination in matters of care and daily living.
- The right to be valued and respected on equal terms with others.

In what follows, the provision of care for people with ASD is considered under three main headings. First, support for families caring for someone with ASD; secondly, residential arrangements and the provision of care outside the family home;

and thirdly, access to the services and rights listed under the bullet points above. Generalisations are necessarily made, which may not hold true for all countries and regions. Terms such as 'government', 'State' (with upper case initial letter, referring to a country; with lower case, referring to subregions of, for example, Australia or America), 'local authority', 'public service' are used variously and loosely to indicate the likely involvement of statutory authorities of one kind or another, while recognising that what is arranged and paid for by government-related authorities in one country or region may not be the responsibility of government-related authorities everywhere. For this reason, references to nation-specific laws or practices are generally avoided. The examples of good practice in caring for people with ASD and their families that are quoted are, however, mainly examples of provision in the UK – because these are the services I know about, not because they do not exist elsewhere.

In the final section of this chapter, which is also the final section of the book, the extent to which the ideals of inclusion have been achieved for people with ASD will be considered.

FAMILIES AND CARE

Roles

Ensuring that an individual with ASD receives the various sorts of care they need and to which they have a right is almost always critically dependent on members of the individual's family.[1]

Parents (or those undertaking the parental role(s)) directly provide for the survival needs of children, and sometimes also of dependent adults (see the first bullet point above). With other family members they also contribute directly and significantly to the provision of quality of life needs (second and third bullet points), although external agencies also have a role here. Health care, intervention and education, etc. (under the fourth bullet point) are generally provided by agencies outside the family. However, parents are likely to be the channel through which these services are accessed and monitored. Parents and other family members may also be involved in delivering health care and intervention to children and dependent adults with ASD, either under the direction of professionals or as initiated by themselves. Finally, it is the parents who bear the brunt of the stigmatising attitudes of society and who fight the battles on behalf of their offspring for recognition of them as valued individuals.

Having a child with ASD introduces unusual stresses into a family (Hayes & Watson, 2013; Nicholas & Kilmer, 2015), and if a family breaks down, the child's

---

[1]The term 'family' is taken to include adoptive, long-term foster and step-families; nuclear families, single-parent families, families based on long-term partnerships between same sex couples, and families in which grandparents or other non-parent family members are the major carers. This discussion will, however, use the terms 'parents', 'mother' and 'father' as conventionally understood when referring to research, most of which has focused on biological families.

or dependent adult's access to all the above forms of care is jeopardised. It is therefore important to identify these sources of stress so that appropriate support can be provided. Supporting families is thus a way of supporting individuals with ASD and ensuring that their care needs are met.

Sources of Stress

Parents

Sources of stress on parents include:

- The time, attention and energy needed to care for the disabled family member.
- Financial costs, often aggravated by loss of earning power.
- Loss of normal family life and leisure activities; changed and disrupted relationships among family members.

These sources of stress may be common to all families caring for a disabled child. However, caring for a child with ASD has been shown to be more stressful, generally speaking, than caring for children with other disabilities (Estes et al., 2009; Hayes & Watson, 2013). Factors that may contribute to this include:

- Behaviour problems including challenging behaviours.
- Lack of emotional responsiveness and poor nonverbal communication.
- Confusion about the nature of autism and its causes, the unpredictability of its developmental course and outcome, and controversy concerning the efficacy of intervention methods.
- The fact that autism falls somewhere between a mental health disorder and a learning disability, aggravating problems of access to provision.

Despite the numerous sources of stress, many families adjust and cope well, showing great resilience in the face of problems associated with caring for a child with ASD (Bitsika et al., 2013). The experience of stress may diminish over time, as family members individually and jointly develop strategies for coping with care for the child with ASD, and with changed family relationships (Gray, 2002). Some individuals with ASD become easier to relate to as they get older, achieving a degree of understanding of others' needs and becoming able to give back not just by being themselves, but in intentional ways. I recall the relationship between a single mother and her adult, moderately learning-impaired autistic son, which was in many ways reciprocal. He addressed her as 'dear', helped with the shopping and made cups of tea, telling her to put her feet up while he did so.

Having said this, a proportion of parents succumb to the stresses, especially in the shorter term, becoming clinically depressed or anxious, or experiencing somatic disorders, partly in response to the difficulties inherent in caring for their child, but also because of the effects on other members of the family (Hastings, Kovshoff, Ward et al., 2005; Montes & Halterman, 2007). Mothers and fathers tend to develop different coping strategies, some of which are more successful than others in maintaining a sense of wellbeing (Hastings, Kovshoff, Brown et al., 2005). Personality traits that have been shown to be protective against the effects of stress include 'optimism', 'hardiness' and 'resilience' (Weiss, 2002; Greenberg et al., 2004; Bitsika et al., 2013). Other factors that have been shown to reduce vulnerability to stress include the presence of a supportive partner or other close family member, and strong friendship groups (Bromley et al., 2004; Hare et al., 2004). A feeling of being in control without having sole or main responsibility can also be protective (Dale et al., 2006), as is secure religious faith (Tarakeshwar & Pargament, 2002).

Siblings

Siblings of children with ASD are also significantly affected by having a child with autism in the family. The few studies of siblings that have been carried out suggest the experience can have both positive and negative effects (Kaminsky & Dewey, 2002; Petalas et al., 2012; Chan & Goh, 2014). This is reflected in Box 13.1 which reproduces some of the verbatim responses of siblings to informal questioning about their experiences of having a brother or sister with ASD. Several first-hand accounts of life with an autistic sibling can be found in the literature (e.g. Konidaris, 2005; Barnhill, 2007), and some practical advice for parents concerning siblings can be found in Ives and Munro (2002). Ariel and Naseef (2005) bring together accounts by various family members, including parents, siblings and grandparents, of their experiences of having someone with ASD in the family.

Box 13.1 Siblings' reactions to having a brother or sister with ASD

Answers to the question 'What is the most difficult part of having a brother/sister with ASD?' included the following:

'Trying to explain to other people what his problem is, 'cos he looks normal.'

'Because he's autistic I have to help my mum more than I might otherwise.'

'You try to play with her and she doesn't like it, and then she gets in a mood 'cos she doesn't get it. She gets angry with herself. And she gets angry with everybody else.'

'If you have a guest he won't take that into account. He'll just carry on shouting. It's quite embarrassing really. Quite often you don't want to have people around, 'cos when he's near, you just don't know what will happen.'

'If I could do something he doesn't like, like play sports or read, it would be all right. But he wants everything the way he likes it. If he's not interested in something, I have to stop it.'

Answers to the question 'What is the best part of having a sibling with ASD?'

Four of the 14 siblings questioned could think of nothing.

Six mentioned the good nature of their brother or sister, describing them as 'fun', 'funny' or 'loving', or described playing and doing things together.

One said that she felt she had grown more mature and understanding as a result of having a sibling with ASD.

(From Mascha, K. (2005), PhD thesis, University of Warwick)

Siblings often take over from their parents the major role of overseeing the continuing care of an adult brother or sister with ASD. In the remainder of this chapter, when care of an adult is discussed, the term 'parent' should be understood as shorthand for 'the responsible family member'.

Support Needs

Post-diagnosis   The period following diagnosis of any chronic childhood disability is one of particularly acute distress and family disturbance. A group of parents that included parents of children with ASD reported that following their child's diagnosis they experienced 'depression, anger, shock, denial, fear, guilt, grief, confusion, and despair'. These feelings were associated with 'uncontrollable crying, sweating, headache and stomach-ache, trembling, and loss of appetite' (Heiman, 2002).

Parents' need for support is therefore acute immediately post-diagnosis, including a need for information, the chance to talk and to express feelings, and advice on treatment methods as well as practical strategies to solve immediate problems and to promote development. An example of good practice in responding to these needs is described in Box 13.2.

Ideally, all aspects of support post-diagnosis should be co-ordinated, with a range of professionals working as a team, as in the example outlined in Box 13.2, or as exemplified in 'Family-Centred-Care' programmes in Canada (Hodgetts et al., 2013; Christon & Myers, 2015). In the US, any child under the age of 3;0 years with a recognised disability qualifies for an Individual Family Service Plan to ensure early intervention and family support. Where an integrated service such as those described above is not available, a Case Manager or Key Worker may be appointed to ensure that a family's needs are met, and to co-ordinate input from different professionals and service agencies. Unfortunately, despite some good provision being in place, many parents report that they felt abandoned post-diagnosis (Selimoglu et al., 2013; Crane et al., 2015).

During childhood   During the years in which a child with ASD is growing up within the family there are particular needs associated with enabling the family as a whole to prosper. The provision of occasional care for the affected child outside the family is particularly important, allowing the rest of the family respite from the caring role. Occasional care may take the form of after-school, weekend or school holiday play and activity groups, short-term residential respite care, or befriending schemes whereby a trusted individual undertakes to look after the child in the home or to take them out on a regular basis. Other family needs during this period include support groups for siblings. These are often organised by local groups of parents who have banded together to support each other, to lobby on behalf of their children, and to plug some of the gaps in formal provision.

Caring for a dependent adult   A study by Anderson et al. (2014) showed that over 87 per cent of young people with ASD were living with parents

---

Box 13.2   An example of good practice in supporting parents of young children with ASD post-diagnosis: Leicestershire County Council's (UK) Autism Outreach (Early Years) Service

The 'Autism Outreach Service' employs a team of specialist teachers and thera-pists to work with parents, extended families and schools to achieve the following stated aims:

To help parents and families make sense of and come to terms with the nature of their child's difficulties.

To help parents to understand their child's autism and to inform them about support services available.

To give information about voluntary organisations that may offer help to the family.

To help parents to develop their child's skills, especially in communication and social interaction.

To help parents understand and manage any challenging behaviours in their child.

To liaise with other services that may be involved with the family and to inform parents about educational possibilities for children with autism in their area.

To provide specialist support and training to parents in the period after diagno-sis so that families can develop their own skills.

To work in partnership with parents so that children with autism reach their full potential.

To offer support and training with regard to Autism Spectrum Disorder to staff in preschool settings and receiving schools.

(From www.leics.gov.uk/autism, with thanks to the Autism Outreach Manager for permission to include this information)

---

in the years immediately following their years in formal education. This per-centage was greater than that of any of the other three disability groups studied. When their autistic child leaves school or full-time college education, the care role for parents increases because the child is no longer out for long periods of the day during term time, and the support offered by school and college staff is no longer available. As a result, parents' need for assistance to obtain work or day care for their son or daughter, and for regular respite care, becomes paramount (Hare et al., 2004). Parents of young adults with ASD may also need to initiate, manage and participate in intervention programmes for their son or daughter. They may also take the lead role in planning and managing their child's move to substitute care.

Not all adults with ASD leave home, however. An American study of older adults reported that 38 per cent of those surveyed were living with their parents (Henninger & Taylor, 2013). This may work well if a settled pattern of routines and relationships can be established, and if the adult with ASD does not have hard-to-manage behavioural problems. However, parents with adult children living at home and who are no longer earning may be in particular need of financial support, not least because lifelong caring has continuously drained their resources. They may also need advice about arrangements, financial and other, for safeguarding their child's future after they die (Hare et al., 2004). More is said about such arrangements in the section on 'Accessing Services and Rights', below.

Lifelong support   For most parents of an autistic child, the information, services, advice and emotional support they need must be sought out as and when needed, and accessed from a variety of sources, adding to the ongoing stresses and strains of caring for an offspring with ASD. I know of only one organisation that offers practical services as well as continuous support for individuals with ASD and their families over the longer term. This is Division TEACCH (Treatment and Education of Autistic and related Communication handicapped CHildren) in North Carolina (Mesibov et al., 2004). Some of the services offered at Division TEACCH are outlined in Box 13.3.

Box 13.3   Long-term services and support to individuals with ASD and their families provided by Division TEACCH

The stated aim of the TEACCH approach to working with families is 'to help parents handle the special stressors that confront them and to support them in their efforts to deal effectively with their child's problems'.

Direct support for families includes:

> Provision of specialist diagnostic and assessment facilities.
>
> Nursery school provision and preschool intervention programmes.
>
> Advice on educational issues and approaches.
>
> Parent counselling.
>
> Parent group activities.

Indirect support for families is provided by services to adults with ASD including:

> Vocational guidance and employment training.
>
> Counselling for those with relationship or mental health problems.

(From Division TEACCH website: http://teacch.com/about-us/what-is-teacch)

OTHER CARE PROVIDERS

Substitute Care for Children

Why substitute care of children may be desirable or necessary

Parents may be unable to care for a child with ASD within the family home for a variety of reasons. These may include the fact that a child has complex disabilities (e.g. comorbid cerebral palsy or severe epilepsy) requiring exceptional levels of care. Parents themselves may have health problems that prevent them from looking after the child at home; or a family may have another child with a disability; or there may be intractable social, economic or emotional problems within the family, making care for the child with autism an intolerable additional undertaking. Children with profound learning difficulties additional to their autism may also require exceptional levels of care, especially if learning difficulties are accompanied by challenging behaviour. These children are frequently excluded from local schools that are not equipped to cope, putting even greater strain on the family. Reasons of these kinds may lead parents to seek whole-year or term-time residential care and education for their children.

Another relatively common reason for a child's living away from home during school terms is the lack of appropriate educational provision locally. High-functioning children in particular may not thrive in their local mainstream school if no provision is made for their special educational, social and other support needs. Finding an appropriate school placement is frequently a source of frustration and concern (Lilley, 2013), and some parents resort to legal action to obtain an appropriate placement (Mayerson, 2014). Figure 13.1 was drawn by a boy I will call 'Adam' to illustrate his distress at being bullied by other students on account of being 'different'. Persuaded that mainstream education was not working well for Adam, the education authority in his local area agreed to help his parents fund a placement in a specialist residential school, where Adam is now thriving.

The experiences of parents seeking residential care for their children through local government agencies are, however, often negative. There is a perception that neither healthcare nor educational or social work agencies will take responsibility administratively or financially, and that cost-saving rather than their children's welfare is the priority (McGill et al., 2006). Parents commonly describe the process of obtaining appropriate residential education and care as 'a battle', and formal appeals against local education authority or State/state funding decisions are common (Loynes, 2001; Mayerson, 2014).

Occasionally a child with ASD may be perceived as being at risk of neglect or abuse within a troubled or dysfunctional family, or at risk simply because a family or family member reaches breaking point (Mandell et al., 2005). Issues of child protection may arise in any family, but more especially in families caring for a child or dependent adult with a disability. Individuals with ASD who cannot communicate, who are hyperactive, needing little sleep, or who have high levels of challenging behaviour may constitute an intolerable burden, and abuse may be the

Figure 13.1 *Picture drawn by 'Adam'*

first sign that a family can no longer cope. In such cases the child may be removed from family care by social services, either temporarily or permanently, and placed in substitute care, with a **guardian ad litem** appointed and a key worker charged with co-ordinating the child's care, education and access to other services in place of the parent(s).

In rare cases, an older child with ASD may be compulsorily detained as a result of having committed an offence or because of a mental health problem that makes them a threat to themselves or others.

Forms of substitute care for children

Whole-year care   Residential homes and boarding schools offering whole-year care may cater specifically for children with ASD or for broader groups of children with special needs that include children with ASD. For example, the combination of severe learning disability with challenging behaviour with or without autism is relatively common, and some care centres cater specifically for this group.

Children with exceptional needs require exceptional residential provision. Specialised provision may include high levels of security (for children with extreme forms of challenging behaviours), modified environments (for children with physical disabilities), on-site medical staff (for children with chronic medical problems) and almost always one-to-one levels of appropriately trained care staff. Whole-year residential provision for children with less complex difficulties, who cannot be looked after at home as a result of family circumstances, need not be so specialised. However, whole-year residential care for any child must provide not only for the child's basic needs, but also for their emotional and social needs. Opportunities for physical, mental and social development must be provided, and access to appropriate education ensured either by locating residential provision as part of a residential school, or by locating provision near to a school or schools able to cater for the children's educational needs.

Necessary as it may sometimes be to place an autistic child or adolescent in a 52-week residential setting, a report by Pinney (2005) commissioned by the UK government noted that there were persistent concerns about:

- The impact on children of growing up away from their family and home community.
- The effectiveness of local arrangements for safeguarding and promoting the welfare of disabled children in residential placements.
- Difficult transitions beyond school and children's services and poor outcomes for some.
- The inappropriate use of residential placements when children's needs could have been met locally.
- The high cost of some placements.

Pinney's report made a number of recommendations, but it is unclear to what extent these have been acted on.

Term-time care Residential schools offering term-time care and education should, like whole-year placements, cater for the full range of children's needs. However, links with families are more likely to be maintained when children are in termly, as opposed to whole-year, care, and major attachment figures and sources of emotional and social support are likely to come from the families rather than the school.

Some residential schools offer education and care specifically for children with ASD. Other residential special schools, for example schools catering for children with language and communication problems, may offer appropriate education for children with high-functioning ASD for whom suitable provision is not available locally. A striking example of successful specialist provision is described in Box 13.4.

Box 13.4   An unusual example of specialist educational provision: Limpsfield Grange, a mainly residential school for girls with ASD

Limpsfield Grange is a mainly residential school catering for girls aged 11–16 with ASD who have been unable to cope with mainstream school environments, even with additional support. All the students at Limpsfield follow the mainstream curriculum and work at approximately age-appropriate levels.

The school aims to provide a range of experiences that 'facilitate interaction, promote social inclusion and independence, and which empower students to understand their autism and celebrate their difference'.

To achieve these aims, the school provides a low arousal environment and a high level of targeted intervention and individualised structured activity throughout the school day. Staff development and training is ongoing, and the different professionals who may be involved in working with any one student plan and work together. Close liaison with parents and carers ensures a continuity of approach across school and home.

The work of the school was recently rated as 'Outstanding' by the relevant government inspectorate in the UK.

(With thanks to the Head Teacher of Limpsfield Grange School for permission to include this information)

Occasionally a local government agency will fund a place for a high-functioning child in a privately run mainstream boarding school, but generally only if there are particular circumstances making it difficult for the child to live at home. Some parents who can afford to do so opt to send their high-functioning child to a private boarding school rather than accepting local provision. They may do this mainly for educational reasons. However, weekly or termly boarding has the additional advantage that it offers respite to other family members, while the holiday periods sustain relationships between the child and the family.

Residential schools catering for children with ASD in countries where autism has long been recognised are run under the auspices of various organisations. These include State-wide or regional education services/authorities, charitable trusts including organisations such as the National Autistic Society in the UK, and schools run by stakeholders such as business organisations, educational trusts and philanthropists. Some specialist schools are, however, run for profit by private companies.

State provision for children at risk, or detained   Children who are removed from their homes for their own or others' safety, or because they have committed a significant offence, may be cared for under the auspices of local authorities in the following types of substitute provision:

- Foster home.
- Residential care home or hostel.

- Residential school.
- Secure mental health unit.
- Young offenders' institution.

Children with ASD form a minority of the total population of 'looked after children' cared for by local authorities, where they are more likely to be placed in residential care homes or schools than in foster homes or other family-type provision (Meltzer et al., 2003).

Older children and adolescents who have fallen foul of the law may be detained in secure units or young offenders institutions. Following some concerns as to the appropriateness of care in some institutions in the UK, the National Autistic Society introduced an accreditation system designed to ensure appropriate levels of staff awareness, understanding and training, as well as ensuring access to education, and to mental health services if needed. Care offered by non-accredited institutions, whether in the UK or elsewhere, is of generally unknown quality and appropriateness (see below).

Advantages and disadvantages of substitute care for children with ASD

It is difficult to generalise about the advantages and disadvantages of substitute care because the reasons why a child is placed in such care, and the kinds of provision made and the quality of provision made, are so varied.

Clearly, where substitute care offers specialised facilities that a family is unable to provide, or where it relieves a family unable to cope for unavoidable reasons, or where it offers protection from neglect or abuse, it has immediate advantages over home care. For children with ASD, the continuity and consistency of approaches to intervention and education made possible by residential schooling (the '24-hour curriculum') may be a further advantage. Termly placement in a residential school may not only benefit the child, but also enable a family to stay together and to provide good home care during school holidays. At its best, residential care and education for children with ASD can work well, for children and for families (McGill et al., 2006).

The major disadvantages of substitute care are cost (usually borne by the State), and the risk of loosening links with a supportive family, especially if substitute care is provided at a significant distance from the child's family home, which is all too often the case. There is also a risk that the care provided, if not conscientiously accredited and monitored, may fail to meet the child's needs in some way. In theory, children living away from home are protected by a raft of laws and government advice on good practice, supposedly enforced by regular monitoring and formal inspection by relevant agencies (health, education and social services). However, these procedures are often inadequately carried out in practice. Some of the shortcomings and risks associated with placing vulnerable children, including those with ASD, into substitute care are highlighted in the book by Smith et al. (2013) and in the review of institutional care for children across Europe, by Hamilton-Giachritsis and Browne (2012).

Residential Arrangements for Adults

Needs of those living away from home

High-functioning adults   High-functioning individuals with ASD may make the transition from living with parents to living independently with relative ease. If the individual has already attended a residential school the break from home will have already been made. For those leaving home for the first time to attend university or college, specialist support from university counsellors or supervisory staff in halls of residence may be available to support and trouble-shoot if necessary.

The ongoing care needs of those high-functioning individuals who move into long-term employment are, at best, no different from those of most neurotypical adults. There is, however, a heightened risk of social isolation and relationship difficulties. The advent of social media has reduced this risk, making it easier for 'Aspies' to form friendships and sometimes life relationships. Despite this, the need for mental health care remains higher than in the neurotypical population (see Chapter 4).

Not all high-functioning individuals can achieve complete independence, however, usually because ASD is not their only disability. An example of someone I once knew who lived largely independently, but who had some special residential, social and occupational care needs, is described in Box 13.5.

Box 13.5   'Adrian': An able man with ASD and moderate visual impairment

Adrian was unable to find paid employment or to live fully independently because he suffered from moderate visual impairment in addition to his autism. He moved out of his parents' home in his mid-20s when his father developed a debilitating illness, and when I knew him he was living in a single bedroom flat in a small block housing adults with a range of disabilities. There was a communal lounge in the block, communal laundry facilities, and an activities room housing computers, a small pool table, a piano and a games console. A warden occupied a ground floor flat with a duty to ensure the safety and wellbeing of tenants. Adrian's flat had been modified to take account of his visual difficulties, and he was able to care for himself in the main, including shopping and cooking his own meals (mostly microwaved 'ready meals', as I recall). His parents lived nearby, and his mother visited once or twice a week to 'keep an eye'. Adrian generally returned the visit after church on Sundays, to see his father and to eat home-cooked Sunday dinner.

Adrian worked for two mornings a week as a volunteer in the offices of his local Autism Support Group, mainly taking telephone calls as they came in. He also attended social gatherings and outings organised by the group. He enjoyed travel and was an expert in those travel firms that offered fully escorted holidays abroad for people with disabilities.

Lower-functioning adults   Lower-functioning adults with ASD have all the care needs and rights listed at the outset of this chapter. During childhood, these needs have usually been met by parents either directly or indirectly. For children in substitute care, essential needs have been met by residential schools, state-run or local authority care homes, foster parents or others 'in loco parentis'. Given good care in childhood, the severity of autism-related behaviours will have diminished by the time the individual leaves school. They will also have acquired some communication capacities as well as daily living routines and some occupational skills. By the time they leave school, therefore, some capacities for independent living should have been established. Nevertheless, complete independence is unlikely to be possible. And for those autistic adults who are most profoundly learning and language impaired, who may also have violent or challenging behaviour, specialist residential care is essential.

Forms of residential provision for lower-functioning adults

Until the middle of the last century, adults with ASD who were unable to care for themselves, and whose parents were not able to care for them at home, were looked after in long-stay hospitals alongside adults with a range of other developmental and mental health disorders. These establishments were generally large and impersonal, catering for basic needs and little else. All such institutions in the UK were closed many decades ago, once their manifold inadequacies were recognised.

Meantime, parent-led organisations had begun to establish specialist residential care homes for adults with ASD.[2] The first such specialist care home was opened in 1974, and continues to offer residential care to severely affected autistic adults (see Box 13.6).

The move described in Box 13.6, from providing residential care for dependent adults in large groups to providing care in individualised or small group settings, reflects further changes in public policy designed to achieve a greater degree of normalisation, and to give adults as much autonomy and control over their lives as is consistent with their health and safety. Individuals with some capacity or potential to care for themselves are now likely to live in small group homes located in the broader community. For example, a small group home might be located in a detached house in a suburban road, offering a home-like environment to six or eight individuals, who are supported by a resident warden and care staff.

'Supported living' schemes take the move towards normalisation one step further, and are increasingly implemented by local authorities in the UK. In these schemes, individuals with disabilities that could include ASD live in their own house or flat, either alone or with a partner or other companion. They are supported by visits from paid carers who may assist with daily living tasks, and by professionals from social service departments who provide assistance of other kinds. These forms of more individualised provision are likely to become increasingly common as legislation drives change from care within large-scale units, into which each individual has,

---

[2]Parents of children with other severe or complex disabilities, such as cerebral palsy or syndromic learning disability, were also setting up residential homes or 'care villages' for their adult children by this time.

Box 13.6 Somerset Court: An example of good practice in the provision of group-based residential care

Somerset Court was established by the UK's National Autistic Society (NAS) in 1974 as the first ever specialist centre for autistic people in the UK.

Originally, residential care was offered to a small group of adults living in the large country house that gives Somerset Court its name. Residential accommodation now consists of seven purpose-built houses designed to enable people to live fulfilling lives in small groups, with the help of specialist staff. The range of living arrangements includes shared bungalows, one-person flats and en-suite bedrooms. Each house has a shared kitchen, living room and dining room, and residents come together for meals and various activities.

Individualised programmes of learning and leisure activities are drawn up which reflect each person's particular interests and needs. Activities include household chores such as shopping, cooking and independent living skills, and leisure activities such as visiting the pub, bowling or going for a walk. People may also choose to do art and craft activities, cooking, IT, music therapy and aromatherapy.

Day Services for autistic adults living in the region are also provided at Somerset Court. Residents can take courses, use sports facilities, or work in the woodwork shop, garden centre or creative studio making high-quality products for sale.

(With thanks to the NAS and the Manager of Somerset Court for permission to include this information)

---

to a greater or lesser extent, to 'fit', towards person-centred care in which support is customised to cater for the needs of each individual.

Financial support for all forms of residential provision for adults with ASD, as outlined above, generally comes from the State directly to the beneficiary or their representative. At the time of writing, the benefits system in the UK is in a state of flux, and there is considerable concern among people with disabilities themselves, their families, and the groups that lobby on behalf of those unable to speak for themselves, concerning possible cuts and reduced quality of life.

On the other hand, recent legislation in the UK and elsewhere has put a statutory obligation on local authorities and health service providers to develop and implement strategies to meet the needs of adults with ASD in their area (the 'Think Autism' directive). State provision for adults with ASD has in the past lagged behind provision for children. When the child leaves school, educational authorities have no further statutory role; only a proportion of individuals with ASD have clinically significant mental health problems such as might make them the responsibility of public health provision; and social service agencies have, historically, offered a generic service with no specialist training or provision for working with people with autism (D'Astous et al., 2014). This situation is, however, in the process of government-led change, as reported below in the section headed 'Accessing Services and Rights'

Problems that can be associated with residential care for lower-functioning adults

Every adult has the right to live as independently as is possible for them, and parents have the right to see their children living as independently as possible, with their needs well catered for, ensuring the best possible quality of life. The examples described above demonstrate that this can be achieved for adults with ASD, whether their needs are borderline, requiring minimal support, or complex, requiring specialised residential care with intensive individualised support.

Many problems can and do arise, however. There is the initial problem of identifying the right kind of substitute provision for any one individual, and finding where the needed provision exists, preferably close to the parental home or close to where a sibling or other involved family member lives. There is the inevitable problem of cost, and issues concerning who will bear costs, especially when specialised residential care is required. There is, as in the case of residential provision for children, the worrying problem that the prescribed processes of licensing and monitoring are not always fully adhered to. Cases of abuse can and do arise, one such having made headline news in the UK in 2011. In this case, appalling abuse occurred in a privately run 'care home' for adults with severe learning difficulties and complex needs, including adults with ASD.

Cases such as the above have increased calls for community-based supported living services to replace institutional services for people with learning disabilities. It would be less than honest, however, to claim that caring for the minority of severely learning disabled people with ASD who are prone to bouts of challenging and sometimes violent behaviour is ever easy, in any setting. It can be done well, using approved and safe methods of restraint and, pre-eminently, intervention to reduce occurrences of such behaviour (see Chapter 12). However, this requires high levels of well-trained staff which, of course, comes at a cost.

Finally, individuals themselves may not want to leave home, and this can make it difficult to achieve an acceptable balance between respecting an adult's right to self-determination and acting in ways agreed by responsible others to be in that adult's best interests. For parents also, and especially for mothers, separation from a dependent child after decades of caring in which a uniquely close type of relationship may have been established can be difficult and painful (Krauss et al., 2005). Sensitive management of the transition period, for both the individual and the parent, or parents, may be critical in determining that the move away from home is experienced positively in the longer term (for discussion of support during transition periods in general, see Smart, 2004).

ACCESSING SERVICES AND RIGHTS

Previous sections of this chapter have dealt with care in the sense of where the child or adult with ASD lives – where is 'home' and who provides for them there. In this section, the autistic individual's access to services and opportunities that are also identified under the principles of inclusion is considered first. The section ends with an appraisal of the extent to which people with disabilities, including those with ASD, enjoy the human rights identified under the principles of inclusion.

Services and Opportunities

Health care

Those with ASD are more vulnerable to health-related problems than most people, including allergies and digestive disturbances, accidental or self-inflicted injury, anxiety and depression (Croen et al., 2006). Frequent visits to clinics and hospital stays have cost implications for families and independent adults, even in societies providing free medical care. Autism-related characteristics may cause additional problems of time and cost in accessing appropriate health care. For example, dental treatment for an individual with poor communication may involve travelling to a specialised clinic or dental hospital, rather than using local services. In addition, lack of up-to-date knowledge and understanding of ASD by many healthcare workers can cause inappropriate interpretation of symptoms, misdiagnosis and inappropriate treatment advice (Heidgerken et al., 2005). This emphasises the need for training, a need that is – albeit belatedly – slowly being recognised and catered for. In the UK, for example, the British Psychological Society and Royal College of General Practitioners now offer postgraduate training courses for professionals working with people with ASD. NHS Scotland has developed an 'Autism Training Framework' outlining the knowledge and skills required by medical staff across the range, from those in generic services through to those working in specialist ASD services. Less encouragingly, a survey of Nurse Practitioners in the US (Will et al., 2013) revealed feelings of inadequacy among those questioned; and specialist training for doctors in the US is also reported to be sparse (Major et al., 2013).

Education

Children with ASD have the same right of access to education as any other child. However, for children with ASD there is no clear division between education in the sense of providing a child with opportunities to acquire knowledge and skills (the goals of education as generally understood) and the provision of interventions designed to provide children with ASD with the skills and strategies they uniquely lack as a consequence of their autism, and to modify non-adaptive behaviours associated with autism (Jordan, 2005). The educational needs of children with ASD are therefore 'special', or 'exceptional', even in the case of high-functioning school-age children or young adults attending college or university.

Appropriate provision for children's and young adults' educational needs could include at least the following:

- Modified environments and equipment (e.g. small classrooms/individualised work stations, secure and specially equipped playgrounds, a sensory room, additional computers).
- Modified curricula and individualised teaching programmes.

- Modified teaching methods (see references to educational methods in Chapter 12).
- Specialist training for teaching staff.
- Parental or key worker involvement to ensure continuity and consistency of educational and intervention approaches across home and school, playgroup or college.

Where and how these needs may best be met in a manner consistent with the principles of inclusion is a hotly debated issue, discussion of which is beyond the scope of this book (see Jordan, 2008, for an account of the issues). However, the principle that no one size fits all is useful to bear in mind. Each individual with ASD has different and changing educational/intervention needs. Each family has different needs, opinions and wishes for their child. Each playgroup or nursery, mainstream or special school, college or university differs in their motivation and capacity to welcome children or students with ASD into their communities. Decisions as to where a child or young adult with ASD should be educated must therefore be made on a case-by-case basis, often constrained by availability. Accessing appropriate education for their children is therefore frequently arduous and frustrating for parents, as noted above. However, where a range of autism-specific forms of provision is provided, parental satisfaction can be high (Department of Education and Science (Ireland), 2006).

Many adults with ASD continue to benefit from education in the sense of intervention to help overcome autism-related limitations and problems or to increase daily living or vocational skills (as described, for example, in Box 13.6, above). Attendance at college courses or evening classes can provide more able adults with the kind of structured social event they are able to cope with, as well as providing stimulation and practical benefits.

Employment

Examples of the kinds of employment or meaningful occupation that may be obtained by individuals with ASD were described in the section on lifespan development in Chapter 5. By 'meaningful occupation' (as opposed to employment) is meant here unpaid, or nominally paid, work, for example household tasks carried out in a residential setting, or work carried out on a voluntary basis or in a sheltered workshop or day care facility. The present section concerns the ability of people with ASD to access paid employment, which they have a right to expect under the principle of inclusion.

Obtaining and keeping paid employment are both problematic for people with ASD, from the least to the most able. Regarding access to employment for less able individuals and those with behavioural problems, the description of Nancy (Box 5.1) provides an example of the kind of setting in which supported employment may be obtained, and the methods used to introduce the individual to a work environment and work practices so as to maintain the individual in their employment. A further example of how environmental modifications and specific task support may enable a less able person with ASD to carry out paid work in a sympathetic setting is described by Hume and Odom (2007). These authors used TEACCH principles of structuring the work environment and providing a visual timetable to enable a young man, Mark, to stay on task and complete work assignments independently of external prompting.

Encouraging as they are, the descriptions of Nancy and Mark serve to underline the difficulties involved for less able individuals to access employment: at the least, it requires sympathetic employers and fellow employees, extensive and painstaking preparation and training, and continued support.

A somewhat different set of problems confronts more able individuals with ASD in accessing and maintaining employment. These are vividly illustrated in quotes from people with AS who were interviewed about their experiences of employment (Hurlburt & Chalmers, 2004). For example, one woman reported:

> I have a degree in political science and am just trying to get a decent job with decent pay and benefits. I have cleaned cat cages, done janitorial work (which is boring, boring, boring), office work ... [been] a telemarketer (which I hated, but I learned how to do public speaking!), and worked in a group home on the early morning shift. (Hurlburt & Chalmers, 2004: 218)

This woman attributed her inappropriate and changing employment to her difficulties in conforming socially. Another woman said that others in the office where she worked 'felt uncomfortable around her and tried to get rid of her'. A young man reported that he had just been laid off his job because of anxiety resulting from his inability to cope with changes in co-workers, supervisors and job coaches (compare the case of 'Mr A', described in Box 4.4).

For reasons such as the above, only a minority of high-functioning people with ASD find paid employment in jobs for which they are well qualified.

However, it has been shown that supported employment schemes for more able individuals can achieve a high level of success with significant benefits to individuals themselves and society in general in terms of cost savings (Mavranezouli et al., 2013). Moreover, ongoing changes in the benefits system in the UK are putting pressure on people with disabilities to find employment, and the 'Think Autism' strategy referred to above places an obligation on local government authorities to support people with ASD into work.

The response of one local authority, working in co-operation with a charity, is outlined in Box 13.7.

Financial assistance

The financial costs to families rearing a child with ASD are considerable (Sharpe & Baker, 2007; Parish et al., 2012) and publicly funded financial assistance to which a family may be legally entitled rarely if ever covers these costs. In addition, accessing the various forms of financial assistance to which a family, or an adult living independently, may be entitled is likely to involve seeking out somewhat inaccessible information, understanding regulations concerning eligibility, filling in complicated forms, and co-operating with intrusive assessments (Grant, 2011). In the UK, at the time of writing, there are eight different forms of allowance or benefit for which families with an autistic child may qualify (NAS website). In the US, the situation for adult claimants is even more complex. Peter Emch, father of an adult with ASD, wrote in 2011:

Box 13.7 An example of good practice in supporting adults with ASD into sustainable employment

Autism Spectrum Disorder Employment Support (ASDES) is a part government-sponsored, part charitable organisation, operating in Wales. Its core aim is to support people with ASD into work. Social gatherings and outings are used to enhance communication and social skills, and to accustom potential job applicants to being out and about in their local community. In addition, a team of counsellors, psychologists and job coaches offers individualised assessment, training, counselling and support to facilitate entry into appropriate sustainable employment. The work carried out by job coaches is critical, and includes the following:

With clients

- Building a relationship with the client in order to identify their strengths and their development needs relating to specific job skills.
- Understanding how their disability affects them personally and considering how their specific needs may be accommodated in the workplace.
- Providing training and support to increase the client's capabilities.
- Ensuring that they have an up-to-date CV and covering letter appropriate to their job goals, and carrying out mock interviews.

With potential employers

- Seeking out appropriate job opportunities.
- Approaching potential employers and arranging interviews.
- Conducting a detailed job analysis at employers' premises in order to match a client to the work.
- Identifying reasonable adjustments for the client in the workplace and negotiating for these adjustments with the employer.
- Escorting the client to interview and acting as their advocate.
- Carrying out ASD staff-awareness sessions with an employer.
- Accompanying the client to work when appointed, until they are settled in.
- Providing follow-up for both the client and the employer, including discussion of issues relating to career development.

(With thanks to the Chairman of ASDES for permission to include this information)

Public support consists of disparate programs, individually legislated sometimes by federal and other times by state governments – some aimed at poverty, others at disability – that are rarely coordinated. The result is a confusing mess. There is no 'U.S. Autism Program'. (autismafter16 website)

Moreover, according to a survey by Parish et al. (2015), private insurance (against medical costs) rarely, if ever, covers actual financial outlay.

Unsuprisingly, families caring for a child or dependent adult with autism find the processes difficult and irksome, and may need assistance with obtaining financial benefits for which they, or their dependent son or daughter, are eligible. National and local ASD support groups may provide helplines, information packs and day courses from which advice can be accessed. Some voluntary organisations also offer free **advocacy** services. However, if a claim goes to an appeal, advice and assistance from paid professionals may be necessary, incurring additional cost.

Professional assistance

Advice and advocacy by professionals such as lawyers, doctors or accountants is needed not only in appeals relating to benefit claims, but also in appeals relating to educational or substitute placements (Mayerson, 2014). Legal and financial expertise are also needed when parents make their Wills, especially in cases where there is a dependent son or daughter. This usually entails setting up a Trust to administer funds for the benefit of the dependent person. Here again, useful information can be obtained from various helplines and websites dealing with issues for families with a dependent disabled child. However, the actual formulation of a legally binding Will, and the establishment and financial management of a legally watertight Trust, require input from lawyers and accountants. Some legal firms specialise in helping families of disabled offspring, and contact details for such firms may be found in relevant publications and websites.

Human Rights

According to the principles of inclusion listed at the outset of the chapter, all humans have a right to self-determination in matters of care and daily living, and the right to be valued and respected on equal terms with others. To what extent are these ideals achieved? And if not achieved, why might this be the case?

The right to self-determination

This human right is generally recognised by authorities regulating substitute care and operating systems of licensing and inspection in developed countries. Substitute care providers generally aspire to recognise this human right, according to their mission statements. However, whether or not this aspiration is met in practice is difficult to ascertain, and the fact that evidence of poor or abusive care continues to emerge via the media suggests that regulatory authorities do not always make adequate checks.

There are also real practical difficulties in cases where an individual does not have the capacity to understand why a decision has been made on their behalf, contrary to their own wishes. A woman I have known since she was a child, who is now in her late 40s, provides an example, although 'Lily', as I will call her, has cerebral palsy and mild to moderate learning difficulty, but not autism – see Box 13.8.

Box 13.8 'Lily': An example of practical difficulty in implementing the right to self-determination

From her early 20s, Lily had lived in great contentment in a group home for physically disabled people. She called the staff and other residents there her 'family', and she was well known and liked by people living and working in the neighbourhood where she was regularly taken to shop, or to a local café, or to 'disabled swimming' sessions.

The time came, however, when the charity running the group care home decided, with the very best of intentions, to move all the residents into their own flats or bed-sits in nearby towns, in accordance with the principles of supported living. Ironically, one of the arguments in favour of supported living arrangements for dependent adults is that it provides greater autonomy for individuals than group living can easily achieve. But Lily was distraught. To her it was compulsory removal from her family and friends, senseless and hurtful. She did not want to live on her own, or with just one other person; nor to take on greater responsibility for her own basic needs.

In the end, and after a prolonged and ultimately unsuccessful campaign by residents' families and friends to keep the group home open, Lily's wishes were partially recognised. She moved into a group home run by a different charity, where she is now in the process of establishing a new 'family' and new friendship groups.

(With thanks to 'Lily' and her mother for permission to include this account)

Regulation and inspection does not of course extend to children or dependent adults living at home. Parents and other family members must make their own compromises concerning their child's, or adult son's or daughter's right to self-determination. Only extreme cases of denial of this right in the context of abuse or neglect would be likely to come to the attention of authorities with the power to improve the situation.

The right to be valued and respected on equal terms with others

The right of disabled people to be valued and respected as much as anyone else involves breaking down barriers of ignorance and prejudice. This is the case for any kind of disability, whether physical or behavioural, that makes an individual noticeably different from the majority. Governments may legislate for inclusive, non-discriminatory provision for people who are perceived as 'different', whether on account of disability, colour, age or religion, but they cannot control the attitudes and reactions of members of the general public.

Parents of children with ASD, even in so-called 'enlightened' societies, frequently report hostile or hurtful reactions to their child from, for example, parents of neurotypical children in mainstream schools, or staff and clientele in supermarkets, restaurants, libraries, swimming pools, and other public places and spaces.

High-functioning children with ASD in mainstream schools are almost invariably victims of bullying. Lower-functioning adults are vulnerable to mockery in the workplace, pub or club. Even something as apparently straightforward as using public transport to travel to school or to work or to see a friend or relative can be difficult and/or unpleasant for individuals and families, provoking hostile or humiliating comments from other transport users.

Why should this be so? The reasons are almost certainly deep-seated and to do with the fact that living in social groups was a crucial factor in the evolution of the human species (Frith, 2013). Living in a group involves differentiating between members of our particular group and those who are not members of our group (Tajfel, 1981). Behaviour towards non-group members, or 'out-groups', is likely to be hostile or at best exclusionary. The human tendency to view the world in terms of in-groups and out-groups at multiple levels is, of course, what all disability rights groups fight against, including the neurodiversity movement referred to in Chapter 12. Ignorance and fear also prevent 'us' (the in-group of non-disabled people) from recognising that the facially disfigured war veteran sitting opposite us on the train, the Tourette's sufferer shouting obscenities in the street, and the autistic child rocking and making strange sounds in the café are all human beings 'like us'.

Getting to know such people as individuals is the best way to combat ignorance and fear, which is one reason why 'autism awareness' is almost always highlighted in strategy documents relating to the wellbeing of people with ASD. Media representations of people with 'Asperger syndrome' as a bit odd but clever to the point of genius have helped those at the high-functioning end of the autism spectrum to gain acceptance and respect. However, the tide of novels, films, TV series and comic strips featuring Aspies has probably made it harder, rather than easier, for people with more debilitating forms of ASD to be respected and valued as much as anyone else: unless they have some savant ability to show off, they are not clever, and their behaviour may be disconcerting or even threatening.

Another reason why people with disabilities are often undervalued and treated with disrespect is that the ideals of normalisation and inclusion have a very short history. Within living memory, parents of a baby with, for example, cerebral palsy or Down syndrome (easy to detect at birth) were commonly advised to 'put him in a home'. In such 'homes' other children with learning disabilities, including those with autism, would also be placed when their difficulties became conspicuous. Basic care needs were provided for, but only those institutions run by the most enlightened voluntary organisations would have perceived any needs for intervention, education or occupation, let alone any legal or moral right to self-determination and respect.

The ideal of 'equal value equal rights' applied to individuals with disabilities is also fragile, since it is only likely to be acted upon in societies that are not under survival pressure. When survival pressures increase as a result of war, famine, epidemic or financial depression, the needs and rights of people with disabilities of any kind, age and infirmity included, are often discounted or ignored, even in so-called civilised societies. Recent examples come all too easily to mind.

In view of the deep-seated roots of prejudice and discrimination, and the relative recency and fragility of the ideals of inclusion, it is not surprising that these ideals have not been fully achieved for people with ASD, even in rich, developed countries. However, within my own lifetime – now long – I have seen immense progress towards making these ideals a reality. There is some way to go. But we should not be pessimistic.

SUMMARY

The principle of inclusion sets the standard for identifying the care needs and rights of people with disabilities, and for judging the degree to which they are met. Identified needs include food, shelter and protection from harm; emotional and social stimulation and support; and opportunities for physical, mental and social development. Rights include access to health care, education and other services, and the right to self-determination and to be valued and respected.

Families are the major providers of care for people with ASD. However, caring for a child or dependent adult with ASD is demanding and stressful, involving unusual amounts of time, energy and money, and entailing loss of normal family life and disruption of within-family relationships. Support for families in their care roles is therefore important. Immediately post-diagnosis of a child, parents need information, emotional support and practical advice. Later, the pre-eminent need is for support that enables the family as a whole to prosper. This could include the provision of respite care, parent counselling and support for siblings. Parents of adults with ASD often have an increased care load when their child leaves full-time education, and the need for work opportunities, day care facilities and respite care for the dependent adult is then paramount. Throughout their lives, parents need advice and practical help in planning their children's future and in accessing available resources and services for them.

'Out-of-home' or 'substitute' care for children may be required for a variety of reasons. For example, a child may have exceptional needs that cannot be catered for at home; a family may be unable to cope for health reasons; appropriate educational provision may not be available locally. Occasionally, a child is considered to be at risk within the family and is taken into care. Substitute care for children takes various forms, from foster care to term-time or whole-year residential care and education. The advantages and disadvantages of substitute care depend on the reasons why an individual has to be cared for, and on the quality of the substitute provision. In all cases, provision is costly, and there is a risk of loosening links between the family and the affected child or adult.

Adults with ASD who are not living at home may at best live completely independently. More commonly, some degree of support is needed to ensure that the individual's needs are met. This ranges from 'keeping an eye' on someone living mainly independently, to providing intensive practical, emotional/social and occupational support to individuals living in small group homes or in individualised accommodation.

Many people with ASD have lifelong needs for the kinds of services and opportunities provided by external agencies. Accessing appropriate services may be difficult for numerous reasons. For example, appropriate health care may be unavailable because of a lack of specialist staff training. Appropriate education for a child with ASD may require modifications of standard environments, curricula, equipment and teaching methods and, again, specialist staff training. Finding and maintaining employment for an adult with ASD may require considerable time and effort from support workers. Accessing much-needed financial benefits and advice is often, again, difficult and frustrating. However, recent legislation underlines the obligations of centrally or locally run authorities to cater for the needs of people with ASD. In addition, autism support networks provide helplines, written advice, and training in advocacy designed to help individuals and carers access services to which they have a right.

The human right of self-determination and the right to be valued and respected are harder to ensure. Enjoyment of these rights is hindered by deep-rooted attitudes within society in general towards people who are perceived as 'different', whether by virtue of skin colour, religion or disability. However, progress in breaking down ignorance and prejudice against people with ASD is being made.

Appendix

ASSIGNMENTS

PART 1 WHAT IS AUTISM?

Chapter 1 Historical Background

1. Choose THREE of the following neurodevelopmental disorders and outline progress that was being made in the period 1950–1980 (approximately) in characterising, defining and understanding these disorders:

   Down syndrome   dyslexia   ADHD   Fragile-X syndrome

   Specific language impairment/developmental dysphasia

2. Take each of 'Creak's Nine Points' and, using the Index of this book (and/or other sources), write summary accounts of current knowledge relating to each of the nine characteristics identified by Creak.

3. Why were the psychoanalytically-based explanations of autism, such as those of Bettelheim and Mahler, taken seriously in the 1950s and 1960s? Why have psychoanalytic/psycho-therapeutic approaches to understanding autism (see, for example, Tustin, 1981/1995, 1991) continued to have a role in the treatment of children and adults with ASD, and in supporting their families?

4. Using an electronic search of peer-reviewed literature published between 1960 and 1980, identify and discuss some of the major topics of interest in the field over this period. Are some or all of these topics still of interest?

Chapter 2 Current Concept and Definition

1. What are the pros and cons of the spectrum concept of ASD as opposed to the subtypes concept? Why might the views of affected individuals themselves and their families, as opposed to the views of academics/researchers, or the views of administrators or practitioners, vary concerning the pros and cons of the two concepts?

2. Popular fiction, including television and stage plays, novels and comic strips have frequently represented individuals who, it is either stated or implied, are autistic. Using one or more example of such fictional representations, state in what ways the representation is accurate and in what ways it might be misleading.

3. Two kinds of 'Descriptors' supplement the diagnostic criteria for ASD in DSM-5. What are these Descriptors and how are they intended to be used? Do you consider them a useful addition? And if so, for whom and why?

4. What are the areas of overlap and the areas of difference between the communicative and other behaviours of a child with ASD as compared to a child with SCD? Give examples of actual behaviours that might contribute to making a differential diagnosis.

5. (a) In what ways do both Mandy and Damien (described in the text) meet the detailed descriptions of SEC impairments and RRBs in DSM-5 (see Box 2.1)? How might DSM-5 Descriptors apply to each of these individuals? (b) From your own knowledge or experience, write one or more further 'thumbnail sketches' indicating ways in which the individual(s) depicted meet DSM-5 criteria.

Chapter 3 The Fuller Picture: Shared Characteristics

1. (a) Watch some real-life and/or filmed two-way interactions between relaxed but wakeful typically developing infants up to 12 months of age (approximately) and their close carers. Use your observations to illustrate the characteristics of dyadic social interaction in infants as described by Trevarthen and Aitken (2001) and/or by Sigman et al. (2004). (b) Do some 'people-watching', for example in a bar or restaurant. In what ways do dyadic interactions between adult couples resemble and/or differ from dyadic interactions between infants and close carers?

2. Read a first-hand account of what it is like to be autistic (there are well-known accounts by, for example, Temple Grandin, Donna Williams – and many others). What does the account tell you about this particular individual's sensory-perceptual experiences, perhaps across several years of their life? What strategies does the individual report using to deal with their particular experiences? Have they benefitted in any way from their unusual experiences?

3. Compare and contrast the behavioural characteristics associated with psychopathy and with autism using, in particular, the concepts and definitions provided in Box 3.1. (This assignment will involve accessing literature beyond the References included in this chapter.)

4. Write an account of one the following 'shared characteristics' of ASD, basing your account on findings from research:

Imagination and creativity	Islets of ability
Motor skills	Sense of self

5. Describe how all four of the above 'shared characteristics' apply, or do not apply, to someone with ASD whom you know well.

Chapter 4 The Fuller Picture: Sources of Diversity

1. (a) It is often said dismissively of intelligence tests that 'they only test what they test'. Working with a fellow-student/friend, test each other on the Wechsler Adult Intelligence Scale (WAIS – any edition). (b) Pool your ideas as to what abilities/capacities are involved in each subtest, starting with, for example, 'vision'. Write an account of your conclusions plus a discussion of the relevance/irrelevance of 'what the WAIS tests' to academic success as indexed by school exams.

2. Compare and contrast the relationship between communication and language in terms of functions, means, etc. Which is the more handicapping, in your view: a social interaction-communication impairment with intact language or a language impairment with intact social interaction-communication? Justify your view.
3. What evidence is there for a raised prevalence in people with ASD of EITHER immune system disorders OR gastrointestinal disorders? Critically assess the evidence.
4. Read/dip-and-skim Lynn Waterhouse's book *Rethinking Autism: Variation and Complexity* (Academic Press, 2013). Write a brief answer to the question 'Is there such a "thing" as "autism"/"ASD"?' referring to some of the arguments and evidence in Waterhouse's book.
5. What is meant by 'challenging behaviours'? Give examples of different kinds of challenging behaviour that can be associated with ASD, drawing on descriptions in the factual or research literature, or from your own experience.

Chapter 5 Facts and Figures: Epidemiology and Lifespan Development

1. Is there an 'epidemic' of ASD in affluent societies? Or can reports of increased prevalence be explained in other ways?
2. What evidence and arguments are there for the suggestion that ASD in females is under-diagnosed? If not under-diagnosed, how might the different distributions of males and females across the spectrum be explained?
3. Awareness of ASD as a relatively common condition is increasing in most low-/middle-income countries. Write an account of autism awareness, diagnostic services and subsequent support and provision for individuals with ASD in one or more low-/middle-income country.
4. The studies by Seltzer et al. (2003), McGovern and Sigman (2005), Levy and Perry (2011), Pellicano (2012c) and others are encouraging concerning the likelihood that SEC impairments and RRBs will diminish in most individuals with ASD over time. What factors increase the chances of this happening? What factors decrease the likelihood?
5. Why do people with ASD have a shorter life expectancy than individuals in the general population? What could be done to increase life expectancy?

PART II WHAT CAUSES AUTISM?

Chapter 6 A Framework for Explaining Autism

1. Figures 6.2a and 6.2b give examples of causal links between facets of ASD-related behaviour that come under the descriptions of 'many-to-one' and 'one-to-many'. Generate and describe some further examples of causal links in ASD to which these descriptions might apply.
2. Three neuropsychological explanations of ASD – impaired mindreading, weak central coherence, and executive dysfunction – were until recently widely considered to be capable of explaining autism-related behaviour. Discuss the current status of each of these theories using material and references from Chapter 9 of this book.

3. In your own words, and giving examples, explain what the following terms mean when used in discussion of the causes of medical, mental health or neurodevelopmental conditions:

    necessary   sufficient   necessary and sufficient

    primacy   specificity   universality

4. Peer-reviewed literature is recommended as a source of information about possible causes of ASD. Peer-review may, however, prevent novel theories from being disseminated. Look up the editorial policy and recent issues of the journal *Medical Hypotheses*. Select a paper that interests you and summarise the hypothesis proposed and the evidence and arguments presented. Is this hypothesis worth pursuing? Justify your response to this question.

5. Identify ways in which understanding the causes of ASD in all its varied manifestations may benefit: (a) individuals; (b) parents and families; (c) practitioners, educators and others working directly with people with ASD; (d) specialists in other fields, for example genetics, pharmacology, toxicology; and (e) society generally.

Chapter 7 Root Causes

1. What do twin and family studies tell us about the role of (a) genes and (b) environmental factors in the etiology of ASD?

2. The capacity to acquire language is genetically determined (given appropriate experience of language in childhood). What specific genes may be involved in the etiology of (a) specific language impairment and (b) language impairment in ASD?

3. What may cases of syndromic autism tell us about the etiology of ASD? Illustrate your argument with detailed reference to the genetic variations underlying at least two syndromes with which ASD may be associated.

4. A couple whom you know are planning to have a child. Members of both families have some marked autistic features of behaviour and your friends are anxious about their own chances of having a child with ASD. What advice would you give them (if asked) regarding any precautions they might take in terms of lifestyle before, during and after the looked-for pregnancy?

5. Why is the hoary 'nature versus nurture'/ 'genes versus environment' controversy untenable in the case of ASD? Why are theories that maintain EITHER that autism is entirely and always genetic in origin OR that autism is entirely and always environmental in origin damaging to individuals and families?

Chapter 8 Brain Bases

1. Animals models are widely used in research into the causes of ASD. Describe their use in increasing our understanding of EITHER the etiology OR the neurobiology of ASD.

2. In what ways has knowledge concerning brain development, structure and function in people with ASD contributed to the development of some of the treatment methods identified in Chapter 12?

3. Substance abuse and most other forms of addiction are rare in people with ASD despite the rigidity and repetitiveness of much of their behaviour. How may an understanding of the neurochemistry of the brain in ASD help to explain this apparent contradiction?

4. What evidence is there concerning abnormal structure and function in individuals with ASD of TWO of the following brain regions/structures?

the prefrontal cortex   the limbic system

the corpus callosum   the cerebellum

Chapter 9 Proximal Causes 1: Diagnostic Behaviours

1. Read Frith's account of the normal development of the human mind, and the anomalous development of the mind in ASD (Frith, U. *Scripta Varia* 121, Vatican City, 2013). Summarise the developments that are described as normally occurring on each of the five floors of the imaginary house. To what extent are developments on any floor innate, according to Frith? To what extent do developments on 'higher' floors build on what has been established on 'lower' floors?

2. What do you understand by the terms 'sensory soothing' and 'sensory seeking'? How may the concepts underlying these terms help to establish links between sensory-perceptual anomalies and RRBs in individuals with autism? What implications might these links have for the treatment of repetitive sensory-motor stereotypies (RSMs)?

3. 'Impaired integration' is cited several times in Chapter 9 as a likely contributory cause of behaviours diagnostic of ASD. Identify and comment on each of these possible causal links and any others that you know of in the autism literature. How might impaired integration at the neuropsychological level derive from brain abnormalities associated with ASD?

4. Facial expression of emotion is a central component of nonverbal communication. What is known about the ability of people with ASD (a) to interpret others' facial expressions of emotion and (b) to use appropriate facial expressions themselves?

5. Watch and listen to one or more filmed conversations between a person with ASD and a non-autistic person. Analyse where and how the conversation is abnormal or unusual. If you have technical understanding of pragmatics, use your knowledge to amplify your answer.

Chapter 10 Proximal Causes 2: Additional Shared Characteristics and Major Specifiers

1. Identify and discuss relationships between RRBs and some of the peaks and troughs of creativity and imagination in autism.

2. Identify ways in which spared, or relatively spared, abilities in people with ASD across the spectrum can be capitalised on – whether automatically and unconsciously by the individual, or with the assistance of others – to benefit the individual. Give practical examples.

3. If you were formulating an exercise regime for an overweight adolescent boy with middle-to-high-functioning ASD, what forms of exercise might you realistically expect him to persist with – and why? How would the regime you describe differ from a regime prescribed for an overweight non-autistic boy of the same age? (Assume the assistance of a supportive adult in both cases.)

4. In what ways may the underlying causes of learning disability in non-autistic individuals (a) overlap with and (b) differ from the underlying causes of learning disability in autism? Support your arguments with reference to research studies.
5. How may (a) SEC impairments and (b) sensory anomalies in infants and young children with ASD contribute to delayed speech/language onset and anomalous language acquisition across the spectrum? Critically appraise evidence for the role of (c) comorbid SLI as a cause of persistently impaired language across the spectrum.

Chapter 11 Assessment, Diagnosis and Screening

1. Describe a variety of methods and procedures that might be used to assess individuals with ASD in any TWO of the following specialisms:

    Occupational Therapy   Educational Psychology

    Paediatrics   Social Work

    Physiotherapy   Clinical Psychology

    How might the assessment methods you describe be relevant and useful?

2. Imagine you are a member of a high-powered debating society and you are to propose the motion that 'This house considers the diagnosis of cases of ASD to be both desirable and necessary'. Write your speech. Then write a speech opposing the motion, responding to points made by yourself as the proposer of the motion. Alternatively, work with someone else to propose/oppose the motion, respectively.
3. Compare and contrast the information elicited by the ADI-R (Box 11.4) and by the DISCO (Box 11.5). What may be the respective advantages and disadvantages of these two highly-respected diagnostic interview formats?
4. There is an ongoing dispute between the American Academy of Pediatrics and the US Preventitive Services Task Force concerning the pros and cons of universal (Level 1) screening of infants and preschool children for ASD. Using scholarly publications and websites as your sources, write an account of both sides of this argument.
5. 'John', an 8;0 year old with middle-functioning ASD, has in the course of one school term been assessed by the school nurse, the special needs teacher who works with him, the speech and language therapist who visits the school, and a researcher investigating working memory in ASD. What may each of these professionals be seeking to learn about John – and why? Are there ways in which these professionals might learn from each other's assessments?

Chapter 12 Intervention

1. Should people with ASD be left essentially 'untreated' and valued for their differences? If treated, should the aim of treatment be to make the affected individual 'more normal' – or to make them 'happier'? Argue the pros and cons of each of these three approaches to intervention, and draw a conclusion.
2. It is widely accepted that early intensive non-physical intervention of certain kinds can – in at least some cases – have positive effects on at least some ASD-related behaviours. What are the common features of many of the programmes on offer? What are some of the differences?

3. Explain why and how each of the following might be appropriately used to treat individuals with ASD:

   Cognitive behavioural therapy   Family therapy

   Psychotropic medication   Psychotherapy

   Illustrate your answer with real-life or imaginary case histories.

4. No medications are available to effectively treat the behavioural anomalies diagnostic of ASD. Why might this be the case?

5. The history of proclaimed cures and treatments for ASD is littered with examples of unsupported claims. Unfortunately this continues, with unsubstantiated claims made for the efficacy of numerous treatments that are on offer. Select any one such 'borderline evidence-based' or 'non-evidence-based' psychosocial/behavioural treatment and design a watertight efficacy study, using the designs and points of method outlined in Boxes 12.1 and 12.2.

Chapter 13 Care

1. Compare and contrast laws relevant to provision for people with ASD (including legislation for disabled people generally) in your own country and one other country, identifying information via the internet.

2. If you ruled the world, what provision would you make for educating people with ASD across the age range and across the spectrum? If possible, check your answer with another student and discuss any differences you have on this question.

3. In the case of very low-functioning and/or significantly behaviourally disturbed individuals on the spectrum, how may a balance be struck between the ideal of inclusion and the realities of catering for each individual's special care needs?

4. Describe the roles of family support groups, whether at neighbourhood level or in the form of large professionally run organisations, in catering for the needs of individuals with ASD and their families in high-income countries.

5. Describe real-life cases, either from your own experience or from your reading, in which individuals with ASD or their families have needed to employ any FOUR of the following professionals:

   specialist lawyer (for criminal cases, employment disputes, Wills, Trusts, etc.)

   financial advisor   tax accountant   insurance consultant

   professionally trained advocate (e.g. for benefit claims)   other

GLOSSARY

Terms included in the Glossary are those indicated in bold typeface the first time they occur in the main text in the usage to be defined, plus some terms that occur in boxes. Italicised words in any definition can be found elsewhere in the Glossary.

Absolute pitch (AP) The ability to recognise the pitch of any given note in music and give its name. Sometimes referred to as 'perfect pitch'.

Acetylcholine (A.CH) See Box 8.1.

Acquired autism A term used to describe cases in which an older child or an adult develops behaviours characteristic of autism after an illness such as *herpes encephalitis* that causes damage to certain areas of the brain. The autistic-like behaviours do not generally persist. Cf. *quasi-autism* and *pseudo-autism*.

Action–outcome monitoring The process of comparing the intended outcome of an action with the actual outcome of that action.

Adaptive behaviour Behaviour that is appropriate and useful for the individual's survival and wellbeing. The opposite to *maladaptive*.

Advocacy Work carried out by groups or individuals with the aim of advocating, or arguing for, the legal rights of individuals with disabilities. May take the form of lobbying for changes within society and the law or making the case for a specific individual's rights, for example to disability allowance or freedom from abuse. Also involved with providing information and advice to individuals and carers, and in training individuals and groups in self-advocacy.

Affect See Box 3.2

Affective To do with emotions.

Affective agnosia   Agnosia means 'not knowing'/'lack of knowledge'. In the current phrase, refers to the inability to perceive and interpret emotions. Colloquially referred to as 'emotion blindness'.

Affective empathy   See Box 3.2. Synonymous with *contagious empathy*.

Akinesia   A neuromuscular condition involving impairment or loss of voluntary movement. Cf. *psychic akinesia*.

Alexithymia   See Box 3.2.

Algorithm   In general terms, a procedure or formula for solving a problem. When used in the context of scoring responses to a complex diagnostic test, an algorithm will involve a set of detailed instructions to be carried out in a specified order.

Alternative and allied healthcare (AAH)   See *complementary and alternative medicine*.

Amodal   Not confined to any one sensory modality: common to all the senses.

Amygdala   An almond-shaped structure in the interior of each *temporal lobe* containing several different *nuclei*. Part of the *limbic system*.

Apoptosis   Death of a cell caused by a chemical signal that activates a genetic mechanism inside the cell.

Apraxia   Complete loss of the ability to perform voluntary movements. Cf. *dyspraxia*.

Arousal   As used in *neuropsychology* and *neurobiology*, generally refers to the state of alertness or readiness of the nervous system to respond, as influenced by the activity of certain brain regions and *neurochemical* systems. See *reticular activating system*.

Articulation   Production of speech sounds (vowels and consonants) by bringing the moving parts of the speech apparatus (tongue, lips, soft palate) into contact with or proximity to other moving parts or non-moving parts (teeth, hard palate). Sometimes inaccurately used in place of *phonology*.

Asperger disorder   Synonymous with *Asperger syndrome* but less commonly used, although preferred in both DSM-IV and ICD-10.

Asperger syndrome (AS)   The autism spectrum disorder characterised by impaired social, emotional and communicative interaction and by restricted, repetitive behaviour and lack of creativity, in people with normal language development and intellectual ability. Synonymous with *Asperger disorder*, as defined in DSM-IV and ICD-10.

Attachment   An emotional tie involving mutual dependence in adults. In young children the term refers to the emotional *bond* between an infant and one or more adults with whom the infant feels secure and on whom s/he depends for the satisfaction of basic and emotional needs.

Attention   As used by psychologists, this term refers to those processes that enable an organism to focus at any one moment on a certain feature or features of their *sensory* or *perceptual* experience to the relative exclusion of other features. These processes include *selective attention* and *attention switching*.

Attention deficit and hyperactivity disorder (ADHD)   A disorder present from childhood involving distractibility, impulsivity and excessive *motor* activity, often leading to academic failure and social difficulties.

Atypical autism   A term used in ICD-10 (1992) synonymously with *pervasive developmental disorder not otherwise specified (PDD-NOS)* in DSM-IV.

Autistic disorder   The term used in DSM-IV to refer to the *pervasive developmental disorder* characterised by impaired social-emotional and communicative interaction with restricted and repetitive behaviour plus impaired or absent language development and *learning disability*. Other terms that have been used in the past to refer to this particular form of ASD include 'Kanner's autism', 'Kanner's syndrome' and 'classic autism'.

Autobiographical memory   Memory of one's own past experiences, contributing to sense of self ('Who I am'). Combines factual knowledge, such as is acquired via *semantic memory*, for example 'I went to France last year', with contextual details, such as are acquired via *episodic* or *relational memory*, for instance 'who one was with', 'what the weather was like', 'how much one enjoyed it', 'how long the trip lasted'.

Autoimmune disorders   Disorders that occur when the immune system attacks normal body components as if they were foreign invaders.

Autonomic nervous system (ANS)   That portion of the *peripheral nervous system* not under conscious control and concerned with vegetative functions, including digestion, circulation and respiration.

Axon   A long threadlike structure leading from the main cell body and branched at the other end that carries information from one cell to other cells.

Basic emotions   See Box 3.2.

Befriending   A method of supporting an individual, couple or family through a friendly relationship established specifically for the purpose of providing social and practical support.

Behaviourist/behavioural   An approach to treatment that conceives of disturbed behaviours as originating in *maladaptive* learning or conditioning, from which it follows that these behaviours can be unlearned by systematic de-conditioning and re-conditioning. Associated with a particular set of terms, such as 'stimulus', 'reinforcement' and 'association'. Sometimes equated with *learning theory* (although this latter term has numerous other uses in psychology).

Biomarker   In medical usage, a reliable biological indicator of the presence in an individual of a specific disease or mental health condition – an 'identity tag'. Biomarkers can take numerous forms including genetic, cellular, neurochemical or structural markers. Ideally they occur *universally* in all cases of the disease/condition and are *specific* to that disease/condition. Cf. *pathognomic*.

Blind trials   A term used in *efficacy studies* to refer to trials (a set of studies or a sequence of tests within a single study) in which neither the actively involved researchers nor the participants (or their families) know whether the participant is receiving the treatment under investigation or a *placebo*. This is termed a *double blind* trial. If only the participants (and families) are unaware of whether they are on the treatment or on *placebo*, this is a *single blind* trial. See Box 12.1.

Body schema   An abstract *representation* of one's own body parts and relations between them. Note: 'body image' is a non-abstract representation of one's own physical appearance.

Bonding/bond   The formation of a strong emotional tie, or 'bond', narrowly used in psychology to describe the relationship formed by the mother (or other very close primary carer) with her newborn infant: the counterpart of the infant's *attachment* to close carers. 'Bonding' is sometimes more loosely used to refer to the reciprocal emotional tie between infants and close carers.

Brain circuit   See *neural network*.

Brain-derived neurotropic factor (BDNF)   See Box 8.1.

Brain stem   The stem, or 'stalk', of the brain leading from the spinal cord and including core structures of the evolutionarily old brain. The most primitive part of the brain, and the earliest part to develop during gestation.

Broader autism phenotype (BAP)   A term used to describe people who have clinically non-significant and partial forms of the behaviours diagnostic of clinically significant autism. Some of the behaviours associated with the BAP may be beneficial to the individual, contributing to superior academic achievement and career success. Synonymous with *lesser variant autism*.

Broken mirror theory   A phrase sometimes used to refer to the theory that the *mirror neuron system* is dysfunctional in ASD.

Candidate genes   Genes for which there is some evidence, or some logical reason, for hypothesing their possible involvement in a particular condition. See Box 7.2.

Catatonia/catatonic state   A condition in which activity effectively ceases, the individual remaining in a fixed position for prolonged periods. Less commonly, catatonia is characterised by ceaseless and chaotic activity.

Central coherence   The tendency to look for meaning in experience. At the sensory-perceptual level this is manifested as a tendency to perceive wholes rather than parts (the whole barking, tail-wagging dog, rather than the sound of the bark or the movement of the tail alone). At the cognitive level the drive for coherence is manifested similarly as a tendency to interpret ongoing experience as wholes rather than as parts (the whole sentence, rather than individual words; the whole film, not just the moment when the boat sank). Cf. *global processing* and *local processing*; see also *weak central coherence*.

Central nervous system (CNS)   That part of the nervous system comprised of the brain and spinal cord.

Cerebellar vermis   A 'wormlike' portion of the *cerebellum* that receives and transmits auditory, visual, tactile, and *kinaesthetic* sensory information.

Cerebellum   A structure situated at the back and lower part of the brain (above the nape of the neck), consisting of two cerebellar hemispheres and covered with cerebellar *grey matter*, or cortex. Importantly involved in *motor skills*, and now known to contribute also to *attention, cognition, language* and possibly emotion.

Cerebral cortex   The outermost layer of *grey matter* (cell bodies and their connections) of the *cerebral hemispheres*.

Cerebral hemispheres   The two (left and right) halves of the *cerebrum*, each consisting of a *frontal, temporal, parietal* and *occipital* lobe, as well as certain subcortical structures.

Cerebrum   The largest part of the brain, divided into a left and a right *cerebral hemisphere* with a fissure between them, but functionally joined together by the *corpus callosum*. Critically involved in mediating most non-vegetative functions.

Challenging behaviour   'Hard-to-handle' behaviours, such as hitting, biting or having a temper tantrum, that occur usually as a result of stress or frustration, associated with inability to express needs, wants and emotions in any other way.

Childhood autism   The term used in ICD-10 corresponding to the term autistic disorder in DSM-IV.

Childhood disintegrative disorder   A rare degenerative disorder (sometimes known as Heller's syndrome), the clinical features of which closely resemble those of autism. However, age of onset is later than the typical age of onset for autism, usually being between the ages of three and five years, following a period of normal development. Most cases involve a severe loss of skills and a persistently low level of functioning.

Childhood psychosis   See *childhood schizophrenia*.

Childhood schizophrenia/early onset schizophrenia/childhood psychosis   Early diagnostic labels for 'autism' used before it was shown that autism/autism spectrum disorder is a *neurodevelopmental* condition in its own right.

Cognitive/cognition   To do with knowing, thinking, reasoning, etc., including *sensation* and *perception*, but excluding emotions, volition and motivation. 'Cognitive'/'cognition' are commonly but incorrectly used by some psychologists and neuroscientists in place of 'psychological'/'psychology', probably under the influence of a conflation between 'psychology' and 'cognitive science'. See Footnote 2 in Chapter 1.

Cognitive empathy   See Box 3.2.

Common pathway   A point at which several *etiological* or *neurobiological* contributory causal factors converge to produce a single *neurobiological* or *neuropsychological* causal factor from which ASD diagnostic behaviours were once hypothesised to derive. Cf. *single factor theory/hypothesis*.

Common variants   See *copy number polymorphisms (CNPs)*.

Comorbid/comorbidity   A medical term describing the co-occurrence in one individual of two or more identifiable conditions or disorders where one is not an integral component of the other.

Complementary and alternative medicines (CAMS)   A broad group of treatments, whether physical or non-physical, that are not considered within a particular culture to have any proven efficacy or to have any theoretical rationale recognised by that particular culture. Synonymous with *alternative and allied healthcare*.

Complex emotions   See Box 3.2.

Comprehensive treatment model (CTM)   An approach to, or method of, treatment designed to alleviate/modify the set of behaviours diagnostic of ASD. CMTs are rooted generally in a conceptual framework which underpins a set of prescribed procedures and instructions as to where and by whom the treatment is best delivered, at what intensity, and over what period of time. Cf. *focused intervention practices (FIPs)*.

Concordance   The occurrence of a particular trait or condition in both members of a twin pair. Cf. *discordance*.

Conjunctive search (test)   A test involving searching for a stimulus that has a unique combination of features among a set of 'distractor' stimuli that have similar but not identical combinations of features.

Connectivity   The structural and/or functional connections between individual *neurons, nuclei* or specific structures in the brain; the structural and/or functional connections within *neural networks/circuits/systems*.

Constructivism–constructivist model   This term originally referred to a model of child development proposed by Piaget, according to which children construct their knowledge and skills on the basis of a minimal set of innate *domain-general* sensory, motor and learning capacities interacting with environmental inputs. Constructivisim (or, as it is sometimes called, *neoconstructivism*) now generally refers to a model of development that seeks to reconcile the Piagetian and the *modularist* theories. This model maintains that children construct their knowledge and skills on the basis of a set of genetically determined *domain-general* learning capacities and *domain-specific* attentional biases and predispositions operating on environmental inputs to produce *domain-specific* modular capacities for, for example, *language* or *mindreading*.

Contagious empathy   See Box 3.2. Synonymous with *emotion contagion* and *affective empathy*.

Continuum   Literally, something that is continuous. When used to describe behaviours that may be associated with autism, the implication is that across individuals there is an unbroken range of ability or difference.

Copy number polymorphisms (CNPs)   Refers to the most commonly occurring copy number variations (CNVs). Synonymous with *common variants*.

Copy number variations/variants (CNVs)   Refers to the fact that the number of copies of a particular gene varies from one individual to the next, with deletions or duplications being common. The most commonly occurring CNVs are referred to as *copy number polymorphisms* or *common variants*.

Corpus callosum   An extended band of *grey matter* consisting of *axons* connecting corresponding regions of the right and left *cerebral hemispheres*.

Cortex   *Grey matter* (predominantly cell bodies) forming the outer layers of both new and old brain structures, including the *cerebral hemispheres*, the *cerebellar* hemispheres and structures within the *limbic system*.

Cortical   Of the cortex (see above).

Cortisol   See Box 8.1.

Counterfactual reasoning   Reasoning based on a fictional/false supposition, for example, 'If the sky were yellow, it would be the same colour as lemons'.

Crossover designs   See Box 12.1.

Crystallised intelligence   A form of intelligence that consists of accumulated knowledge, the acquisition of which depends on culture and learning opportunities. Cf. *fluid intelligence*.

Cytokines   Proteins secreted by specific cells of the immune system to mediate and regulate immunity, and to counteract infection, inflammation and some forms of disease. They also have a role in reproduction.

Declarative memory   Conscious or 'explicit' forms of memory that can be reflected on and reported. Includes memory for personally experienced events (*episodic memory*) and factual memories/knowledge (*semantic memory*).

Default mode network (DMN)   A neural circuit that is activated when the individual is awake but not engaged in any outward-directed task. They may be thinking about themselves, thinking about others, recalling past events, thinking about the future, or thinking about nothing in particular. The DMN consists of a known set of interconnected brain regions. However, different but overlapping groups of structures may be involved in thinking about self, thinking about others, and in thinking about past and future.

Deixis/deictic terms   A term used by linguists to refer to words the meaning of which is dependent on the identity of the speaker, and where and when they are speaking. Examples include 'you', 'here' and 'now'.

Dendrites   Branch-like structures attached to *neurons*, which receive information from the *axons* of other neurons.

Descriptors   A term introduced in the DSM-5 definition of ASD to cover, first, the severity of the diagnostic behaviours as they occur in any individual, and secondly, the presence of any significant additional condition or factor. Cf. *specifiers*.

Design fluency test   A test of the ability to *generate* a varied range of patterns, shapes or representations of objects utilising a limited number of given constituents. See *fluency*.

Developmental dyslexia   Inability to learn to read to the expected standard in the absence of any obvious cause, such as significant visual impairment, *learning disability* or lack of learning opportunity. Often associated with poor spelling and writing, and sometimes with poor arithmetical ability.

Developmental trajectory   The passage or course of development and change over the lifespan.

Diagnostic pathway   'Pathway', as used here, refers to a set of recommendations relating to procedures and practices, the succession and timing of these, and the personnel involved, designed to ensure best practice in health care. Recommended diagnostic pathways may differ across regions and countries, and also across time, according to current knowledge, culture and available services.

Differential diagnosis   Diagnosis that includes consideration not only of what a condition is, but also what it is not: distinguishing one condition from another.

Discordance   The occurrence of a particular trait or condition in one member of a twin pair but not the other. Cf. *concordance*.

Dissociable/dissociation   If psychological or *neuropsychological* phenomenon A can occur independently of phenomenon B, then A and B can be described as dissociable. If B can also occur independently of A, A and B can be described as 'doubly dissociable' or constituting an example of a 'double dissociation'. Hearing impairment and visual impairment are doubly dissociable. Communication impairment and language impairment in autism, however, are merely dissociable (because communication impairment can occur without language impairment, but not vice versa).

Distal   Most distant; furthest away. The opposite of *proximal*.

Dizygotic (DZ) (twins)   Twins who develop from different fertilised eggs and who do not share identical *genotypes*. Cf. *monozygotic* twins.

Domain-general   Pertaining to a broad range of skills and knowledge, and/or the acquisition of such skills/knowledge. For example, sensory capacities, attention, representational abilities, memory.

Domain-specific   Pertaining to a particular area of knowledge and/or set of skills, for example *language*, mathematics, music or *mindreading/theory of mind*. Associated with *modularist* models of brain/mind organisation and development.

Dopamine   See Box 8.1.

Double blind trials   See *blind trials*.

Down (Down's) syndrome   A developmental condition identified by Dr Langdon-Down in the nineteenth century, resulting from abnormal genetic material on chromosome 21. Characterised by a distinctive set of physical, psychological and health anomalies, not all of which are present in all cases, allowing a broad range of developmental outcomes. See also Box 7.1.

Dyadic interaction   In social psychology, a face-to-face encounter or interaction between two people referred to as a 'dyad', for instance mother–child dyad or husband–wife dyad. In developmental psychology, closely similar in meaning to *primary intersubjectivity*, though with less emphasis on shared *affect* and awareness of *self–other correspondence*.

Dyspraxia   Partial loss of the ability to perform voluntary movements. Cf. *verbal apraxia*.

Echolalia   Speech in which the words used by another person are repeated more or less exactly, with the same stress and inflexion, either immediately ('immediate echolalia', which is usually reflexive) or some time later ('delayed echolalia', which may be used communicatively).

Efficacy study   A scientific study of the effectiveness of a treatment or other form of intervention designed to cure or alleviate a medical condition or disorder. See Boxes 12.1 and 12.2.

Elective mutism   See *selective mutism*.

Electroencephalography (EEG)   A method of recording electrical activity in the brain involving placing electrodes on the scalp that pick up changes in electrical potentials in underlying brain regions.

Embryo   The developing organism *in utero* from two to eight weeks post-conception (in humans). Cf. *fetus*.

Emotion contagion   See Box 3.2. Syonymous with *affective* or *contagious empathy*.

Empathising system   See Box 3.2. NB: The Empathising SyStem (TESS) is sometimes used narrowly by Baron-Cohen to refer one of the set of hypothetical *modular* capacities underlying *mindreading*.

Empathy   See Box 3.2 and the asterisked footnote.

Enhanced discrimination–reduced generalisation theory   A theory proposed by Plaisted and colleagues based on the observation that, whereas unique combinations of features of a stimulus are discriminated better by individuals with ASD than by non-autistic individuals, shared or similar features are less salient than for non-autistic individuals.

Enhanced perceptual function (EPF) theory   A theory first proposed by Mottron and Burack in 2001, the main tenet of which is that superior low-level *perceptual* functioning leads to a restriction of interests in favour of preoccupation with perceptual processing within a selected domain.

Epidemiology   The study of the *incidence, prevalence* and distribution of diseases.

Epigenetic   To do with changes in gene expression caused by external factors rather than by changes in the DNA sequence.

Episodic memory   See Box 9.3. Synonymous with *relational memory*.

Etiology/etiological   The study of the initial or first causes of a disease or disorder. (Sometimes spelt 'aetiology'.)

Executive functions   The set of cognitive processes that are involved in the organisation and control of mental and physical activity, including *attention, generativity*, inhibition and action monitoring. Derives from an analogy with computers, in which a master program controls and directs all the software programs on the machine.

Explanatory power   The capacity of a hypothesis or theory to explain its subject matter. Explanatory power varies according to the strength of the evidence and arguments adduced in support of a theory, the precision and parsimony of the theory, and its predictive power (among other measures).

Explicit theory of mind   Conscious knowledge of another person's *mental state*, for example what another person has seen, is feeling, knows etc., as well as conscious knowledge of one's own mental states, plus the ability to reflect on one's own and others' mental states and to predict (verbally, if requested) another person's behaviour in the light of this knowledge.

Extreme male brain (EMB) theory   The theory that autism is associated with an extreme version of the typical male brain, including an abnormally strong capacity for *systemising* and an abnormally weak capacity for *empathising*.

False belief test/task   Any test of the ability to understand that another person may believe something to be true that is in fact false, and to predict the other person's behaviour on the basis of their false belief.

False negative   When used in the context of screening or diagnosis, this refers to a failure to identify the presence of a particular disease or condition in an individual who is suffering from that disease/condition.

False positive   When used in the context of screening or diagnosis, this refers to the incorrect identification of a particular disease or condition in an individual who is not affected by that disease/condition.

Familial   Characteristic of a family. Inherited characteristics that are familial are those that tend to run in families, as opposed to those that occur as a result of *sporadic* variation or damage to genetic material.

Fetus   The developing organism *in utero* from the eighth week post-conception (in humans). Cf. *embryo*.

Fidelity   This term has various meanings within psychology. When used in relation to *psychosocial* or *behavioural* treatments, it refers to the extent to which a treatment is carried out in conformity with the precise instructions relating to that intervention.

Fine cuts   A term coined by Frith and Happé to refer to the phenomenon, which is striking in autism, of two closely related abilities being unimpaired in one case and impaired in the other (e.g. *protoimperative* and *protodeclarative pointing*).

First-degree relatives   An individual's biological parents and biological siblings.

Fluency/fluency tests. As used by psychologists, 'fluency' generally means the ability to produce a number and variety of words, images or ideas in response to a prompt or cue. Synonymous with *generativity* in the sense of capacity to produce novel outputs.

Fluid intelligence   A form of intelligence that involves the ability to perceive relationships between stimuli and to reason logically and abstractly. Thought to be genetically determined, at least in part, rather than critically dependent on culture or learning opportunities. Synonymous with *general intelligence ('g')*. Cf. *crystallised intelligence*.

Focused intervention practice (FIP)   FIPs are designed to instantiate or strengthen specific *adaptive* skills/abilities or to alleviate or eliminate specific *maladaptive* habits/behaviour problems. Most FIPs are based on a conceptual framework and methods adopted from *learning theory*. Cf. *comprehensive treatment model*.

Formulaic language/formulaicity   Rigid, invariable phrases, expressions or grammatical 'frames'. For example, 'Many happy returns of the day', 'Dead as a dodo', 'Want (Mummy, Daddy, X, Y, Z) do it'.

Fragile-X (FRA-X) syndrome   The most common inherited cause of mild to moderate *learning disability*, resulting from an abnormality on the X-chromosome and therefore manifesting differently in males and females (see *sex-linked*). Also characterised by a number of physical and behavioural anomalies, some of the latter resembling behaviours seen in autism. See also Box 7.1.

Frontal lobe(s)   The lobe that lies at the front of each *cerebral hemisphere*. See Figure 8.1. The most recently evolved component of the *cerebral cortex*, involved in several higher-order or human-unique functions, including *language* and *theory of mind*.

Functional magnetic resonance imaging (fMRI)   A method of assessing brain activity. See Box 8.4.

Functional pretend play/pretence   Pretend play in which either real-life objects or miniature versions of real-life objects are used with their conventional functions, for example a real comb, or a doll-sized comb, used to 'do dolly's hair'. Cf. *symbolic play/pretence*.

Future thinking   Thinking forwards in time as the converse of episodic memory, which involves 'thinking backwards in time'. Future thinking and episodic memory may be envisaged as involving 'mental time travel'. Both are subserved by the *default mode network*.

Gamma-amino-butyric acid (GABA)   The most important inhibitory neurotransmitter in the brain. See Box 8.1.

Gaze following   The strong tendency among typically developing infants to turn to look in the same direction in which another person turns their head to look. Sometimes referred to as 'gaze monitoring'.

General intelligence ('g')   A predominantly innate capacity for learning, reasoning, problem solving and abstract thinking that makes a measurable contribution to performance on all tests of intelligence. Often referred to as 'g'. Synonymous with *fluid intelligence*.

Generalise/generalisation   The process of extending knowledge or skills gained from a limited set of stimuli or life experiences to include other related, but non-identical, stimuli or experiences.

Generativity   A term borrowed from linguistics, where it refers to the fact that an infinite number of different sentences can be generated from a finite set of words and grammatical rules. More loosely, 'productivity' and, in psychology, *fluency*.

Genetic variant/variation   Any variations within a gene, including a *copy number variation (CNV)*, a *single-nucleotide polymorphism (SNP)* or a mutation.

Genome   The full set of genes of any individual organism.

Genotype   The genetic constitution of an organism; a set of hereditary factors that influences, but does not fully determine, the development of an organism. Sometimes used to refer to the genetic make-up of a particular group of organisms/individuals.

Glial cells/glia   The supporting cells in the *central nervous system* that serve protective, nutritional and other 'housekeeping' functions for the information-carrying neurons and their projections.

Global network   A *neural network* made up of the co-ordinated activity of several *local networks*, and mediating complex, multidimensional and multimodal experience.

Global processing A term used in the psychology of *perception*, referring to the tendency to perceive complex stimuli as wholes rather than to perceive individual parts of a stimulus. Cf. *local processing*, also *central coherence*.

Glutamate The most important excitatory *neurotransmitter* in the brain. See Box 8.1.

Grey literature Literature (in print or electronic form) within a field of study that has not been authoritatively *peer-reviewed* prior to publication.

Grey/gray matter Brain tissue made up of cell bodies that are greyish-brown in colour. Cf. *white matter*.

Guardian ad litem An individual with legal responsibility to care for the interests of another person who, for whatever reason, is deemed unable to do this for themselves.

Gyrus/gyri Ridges on the cortical surfaces of the brain which, in combination with *sulci*, significantly extend the cortical surface area.

Herpes encephalitis Inflammation in the brain, usually including regions of the *limbic system*, caused by one of the several herpes viruses.

Heterogeneous/heterogeneity Variety or difference. The opposite of *homogeneous*.

Hippocampus A seahorse-shaped structure in the interior of each *temporal lobe*. Part of the *limbic system*.

Homogeneous/homogeneity Similarity or overall sameness. The opposite of *heterogeneous*.

Hyperacusis/hyperacusic Excessively sensitive hearing, sometimes restricted to certain sounds or groups of sounds, capable of causing actual distress.

Hypercalculia A specific developmental condition in which the ability to perform mathematical calculations is significantly superior to general learning ability and to school attainment in maths.

Hyperlexia A specific developmental condition in which the ability to read aloud with reasonable accuracy is significantly superior to reading comprehension. Cf. *mechanical reading*.

Hypersystemising Unusually strong tendencies to *systemise*.

Hypertonia/hypertonic Excessive muscle tone, i.e. tension or rigidity in the muscles. The opposite of *hypotonia*.

Hypo-priors   Poorly defined or narrowed *prototypes* or *priors*.

Hypothalamic-pituitary-adrenal axis (HPA)   An interactive system comprising the hypothalamus and the pituitary gland in the brain, and the adrenal glands on the kidneys, that is a major part of the neuroendocrine system that controls reactions to stress and regulates various bodily processes.

Hypotonia   Lack of normal muscle tone, i.e. floppiness and lack of power in the muscles. The opposite of *hypertonia*.

Ideational fluency test   A test of the ability to generate a varied range of functions or uses of a limited number of given constituents. See *fluency*.

Idiopathic   Describes any medical condition or disorder that arises from within the individual, or some part of the individual, in the absence of any known external factor. More loosely, the term is used to describe conditions the causes of which are unknown.

Immediate memory   See Box 9.3.

Implicit theory of mind   Unconscious knowledge of another person's *mental state*, for instance what another person has seen, is feeling, knows, etc.

Incidence   Refers to the number of new cases of a disease or disorder reported in a given period of time.

Inclusion   As used here, this term refers to the moral right of every person to be included as a valued member of their society and not discriminated against because of difference.

Insistence on sameness (IS)   That kind of repetitive-restricted behaviour that manifests as a strong preference for environments and behaviours that reduce novelty and promote predictability for the individual. Resistance to change.

Intelligence quotient (IQ)   The number derived either from a table (as in the Wechsler scales) or from dividing an individual's *mental age* as measured on an intelligence test by their chronological age and multiplying by 100. Note that in the Wechsler scales, 'IQ' is referred to as 'Full Scale IQ' (FS-IQ). See Box 4.1.

Joint attention   A state of attention in which two (or more) individuals are not only attending to the same object, person or event, but also know that the other person is attending to it; thus they have knowledge of the other person's *mental state*. Synonymous with *shared attention*. Cf. also *triadic interaction/relating*.

Joint laxity   A condition in which the ligaments of a joint do not hold the joint tightly in place, allowing for 'hypermobility', colloquially 'double jointedness'.

Kinaesthesia/kinaesthetic   A feeling of movement; to do with the experience of one's own body movements. A specific component of *proprioception*.

Lateralisation   The process by which different functions and processes come to be mediated by one or the other side of the brain.

Learning disability   The currently preferred term for what used to be referred to (and sometimes still is) as 'mental retardation', 'general learning disability' or 'intellectual disability'. All these terms are defined in terms of a combination of subaverage intelligence (as measured on *standardised* tests) and poor day-to-day *adaptive*, or coping, abilities. Note that in the UK the term 'specific learning impairment' refers to selective, as opposed to generalised, learning difficulty (as in, for example, *developmental dyslexia* or *specific language impairment*).

Learning theory   A term used with various meanings by psychologists (and others). In the context of non-physical treatments for ASD, however, the term is generally associated with *behaviourist* methods of intervention in which learning is conceptualised as a form of conditioning.

Lesion   Any impairment or flaw in body tissue produced by an injury, disease or surgery.

Lesser variant autism   See *broader autism phenotype*.

Lexical semantics   See *semantics*.

Limbic system   A set of evolutionarily old structures in the interior of the brain including the *amygdala* and *hippocampus*; important for emotion, motivation and *declarative memory*.

Local network   A circuit involving relatively few *nuclei* situated close together in the brain.

Local processing   A term used in the psychology of *perception* referring to the tendency to perceive the individual parts of a complex stimulus rather than to perceive wholes. Cf. *global processing* and *central coherence*.

Macrocephaly   A condition in which the head is notably enlarged.

Maladaptive behaviour   Behaviour that is inappropriate and ultimately not conducive to the individual's survival and wellbeing, though it may achieve immediate or short-term goals. Cf. *adaptive behaviour*.

Manifest behaviour   Instances of any individual's day-to-day behaviour such as might come under generalised headings such as 'impaired social interaction', 'lack of emotional reciprocity', 'restricted and repetitive behaviour', etc.

Mechanical reading   Reading aloud with correct pronunciation, but without comprehension. A form of *hyperlexia*.

Mental age (MA)   Level of development or achievement expressed in terms of the chronological age (CA) at which this level would be average or prototypical. In a completely average child MA = CA; in a child with superior ability MA > CA; in a child with developmental delay MA < CA. Sometimes referred to as 'age equivalent' or 'developmental age'.

Mental set   A state of mind in which there is a preparedness to respond in a particular way (e.g. to press the buzzer when a circle (but not a square) appears; to perceive a particular face (not others) in a crowd).

Mental state   A perception, feeling, desire, thought, belief or other item of knowledge or feeling that, according to *representational* models, exists in the mind and corresponds to a specific pattern of neural activity in the brain.

Mentalising ability   The ability to form *representations* of other people's and one's own *mental states*.

Meta-analysis   An analysis of the results of several research studies investigating a particular phenomenon.

Metarepresentation   Crudely, 'a representation of a representation'. For example, a drawing of a house is a *representation* of a house; but a photograph of the drawing is a metarepresentation. Metarepresentation of mental states, our own and those of others, enables us to compare an original representation with its re-representation, to reflect on and reason about them, and to make predictions about others' behaviour based on similarities and differences between the status of the original and that of the 'copy'.

Mindreading   Colloquially, the ability to 'read' other people's thoughts. In the psychological and especially the autism literatures, the term has the broader meaning of the capacity to represent in one's own mind the perceptions, thoughts, feeling of oneself and others, either unconsciously (see *implicit ToM*) or consciously (see *explicit ToM*). Explicit mindreading/theory of mind ability enables the individual to reason about, and to explicitly predict, others' behaviour. Dependent on the ability to *mentalise*.

Minicolumn   A column of around 100 interconnected neurons running vertically through cortical layers of the brain. Thought to play an essential role in the organisation of cortical pathways and functional connections. There are an estimated 200 million of these microscopic structures in human cortex.

Mirror neurons/mirror neuron system (MNS)   A set of motor neurons that fire when an individual performs an action, and which are also active when the same action is seen to be performed by another individual of the same species (human or primate, according to current research). See also *broken mirror theory*.

Module/modular/modularism/modularist   Modularism is the theory that the brain/mind is largely organised in the form of discrete *domain-specific*, genetically specified processing systems (modules), associated with particular neural structures and circuits that are innately *programmed* to develop at a particular time and in a predictable sequence in all individuals of a particular species. Contrasts with *(neo)constructivism*.

Monotropic attention   Attention to *sensory* inputs from one modality only, to the exclusion of information from other sensory channels.

Monozygotic (MZ) (twins)   Twins who develop from the same fertilised egg, and who have identical *genotypes*. Cf. *dizygotic* (twins).

Morphology/morphemes/morphosyntax   See Box 4.2.

Motor (skills)   To do with bodily positioning and movement; the set of capacities and processes involved in the initiation, execution and control of bodily posture and movement.

Multiplex families   Families in which more than one person has ASD, and/or close relatives fall within the *broader autism phenotype*.

Myelin sheath   The whiteish-coloured tube made up of *glial cells* that protects an *axon* and insulates it from other axons.

Necessary cause   Any causal factor without which a particular effect cannot occur. Cf. *sufficient cause*.

Neoconstructivism   See *constructivism*.

Neologism   A made-up word; a newly invented expression.

Nerve tract   A bundle of myelinated nerve fibres following a path through the brain.

Neural network/circuit/system   A set of brain *nuclei*, or brain structures, and their neural connections, subserving a particular function or related set of functions. Analogous to an electrical circuit dedicated to a specific function or set of functions.

Neurobiology/neurobiological   Branch of biology that deals with the structure and function of the nervous system including the brain.

Neurochemistry   Study of the chemical constituents of the nervous system, their processes and functions.

Neurodevelopmental disorder Any brain-based condition that manifests from early childhood by disrupting normal psychological development, generally in ways that may be termed 'specific' or 'selective'. Thus, conditions such as *specific language disorder* or *attention deficit disorder* fall under the heading of 'neurodevelopmental disorder', whereas pervasive *learning disability* (*mental retardation*) is less likely to be so described.

Neurodiversity Refers to the belief, or argument, that many conditions conventionally considered pathological, including ASD, result from normal variations within the human genome comparable to those that contribute to variations in sexual orientation or ethnicity. It follows that people with such conditions should be accepted and valued as 'different' rather than being described as 'sick' or 'disabled'.

Neuromodulator A naturally secreted substance (usually a *neuropeptide*, e.g. *oxytocin, vasopressin*) that acts like a *neurotransmitter* except that its operates not only at *synapses* but also more widely, and often over whole *neural circuits/networks*.

Neurons The information-processing and information-transmitting elements of the nervous system. Synonymous with 'nerve cell'.

Neuropsychology/neuropsychological Study of the interface between brain and mind, where fundamental/irreducible psychological processes or behaviours can be identified with the structures and functions of the brain that subserve them.

Neuroreceptors Molecules within *neurons* that are selectively responsive to particular *neurotransmitters*.

Neurosis A personality or mental disturbance not resulting from any known biological cause. Sometimes equated with any mental health disorder in which an individual does not lose touch with reality (in contrast to *psychosis*).

Neurotransmitter Chemical substances released by one *neuron* to stimulate or inhibit activity in other neurons.

Neurotrophins Chemical substances that influence the growth of *neurons* and their connections.

Neurotypical Neurobiologically normal, especially in terms of brain structure and function. Cf. *typicality/typical/typically developing*.

Nicotinic receptors Proteins that respond to acetylcholine and also to some drugs, including nicotine. Widely distributed in both the *CNS* and the *PNS* with multiple functions within the autonomic nervous system and also the *motor output system*.

Non-specific factors Factors that may influence the outcome of a piece of research (e.g. an *efficacy study*) that are not controlled for in the research. Such factors are often ongoing, or background, factors, such as the motivation of an individual to participate or their expectations of the outcome.

Nonverbal abilities/nonverbal intelligence Reasoning and problem solving abilities that are not dependent on the use of language, for instance visual-spatial constructional skills, pattern perception and manipulation. For examples of tests of nonverbal intelligence, see Box 4.1.

Nonverbal communication *Communication* achieved by means other than *language*, for example by facial expressions; body postures, orientation and movement; body odours or odours of specially emitted body substances; touch; vocalisation and other sounds.

Nonverbal IQ/NVQ See Box 4.1. NB: in the Wechsler tests, nonverbal IQ/NVQ are referred to as 'performance IQ/PQ'.

Noradrenalin/norepinephrine See Box 8.1.

Normalisation The principle according to which people with disabilities should be enabled to have lives as similar as possible to those of people without disabilities; they should be enabled to achieve good quality of life; and they should have the same human rights as people without disabilities.

Nucleus The central region of a cell, containing the chromosomes; or a cluster of neurons, all of which are involved in transmitting and receiving the same information.

Nuclei Plural of *nucleus* in either sense, but most commonly used to refer to clusters of neurons.

Obsessive-compulsive disorder (OCD) A specific form of anxiety disorder characterised by recurrent and persistent thoughts and compulsions to carry out repetitive and ritualised behaviours.

Occipital lobe(s) One of the lobes of the cerebrum, situated at the back of the skull (see Figure 8.1). Contains the primary visual cortex, where visual information is processed.

Open/open label designs See Box 12.1.

Oppositional defiant disorder (ODD) Defined in DSM-5 as a persistent pattern of angry/irritable mood, argumentative/defiant behaviour, or vindictiveness.

Optimal outcome (OO) The term used to refer to instances of recovery from ASD, i.e. instances where a person who was once diagnosed with ASD no longer qualifies for this diagnosis.

Oscillations   Rhythmic electrical activity generated spontaneously and in response to stimuli within the central nervous system, colloquially referred to as 'brain waves'.

Over-focused attention   See *over-selective attention*.

Over-selective attention   Attention directed at a single feature of a stimulus when it would be more usual or appropriate to attend to a broader range of features. For example, focusing solely on the colour of an object instead of seeing the object as a whole, including colour, shape, size, texture, etc. Synonymous with *over-focused attention*; see also *selective attention*.

Oxytocin   See Box 8.1.

Parallel design   See Box 12.1.

Parietal lobe(s)   One of the lobes of the cerebrum situated behind the *frontal lobe*, above the *temporal lobe*, and in front of the *occipital lobe* (see Figure 8.1). The primary sensory areas for pain, pressure, and touch. Also involved in spatial orientation, *language* development and *attention*.

Pathognomic   A description of physical or behavioural 'trademark' signs of a specific disease or mental health condition. Cf. *biomarker*.

Peer review   The process by which scholarly articles are critically assessed by other experts in the same field when submitted for publication. Determines whether or not an article is accepted for publication, and acceptance is often subject to conditions designed to improve the work reported or the report itself, as suggested by the reviewers.

Perception   The processes that give coherence and meaning to sensory input.

Perceptual memory   See Box 9.3.

Peripheral nervous system (PNS)   That part of the nervous system that is not contained within the brain and spinal cord. Connects the *central nervous system (CNS)* with the rest of the body.

Peripheral vision   Vision using the peripheral parts of the retina (colloquially, seeing things out of the corners of the eyes).

Perseveration/perseverative   The tendency to continue to do something or continue in a particular line of thought inappropriately, with the implication that the persistence or repetition is *maladaptive*/pathological.

Pervasive developmental disorder not otherwise specificied (PDD-NOS)   A diagnostic term used in DSM-IV to describe individuals with mild, partial or atypical forms of autism-related behaviours. Synonymous with *atypical autism* in ICD-10.

Pervasive developmental disorders (PDDs)   A group of five disorders charac-terised by delays in the development of multiple basic functions including social-isation and *communication*. According to DSM-IV, the group consists of *autistic disorder*, *Asperger syndrome*, *pervasive developmental disorder not otherwise specified*, *Rett syndrome* and *childhood disintegrative disorder*.

Pervasive mutism   A poorly understood and little-researched condition in which an individual understands at least some language but is unable to produce any voluntary and intentional form of communicative output.

Phenotype   The outcome of the interaction between a *genotype* and environmen-tal factors in an individual, as manifested in the structure, function and behaviour of the individual. Sometimes used to refer to outcomes characteristic of a particu-lar group of individuals, for example *autism phenotype*, *broader autism phenotype*.

Phenylketonuria (PKU)   An inherited disorder of protein metabolism which, if untreated, arrests brain development and causes *learning disability*. See also Box 7.1.

Phoneme/phonology/phonotactics   See Box 4.2.

Phonological loop   See Box 9.3.

Pica   A compulsion to eat non-edible substances, for example grass, earth, paper.

Placebo   A substance with no medicinal properties, administered as a control condition in efficacy studies of drug or dietary treatments (see Box 12.1). Also sometimes used by doctors for the psychological benefit of a person complaining of a condition for which there is no detectable organic cause, or in cases where medication is likely to be ineffective or inappropriate.

Plasticity   A term used in *neurobiology* to refer to the adaptability of the brain in terms of which *nuclei/circuits/*regions carry out specific functions.

Pleiotropic   A term used in genetics to refer to any gene that contributes to many different *phenotypic* outcomes.

Polydipsia   Excessive thirst; a pathological compulsion to ingest liquids.

Polygenic   A pattern of inheritance involving many genes that applies to charac-teristics which vary continuously, such as height, gender orientation, intelligence.

Prader-Willi syndrome   An inherited condition manifesting from birth and char-acterised by learning disability, immature physical development, emotional insta-bility, *hypotonia* and excessive appetite. See also Box 7.1.

Pragmatics   Knowledge of the rules and conventions governing the choice of words and word forms used in any instance of actual conversation.

Predictive value   A measure of the efficacy of a *screening* test based on the accuracy with which a particular test predicts the proportion of individuals in the general population who have a particular disease or disorder as compared to the proportion who do not.

Prevalence   The total number of cases of a disease or disorder in a specified population at a particular point in time.

Primacy criterion   A yardstick for assessing the *validity* of a theory/hypothesis concerning the causes of a disorder or a particular facet of a disorder based on the fact that cause always precedes effect.

Primary intersubjectivity   The earliest forms of one-to-one co-ordinated interaction between infants and carers, in which infants indicate some awareness of the sameness between themselves and other people (self-equivalence). Similar to *dyadic interaction*, but with greater emphasis on emotion sharing. See also *secondary intersubjectivity*.

Priors   A term introduced and used by Pellicano and colleagues in their '*hypopriors' theory*. Synonymous with *prototypes*.

Proband   A term used in studies of the genetic origins of mental or physical disorders to refer to the affected individual within a family.

Procedural memory   See Box 9.3.

Prodromal autism   A developmental stage that precedes diagnosable ASD, but during which some early indications of ASD may be retrospectively detectable (e.g. from home videos). Synonymous with 'incipient autism'.

Prognosis   The predicted course and eventual outcome of a particular disease or disorder in medical terminology.

Programmed   Genetically determined to occur at a certain time in a certain sequence. An expression used in discussions of development and behaviour, based on an analogy between brains and computers. Synonymous with 'hardwired'.

Proprioception/proprioceptive   A general term used to refer to all those *sensory* systems that are involved in providing information about position, location, orientation, and movement of one's own body/body parts.

Prosody   See Box 4.2.

Prospective studies   Research studies of groups selected before there are any signs of the onset of a particular condition, then studied to determine if, when and how a condition such as ASD first manifests. Groups participating in prospective studies are often selected on grounds of likely risk, for example younger siblings of a child with ASD. Cf. *retrospective studies*.

Protoconversation   Conversation-like, turn-taking exchanges of vocalisations and other *nonverbal communication* signals between prelinguistic infants and carers, often initiated as well as maintained by the infant.

Protodeclarative (pointing)   *Communication* for the sake of sharing something of interest with another person, often by pointing at the object or event of interest; but it can also involve bringing something to show another person or drawing attention to something using language. Associated with *joint/shared attention*.

Protoimperative (pointing)   *Communication* designed to obtain something an individual needs or wants, sometimes by pointing, sometimes by asking, sometimes by taking another person towards a wanted object or guiding their hand towards it.

Prototype   An abstract representation of the most typical instance of a class or category of things, based on the shared features or functions of individual instances of the class or category.

Proximal   Nearest; most immediate. The opposite of *distal*.

Pseudo-autism   A term used to describe cases in which an individual has the behaviours characteristic of autism or resembling those of autism, but where the causes and course of those behaviours differ from those of ASD. So, for example, 'autism' or 'autistic-like behaviours' associated with blindness or with extreme deprivation in early childhood may be described as cases of pseudo-autism. Synonymous with *quasi-autism*.

Psychic akinesia   A rare neurological condition characterised by extreme passivity, apathy and profound generalised loss of self-motivation; affected individuals describe themselves as having a complete mental void or blank. However, complex physical and mental tasks can be carried out under instruction, and with prompts to continue.

Psychosis/psychotic   A severe personality or mental disturbance, usually of biological origin though precipitating experiences may also be involved. Sometimes equated with any mental health disorder in which an individual loses touch with reality (in contrast to *neurosis*).

Psychosocial (interventions)   Interventions in which social interaction is the main vehicle for changing behaviour. Overlaps with *behavioural* interventions, in which there is less emphasis on social interaction.

Purkinje cells   Large branching neurons found in the *cortex* of the *cerebellum*.

Quasi-autism   See *pseudo-autism*.

Randomised control trial (RCT)   See Box 12.1.

Reelin   See Box 8.1.

Referent   The entity, or 'thing' in the real world that a word stands for.

Regressive autism   A diagnostic or descriptive term used to describe cases in which behaviours associated with autism appear in children, usually after the age of three years, and following ostensibly normal early development. Synonymous with *late-onset autism*.

Relational memory   Memory for complex, multimodal stimuli and events, including contextual information. Synonymous with *episodic memory*.

Reliable/reliability   When used to describe an assessment procedure or diagnostic test, implies that the test in question produces consistent results when used under different conditions, for example when administered to an individual by different testers or to an individual on different occasions. Various aspects of test reliability can be assessed statistically. Cf. *valid*.

Repetitive sensory-motor stereotypies (RSMs)   That group of repetitive-restricted behaviours which consists of movements or self-stimulatory behaviours such as hand-flapping, rocking, or habitually sifting sand through the fingers.

Representation   A construct used in philosophical and some psychological theories concerning the mind, its properties and functions. Such theories envisage the mind as furnished with images or 'copies' representing, or standing for, things in the external world, experienced feelings, abstract ideas, etc. Cf. *metarepresentation*.

Respite care   Care of an individual by someone or some organisation outside the family (or other full-time carer(s)), for a period of time, often on a regular basis (e.g. one night a week for a child). Provides carers with some respite from their responsibilities to the individual, and provides the individual with the opportunity to extend their social relationships and life experiences.

Reticular activating system   A brain system originating within the *brain stem* that modulates *arousal* levels among other functions.

Retrospective studies   Research studies that use information from the past to identify the earliest signs of, or risk factors for, a disease or mental health condition.

Rett (Rett's) syndrome   A rare degenerative disorder occurring only in girls, and which at various stages in its course involves hand stereotypies resembling those that occur in some people with autism, and also loss of language and some degree of social withdrawal.

Salience network   This relatively recently identified *brain circuit* is thought to mediate the allocation of attention to whatever stimuli are most relevant, or 'salient', at any one particular time; to modulate autonomic responses to salient stimuli; and to link with the *motor* system to initiate stimulus-appropriate action. Key brain structures are the insula (which detects salient events and initiates autonomic responses) and the anterior cingulate cortex (which links to the *motor* system).

Savant   Someone with *savant abilities*.

Savant abilities   Abilities that are outstanding by comparison with those of members of the general population, and even more striking because they occur in individuals with modest or low intellectual ability and, frequently, autistic features of behaviour. Examples of savant abilities have been documented in the fields of arithmetical calculation, drawing, musical memory and improvisation, foreign language learning, and poetry writing.

Schizoid personality disorder   A mental health disorder characterised by emotional coldness and impaired reciprocal social interaction, abnormalities of verbal and *nonverbal communication*, and obsessive interests. See Box 2.1.

Screening   A process of administering clinical tests either to whole populations or to selected populations with the purpose of either making a provisional diagnosis of the presence/absence of a particular disease or disorder in individuals within the population tested or to estimate the probability that certain individuals within the population have, or may later be found to have, a particular disease or disorder.

Secondary intersubjectivity   Essentially synonymous with *triadic relating*, but with greater allowance for the role of emotion sharing. Cf. *primary intersubjectivity*.

See-saw effect   Refers to the compensatory use of an intact capacity when a related capacity is absent or impaired.

Selective attention   The process involved in situations involving complex stimuli from which a single stimulus or stimulus feature is selected as the attentional focus. Cf. *over-selective/over-focused attention*.

Selective mutism   A rare condition in which an individual who understands and can use language normally is inhibited (usually by pathological anxiety) from speaking to particular individuals or in particular locations or contexts, whereas they speak normally in other situations. Synonymous with *elective mutism*.

Self-injurious behaviours (SIBs)   A form of *repetitive sensory-motor stereotypy (RSM)* which causes physical injury to the person engaging in the RSM.

Self-monitoring   The process of comparing one's intended action with the actual ongoing action one is carrying out. Differentiate from *action–outcome monitoring*.

Self–other equivalence mapping The unconscious identification of sameness, or equivalence, between oneself/one's own body parts and other members of the human species/their body parts. Possibly mediated by *mirror neurons*.

Self-regulation/self-regulatory system In psychology and physiology, a mechanism operating to maintain an organism or some facet of an organism's functions in *adaptive* equilibrium with its environment.

Semantic memory See Box 9.3.

Semantic-pragmatic language disorder A form of *specific language impairment* in which *semantics* and *pragmatics* are selectively impaired, leaving *phonology/articulate* and *syntax* relatively intact.

Semantics/lexical semantics 'Semantics' may be used to refer to the network of conceptual knowledge underlying language. However, 'semantics' is also commonly used to refer to knowledge of linguistic meaning, whether at the level of individual words, phrases or sentences. 'Lexical semantics' refers only to knowledge of linguistic meaning.

Sensation/sensory processing The processing of raw data from the senses prior to the processes associated with *perception*.

Sensitivity (As used in the context of *screening* tests.) A measure of the efficacy of a screening test based on the proportion of those tested who are correctly identified as having the disease or disorder being screened for, relative to the proportion who have the disorder but are not identified. Associated with a low level of *false negatives*. High sensitivity (i.e. a high proportion) is desirable.

Sensory modulation Variation of the impact of incoming experience on the senses, for instance increasing or decreasing sensitivity to a particular sound or class of sounds. Partly physiologically determined by states of *arousal*, but may be partly controlled by attentional processes.

Sensory seeking An interpretation of repetitive, self-stimulatory actions or activities in terms of a way of compensating for hypo-responsivity to sensory stimuli.

Sensory soothing An interpretation of repetitive, self-stimulatory actions or activities in terms of a way of compensating for hyper-responsivity to sensory stimuli.

Serotonin/5-hydroxytryptamine/5-HT See Box 8.1.

Serotonin transporter substance/SERT/5-HTT A protein with a known genetic origin thought to be involved in susceptibility to depression, and the target of many antidepressant medications.

Shared attention   See *joint attention*.

Shutdown   A self-explanatory term often used by high-functioning people with ASD to describe the defence mechanism they use to avoid over-*arousal* by excessive sensory-perceptual stimulation. See Box 3.3.

Simplex families   Families in which an isolated, or *sporadic*, case of ASD occurs.

Single blind trial. See *blind trials*.

Single factor theory/hypothesis   Theories/hypotheses that propose that all the diagnostic behaviours associated with ASD derive from a single causal factor at one or another level of explanation. Cf. *common pathway* theories.

Single-nucleotide polymorphisms (SNPs)   A difference within a single DNA building block, called a nucleotide. SNPs (pronounced 'SNiPs') occur normally throughout a person's DNA, and are the most common type of *genetic variation* among people. Most SNPs have no effect on health or development. However, some may be associated with disease.

Single subject experimental design (SSED)   See Box 12.1.

Social anxiety disorder   A term introduced in DSM-5 to replace *social phobia* as in DSM-IV. Refers to pathological shyness, characterised by extreme discomfort anxiety or fear in social situations, sufficient to interfere with everyday living.

Social brain. The neural basis of social experience, knowledge and interaction.

Social communication disorder (SCD)   A newly identified condition in DSM-5. For an abbreviated summary of diagnostic criteria for SCD see Chapter 2.

Social orienting. The innate bias of neonates and very young babies to attend preferentially to social stimuli, in particular to human faces and voices.

Social phobia   See *social anxiety disorder*.

Socio-economic status (SES)   Refers to the social standing or class of an individual or group most commonly assessed in terms of education, income and occupation.

Specific language impairment (SLI)   Significant delay or anomaly in the acquisition of a first language system, that cannot be explained by learning disability, sensory impairment, environmental deprivation, autism or other obvious cause.

Specificity   (As used in the context of *screening* tests.) A measure of the efficacy of a screening test based on the proportion of those tested who are correctly identified as having the disease or disorder being screened for relative to the proportion who are incorrectly identified as having the disorder. Associated with a low level of *false positives*. High specificity is desirable.

Specificity criterion   A yardstick for assessing the *validity* of any theoretical explanation of a *neurodevelopmental disorder* or facet of a disorder, for exmple autism. The criterion states that, if a theory proposes that a particular causal factor is both *necessary* and *sufficient* for autism or a particular facet of autism to occur, then that factor must occur only in individuals with autism (or the facet of autism identified in the theory).

Specifiers   One of the two kinds of *descriptor* introduced in the DSM-5 description of ASD. Refers to any additional condition or significant factor that is present. Cf. *Descriptors*.

Sporadic   A term used to differentiate between genetic disorders that are inherited via chance abnormality or variation of genetic material in eggs or sperm, as opposed to genetic disorders that are *familial*, i.e. that run in families.

Standardised   (As in 'standardised tests'.) A formal test (usually of some psychological capacity, i.e. a 'psychometric' test) that has been carried out in rigorous conditions and with large groups of individuals, and the results statistically analysed to yield norms for the population being studied. The test will also have been shown to produce results that are *reliable* and *valid*.

Statistical power   A technical term that refers to the probability, in statistical terms, that a research study will detect evidence in support of a hypothesis when that hypothesis is in fact correct. Various factors affect this probability, including the number of participants (or other entities to be examined) included in a study, and how common or marked are the phenomena predicted by the hypothesis (i.e. how easy they are to detect). See Box 12.2.

Structural magnetic resonance imaging (sMRI)   A method of assessing the neuroanatomy of the brain at gross structural, volumetric or cellular levels by utilising *magnetic resonance imaging*. See Box 8.2.

Subcortical   Parts of the brain that are not part of the *cerebral cortex*. Evolutionarily older than much of the cerebral cortex and subserving vital but 'lower-order' processes.

Sufficient cause   Any causal factor, or set of causal factors, that, if present, will invariably cause a particular effect/disorder/condition to occur. Cf. *necessary cause*.

Sulcus/sulci   Grooves, or furrows, on the cortical surfaces of the brain which, in combination with *gyri*, significantly extend the cortical surface area.

Supported living   A principled method of enabling people with disabilities to live in their own homes, whether a bedsit flat or house, with or without others according to their preference, by providing the ongoing support necessary to make this possible.

Susceptibility genes   Genes that increase the likelihood of an individual developing a particular characteristic or condition.

Symbol/symbolic/symbolise   A symbol is something that stands for, or represents, something else. The relationship between a symbol and what it stands for can be arbitrary, for example most words and their *referents*. Alternatively, symbol and *referent* can be meaningfully linked, for instance a crucifix and the Christian religion; the storm in 'King Lear' and the state of Lear's mind; a blue cloth and a pretend 'river'.

Symbolic pretend play/pretence   Play in which either one thing is used to stand for another (e.g. a box for 'a house'; water for 'tea') or something is imagined to be present though not actually present (e.g. throwing an imaginary ball; pretending to be a lion). Cf. *functional pretend play*.

Sympathy   See Box 3.2 and the asterisked footnote.

Synaesthesia   A neurological condition in which inputs from the different senses become confused, for example a sound triggering the experience of a particular colour.

Synapse   The junction between the end point of an *axon* from one *neuron* and the *dendrites* of another neuron, across which information is transmitted in the form of electrical impulses.

Synaptic pruning   Loss of less-used connective fibres (*axons* and *dendrites*) and their synapses following early proliferation of fibres. See (brain) *sculpting*.

Synaptogenesis   The formation and development of *synapses*.

Syndrome   A cluster of often seemingly unrelated symptoms or characteristics that may be psychological, physical or health-related and are sometimes, but not always, assumed to have a single ultimate cause.

Syndromic autism   A term used to refer to ASD when it occurs in combination with a known medical syndrome usually congenital and genetic in origin, for example *Fragile-X syndrome, Turner syndrome*.

Syntax   See Box 4.2.

Systemise/systemising mechanism   A tendency (and the hypothetical mechanism underlying this tendency) identified in Baron-Cohen's *extreme male brain* theory, to look for lawful regularities in experience that can be used to predict or calculate outcomes, occurrences, events, etc. Stronger in males than in females, as a general rule. See also *hypersystemising*.

Temporal lobe(s)   One of the lobes of the cerebrum, situated below the *frontal* and *parietal lobes* within the lower sides of the skull (see Figure 8.1). Involved in hearing, language comprehension, the integration of information from several senses, and memory processing.

Teratogen   Any environmental agent that causes damage to the *embryo* or *fetus in utero*.

Testosterone   See Box 8.1.

Theory of mind (ToM)   The ability to represent in one's own mind the mental states of others and also onself and to act in accordance with such mental-state knowledge. Often used synonymously with *mindreading*. In this book, the term is used only in the phrases *implicit ToM* or *explicit ToM*.

Thimerosal   A substance containing mercury that was for a time used as a preservative in vaccines.

Tourette's syndrome   A neurological disorder characterised by uncontrolled tics, body movements and vocalisations or other utterances (often obscenities).

Triadic relating/triadic social interaction   An early developing form of social inter-action in which two (or more) individuals attend to a third person, object, action or event and are aware that the person with whom they are interacting is having a similar perceptual/cognitive/emotional experience of their own. In developmental psychology, closely similar in meaning to *secondary intersubjectivity*, though with less emphasis on shared *affect*.

Trichotillomania   Compulsive pulling out of one's own hair.

Tuberous sclerosis   A rare genetic disorder in which benign growths occur in various organs of the body, including the brain. It is frequently associated with seizures, *learning disability*, and autistic features of behaviour. See also Box 7.1.

Turner syndrome   An inherited condition manifesting in females and caused by the absence or abnormality of one of the X-chromosomes. Numerous and variable characteristics include physical anomalies, absence or underdevelop-ment of female reproductive organs, and secondary sexual characteristics and functions, and in some cases mild *learning disability* and autistic tendencies. See also Box 7.1.

Typicality/typical/typically developing   Used in place of 'normality'/'nor-mal'/'normally developing' to avoid the associated stigmatising terms 'abnormal' or 'subnormal', replacing them with the less-stigmatising terms 'non-typical', 'atypical' or 'different'.

Unitary disorder   A disorder or condition resulting from a single cause or set of closely related causes with generally *homogeneous* and predictable symptoms, course, outcome and response to treatment.

Universality criterion   A yardstick for assessing the *validity* of any theoretical explanation of a disorder, or facet of a disorder, for example autism. The criterion states that if a theory proposes a particular causal factor is a *necessary* cause of autism, or of some facet of autism, then that causal factor must occur universally in all individuals with autism (or with the facet of autism identified in the theory).

Valid/validity   The property of being true, correct, in conformity with reality. Thus, a valid theory is one that fits well with what is seen in practice or with the findings from research. A valid test or assessment is one that measures what it purports to measure. This can only be judged by comparing the outcomes of a particular test or procedure with the outcomes of other *reliable* tests or procedures used to measure the same thing.

Vasopressin   See Box 8.1.

Vegetative functions   Bodily processes directly concerned with maintenance of life, for example eating and digestion, excretion, sleeping and waking, sexual and other hormonal functions.

Verbal abilities/verbal intelligence   Those aspects of intelligence measured using tests that assess knowledge of language directly; or that require the use of language in the form of verbal mediation ('inner speech') or response output; or that assess the kinds of knowledge obtained via language-mediated learning. For examples of tests of verbal intelligence, see Box 4.1.

Verbal apraxia/dyspraxia   Complete loss (apraxia) or impairment (dyspraxia) of the ability to voluntarily perform the movements required for speech, in the absence of any significant muscular or neuromuscular abnormalities. May result from a brain-based impairment of *motor* output planning and/or the ability to initiate the required movements.

Verbal fluency test   A test of the ability to generate as many words as possible in reponse to a given cue, such as an initial letter or named category (flowers, animals). See *fluency*.

Verbal intelligence   See *verbal abilities*.

Verbal IQ/VQ   See Box 4.1.

Vermis   See *cerebellar vermis*.

Weak central coherence (WCC)   An unusual degree of weakness in the normal drive for *central coherence*, resulting in a tendency to process complex perceptual stimuli as parts rather than as wholes, and a failure to integrate the component parts of higher-order experience, such as narratives or events, into meaningful wholes.

White matter   Brain tissue consisting of concentrations of *axons*, each covered in a whiteish-coloured *myelin sheath* made up of *glial cells*.

Williams syndrome   A rare *sporadic* (i.e. not *familial*) genetic disorder character-ised by 'elfin' facial features and other physical anomalies, and generally accom-panied by *learning disability* but relatively spared social interaction and language.

Working memory   See Box 9.3.

REFERENCES

Abdallah, M., Larsen, N., Grove, J. …. Mortensen, E. (2013). Neonatal chemokine levels and risk of autism spectrum disorders. *Cytokine, 61*, 370–376.

Abrams, D., Lynch, C., Cheng, K. …. Menon, V. (2013). Underconnectivity between voice-selective cortex and reward circuitry in children with autism. *Proceedings of the National Academy of Sciences, 110*, 12060–12065.

Accardo, P. & Barrow, W. (2015). Toe walking in autism. *Journal of Child Neurology, 30*, 606–609.

Adams, M. (2013). Explaining the theory of mind deficit in autism spectrum disorder. *Philosophical Studies, 163*, 233–249.

Adolphs, R. (2009). The social brain. *Annual Review of Psychology, 60*, 693–716.

Alcántara, J., Weisblatt, E., Moore, B., & Bolton, P. (2004). Speech-in-noise perception in high-functioning individuals with autism or Asperger's syndrome. *Journal of Child Psychology and Psychiatry, 45*, 1107–1114.

Allely, C. (2013). Pain sensitivity and observer perception of pain in individuals with autistic spectrum disorder. *Scientific World Journal*, 916178.

Allman, M. J. (2011). Deficits in temporal processing associated with autistic disorder. *Frontiers in Integrative Neuroscience, 5*, 2.

Alvarez, A. (1996). Addressing the element of deficit in children with autism: Psychotherapy which is both psychoanalytically and developmentally informed. *Clinical Child Psychology and Psychiatry, 1*, 525–537.

Alvarez, A. & Reid, S. (1999). *Autism and Personality: Findings from the Tavistock Autism Workshop*. London: Routledge.

American Psychiatric Association (1980). *Diagnostic and Statistical Manual of Mental Disorders* (3rd edn) (DSM-III). Washington, DC: APA.

American Psychiatric Association (1987). *Diagnostic and Statistical Manual of Mental Disorders* (3rd edn Revised) (DSM-III-R). Washington, DC: APA.

American Psychiatric Association (1994). *Diagnostic and Statistical Manual of Mental Disorders* (4th edn) (DSM-IV). Washington, DC: APA.

American Psychiatric Association (2000). *Diagnostic and Statistical Manual of Mental Disorders* (4th edn, Text Revised) (DSM-IV-TR). Washington, DC: APA.

American Psychiatric Association (2013). *Diagnostic and Statistical Manual of Mental Disorders* (5th edn) (DSM-5). Washington, DC: APA.

Ames, C. & Fletcher-Watson, S. (2010). A review of methods in the study of attention. *Developmental Review, 30*, 52–73.

Anagnostou, E., Zwaigenbaum, L., Szatmari, P. …. Buchanan, J. (2014). Autism spectrum disorder: Advances in evidence-based practice. *Canadian Medical Association Journal, 186*, 509–519.

Anderson, D., Liang, J., & Lord, C. (2013). Predicting young adult outcome among more or less cognitively able individuals with autism spectrum disorders. *Journal of Child Psychology and Psychiatry, 55,* 485–494.

Anderson, G. (2014). Biochemical biomarkers for autism spectrum disorder. In F. Volkmar, S. Rogers, R. Paul & K. Pelphrey (Eds.), *Handbook of Autism and Pervasive Developmental Disorders* (Vol. 2, 4th edn) (pp. 457–481). Hoboken, NJ: Wiley & Sons.

Anderson, K., Shattuck, P., Cooper, B., Roux, A., & Wagner, M. (2014). Prevalence and correlates of postsecondary residential status among young adults with autism spectrum disorder. *Autism, 18,* 562–570.

Ariel, C. & Naseef, R. (2005). *Voices from the Spectrum: Parents, Grandparents, Siblings, People with Autism and Professionals Share their Wisdom.* London: Jessica Kingsley.

Arndt, T., Stodgell, C., & Rodier, P. (2005). The teratology of autism. *International Journal of Developmental Neuroscience, 23,* 189–199.

Ashwood, P. & Van de Water, J. (2004). Is autism an autoimmune disease? *Autoimmunity Reviews, 3,* 557–562.

Asperger, H. (1944/1991). 'Autistic psychopathy' in childhood. Translated in U. Frith (Ed.), *Autism and Asperger Syndrome* (pp. 37–92). Cambridge: Cambridge University Press.

Assaf, M., Jagannathan, K., Calhoun, V. .... Pearlson, G. (2010). Abnormal functional connectivity of default mode sub-networks in autism spectrum disorder patients. *NeuroImage, 53,* 247–256.

Aston, M. (2001). *The Other Half of Asperger Syndrome.* London: National Autistic Society.

Attwood, T. (1998). *Asperger's Syndrome: A Guide for Parents and Professionals.* London and Philadelphia, PA: Jessica Kingsley Publishers.

Auyeung, B., Baron-Cohen, S., Wheelwright, S., & Allison, C. (2008). The Autism Spectrum Quotient: Children's version (A Q-Child). *Journal of Autism and Developmental Disorders, 38,* 1230–1240.

Bachevalier, J. (1994). Medial temporal lobe structures and autism. *Neuropsychologia, 32,* 627–648.

Bachevalier, J. (2008). Temporal lobe structures and memory in non-human primates: Implications for autism. In J. Boucher & D. M. Bowler (Eds.), *Memory in Autism.* Cambridge: Cambridge University Press.

Baddeley, A. (1986). *Working Memory.* Oxford: Oxford University Press.

Baddeley, A. (2000). The episodic buffer: A new component of working memory? *Trends in Cognitive Science, 4,* 417–423.

Bailey, A., Le Couteur, A., Gottesman, I. .... Rutter, M. (1995). Autism as a strongly genetic disorder: Evidence from a British twin study. *Psychological Medicine, 25,* 63–77.

Baird, G., Charman, T., Baron-Cohen, S. .... Drew, A. (2000). A screening instrument for detecting autism at 18 months of age: A six-year follow-up study. *Journal of the American Academy of Child and Adolescent Psychiatry, 39,* 694–702.

Baird, G., Simonoff, E., Pickles, A. .... Charman, T. (2006). Prevalence of disorders of the autism spectrum in a population cohort of children in South Thames: The Special Needs and Autism Project (SNAP). *The Lancet, 368,* 210–215.

Baranek, G., Little, L., Parham, D., Ausderau, K., & Sabatos-De Vito, M. (2014). Sensory features in autism spectrum disorders. In F. Volkmar, S. Rogers, R. Paul & K. Pelphrey (Eds.), *Handbook of Autism and Pervasive Developmental Disorders* (Vol. 2, 4th edn) (pp. 378–407). Hoboken, NJ: Wiley & Sons.

Barbaro, J., & Dissanayake, C. (2013). Early markers of autism spectrum disorders in infants and toddlers prospectively identified in the Social Attention and Communication Study. *Autism, 17,* 64–86.

Barbeau, E., Soulières, I., Dawson, E. .... Mottron, L. (2013). The level and nature of autistic intelligence III. *Journal of Abnormal Psychology, 122,* 295–301.

Barnard-Brak, L., Sulak, T., & Hatz, J. (2011). Macrocephaly in children with autism spectrum disorders. *Pediatric Neurology, 44*, 97–100.

Barnevik-Olsson, M., Gillberg, C., & Fernell, E. (2010). Prevalence of autism in children of Somali origin living in Stockholm. *Developmental Medicine and Child Neurology, 52*, 1167–1168.

Barnhill, A. Clinard (2007). *At Home in the Land of Oz: My Sister, Autism and Me.* London: Jessica Kingsley.

Baron-Cohen, B., Johnson, D., Asher, J. …. Allison, C. (2013). Is synaesthesia more common in autism? *Molecular Autism, 4*, 1–6.

Baron-Cohen, S. (1989). The autistic child's theory of mind: A case of specific developmental delay. *Journal of Child Psychology and Psychiatry, 30*, 285–298.

Baron-Cohen, S. (1991). Do people with autism understand what causes emotion? *Child Development, 62*, 385–395.

Baron-Cohen, S. (1995). *Mindblindness: An Essay on Autism and Theory of Mind.* Cambridge, MA: The MIT Press.

Baron-Cohen, S. (2005). The Empathizing System: A revision of the 1994 model of the Mindreading System. In B. Ellis & D. Bjorklund (Eds.), *Origins of the Social Mind* (pp. 468–492). New York: Guilford Press.

Baron-Cohen, S. (2009). Autism: The empathizing–systemizing (E–S) theory. *Annals of the New York Academy of Sciences, 1156*, 68–80.

Baron-Cohen, S., Baldwin, D., & Crowson, M. (1997). Do children with autism use the speaker's direction of gaze strategy to crack the code of language? *Child Development, 68*, 48–57.

Baron-Cohen, S. & Hammer, J. (1997). Is autism an extreme form of the male brain? *Advances in Infancy Research, 11*, 193–218.

Baron-Cohen, S., Hoekstra, R., Knickmeyer, R., & Wheelwright, S. (2006). The Autism-Spectrum Quotient (AQ) – Adolescent version. *Journal of Autism and Developmental Disorders, 36*, 343–350.

Baron-Cohen, S., Jolliffe, T., Mortimore, C., & Robertson, M. (1997). Another advanced test of theory of mind: Evidence from very high functioning adults with autism or Asperger syndrome. *Journal of Child Psychology and Psychiatry, 38*, 813–822.

Baron-Cohen, S., Knickmeyer, R., & Belmonte, M. (2005). Sex differences in the brain: Implications for explaining autism. *Science, 310* (5749), 819–823.

Baron-Cohen, S., Leslie, A., & Frith, U. (1985). Does the autistic child have a 'theory of mind'? *Cognition, 21*, 37–47.

Baron-Cohen, S., Richler, J., Bisarya, D., Gurunathan, N., & Wheelwright, S. (2003). The systemizing quotient: An investigation of adults with Asperger syndrome or high-functioning autism, and normal sex differences. *Philosophical Transactions of the Royal Society of London B: Biological Sciences, 358*, 361–374.

Baron-Cohen, S., Wheelwright, S., Skinner, R., Martin, J., & Clubley, E. (2001). The Autism Spectrum Quotient (AQ): Evidence from Asperger syndrome/high functioning autism, males and females, scientists and mathematicians. *Journal of Autism and Developmental Disorders, 31*, 5–18.

Barrow, W., Jaworski, M., & Accardo, P. (2011). Persistent toe walking in autism. *Journal of Child Neurology, 26*, 619–621.

Bartak, L., Rutter, M., & Cox, A. (1975). A comparative study of infantile autism and specific developmental receptive language disorder. *The British Journal of Psychiatry, 126*, 127–145.

Bartak, L., Rutter, M., & Cox, A. (1977). A comparative study of infantile autism and specific developmental receptive language disorders III: Discriminant function analysis. *Journal of Autism and Childhood Schizophrenia, 7*, 383–396.

Bates, E. (1990). Language about me and you: Pronominal assessment and the emerging concept of self. In D. Cicchetti & M. Beeghly (Eds.), *The Self in Transition: Infancy to Childhood* (pp. 165–182). Chicago, IL: University of Chicago Press.

Bauminger, N. & Shulman, C. (2003). The development and maintenance of friendship in high-functioning children with autism: Maternal perceptions. *Autism, 7*, 81–97.

Bee, H. & Boyd, D. (2012). *The Developing Child* (13th edn). Harlow: Pearson.

Beers, A., McBoyle, M., Kakande, E., Dar Santos, R., & Kozak, F. (2014). Autism and peripheral hearing loss: A systematic review. *International Journal of Pediatric Otolaryngology, 78*, 96–101.

Begeer, S., Terwogt, M., Lunenburg, P., & Stegge, H. (2009). Additive and subtractive counterfactual reasoning of children with high-functioning autism spectrum disorders. *Journal of Autism and Developmental Disorders, 39*, 1593–1597.

Belmonte, M., Allen, G., Beckel-Mitchener, A. …. Webb, S. (2004). Autism and abnormal development of brain connectivity. *The Journal of Neuroscience, 24*, 9228–9231.

Belmonte, M. & Carper, R. (2006). Monozygotic twins with Asperger syndrome: Differences in behaviour reflect variations in brain structure and function. *Brain and Cognition, 61*, 110–121.

Belmonte, M., Cook, E., Anderson, G. …. Tierney, E. (2004). Autism as a disorder of neural information processing: Directions for research and targets for therapy. *Molecular Psychiatry, 9*, 646–663.

Ben Shalom, D. (2000). Autism: Emotions without feelings. *Autism, 4*, 205–207.

Ben Shalom, D., Mostofsky, M., Hazlett, R. …. Hoehn-Saric, R. (2006). Normal physiological emotions but differences in expressions of conscious feelings in high-functioning autism. *Journal of Autism and Developmental Disorders, 36*, 395–400.

Bender, L. (1956). Schizophrenia in childhood: Its recognition, description and treatment. *American Journal of Orthopsychiatry, 26*, 499–506.

Bennett, H., Wood, C., & Hare, D. (2005). Providing care for adults with autistic spectrum disorders in learning disability services: Needs-based or diagnosis-driven? *Journal of Applied Research in Intellectual Disabilities, 18*, 51–64.

Bent, C. A., Dissanayake, C., & Barbaro, J. (2015). Mapping the diagnosis of autism spectrum disorders in children aged under 7 years in Australia, 2010–2012. *The Medical Journal of Australia, 202*, 317–320.

Berk, L. & Meyers, A. (2015). *Infants and Children* (8th edn). Harlow: Pearson.

Bernier, R., Gerdts, J., Munson, J., Dawson, G., & Estes, A. (2012). Evidence for broader autism phenotype characteristics in parents from multi-incidence autism families. *Autism Research, 5*, 13–20.

Bertone, A., Mottron, L., Jelenic, P., & Faubert, J. (2005). Enhanced and diminished visuo-spatial information processing in autism depends on stimulus complexity. *Brain, 128*, 2430–2441.

Betancur, C. (2011). Etiological heterogeneity in autism spectrum disorders. *Brain Research, 1380*, 42–77.

Bettelheim, B. (1967). *The Empty Fortress: Infantile Autism and the Birth of Self.* New York: The Free Press.

Bigham, S., Boucher, J., Mayes, A., & Anns, S. (2010). Assessing recollection and familiarity in autistic spectrum disorders: Methods and findings. *Journal of Autism and Developmental Disorders, 40*, 878–889.

Bilder, D., Botts, E., Smith, K. …. Coon, H. (2013). Excess mortality and causes of death in autism spectrum disorders. *Journal of Autism and Developmental Disorders, 43*, 1196–1204.

Binnie, J. & Blainey, S. (2013). The use of cognitive behavioural therapy for adults with autism spectrum disorders: A review of the evidence. *Mental Health Review Journal, 18*, 93–104.

Bishop, D. (2010). Overlaps between autism and language impairment: Phenomimicry or shared etiology? *Behavior Genetics, 40,* 618–629.

Bishop, D. & Norbury, C. (2002). Exploring the borderlands of autistic disorder and specific language impairment: A study using standardised diagnostic instruments. *Journal of Child Psychology and Psychiatry, 43,* 917–929.

Bishop-Fitzpatrick, L., Minshew, N., & Eack, S. (2014). A systematic review of psychosocial interventions for adults with autism spectrum disorders. In F. Volkmar, B. Reichow & J. McPartland (Eds.), *Adolescents and Adults with Autism Spectrum Disorders* (pp. 315–327). New York: Springer.

Bitsika, V., Sharpley, C., & Bell, R. (2013). The buffering effect of resilience upon stress, anxiety and depression in parents of a child with an autism spectrum disorder. *Journal of Developmental and Physical Disabilities, 25,* 533–543.

Blair, R. (1999). Psychophysiological responsiveness to the distress of others in children with autism. *Personality and Individual Differences, 26,* 477–485.

Blatt, G. (2012). Inhibitory and excitatory systems in autism spectrum disorders. In J. Buxbaum & P. Hof (Eds.), *The Neuroscience of Autism Spectrum Disorders* (pp. 335–347). Amsterdam: Elsevier.

Bloom, P. (2000). *How Children Learn the Meanings of Words.* Cambridge, MA: The MIT Press.

Bodison, S. & Mostofsky, S. (2014). Motor control and motor learning processes in autism spectrum disorders. In F. Volkmar, S. Rogers, R. Paul & K. Pelphrey (Eds.), *Handbook of Autism and Pervasive Developmental Disorders* (Vol. 2, 4th edn) (pp. 354–377). Hoboken, NJ: Wiley & Sons.

Bókkon, I., Salari, V., Scholkmann, F., Dai, J., & Grass, F. (2013). Interdisciplinary implications on autism, savantism, Asperger syndrome and the biophysical picture representation: Thinking in pictures. *Cognitive Systems Research, 22,* 67–77.

Bölte, S. (2014). Is autism curable? *Developmental Medicine and Child Neurology, 56,* 927–931.

Bolton, S., McDonald, D., Curtis, E., Kelly, S., & Gallagher, L. (2014). Autism in a recently arrived immigrant population. *European Journal of Pediatrics, 173,* 337–343.

Bondy, A. & Frost, L. (2001). The picture exchange communication system. *Behavior Modification, 25,* 725–744.

Bonnel, A., McAdams, S., Smith, B. .... Mottron, L. (2010). Enhanced pure-tone pitch discrimination among persons with autism but not Asperger syndrome. *Neuropsychologia, 48,* 2465–2475.

Botting, N. & Conti-Ramsden, G. (2003). Autism, primary pragmatic difficulties, and specific language impairment: Can we distinguish them using psycholinguistic markers? *Developmental Medicine and Child Neurology, 45,* 515–524.

Boucher, J. (1976). Articulation in early childhood autism. *Journal of Autism and Childhood Schizophrenia, 6,* 297–302.

Boucher, J. (1988). Word fluency in high functioning autistic children. *Journal of Autism and Developmental Disorders, 18,* 637–645.

Boucher, J. (1996). The inner life of children with autistic difficulties. In V. Varma (Ed.). *The Inner Life of Children with Special Needs* (pp. 81–94). London: Whurr.

Boucher, J. (2001). Lost in a sea of time: Time-parsing and autism. In C. Hoerl & T. McCormack (Eds.), *Time and Memory* (pp. 111–135). Oxford: Clarendon Press.

Boucher, J. (2011). Redefining the concept of autism as a unitary disorder: Multiple causal deficits of a single kind? In D. Fein (Ed.), *The Neuropsychology of Autism* (pp. 469–482). Oxford: Oxford University Press.

Boucher, J. (2012). Structural language in autistic spectrum disorder. *Journal of Child Psychology and Psychiatry, 53,* 219–233.

Boucher, J., Cowell, P., Howard, M. …. Mayes, A. (2005). A combined clinical neu-ropsychological and neuroanatomical study of adults with high-functioning autism. *Cognitive Neuropsychiatry*, *10*, 165–214.

Boucher, J., Lewis, V., & Collis, G. M. (1998). Familiar face and voice matching and recog-nition in children with autism. *Journal of Child Psychology and Psychiatry*, *39*, 171–181.

Boucher, J., Lewis, V., & Collis, G. M. (2000). Voice processing abilities in children with autism, children with specific language impairments, and young typically developing children. *Journal of Child Psychology and Psychiatry*, *41*, 847–857.

Boucher, J., Mayes, A., & Bigham, S. (2008). Memory, language, and intellectual ability in low functioning autism. In J. Boucher & D. M. Bowler (Eds.), *Memory in Autism* (pp. 268–290). Cambridge: Cambridge University Press.

Boucher, J., Mayes, A., & Bigham, S. (2012). Memory in autistic spectrum disorder. *Psychological Bulletin*, *138*, 458.

Bouvet, L., Mottron, L., Valdois, S., & Donnadieu, S. (2014). Auditory stream segregation in autism spectrum disorder. *Journal of Autism and Developmental Disorders*, Feb1–9.

Bowler, D., Gaigg, S., & Gardiner, J. (2008). Subjective organisation in the free recall of adults with Asperger's syndrome. *Journal of Autism and Developmental Disorders*, *38*, 104–113.

Bowler, D., Gaigg, S., & Gardiner, J. (2014). Binding of multiple features in memory by high-functioning adults with autism spectrum disorder. *Journal of Autism and Developmental Disorders*, *44*, 2355–2362.

Bowler, D., Gaigg, S., & Lind, S. (2011). Memory in autism: Binding, self, and brain. In I. Roth & P. Rezaie (Eds.), *Researching the Autistic Spectrum: Contemporary Perspectives* (pp. 316–347). Cambridge: Cambridge University Press.

Boyd, B., Baranek, G., Sideris, J. …. Miller, H. (2010). Sensory features and repetitive behav-iour in children with autism and developmental delays. *Autism Research*, *3*, 78–87.

Boyd, B., Hume, K., McBee, M. …. Odom, S. L. (2014). Comparative efficacy of LEAP, TEACCH and non-model-specific special education programs for preschoolers with autism spectrum disorders. *Journal of Autism and Developmental Disorders*, *44*, 366–380.

Braiden, H., Bothwell, J., & Duffy, J. (2010). Parents' experience of the diagnostic process for autistic spectrum disorders. *Child Care in Practice*, *16*, 377–389.

Brent, J. (2013). Commentary on the abuse of metal chelation therapy in patients with autism spectrum disorders. *Journal of Medical Toxicology*, *9*, 370–372.

Brock, J., Brown, C., Boucher, J. & Rippon, G. (2002). The temporal binding deficit hypoth-esis of autism. *Development and Psychopathology*, *14*, 209–224.

Bromley, J., Hare, D., Davison, K., & Emerson, E. (2004). Mothers supporting children with autistic spectrum disorders: Social support, mental health status and satisfaction with services. *Autism*, *8*, 409–423.

Brown, J., Aczel, B., Jiménez, L., Kaufman, S., & Grant, K. (2010). Intact implicit learning in autism spectrum conditions. *The Quarterly Journal of Experimental Psychology*, *63*, 1789–1812.

Buckner, R., Andrews-Hanna, J., & Schacter, D. (2008). The brain's default network. *Annals of the New York Academy of Sciences*, *1124*, 1–38.

Buie, T., Campbell, D., Fuchs, G. …. Winter, H. (2010). Evaluation, diagnosis and treatment of gastrointestinal disorders in individuals with ASDs. *Pediatrics*, *125*, S1–18.

Buxbaum, J. & Hof, P. (2012). *The Neuroscience of Autism Spectrum Disorders*. Amsterdam: Academic Press/Elsevier.

Byford, S., Cary, M., Barrett, B. …. Pickles, A. (2015). Cost-effectiveness analysis of a communication-focused therapy for pre-school children with autism. *BMC Psychiatry*, *15*, 1.

Cadogan, S. & McCrimmon, A. (2015). Pivotal response treatment for children with autism spectrum disorder: A systematic review of research quality. *Developmental Neurorehabilitation, 18*, 137–144.

Camarata, S. (2014). Early identification and early intervention in autism spectrum disorders: Accurate and effective? *International Journal of Speech-Language Pathology, 16*, 1–10.

Capps, L., Yirmiya, N., & Sigman, M. (1992). Understanding of simple and complex emotions in non-retarded children with autism. *Journal of Child Psychology and Psychiatry, 33*, 1169–1182.

Carlson, N. (2012). *Physiology of Behaviour* (11th edn). Harlow: Pearson.

Carr, E. & Durand, V. (1985). Reducing behavior problems through functional communication training. *Journal of Applied Behavior Analysis, 18*(2), 111–126.

Carrington, S., Kent, R., Maljaars, J. .... Leekam, S. (2014). DSM-5 Autism Spectrum Disorder: In search of essential behaviours for diagnosis. *Research in Autism Spectrum Disorders, 8*, 701–715.

Carrington, S., Leekam, S., Kent, R. .... Noens, I. (2015). Signposting for diagnosis of autism spectrum disorder using the Diagnostic Interview for Social and Communication Disorders (DISCO). *Research in Autism Spectrum Disorders, 9*, 45–52.

Carruthers, P. (2009). How we know our own minds: The relationship between mindreading and metacognition. *Behavioral and Brain Sciences, 32*, 121–138.

Carruthers, P. (2013). Mindreading in infancy. *Mind and Language, 28*, 141–172.

Carson, K., Gast, D., & Ayres, K. (2008). Effects of a photo activity schedule book on independent task changes by students with intellectual disabilities in community and school job sites. *European Journal of Special Needs Education, 23*, 269–279.

Carter, A., Messinger, D., Stone, W. .... Yoder, P. (2011). A randomized controlled trial of Hanen's 'More Than Words' in toddlers with early autism symptoms. *Journal of Child Psychology and Psychiatry, 52*, 741–752.

Carter, A., Volkmar, F., Sparrow, S. .... Schopler, E. (1998). The Vineland Adaptive Behaviour Scales: Supplementary norms for individuals with autism. *Journal of Autism and Developmental Disorders, 28*, 287–302.

Casanova, M. (2012). The minicolumnopathy of autism. In J. Buxbaum & P. Hof (Eds.), *The Neuroscience of Autism Spectrum Disorders* (pp. 327–333). Amsterdam: Elsevier.

Cesaroni, L. & Garber, M. (1991). Exploring the experience of individuals through first-hand accounts from high-functioning individuals with autism. *Journal of Autism and Developmental Disorders, 21*, 303–314.

Chaffin, M., Hanson, R., Saunders, B. .... LeTourneau, E. (2006). Report of the APSAC task force on attachment therapy, reactive attachment disorder, and attachment problems. *Child Maltreatment, 11*, 76–89.

Chan, G. & Goh, E. (2014). 'My parents told us that they will always treat my brother differently because he is autistic': Are siblings of autistic children the forgotten ones? *Journal of Social Work Practice, 28*, 155–171.

Charman, T., Pickles, A., Simonoff, E. .... Baird, G. (2010). IQ in children with autism spectrum disorders. *Psychological Medicine, 41*, 619–627.

Chaste, P. & Leboyer, M. (2012). Autism risk factors: Genes, environment, and gene-environment interactions. *Dialogues in Clinical Neuroscience, 14*, 281–92.

Chawarska, K., Campbell, D., Chen, L., ... Chang, J. (2011). Early generalized overgrowth in boys with autism. *Archives of General Psychiatry, 68*, 1021–1031.

Cheuk, D., Wong, V., & Chen, W. (2011). Acupuncture for people with autism spectrum disorders. *Cochrane Database Systemic Review, 7*.

Chevallier, C., Kohls, G., Troiani, V., Brodkin, E., & Schultz, R. (2012). The social motivation theory of autism. *Trends in Cognitive Sciences, 16*, 231–239.

Chomiak, T. & Hu, B. (2013). Alterations of neocortical development and maturation in autism: Insights from Valproic acid exposure and animal models. *Neurotoxicology and Teratology, 36*, 57–66.

Christensen, J., Grønborg, T., Sørensen, M. .... Vestergaard, M. (2013). Prenatal valproate exposure and risk of autism spectrum disorders. *JAMA, 309*, 1696–1703.

Christon, L. & Myers, B. (2015). Family-centered care practices in a multidisciplinary sample of pediatric professionals providing autism spectrum disorder services in the United States. *Research in Autism Spectrum Disorders, 20*, 47–57.

Churchill, D. W. (1972). The relation of infantile autism and early childhood schizophrenia to developmental language disorders of childhood. *Journal of Autism and Childhood Schizophrenia, 2*, 182–197.

Cleland, J., Gibbon, F., Peppé, S., O'Hare, A., & Rutherford, M. (2010). Phonetic and phonological errors in children with high-functioning autism and Asperger syndrome. *International Journal of Speech and Language Pathology, 12*, 69–76.

Cline, T. & Baldwin, S. (2004). *Selective Mutism in Children.* London: Whurr.

Coben, R., Mohammad-Rezazadeh, I., & Cannon, R. (2014). Using quantitative and analytic EEG methods in the understanding of connectivity in autism spectrum disorders: A theory of mixed over- and under-connectivity. *Frontiers in Human Neuroscience, 8.*

Collacott, R., Cooper, S., Branford, D., & McGrother, C. (1998). Epidemiology of self-injurious behaviour in adults with learning disabilities. *British Journal of Psychiatry, 173*, 428–432.

Colombi, C., Vivanti, G., & Rogers, S. (2012). Imitation in ASD. In D. Fein (Ed.), *The Neuropsychology of Autism* (pp. 243–266). Oxford: Oxford University Press.

Coman, D., Alessandri, M., Gutierrez, A. .... Odom, S. (2013). Commitment to classroom model philosophy and burnout symptoms among high fidelity teachers implementing preschool programs for children with autism spectrum disorders. *Journal of Autism and Developmental Disorders, 43*, 345–360.

Constantino, J., Davis, S., Todd, R. .... Reich, W. (2003). Validation of a brief quantitative measure of autistic traits: Comparison of the Social Responsiveness Scale with the ADI-R. *Journal of Autism and Developmental Disorders, 33*, 427–433.

Constantino, J., Zhang, Y., Frazier, T., Abbacchi, A., & Law, P. (2010). Sibling recurrence and the genetic epidemiology of autism. *American Journal of Psychiatry, 167*, 1349–1356.

Costa, L., Cole, T., Coburn, J. .... Roque, P. (2014). The effect of air pollution on the brain. *BioMedical Research*, Article ID 736385.

Courchesne, E. (2004). Brain development in autism: Early overgrowth followed by premature arrest of growth. *Mental Retardation and Developmental Disabilities Research Reviews, 10*, 106–111.

Courchesne, E., Campbell, K., & Solso, S. (2011). Brain growth across the life span in autism. *Brain Research, 1380*, 138–145.

Courchesne, E. & Pierce, K. (2005). Why the frontal cortex in autism might be talking only to itself: Local over-connectivity but long-distance disconnection. *Current Opinion in Neurobiology, 15*, 225–230.

Cowell, P., Sluming, V., Wilkinson, I. .... Roberts, N. (2007). Effects of sex and age on regional prefrontal brain volume in two human coherts. *European Journal of Neuroscience, 25*, 307–318.

Crane, L., Chester, J., Goddard, L., Henry, L., & Hill, E. (2015). Experiences of autism diagnosis: A survey of over 1000 parents in the United Kingdom. *Autism*, 1362361315573636.

Crane, L., & Goddard, L. (2008). Episodic and semantic autobiographical memory in adults with autism spectrum disorders. *Journal of Autism and Developmental Disorders, 38*, 498–506.

Crane, L., Goddard, L., & Pring, L. (2009). Specific and general autobiographical knowledge in autism spectrum disorders. *Memory, 17*, 557–576.

Creak, M. (1961). Schizophrenic syndrome in childhood: Progress report of a working party. *Cerebral Palsy Bulletin, 3*, 501–504.

Croen, L., Najjar, D., Ray, G., Lotspeich, L., & Bernal, P. (2006). A comparison of health-care utilization and costs in children with and without autism spectrum disorders in a large-group model health plan. *Pediatrics, 118*, 1203–1211.

Cross-Disorder Group of the Psychiatric Genomics Consortium (2013). Identification of risk loci with shared effects on five major psychiatric disorders. *The Lancet, 381*, 1371–1379.

Cummings, L. (2013). Clinical pragmatics and theory of mind. In F. Piparo & M. Carapezza (Eds.), *Perspectives on Linguistic Pragmatics* (pp. 23–56). New York: Springer.

Curcio, F. (1978). Sensorimotor functioning and communication in mute autistic children. *Journal of Autism and Childhood Schizophrenia, 2*, 264–287.

Dadds, M., MacDonald, E., Cauchi, A., Williams, K., Levy, F., & Brennan, J. (2014). Nasal oxytocin for social deficits in childhood autism: A randomized controlled trial. *Journal of Autism and Developmental Disorders, 44*, 521–531.

Dakin, S. & Frith, U. (2005). Vagaries of visual perception in autism. *Neuron, 48*, 497–507.

Dale, E., Jahoda, A., & Knott, F. (2006). Mothers' attributions following their child's diagnosis of autistic spectrum disorder: Exploring links with maternal levels of stress, depression and expectations about their child's future. *Autism, 10*, 463–479.

Damasio, A. & Maurer, R. (1978). A neurological model for childhood autism. *Archives of Neurology, 35*, 777–786.

Danial, J. & Wood, J. (2013). Cognitive behavioral therapy for children with autism: Review and considerations for future research. *Journal of Developmental and Behavioral Pediatrics, 34*, 702–715.

D'Astous, V., Manthorpe, J., Lowton, K., & Glaser, K. (2014). Retracing the historical social care context of autism. *British Journal of Social Work, 46*, 789–807.

Davis, G. & Plaisted-Grant, K. (2015). Low endogenous neural noise in autism. *Autism, 19*, 351–362.

Davis, T., O'Reilly, M., Kang, S. …. Mulloy, A. (2013). Chelation treatment for autism spectrum disorders: A systematic review. *Research in Autism Spectrum Disorders, 7*, 49–55.

Dawson, G., Jones, E. J., Merkle, K. …. Smith, M. (2012). Early behavioral intervention is associated with normalized brain activity in young children with autism. *Journal of the American Academy of Child and Adolescent Psychiatry, 51*, 1150–1159.

Dawson, G. & McKissick, F. (1984). Self-recognition in autistic children. *Journal of Autism and Developmental Disorders, 14*, 383–394.

Dawson, G., Rogers, S., Munson, J. …. Varley, J. (2010). Randomized, controlled trial of an intervention for toddlers with autism: The Early Start Denver Model. *Pediatrics, 125*, e17–e23.

Dawson, G., Toth, K., Abbott, R. …. McPartland, J. (2004). Early social attention impairments in autism: Social orienting, joint attention, and attention to distress. *Developmental Psychology, 40*, 271–283.

Dawson, G., Webb, S., Schellenberg, G. …. Friedman, S. (2002). Defining the broader phenotype of autism: Genetic, brain, and behavioural perspectives. *Development and Psychopathology, 14*, 581–611.

Dawson, M., Mottron, L., & Gernsbacher, M. (2008). Learning in autism. In J. Byrne & H. Roediger (Eds.), *Learning and Memory: A Comprehensive Reference, Vol. III: Cognitive Psychology* (pp. 759–772). Oxford: Elsevier.

Dawson, M., Soulières, I., Gernsbacher, M., & Mottron, L. (2007). The level and nature of autistic intelligence. *Psychological Science, 18*, 657–662.

de Bildt, A., Sytema, S., Zander, E. …. Green, J. (2015). Autism Diagnostic Interview-Revised (ADI-R) algorithms for toddlers and young preschoolers: Application in a non-US sample of 1,104 children. *Journal of Autism and Developmental Disorders, 45*, 2076–2091.

De Rubeis S., & Buxbaum J. (2015). Genetics and genomics of autism spectrum disorder. *Human Molecular Genetics*. July:ddv273.

DeLong, G., Bean, C., & Brown, F. (1981). Acquired reversible autistic syndrome in acute encephalitic illness in children. *Archives of Neurology, 38*, 191–194.

DeMyer, M., Barton, S., Alpern, G. …. Steele, R. (1974). The measured learning abilities of autistic children. *Journal of Autism and Childhood Schizophrenia, 4*, 42–60.

Department of Education and Science (Ireland) (2006). *An Evaluation of Educational Provision for Children with Autistic Spectrum Disorders*. www.education.ie/servlet/ blob-servlet/des_autismreport_foreword.htm

DeSoto, M. & Hitlan, R. (2012). Synthetic folic acid supplementation during pregnancy may increase the risk of developing autism. *Journal of Pediatric Biochemistry, 2*, 251–261.

Deutsch, S., Schwartz, B., Urbano, M. …. Herndon, A. (2014). Nicotinic acetylcholine receptors in autism spectrum disorders. In V. Patel, V. Preedy & C. Martin (Eds.), *Comprehensive Guide to Autism* (pp. 755–777).New York: Springer.

Di Martino, A., Ross, K., Uddin, L. …. Milham, M. (2009). Functional brain correlates of social and non-social processes in autism spectrum disorders. *Biological Psychiatry, 65*, 63–74.

Di Martino, A., Yan, C.-G., Li, Q. …. Milham, M. (2014). The autism brain imaging data exchange. *Molecular Autism, 19*, 659–667.

Doja, A. & Roberts, W. (2006). Immunizations and autism. *Canadian Journal of Neurological Sciences, 33*, 341–346.

Donnellan, A., Hill, D., & Leary, M. (2015). Rethinking autism: Implications of sensory and movement differences for understanding and support. In E. Torres & A. Donnellan (Eds.), *Autism: The Movement Perspective*. Lausanne: Frontiers Media SA.

Dumont-Mathieu, T. & Fein, D. (2005). Screening for autism in young children: The Modified Checklist for Autism in Toddlers (M-CHAT) and other measures. *Mental Retardation and Developmental Disabilities Research Reviews, 11*, 253–262.

Durkin, M., Maenner, M., Meaney, F. …. Schieve, L. (2010). Socioeconomic inequality in the prevalence of autism spectrum disorder. *PLoS One, 5*, e11551.

Dworzynski, K., Ronald, A., Bolton, P., & Happé, F. (2012). How different are boys and girls above and below the threshold for autism spectrum disorders? *Journal of the American Academy of Child and Adolescent Psychiatry, 51*, 788–797.

Dziuk, A., Larson, J., Apostu, A. …. Mostofsky, S. (2007). Dyspraxia in autism: Association with motor, social, and communicative deficits. *Developmental Medicine and Child Neurology, 49*, 734–739.

Easson, A. & Woodbury-Smith, M. (2014). The role of prenatal immune activation in the pathogenesis of autism and schizophrenia. *Research in Autism Spectrum Disorders, 8*, 312–316.

Ecker, C., Ginestet, C., Feng, Y. …. Murphy, D. (2013). Brain surface anatomy in adults with autism. *JAMA Psychiatry, 70*, 59–70.

Eigsti, I., Bennetto, L., & Dadlani, M. (2007). Beyond pragmatics: Morphosyntactic development in autism. *Journal of Autism and Developmental Disorders, 37*, 1573–3432.

Eigsti, I., de Marchena, A., Schuh, J., & Kelley, E. (2011). Language acquisition in autism spectrum disorders: A developmental review. *Research in Autism Spectrum Disorders, 5*, 681–691.

Eigsti, I. & Fein, D. (2013). More is less: Pitch discrimination and language delays in children with optimal outcomes from autism. *Autism Research, 6*, 605–613.

El-Ghoroury, N. & Krackow, E. (2011). A developmental–behavioral approach to outpatient psychotherapy with children with autism spectrum disorders. *Journal of Contemporary Psychotherapy, 41*, 11–17.

Elia, M., Ferri, R., Musumeci, A. …. Gruber, J.-C. (2000). Sleep in subjects with autistic disorder. *Brain Development, 22*, 88–92.

Elman, J., Bates, E., Johnson, M. …. Plunkett, K. (1996). *Rethinking Innateness: A Connectionist Perspective on Development.* Cambridge, MA: The MIT Press.

Elsabbagh, M., Divan, G., Koh, Y.-J. …. Fombonne, E. (2012). Global prevalence of autism and other pervasive developmental disorders. *Autism Research, 5,* 160–179.

Erickson, C., Stigler, K., Corkins, M., Posey, D., Fitzgerald, J., & McDougle, C. (2005). Gastrointestinal factors in autistic disorder: A critical review. *Journal of Autism and Developmental Disorders, 35,* 713–727.

Estes, A., Munson, J., Dawson, G. …. Abbott, R. (2009). Parenting stress and psychological functioning among mothers of preschool children with autism and developmental delay. *Autism, 13,* 375–387.

Faherty, C. (2008). *Understanding Death and Illness.* Arlington, TX: Future Horizons.

Falter, C., Plaisted, K., & Davis, G. (2008). Visuo-spatial processing in autism – testing the predictions of the extreme male brain theory. *Journal of Autism and Developmental Disorders, 38,* 507–515.

Faran, Y. & Ben Shalom, D. (2008). Possible parallels between memory and emotion processing in autism: A neuropsychological perspective. In J. Boucher & D. M. Bowler (Eds.), *Memory in Autism* (pp. 86–102). Cambridge: Cambridge University Press.

Farley, M., McMahon, W., Fombonne, E. …. Coon, H. (2009). Twenty-year outcome for individuals with autism and average or near-average cognitive abilities. *Autism Research, 2,* 109–118.

Farrant, B., Mattes, E., Keelan, J., Hickey, M., & Whitehouse, A. (2013). Fetal testosterone, socio-emotional engagement and language development. *Infant and Child Development, 22,* 119–132.

Fatemi, S. H., Aldinger, K., Ashwood, P. …. Welsh, J. P. (2012). Pathological role of the cerebellum in autism. *The Cerebellum, 11,* 777–807.

Fay, W. & Schuler, A. (1980). *Emerging Language in Autistic Children.* London: Edward Arnold.

Fein, D., Barton, M., Eigsti, M. ….Tyson, K. (2013). Optimal outcome in individuals with a history of autism. *Journal of Child Psychology and Psychiatry, 54,* 195–205.

Feldman, R. (2007). Parent–infant synchrony and the construction of shared timing: Physiological precursors, developmental outcomes, and risk conditions. *Journal of Child Psychology and Psychiatry, 48,* 329–354.

Fernández, C. (2013). Mindful storytellers: Emerging pragmatics and theory of mind development. *First Language, 33,* 20–46.

Fernell, E., Bejerot, S., Westerlund, J. …. Humble, M. (2015). Autism spectrum disorder and low vitamin D at birth. *Molecular Autism, 6,* 1.

Ferster, C. (1961). Positive reinforcement and behavioural deficits of autistic children. *Child Development, 32,* 437–456.

Fisher, N., Happé, F., & Dunn, J. (2005). The relationship between vocabulary, grammar, and false belief task performance in children with autistic spectrum disorders and children with moderate learning difficulties. *Journal of Child Psychology and Psychiatry, 46,* 409–419.

Flippin, M., Reszka, S., & Watson, L. (2010). Effectiveness of the Picture Exchange Communication System (PECS) on communication and speech for children with autism spectrum disorders. *American Journal of Speech-Language Pathology, 19,* 178–195.

Florian, L., Dee, L., Byers, R., & Maudslay, L. (2000). What happens after the age of 14? Mapping transition for pupils with profound and complex learning difficulties. *British Journal of Special Education, 27,* 124–128.

Fodor, J. (1983). *The Modularity of Mind.* Cambridge, MA: The MIT Press.

Fombonne, E. (1999). The epidemiology of autism. *Psychological Medicine, 29,* 769–787.

Forti, S., Valli, A., Perego, P. …. Molteni, M. (2011). Motor planning and control in autism: A kinematic analysis of preschool children. *Research in Autism Spectrum Disorders, 5,* 834–842.

Foti, F., De Crescenzo, F., Vivanti, G., Menghini, D., & Vicari, S. (2015). Implicit learning in individuals with autism spectrum disorders: A meta-analysis. *Psychological Medicine*, *45*, 897–910.

Fountain, C., King, M., & Bearman, P. (2011). Age of diagnosis for autism: Individual and community factors across 10 birth cohorts. *Journal of Epidemiology and Community Health*, *65*, 503–510.

Fournier, K., Hass, C., Naik, S., Lodha, N., & Cauraugh, J. (2010). Motor co-ordination in autism spectrum disorders. *Journal of Autism and Developmental Disorders*, *40*, 1227–1240.

Foxx, R. M. & Mulick, J. A. (Eds.) (2015). *Controversial Therapies for Autism and Intellectual Disabilities: Fad, Fashion, and Science in Professional Practice*. London: Routledge.

Frans, E., Sansin, S., Reichenberg, A. …. Hultman, C. (2013). Autism risk across generations. *JAMA Psychiatry*, *70*, 516–521.

Freeth, M., Milne, E., Sheppard, E., & Ramachandran, R. (2014). Autism across cultures. In F. Volkmar, S. Rogers, R. Paul & K. Pelphrey (Eds.), *Handbook of Autism and Pervasive Developmental Disorders* (Vol. 2, 4th edn) (pp. 997–1013). Hoboken, NJ: Wiley & Sons.

Freitag, C., Staal, W., Klauck, S., Duketis, E., & Waltes, R. (2010). Genetics of autistic disorders. *European Journal of Child and Adolescent Psychiatry*, *19*, 169–178.

Frenette, P., Dodds, L., MacPherson, K. …. Bryson, S. (2013). Factors affecting the age at diagnosis of autism spectrum disorders in Nova Scotia, Canada. *Autism*, *17*, 184–195.

Friston, K., Lawson, R., & Frith, C. (2013). On hyperpriors and hypopriors: Comment on Pellicano and Burr. *Trends in Cognitive Sciences*, *17*, 10–16.

Frith, U. (1989). *Autism: Explaining the Enigma*. Oxford: Blackwell.

Frith, U. (2003). *Autism: Explaining the Enigma* (2nd edn). Oxford: Blackwell.

Frith, U. (2013). Are there innate mechanisms that make us social beings? *Scripta Varia 121*.

Frith, U. & Frith, C. (2003). Development and neurophysiology of mentalizing. *Philosophical Transactions of the Royal Society of London B: Biological Sciences*, *358*, 459–473.

Frith, U. & Frith, C. (2010). The social brain: Allowing humans to boldly go where no other species has been. *Philosophical Transactions of the Royal Society of London B: Biological Sciences*, *365*, 165–176.

Frith, U. & Happé, F. (1999). Theory of mind and self-consciousness: What is it like to be autistic? *Mind and Language*, *14*, 1–22.

Frith, U., Morton, J., & Leslie, A. (1991). The cognitive basis of a biological disorder: Autism. *Trends in Neurosciences*, *14*, 433–438.

Frost, L. & Bondy, A. (2011). *A Clear Picture: The Use and Benefits of PECS*. Brighton: Pyramid Educational Consultants.

Gabriele, S., Sacco, R., & Persico, A. (2014). Blood serotonin levels in autism spectrum disorder. *European Neuropsychopharmacology*, *24*, 919–929.

Gabriels, R., Agnew, J., Miller, L. …. Hooks, E. (2008). Is there a relationship between restricted, repetitive, stereotyped behaviours and abnormal sensory response in children with autism spectrum disorders? *Research in Autism Spectrum Disorders*, *2*, 660–670.

Gadow, K., Pinsonneault, J., Perlman, G., & Sadee, W. (2014). Association of dopamine gene variants, emotion dysregulation and ADHD in autism spectrum disorder. *Research in Developmental Disorders*, *35*, 1658–1665.

Gaigg, S. (2012). The interplay between emotion and cognition in autism spectrum disorder: Implications for developmental theory. *Frontiers in Integrative Neuroscience*, *4*, 113.

Gaigg, S., Bowler, D., Ecker, C., Calvo-Merino, B., & Murphy, D. (2015). Episodic recollection difficulties in ASD result from atypical relational encoding: Behavioral and neural evidence. *Autism Research*, *8*, 317–327.

Gaigg, S., Bowler, D., & Gardiner, J. M. (2014). Episodic but not semantic order memory difficulties in autism spectrum disorder: Evidence from the Historical Figures Task. *Memory*, *22*, 669–678.

Gal, E., Dyke, M., & Passmore, A. (2002). Sensory differences and stereotyped movements in children with autism. *Behavioural Change, 19*, 207–219.

Gallagher, S. (2004). Understanding interpersonal problems in autism. *Philosophy, Psychiatry and Psychology, 11*, 199–217.

Gallese, V., Rochat, M., & Berchio, C. (2013). The mirror mechanism and its potential role in autism. *Developmental Medicine and Child Neurology, 55*, 15–22.

García-Primo, P., Hellendoorn, A., Charman, T. …. Moilanen, I. (2014). Screening for autism spectrum disorders: State of the art in Europe. *European Child and Adolescent Psychiatry, 23*, 1005–1021.

Gargaro, B., Rinehart, N., Bradshaw, J., Tonge, B., & Sheppard, D. (2011). Autism and ADHD. *Neuroscience and Biobehavioural Reviews, 35*, 1081–1088.

Gepner, B. & Mestre, D. (2002). Rapid visual motion integration deficit in autism. *Trends in Cognitive Sciences, 6*, 255.

Gerhardt, P., Cicero, F., & Mayville, E. (2014). Employment and related service for adults with ASD. In F. Volkmar, S. Rogers, R. Paul & K. Pelphrey (Eds.), *Handbook of Autism and Pervasive Developmental Disorders* (Vol. 2, 4th edn) (pp. 907–917). Hoboken, NJ: Wiley & Sons.

German, T. & Leslie, A. (2004). No (social) construction without (meta-) representation: Modular mechanisms as a basis for the capacity to acquire an understanding of mind. *Behavioral and Brain Sciences, 27*, 106–107.

Gernsbacher, G., Sauer, E., Geye, H., Schweigert, E., & Goldsmith, H. (2008). Infant and toddler oral- and manual-motor skills predict later speech fluency in autism. *Journal of Child Psychology and Psychiatry, 49*, 43–50.

Gerrans, P. & Stone, V. (2008). Generous or parsimonious cognitive architecture? Cognitive neuroscience and theory of mind. *The British Journal for the Philosophy of Science, 59*, 121–141.

Geschwind, D. (2011). Genetics of autism spectrum disorders. *Trends in Cognitive Sciences, 15*, 409–416.

Getso, B. & Ibrahim, S. (2014). Impact of endocrine disruptions on man. *Bayero Journal of Pure and Applied Sciences, 7*, 93–100.

Ghanizadeh, A. (2012). Hyperbaric oxygen therapy for treatment of children with autism: A systematic review of randomized trials. *Medical Gas Research, 2*, 13.

Ghaziuddin, M., Al-Khouri, I., & Ghaziuddin, N. (2002). Autistic symptoms following herpes encephalitis. *European Journal of Child and Adolescent Psychiatry, 11*, 142–146.

Gillberg, C. (1986). Onset at age 14 of a typical autistic syndrome. *Journal of Autism and Developmental Disorders, 16*, 369–375.

Goines, P. & Ashwood, P. (2013). Cytokine dysregulation in autism spectrum disorders. *Neurotoxicology and Teratology, 36*, 67–81.

Golan, O., Sinai-Gavrilov, Y., & Baron-Cohen, S. (2015). The Cambridge Mindreading Face-Voice Battery for Children (CAM-C): Complex emotion recognition in children with and without autism spectrum conditions. *Molecular Autism, 6*, 1.

Goldani, A., Downs, S., Widjaja, F., Lawton, B., & Hendren, R. (2014). Biomarkers in autism. *Frontiers in Psychiatry, 5*, 100.

González-Alzaga, B., Lacasaña, M., Aguilar-Garduño, C. …. Hernández, A. (2014). A systematic review of the effects of prenatal and postnatal organophosphate pesticide exposure. *Toxicology Letters, 230*, 104–121.

Gordon, I., Vander Wyk, B., Bennett, R. …. Pelphrey, K. A. (2013). Oxytocin enhances brain function in children with autism. *Proceedings of the National Academy of Sciences, 110*, 20953–20958.

Gould, J. & Ashton-Smith, J. (2011). Missed diagnosis or misdiagnosis? Girls and women on the autism spectrum. *Good Autism Practice, 12*, 34–41.

Gould, K. (2011). Fantasy play as the conduit for change in the treatment of a six-year-old boy with Asperger's Syndrome. *Psychoanalytic Inquiry, 31*, 240–251.

Gowen, E. & Hamilton, A. (2013). Motor abilities in autism. *Journal of Autism and Developmental Disorders, 43*, 323–344.

Grandin, T. & Scariano, M. (1986). *Emergence Labelled Autistic*. Novato, CA: Arena Press.

Grandjean, P. & Landigren, P. (2014). Neurobehavioural effects of developmental toxicity. *The Lancet: Neurology, 13*, 330–338.

Granpeesheh, D., Tarbox, J., & Dixon, D. R. (2009). Applied behavior analytic interventions for children with autism: A description and review of treatment research. *Annals of Clinical Psychiatry, 21*, 162–173.

Grant, A. (2011). Fear, confusion and participation: Incapacity benefit claimants and (compulsory) work focused interviews. *Research, Policy and Planning, 28*, 161–171.

Gray, D. (2002). Ten years on: A longitudinal study of families of children with autism. *Journal of Intellectual and Developmental Disability, 27*, 215–222.

Green, J., Charman, T., McConachie, H. .... Barrett, B. (2010). Parent-mediated communication-focused treatment in children with autism (PACT): A randomised controlled trial. *The Lancet, 375*, 2152–2160.

Green, J., Charman, T., Pickles, A. .... Jones, E. (2015). Parent-mediated intervention versus no intervention for infants at high risk of autism. *The Lancet Psychiatry, 2*, 133–140.

Green, S. & Ben-Sasson, A. (2010). Anxiety disorders and sensory over-responsivity in children with autism spectrum disorders: Is there a causal relationship? *Journal of Autism and Developmental Disorders, 40*, 1495–1504.

Green, S., Ben-Sasson, A., Soto, T., & Carter, A. (2012). Anxiety and sensory over-responsivity in toddlers with autism spectrum disorders: Bidirectional effects across time. *Journal of Autism and Developmental Disorders, 42*, 1112–1119.

Greenberg, J., Krauss, M., Seltzer, M., Chou, R., & Hong, J. (2004). The effect of quality of the relationship between mothers and adult children with schizophrenia, autism, or Down syndrome on maternal well-being: The mediating role of optimism. *American Journal of Orthopsychiatry, 74*, 14–25.

Greenspan, S. & Wieder, S. (1999). A functional developmental approach to autism spectrum disorders. *Research and Practice for Persons with Severe Disabilities, 24*, 147–161.

Greenspan, S. & Wieder, S. (2009). *Engaging Autism: Using the Floortime Approach to Help Children Relate, Communicate, and Think*. Boston, MA: Da Capo Press.

Greimel, E., Nehrkom, B., Schulte-Ruther, M. .... Eickhoff, S. B. (2013). Changes in gray matter development in autism spectrum disorder. *Brain Structure and Function, 218*, 929–942.

Griffith, E., Pennington, B., Wehner, E., & Rogers, S. (1999). Executive functions in young children with autism. *Child Development, 70*, 817–832.

Grigorenko, E., Klin, A., Pauls, D. .... Volkmar, F. (2002). A descriptive study of hyperlexia in a clinically referred sample of children with developmental delays. *Journal of Autism and Developmental Disorders, 32*, 3–12.

Grzadzinski, M., Luyster, R., Spencer, A., & Lord, C. (2014). Attachment in young children with autism spectrum disorders. *Autism, 18*, 85–96.

Grzadzinski, R., Huerta, M., & Lord, C. (2013). DSM-5 and autism spectrum disorders (ASDs): An opportunity for identifying ASD subtypes. *Molecular Autism, 4*, 12.

Guilmatre, A., Dubourg, C., Mosca, A. L. .... Campion, D. (2009). Recurrent rearrangements in synaptic and neurodevelopmental genes and shared biologic pathways in schizophrenia, autism, and mental retardation. *Archives of General Psychiatry, 66*, 947–956.

Gunnes, N., Surén, P., Bresnahan, M. .... Stoltenberg, C. (2013). Inter-pregnancy interval and risk of autism spectrum disorder. *Epidemiology, 24*, 906–912.

Guthrie, W., Swineford, L., Wetherby, A., & Lord, C. (2013). Comparison of DSM-IV and DSM-5 factor structure models for toddlers with autism spectrum disorder. *Journal of the American Academy of Child & Adolescent Psychiatry, 52*, 797–805.

Gutstein, S. (2000). *Solving the Relationship Puzzle: A New Developmental Program that Opens the Door to Lifelong Social and Emotional Growth*. Arlington, TX: Future Horizons.

Gutstein, S., Burgess, A., & Montfort, K. (2007). Evaluation of the relationship development intervention program. *Autism, 11*, 397–411.

Hahamy, A., Behrmann, M., & Malach, R. (2015). The idiosyncratic brain. *Nature Neuroscience, 18*, 302–309.

Halepoto, D., AI-Ayadhi, L., & Salam, A. (2014). Therapeutic use of hyperbaric oxygen therapy for children with autism spectrum disorder. *Journal of the College of Physicians and Surgeons Pakistan, 24*, 508–514.

Halepoto, D., Bashir, S., & AI-Ayadhi, L. (2014). Possible role of brain-derived neurotrophic factor (BDNF) in autism spectrum disorder. *Journal of the College of Physicians and Surgeons Pakistan, 24*, 274–278.

Halfon, N. & Kuo, A. (2013). What DSM-5 could mean to children with autism and their families. *Journal of the American Academy of Pediatrics, 167*, 608–613.

Hamilton, A. (2013). Reflecting on the mirror neuron system in autism. *Developmental Cognitive Neuroscience, 3*, 91–105.

Hamilton-Giachritsis, C. & Browne, K. (2012). Forgotten children? An update on young children in institutions across Europe. *Early Human Development, 88*, 911–914.

Hansen, S., Schendel, D., & Parner, E. (2015). Explaining the increase in the prevalence of autism spectrum disorders. *JAMA Pediatrics, 169*, 56–62.

Happé, F. (1994). *Autism: An Introduction to Psychological Theory*. London: UCL Press.

Happé, F. (1995). Understanding minds and metaphors. *Metaphor and Symbolic Activity, 10*, 275–295.

Happé, F. (2003). Theory of mind and the self. *Annals of the New York Academy of Sciences, 1001*, 134–144.

Happé, F. (2011). Criteria, categories, and continua: Autism and related disorders in DSM-5. *Journal of the American Academy of Child and Adolescent Psychiatry, 50*, 540–542.

Happé, F. & Frith, U. (2006). The weak coherence account: Detail-focused cognitive style in autism spectrum disorders. *Journal of Autism and Developmental Disorders, 36*, 5–23.

Happé, F. & Frith, U. (2010). *Autism and Talent*. Oxford: Oxford University Press.

Happé, F. & Frith, U. (2014). Annual research review: Towards a developmental neuroscience of atypical social cognition. *Journal of Child Psychology and Psychiatry, 55*, 553–577.

Happé, F., Ronald, A., & Plomin, R. (2006). Time to give up on a single explanation for autism. *Nature Neuroscience, 9*, 1218–1220.

Hare, D. & Malone, C. (2004). Catatonia and autistic spectrum disorders. *Autism, 8*, 183–195.

Hare, D., Gould, J., Mills, R., & Wing, L. (1999). *A Preliminary Study of Individuals with ASDs in Three Special Hospitals in England*. London: National Autistic Society.

Hare, D., Pratt, C., Burton, M., Bromley, J., & Emerson, E. (2004). The health and social care needs of family carers supporting adults with autistic spectrum disorders. *Autism, 8*, 425–444.

Harms, M., Martin, A., & Wallace, G. (2010). Facial emotion recognition in autistic spectrum disorders: A review of behavioural and neuroimaging studies. *Neuropsychology Review, 20*, 290–322.

Hastings, R., Kovshoff, H., Brown, T. .... Remington, B. (2005). Coping strategies in mothers and fathers of preschool and school-age children with autism. *Autism, 9*, 377–391.

Hastings, R., Kovshoff, H., Ward, N. .... Remington, B. (2005). Systems analysis of stress and positive perceptions in mothers and fathers of pre-school children with autism. *Journal of Autism and Developmental Disorders, 35*, 635–644.

Hayes, S. & Watson, S. (2013). The impact of parenting stress: A meta-analysis of studies comparing the experience of parenting stress in parents of children with and without autism spectrum disorder. *Journal of Autism and Developmental Disorders, 43*, 629–642.

Hazen, E., McDougle, C., & Volkmar, F. (2013). Changes in the diagnostic criteria for autism in DSM-5: Controversies and concerns. *Journal of Clinical Psychiatry*, *74*, 739.

Hazlett, H., Poe, M., Gerig, G. …. Piven, J. (2011). Early brain overgrowth in autism associated with an increase in cortical surface area before age 2 years. *JAMA Psychiatry*, *68*, 467–476.

Heaton, P. (2003). Pitch memory, labelling and disembedding in autism. *Journal of Child Psychology and Psychiatry*, *44*, 543–551.

Heaton, P., Hermelin, B., & Pring, L. (1998). Autism and pitch processing: A precursor for savant ability? *Music Perception*, *15*, 291–305.

Heidgerken, A., Geffken, G., Modi, A., & Frakey, L. (2005). A survey of autism knowledge in a health care setting. *Journal of Autism and Developmental Disorders*, *35*, 323–330.

Heiman, T. (2002). Parents of children with disabilities: Resilience, coping and future expectations. *Journal of Developmental and Physical Disabilities*, *14*, 159–171.

Heinrichs, M. & Domes, G. (2008). Neuropeptides and social behaviour: Effects of oxytocin and vasopressin in humans. *Progress in Brain Research*, *170*, 337–350.

Henninger, N. & Taylor, J. (2013). Outcomes in adults with autism spectrum disorders. *Autism*, *17*, 103–116.

Herbert, J. & Brandsma, L. (2002). Applied behavior analysis for childhood autism: Does the emperor have clothes? *The Behavior Analyst Today*, *3*, 45.

Herbert, M. & Weintraub, K. (2013). *The Autism Revolution: Whole-Body Strategies for Making Life All It Can Be*. New York: Ballantine Books.

Hermann, I., Haser, V., van Elst, L. …. Konieczny, L. (2013). Automatic metaphor processing in adults with Asperger syndrome. *European Archives of Psychiatry and Clinical Neuroscience*, *263*, S177–S187.

Hermelin, B. (2001). *Bright Splinters of the Mind*. London: Jessica Kingsley.

Hermelin, B. & O'Connor, N. (1970). *Psychological Experiments with Autistic Children*. Oxford: Pergamon Press.

Hermelin, B. & O'Connor, N. (1985). Logico-affective states and non-verbal language. In E. Schopler & G. Mesibov (Eds.), *Communication Problems in Autism* (pp. 293–309). New York: Plenum Press.

Hertz-Picciotto, I. & Delwiche, L. (2009). The rise in autism and the role of age at diagnosis. *Epidemiology*, *20*, 84–90.

Hess, E. (2013). DIR®/Floortime™: Evidence-based practice towards the treatment of autism and sensory processing disorder in children and adolescents. *International Journal of Child Health and Human Development*, *6*, 267–274.

Hill, A., Zuckerman, K., & Fombonne, E. (2014). Epidemiology of autism spectrum disorders. In F. Volkmar, S. Rogers, R. Paul & K. Pelphrey (Eds.), *Handbook of Autism and Pervasive Developmental Disorders* (Vol. 2, 4th edn) (pp. 3–27). Hoboken, NJ: Wiley & Sons.

Hill, E. (2004). Evaluating the theory of impairments of executive function in autism. *Developmental Review*, *24*, 189–233.

Hill, E., Berthoz, S., & Frith, U. (2004). Brief report: Cognitive processing of own emotions in individuals with autistic spectrum disorder and in their relatives. *Journal of Autism and Developmental Disorders*, *34*, 229–235.

Hill, S., Wagner, E., Shedlarski, J., & Sears, S. (1977). Diurnal cortisol and temperature variation of normal and autistic children. *Developmental Psychobiology*, *10*, 579–583.

Hobson, R. P. (1990). On the origins of self and the case of autism. *Development and Psychopathology*, *2*, 163–181.

Hobson, R. P. (1993). *Autism and the Development of Mind*. Hove: Lawrence Erlbaum Associates.

Hobson, R. P. (2014). Autism and emotion. In F. Volkmar, S. Rogers, R. Paul & K. Pelphrey (Eds.), *Handbook of Autism and Pervasive Developmental Disorders* (Vol. 2, 4th edn) (pp. 332–353). Hoboken, NJ: Wiley & Sons.

Hobson R. P., Chidambi G., Lee A. & Racine T. (2006). Foundations for self-awareness: An exploration through autism. *Monographs of the Society for Research in Child Development.* Jan 1: i–166.

Hobson, R. P., García-Pérez, R., & Lee, A. (2010). Person-centred (deictic) expressions and autism. *Journal of Autism and Developmental Disorders, 40,* 403–415.

Hobson, R. P. & Lee, A. (2010). Reversible autism among congenitally blind children? A controlled follow-up study. *Journal of Child Psychology and Psychiatry, 51,* 1235–1241.

Hobson, R. P., Ouston, J., & Lee, A. (1989). Naming emotion in faces and voices: Abilities and disabilities in autism and mental retardation. *British Journal of Developmental Psychology, 7,* 237–250.

Hodgetts, S., Nicholas, D., Zwaigenbaum, L., & McConnell, D. (2013). Parents' and professionals' perceptions of family-centered care for children with autism spectrum disorder across service sectors. *Social Science and Medicine, 96,* 138–146.

Hofvander, B., Delorme, R., Chaste, P. .... Leboyer, M. (2009). Psychiatric and psychosocial problems in adults with normal-intelligence autism spectrum disorders. *BMC Psychiatry, 9,* 1.

Hosenbocus, S. & Chahal, R. (2012). A review of executive function deficits and pharmacological management in children and adolescents. *Journal of the Canadian Academy of Child and Adolescent Psychiatry, 21,* 223–229.

Houghton, K., Schuchard, J., Lewis, C., & Thompson, C. (2013). Promoting child-initiated social-communication in children with autism: Son-Rise Program intervention effects. *Journal of Communication Disorders, 46,* 495–506.

Howlin, P. (2000). Outcome in adult life for more able individuals with autism or Asperger syndrome. *Autism, 4,* 63–83.

Howlin, P., Alcock, J., & Burkin, J. (2005). An 8-year follow-up of a specialist supported employment service for high-ability adults with autism or Asperger syndrome. *Autism, 9,* 533–569.

Howlin, P., Goode, S., Hutton, J., & Rutter, M. (2004). Adult outcome for children with autism. *Journal of Child Psychology and Psychiatry, 45,* 212–229.

Howlin, P., Savage, S., Moss, P., Tempier, A., & Rutter, M. (2014). Cognitive and language skills in adults with autism. *Journal of Child Psychology and Psychiatry, 55,* 49–58.

Hubbard, A., McNealy, K., Zeeland, S. .... Dapretto, M. (2012). Altered integration of speech and gesture in children with autism spectrum disorders. *Brain and Behavior, 2,* 606–619.

Huerta, M., Bishop, S., Duncan, A., & Lord, C. (2012). Application of DSM-5 criteria for autism spectrum disorder to three samples of children with DSM-IV diagnoses of pervasive developmental disorders. *American Journal of Psychiatry, 169,* 1056–1064.

Hughes, C. (1996). Brief report: Planning problems in autism at the level of motor control. *Journal of Autism and Developmental Disorders, 26,* 99–107.

Hughes, P. J. (2007). *Reflections: Me and Planet Weirdo.* London: ChipmunkPublishing.

Hultman, C., Sandin, S., Levine, S., Lichtenstein, P., & Reichenberg, A. (2011). Advancing paternal age and risk of autism. *Molecular Psychiatry, 16,* 1203–1212.

Hume, K. & Odom, S. (2007). Effects of an individual work system on the independent functioning of students with autism. *Journal of Autism and Developmental Disorders, 37,* 1166–1180.

Hurlburt, K. & Chalmers, L. (2004). Employment and adults with Asperger syndrome. *Focus on Autism and Other Developmental Disabilities, 19,* 215–222.

Hussman, J. (2001). Suppressed GABAergic inhibition as a common factor in suspected etiologies of autism. *Journal of Autism and Developmental Disorders, 31,* 247–248.

Hutt, S., Hutt, C., Lee, D., & Ounsted, C. (1964). Arousal and childhood autism. *Nature, 204,* 908.

Hutt, S., Hutt, C., Ounsted, C., & Lee, D. (1965). A behavioural and electroencephalographic study of autistic children. *Journal of Psychiatry Research, 3,* 181–197.

Iarocci, G. & McDonald, J. (2006). Sensory integration and the perceptual experience of persons with autism. *Journal of Autism and Developmental Disorders, 36,* 77–90.

Ibrahim, S., Voigt, R., Katusic, S., Weaver, A., & Barbaresi, W. (2009). Incidence of gastrointestinal symptoms in children with autism. *Pediatrics, 124,* 680–684.

Isanon, A. (2001). *Spirituality and the Autistic Spectrum: Of Falling Sparrows.* London: Jessica Kingsley.

Itahashi, T., Yamada, T., Nakamura, M. …. Hashimoto, R. (2015). Linked alterations in gray and white matter in adults with high-functioning autism spectrum disorder. *NeuroImage: Clinical, 7,* 155–169.

Ives, M. & Munro, N. (2002). *Caring for a Child with Autism.* London: Jessica Kingsley.

Jarrold, C. (2003). A review of research into pretend play in autism. *Autism, 7,* 379–390.

Jarrold, C., Boucher, J., & Smith, P. K. (1996). Generativity deficits in pretend play in autism. *British Journal of Developmental Psychology, 14,* 275–300.

Jarrold, C., Butler, D., Cottington, E., & Jimenez, F. (2000). Linking theory of mind and central coherence bias in autism and in the general population. *Developmental Psychology, 36,* 126–138.

Järvinen-Pasley, A., Wallace, G., Ramus, F., Happé, F., & Heaton, P. (2008). Enhanced perceptual processing of speech in autism. *Developmental Science, 11,* 109–121.

Jones, A., Happé, F., Gilbert, F., Burnett, S., & Viding, E. (2010). Feeling, caring, knowing: Different types of empathy in boys with psychopathic tendencies and autism spectrum disorder. *Journal of Child Psychology and Psychiatry, 51,* 1188–1197.

Jones, C., Happé, F., Golden, H. …. Charman, T. (2009). Reading and arithmetic in adolescents with autism spectrum disorders. *Neuropsychology, 23,* 718–728.

Jones, E., Gliga, T., Bedford, R., Charman, T., & Johnson, M. (2014). Developmental pathways to autism: A review of prospective studies of infants at risk. *Neuroscience and Biobehavioural Reviews, 39,* 1–33.

Jones, W., Carr, K., & Klin, A. (2008). Absence of preferential looking to the eyes of approaching adults predicts level of social disability in 2-year-old toddlers with autism spectrum disorder. *Archives of General Psychiatry, 65,* 946–954.

Jordan, R. (2001). Effects of culture on service provision for people with autistic spectrum disorders. *Good Autism Practice, 2,* 332–338.

Jordan, R. (2005). Managing autism and Asperger's syndrome in current educational provision. *Developmental Neurorehabilitation, 8,* 104–108.

Jordan, R. (2008). Autism spectrum disorders: A challenge and a model for inclusion in education. *British Journal of Special Education, 35,* 11–15.

Jordan, R. & Powell, S. (1995). *Understanding and Teaching Children with Autism.* Chichester: John Wiley & Sons.

Josefi, O. & Ryan, V. (2004). Non-directive play therapy for young children with autism: A case study. *Clinical Child Psychology and Psychiatry, 9,* 533–551.

Kahane, L. & El-Tahir, M. (2015). Attachment behavior in children with Autistic Spectrum Disorders. *Advances in Mental Health and Intellectual Disabilities, 9,* 79–89.

Kakooza-Mwesige, A., Wachtel, L., & Dhossche, D. (2008). Catatonia in autism. *European Journal of Child and Adolescent Psychiatry, 17,* 327–335.

Kalkbrenner, A., Schmidt, R., & Penlesky, A. (2014). Environmental chemical exposures and autism spectrum disorders. *Current Problems in Pediatric and Adolescent Health Care, 44,* 277–318.

Kaminsky, L. & Dewey, D. (2002). Psychosocial adjustment in siblings of children with autism. *Journal of Child Psychology and Psychiatry, 43,* 225–232.

Kana, R., Uddin, L., Kenet, T., Chugani, D., & Muller, R.-A. (2014). Brain connectivity in autism. *Frontiers in Human Neuroscience, 8,* 1–4.

Kanner, L. (1943). Autistic disturbances of affective contact. *Nervous Child, 2,* 217–250.

Kapp, S., Gillespie-Lynch, K., Sherman, L., & Hutman, T. (2013). Deficit, difference, or both? Autism and neurodiversity. *Developmental Psychology, 49*, 59.

Karmiloff-Smith, A. (1992). *Beyond Modularity*. Cambridge, MA: The MIT Press.

Karmiloff-Smith, A. (2006). The tortuous route from genes to behavior: A neuroconstructivist approach. *Cognitive, Affective and Behavioral Neuroscience, 6*, 9–17.

Kasarpalkar, N., Kothan, S., & Dave, U. (2014). Brain-derived neurotrophic factor (BDNF) in children with autism spectrum disorder. *Annals of Neuroscience, 21*, 129-133.

Kasirer, A. & Mashal, N. (2014). Verbal creativity in autism. *Frontiers in Human Neurosciences, 8*, 615.

Kates, W., Burnette, C., Eliez, S. …. Pearlson, G. (2004). Neuroanatomic variation in monozygotic twin pairs discordant for the narrow phenotype for autism. *American Journal of Psychiatry, 161*, 539–546.

Kato, K., Mikami, K., Akama, F. …. Matsumoto, H. (2013). Clinical features of suicide attempts in adults with autism spectrum disorders. *General Hospital Psychiatry, 35*, 50–53.

Kaufman, B. & Kaufman, S. (1976). *Son-Rise*. New York: Harper Collins.

Keen, D., Reid, F., & Arnone, D. (2010). Autism, ethnicity and maternal immigration. *British Journal of Psychiatry, 196*, 274–281.

Kelley, E. (2011). Language in ASD. In D. Fein (Ed.), *The Neuropsychology of Autism* (pp. 123–137). Oxford: Oxford University Press.

Kelley, E., Paul, J., Fein, D., & Naigles, L. (2006). Residual language deficits in optimal outcome children with a history of autism *Journal of Autism and Developmental Disorders, 36*, 807–828.

Kemper, T. & Bauman, M. (1998). Neuropathology of infantile autism. *Journal of Neuropathology and Experimental Neurology, 57*, 645–652.

Kenny, L., Molins, B., Buckley, C. … Pellicano, E. (2015). Which terms should be used to describe autism? Perspectives from the UK autism community. *Autism, 19*, 1–21.

Kent, R., Carrington, S., Le Couteur, A. …. Leekam, S. (2013). Diagnosing autism spectrum disorder: Who will get a DSM-5 diagnosis? *Journal of Child Psychology and Psychiatry, 54*, 1242–1250.

Kern, J., Geier, D., & Geier, M. (2014). Evaluation of regression in autism spectrum disorder based on parental reports. *North American Journal of Medical Sciences, 6*, 41–47.

Kern, J., Geier, D., Sykes, L., & Geier, M. (2013). Evidence of neurodegeneration in autism spectrum disorder. *Translational Neurodegeneration, 2*, 1.

Kim, S. & Lord, C. (2010). Restricted and repetitive behaviors in toddlers and preschoolers with autism spectrum disorders based on the Autism Diagnostic Observation Schedule (ADOS). *Autism Research, 3*, 162–173.

Kim, S. & Lord, C. (2012a). New autism diagnostic interview-revised algorithms for toddlers and young preschoolers from 12 to 47 months of age. *Journal of Autism and Developmental Disorders, 42*, 82–93.

Kim, S. & Lord, C. (2012b). Combining information from multiple sources for the diagnosis of autism spectrum disorders for toddlers and young preschoolers from 12 to 47 months of age. *Journal of Child Psychology and Psychiatry, 53*, 143–151.

Kim, S. H., Paul, R., Tager-Flusberg, H., & Lord, C. (2014). Language and communication in autism. In F. Volkmar, S. Rogers, R. Paul & K. Pelphrey (Eds.), *Handbook of Autism and Pervasive Developmental Disorders* (Vol. 2, 4th edn.) (pp. 230–262). Hoboken, NJ: Wiley & Sons.

Kimhi, Y., Shoam-Kugelmas, D., Ben-Artzi, …. Bauminger-Zviely, N. (2014). Theory of mind and executive function in preschoolers with typical development versus intellectually able preschoolers with autism spectrum disorder. *Journal of Autism and Developmental Disorders, 44*, 2341–2354.

Kimura, M., Hanaie, R., Mohri, I. …. Masako, T. (2013). Altered microstructural connectivity of the arcuate fasciculus is related to language disability in children with autism spectrum disorder. *Journal of Brain Sciences, 42*, 21–42.

King, B. & Lord, C. (2011). Is schizophrenia on the autistic spectrum? *Brain Research, 1380*, 34–41.

Kjelgaard, M. & Tager-Flusberg, H. (2001). An investigation of language profiles in autism: Implications for genetic subgroups. *Language and Cognitive Processes, 16*, 287–308.

Klei, L., Sanders, S., Murtha, M. …. Devlin, B. (2012). Common genetic variants, acting additively are a major risk factor for autism. *Molecular Autism, 3*, 1–9.

Klein, K. & Diehl, E. (2004). Relationship between MMR vaccine and autism. *Annals of Pharmacotherapy, 38*, 1297–1300.

Klintwall, L., & Eikeseth, S. (2014). Early and Intensive Behavioral Intervention (EIBI) in autism. In V. Patel, V. Preedy & C. Martin (Eds.), *Comprehensive Guide to Autism* (pp. 117–137). New York: Springer.

Koegel, R., Kern, L., & Koegel, L. (2006). *Pivotal Response Treatments for Autism: Communication, Social, and Academic Development.* Baltimore, MD: Paul H. Brookes.

Koegel, R. & Koegel, L. (2012). *The PRT Pocket Guide.* Baltimore, MD: Paul H. Brookes.

Kolvin, I. (1971). Studies in childhood psychoses, I: Diagnostic criteria and classification. *British Journal of Psychiatry, 118*, 381–384.

Konidaris, J. (2005). A sibling's perspective on autism. In F. Volkmar, R. Paul, A. Klin & D. Cohen (Eds.), *Handbook of Autism and Pervasive Developmental Disorders* (Vol. 2, 3rd edn) (pp. 1265–1275). Hoboken, NJ: John Wiley & Sons.

Kovács, A., Téglás, E., & Endress, A. (2010). The social sense: Susceptibility to others' beliefs in human infants and adults. *Science, 330*(6012), 1830–1834.

Kraijer, D. (2000). Review of adaptive behaviour studies in mentally retarded persons with autism/pervasive developmental disorder. *Journal of Autism and Developmental Disorders, 30*, 39–48.

Krause, I., He, X., Gershwin, M., & Schoenfeld, Y. (2002). Review of autoimmune factors in autism. *Journal of Autism and Developmental Disorders, 32*, 337–345.

Krauss, M. & Seltzer, M. (2000). An unanticipated life: The impact of lifelong caregiving. In H. Bersani (Ed.), *Responding to the Challenge: International Trends and Current Issues in Developmental Disabilities* (pp. 173–188). Northampton, MA: Brookline Books.

Krauss, M., Seltzer, M., & Jacobson, H. (2005). Adults with autism living at home or in non-family settings: Positive and negative aspects of residential status. *Journal of Intellectual Disability Research, 49*, 111–124.

Krcek, T. E. (2013). Deconstructing disability and neurodiversity: Controversial issues for autism and implications for social work. *Journal of Progressive Human Services, 24*, 4–22.

Kriette, T. & Noelle, D. (2015). Dopamine and the development of executive function in autism spectrum disorders. *PLoS One, 10*, e0121605.

Krug, D., Arick, J., & Almond, P. (1978). *ABC—Autism Behaviour Checklist.* Portland, OR: ASIEP Education Co.

Kumsta, R., Kreppner, J., Kennedy, M. …. Sonuga-Barke, E. (2015). Psychological consequences of early global deprivation. *European Psychologist, 20*, 138–151.

Kurtz, P., Boelter, E., Jarmolowicz, D., Chin, M., & Hagopian, L. (2011). An analysis of functional communication training as an empirically supported treatment for problem behavior displayed by individuals with intellectual disabilities. *Research in Developmental Disabilities, 32*, 2935–2942.

Kyrkou, M. (2005). Health issues and quality of life in women with intellectual disability. *Journal of Intellectual Disability Research, 49*, 770–777.

Lai, M.-C., Lombardo, M., Chakrabarti, B., & Baron-Cohen, S. (2013). Subgrouping the autism 'Spectrum': Reflections on DSM-5. *PLoS Biology, 11*, e1001544.

Lam, J., Sutton, P., Kalkbrenner, A., …. Woodruff, T. (2016). A systematic review and meta-analysis of multiple airborne pollutants and autism spectrum disorder. *PLoS One, 11*(9), e0161851.

Lang, R., O'Reilly, M., Healy, O. …. Didden, R. (2012). Sensory integration therapy for autism spectrum disorders: A systematic review. *Research in Autism Spectrum Disorders, 6*, 1004–1018.

Lawson, R., Rees, G., & Friston, K. (2014). An aberrant precision account of autism. *Frontiers in Human Neurosciences, 8.*

Le Couteur, A., Bailey, A., Goode, S., Pickles, A. …. Rutter, M. (1996). A broader phenotype of autism: The clinical spectrum in twins. *Journal of Child Psychology and Psychiatry, 37*, 785–801.

Le Couteur, A., Baird, G., & National Initiative for Autism Screening and Assessment (NIASA) (2003). *National Autism Plan.* London: National Autistic Society.

Leary, M. & Hill, D. A. (1996). Moving on: Autism and movement disturbance. *Mental Retardation, 34*, 39–53.

LeClerc, S. & Easley, D. (2015). Pharmacological therapies for autism spectrum disorder. *Pharmacy and Therapeutics, 40*, 389.

LeDoux, J. (1998). *The Emotional Brain: The Mysterious Underpinnings of Emotional Life.* New York: Simon & Schuster.

Lee, A. & Hobson, R. P. (1998). On developing self concepts: A controlled study of children and adolescents with autism. *Journal of Child Psychology and Psychiatry, 39*, 1131–1141.

Lee, M. S., Choi, T. Y., Shin, B. C., & Ernst, E. (2012). Acupuncture for children with autism spectrum disorders: A systematic review of randomized clinical trials. *Journal of Autism and Developmental Disorders, 42*, 1671–1683.

Leekam, S., Prior, M., & Uljarevic, M. (2011). Restricted and repetitive behaviors in autism spectrum disorders: A review of research in the last decade. *Psychological Bulletin, 137*, 562–593.

Leekam, S. & Ramsden, C. (2006). Dyadic orienting and joint attention in preschool children with autism. *Journal of Autism and Developmental Disorders, 36*, 185–197.

Leinonen, E., Letts, C., & Smith, B. R. (2000). *Children's Pragmatic Communication Difficulties.* London: Whurr.

Leonard, L. (2000). *Children with Specific Language Impairment.* Cambridge, MA: The MIT Press.

Lerna, A., Esposito, D., Conson, M., & Massagli, A. (2014). Long-term effects of PECS on social–communicative skills of children with autism spectrum disorders. *International Journal of Language and Communication Disorders, 49*, 478–485.

Leslie, A. (1987). Pretense and representation in infancy: The origins of theory of mind. *Psychological Review, 94*, 412–427.

Levy, A. & Perry, A. (2011). Outcomes in adolescents and adults with autism. *Research in Autism Spectrum Disorders, 5*, 1271–1282.

Levy, S., Giarelli, E., Lee, L.-C. …. Rice, C. (2010). Autism spectrum disorder and co-occurring developmental, psychiatric and medical conditions among children in multiple populations of the United States. *Developmental and Behavioural Pediatrics, 31*, 267–275.

Lewis, V. & Boucher, J. (1988). Spontaneous, instructed, and elicited play in relatively able autistic children. *British Journal of Developmental Psychology, 6*, 325–339.

Lewis, V. & Boucher, J. (1991). Skill, content, and generative strategies in autistic children's drawings. *British Journal of Developmental Psychology, 9*, 393–416.

Li, H., Xue, Z., Ellmore, T., Frye, R., & Wong, S. (2014). Network-based analysis reveals stronger local diffusion-based connectivity … in brains of high-functioning children with autism spectrum disorders. *Human Brain Mapping, 35*, 396–413.

Li, W., Mai, X., & Liu, C. (2014). The default mode network and social understanding of others: What do brain connectivity studies tell us? *Frontiers in Human Neuroscience*, *8*, 74ff.

Libero, L., DeRamus, T., Deshpande, H., & Kana, R. (2014). Surface-based morphometry of the cortical architecture of autism spectrum disorders. *Neuropsychologia*, *62*, 1–10.

Lidstone, J., Uljarevic, M., Sullivan, J. …. Leekam, S. (2014). Relations among restricted and repetitive behaviours, anxiety and sensory features in children with autism spectrum disorders. *Research in Autism Spectrum Disorders*, *8*, 82–92.

Lilley, R. (2013). It's an absolute nightmare: Maternal experiences of enrolling children diagnosed with autism in primary school in Sydney, Australia. *Disability and Society*, *28*, 514–526.

Lincoln, A. J., Allen, M., & Killman, A. (1995). The assessment and interpretation of intellectual abilities in people with autism. In E. Schopler & G. Mesibov (Eds.), *Learning and Cognition in Autism* (pp. 89–118). New York: Plenum Press.

Lind, S. (2010). Memory and the self in autism. *Autism*, *14*, 430–456.

Lind, S. & Bowler, D. (2010). Episodic memory and episodic future thinking in adults with autism. *Journal of Abnormal Psychology*, *119*, 896–905.

Lind, S., Williams, D., Bowler, D., & Peel, A. (2014). Episodic memory and episodic future thinking impairments in high-functioning autism spectrum disorder: An underlying difficulty with scene construction or self-projection? *Neuropsychology*, *28*, 55.

Lindell, A. & Hudry, K. (2013). Atypicalities in cortical structure, handedness, and functional lateralisation for language in autism spectrum disorders. *Neuropsychology Review*, *23*, 257–270.

Liss, M., Saulnier, C., Fein, D., & Kinsbourne, M. (2006). Sensory and attention abnormalities in autistic spectrum disorders. *Autism*, *10*, 155–172.

Liu, J., McErlean, R., & Dadds, M. (2012). Are we there yet? The clinical potential of intranasal oxytocin in psychiatry. *Current Psychiatry Reviews*, *8*, 37–48.

Liu, M.-J., Shih, W.-L., & Ma, L.-Y. (2011). Are children with Asperger syndrome creative in divergent thinking and feeling? *Research in Autism Spectrum Disorders*, *85*, 294–298.

Lombardo, M., Ashwin, E., Auyeung, B. …. Baron-Cohen, S. (2012). Fetal programming effects of testosterone on the reward system and behavioural approach tendencies in humans. *Biological Psychiatry*, *72*, 839–847.

Lombardo, M., Barnes, S., Wheelwright, S., & Baron-Cohen, S. (2007). Self-referential cognition and empathy in autism. *PLoS One*, *2*, e883.

Lombardo, M. & Baron-Cohen, S. (2011). The role of the self in mindblindness in autism. *Consciousness and Cognition*, *20*, 130–140.

LoParo, D. & Waldman, I. (2014). The oxytocin receptor gene (OXTR) is associated with autism spectrum disorder. *Molecular Psychiatry*, *20*, 640–646.

Lord, C., Cook, E., Blumenthal, B., & Amarel, D. (2000). Autistic spectrum disorders. *Neuron*, *28*, 355–363.

Lord, C. & Costello, C. (2005). Diagnostic instruments in autistic spectrum disorders. In F. Volkmar, R. Paul, A. Klin & D. Cohen (Eds.), *Handbook of Autism and Pervasive Developmental Disorders* (Vol. 2, 3rd edn) (pp. 730–771). Hoboken, NJ: John Wiley & Sons.

Lord, C. & Paul, R. (1997). Language and communication in autism. In D. Cohen & F. Volkmar (Eds.), *Handbook of Autism and Pervasive Developmental Disorders* (2nd edn) (pp. 195–225). New York: John Wiley.

Lord, C., Risi, S., DiLavore, P. …. Pickles, A. (2006). Autism from 2 to 9 years of age. *Archives of General Psychiatry*, *63*, 694–701.

Lord, C., Rutter, M., DiLavore, P., & Risi, S. (1999). *Autism Diagnostic Observation Schedule*. Los Angeles, CA: Western Psychological Services.

Loucas, T., Charman, T., Pickles, A. .... Baird, G. (2008). Autistic symptomatology and language ability in autism spectrum disorder and specific language impairment. *Journal of Child Psychology and Psychiatry, 49*, 1184–1192.

Lovaas, I., Calouri, K., & Jada, J. (1989). The nature of behavioral treatment and research with young autistic persons. In C. Gillberg (Ed.), *Diagnosis and Treatment of Autism* (pp. 285–305). New York: Springer.

Loveland, K. & Landry, S. (1986). Joint attention in autism and developmental language delay. *Journal of Autism and Developmental Disorders, 16*, 335–349.

Low, J., Goddard, E., & Melser, J. (2009). Generativity and imagination in autism spectrum disorder: Evidence from individual differences in children's impossible entities drawings. *British Journal of Developmental Psychology, 27*, 425–444.

Loynes, F. (2001). *The Rising Challenge: A Survey of Local Education Authorities on Educational Provision for Pupils with Autistic Spectrum Disorders*. London: All Party Parliamentary Group on Autism.

Lundin, A. & Dwyer, J. (2014). Autism: Can dietary interventions and supplements work? *Nutrition Today, 49*, 196–206.

Luyster, R., Gotham, K., Guthrie, W. .... Richler, J. (2009). The Autism Diagnostic Observation Schedule–Toddler Module: A new module of a standardized diagnostic measure for autism spectrum disorders. *Journal of Autism and Developmental Disorders, 39*, 1305–1320.

Luyster, R., Kadlec, M., Carter, A., & Tager-Flusberg, H. (2008). Language assessment and development in toddlers with autism spectrum disorder. *Journal of Autism and Developmental Disorders, 38*, 1426–1438.

Luyster, R., Seery, A., Talbott, M., & Tager-Flusberg, H. (2011). Identifying early-risk markers and developmental trajectories for language impairment in neurodevelopmental disorders. *Developmental Disabilities Research Reviews, 17*, 151–159.

Lyall, K., Munger, K., O'Reilly, E., Santangelo, S., & Ascherio, A. (2013). Maternal dietary fat intake in association with autism spectrum disorders. *American Journal of Epidemiology, 178*, 209–220.

Lyall, K., Schmidt, R., & Hertz-Picciotto, I. (2014). Environmental factors in the preconception and prental periods in relation to risk for ASD. In F. Volkmar, S. Rogers, R. Paul & K. Pelphrey (Eds.), *Handbook of Autism and Pervasive Developmental Disorders* (Vol. 2, 4th edn) (pp. 424–456). Hoboken, NJ: Wiley & Sons.

Lyall, S., Pauls, D., Spiegelman, D., Ascherio, A., & Santangelo, S. (2012). Pregnancy complications and obstetric suboptimality in association with autism spectrum disorders in children. *Autism Research, 5*, 21–30.

Lyons, V. & Fitzgerald, M. (2013). Critical evaluation of the concept of autistic creativity. In M. Fitzgerald (Ed.), *Recent Advances in Autism Spectrum Disorders* (Vol. 1). InTech, DOI: 10.5772/54465. Available from www.intechopen.com/books.

Mackintosh, N. (2011). *IQ and Human Intelligence* (2nd edn). Oxford: Oxford University Press.

MacNeil, L. & Mostofsky, S. (2012). Specificity of dyspraxia in children with autism. *Neuropsychology, 26*, 165–171.

Maddox, B. & White, S. (2015). Comorbid social anxiety disorder in adults with autism spectrum disorder. *Journal of Autism and Developmental Disorders, 45*, 3949–3960.

Mahler, M. (1952). On child psychosis and schizophrenia: Autistic and symbiotic psychosis. *Psychoanalytic Study of the Child, 7*, 286–305.

Major, N., Peacock, G., Ruben, W., Thomas, J., & Weitzman, C. (2013). Autism training in pediatric residency. *Journal of Autism and Developmental Disorders, 43*, 1171–1177.

Makris, M., Polyzos, K., Mavros, M. .... Falagas, M. (2012). Safety of hepatitis B, pneumococcal polysaccharide and meningococcal polysaccharide vaccines in pregnancy. *Drug Safety, 35*, 1–14.

Mandell, D., Knashawn H., Ming Xie .... Marcus, S. (2010). County-level variation in the prevalence of Medicaid-enrolled children with autism spectrum disorders. *Journal of Autism and Developmental Disorders*, *40*, 1241–1246.

Mandell, D., Walrath, C., Manteuffel, B., Sgro, G., & Pinto-Martin, J. (2005). The prevalence and correlates of abuse among children with autism served in comprehensive community-based mental health settings. *Child Abuse and Neglect*, *29*, 1359–1372.

Mannion, A. & Leader, G. (2014). Sleep problems in autism spectrum disorder: A literature review. *Review Journal of Autism and Developmental Disorders*, *1*, 101–109.

Marcus, A., Sinnott, B., Bradley, S., & Grey, I. (2010). Treatment of idiopathic toe-walking in children with autism using GaitSpot auditory speakers and simplified habit reversal. *Research in Autism Spectrum Disorders*, *4*, 260–267.

Masi, A., Lampit, A., Glozier, N., Hickie, I., & Guastella, A. (2015). Predictors of placebo response in pharmacological and dietary supplement treatment trials in pediatric autism spectrum disorder: A meta-analysis. *Translational Psychiatry*, *5*, e640.

Matson, J., Adams, H., Williams, L., & Rieske, R. D. (2013). Why are there so many unsubstantiated treatments in autism? *Research in Autism Spectrum Disorders*, *7*, 466–474.

Matson, J. & Neal, D. (2009). Seizures and epilepsy and their relation to autism spectrum disorders. *Research in Autism Spectrum Disorders*, *3*, 999–105.

Matson, J., Sipes, M., Fodstad, J., & Fitzgerald, M. (2011). Issues in the management of challenging behaviours of adults with autism spectrum disorder. *CNS Drugs*, *25*, 597–606.

Mavranezouli, I., Megnin-Viggars, O., Cheema, N. .... Pilling, S. (2013). The cost-effectiveness of supported employment for adults with autism in the United Kingdom. *Autism,18*, 975–984.

Maximo, J., Cadena, E., & Kana, R. (2014). The implications of brain connectivity in the neuropsychology of autism. *Neuropsychology Review*, 24, 16–31.

Mayerson, G. (2014). Autism in the courtroom. In F. Volkmar, S. Rogers, R. Paul & K. Pelphrey (Eds.), *Handbook of Autism and Pervasive Developmental Disorders* (Vol. 2, 4th edn) (pp. 1036–1050). Hoboken, NJ: Wiley & Sons.

Mayes, S. & Calhoun, S. (2003). Analysis of WISC-III, Stanford-Binet:4, and academic achievement test scores in children with autism. *Journal of Autism and Developmental Disorders*, *33*, 329–341.

Mayes, S., Calhoun, S., Mayes, R., & Molitoris, S. (2012). Autism and ADHD. *Research in Autism Spectrum Disorders*, *6*, 277–285.

Mayes, S., Calhoun, S., Murray, M., ... Tierney, C. (2014). Final DSM-5 under-identifies mild autism spectrum disorder: Agreement between the DSM-5, CARS, CASD, and clinical diagnoses. *Research in Autism Spectrum Disorders*, *8*, 68–73.

Mayes, S., Calhoun, S., Murray, M., & Zahid, J. (2011). Variables associated with anxiety and depression in children with autism. *Journal of Developmental and Physical Disabilities*, *23*, 325–337.

Mayes, S., Gorman, A., Hillwig-Garcia, J., & Syed, E. (2013). *Research in Autism Spectrum Disorders*, *7*, 109–119.

Mazza, M., Pino, M., Mariano, M. .... Valenti, M. (2014). Affective and cognitive empathy in adolescents with autism spectrum disorder. *Frontiers in Human Neuroscience*, *8*, 791.

Mazzone, L., Posterino, V., Valeri, G., & Vicari, S. (2014). Catatonia in patients with autism. *CNS Drugs*, *28*, 205–215.

Mazzone, L., Ruta, L., & Reale, L. (2012). Psychiatric comorbidities in Asperger syndrome and high-functioning autism. *Annals of General Psychiatry*, *11*, 16.

McClimens, A., Brennan, S., & Hargreaves, P. (2015). Hearing problems in the learning disability population: Is anybody listening? *British Journal of Learning Disabilities*, *43*, 153–160.

McClure, I. (2014). Developing and implementing practice guidelines. In F. Volkmar, S. Rogers, R. Paul & K. Pelphrey (Eds.), *Handbook of Autism and Pervasive Developmental Disorders* (Vol. 2, 4th edn) (pp. 1014–1035). Hoboken, NJ: Wiley & Sons.

McDougle, C., Landino, S., Vahabzadeh, A. .... Carlezon, W. (2015). Toward an immune-mediated subtype of autism spectrum disorder. *Brain Research, 1617,* 72–92.

McGee, G., Daly, T., & Jacobs, H. (1994). The Walden preschool. In S. L. Harris & J. S. Handleman (Eds.), *Preschool Education Programs for Children with Autism* (pp. 127–162). Austin, TX: PRO-ED.

McGee, G., Morrier, M., & Daly, T. (1999). An incidental teaching approach to early intervention for toddlers with autism. *Research and Practice for Persons with Severe Disabilities, 24,* 133–146.

McGill, P., Tennyson, A., & Cooper, V. (2006). Parents whose children with learning disabilities and challenging behaviour attend 52-week residential schools: Their perception of services received and expectations for the future. *British Journal of Social Work, 36,* 597–616.

McGovern, C. & Sigman, M. (2005). Continuity and change from early childhood to adolescence in autism. *Journal of Child Psychology and Psychiatry, 46,* 401–408.

McKeague, I., Brown, A., Bao, Y. .... Sourander, A. (2015). Autism with intellectual disability related to dynamics of head circumference growth during early infancy. *Biological Psychiatry, 77,* 833–840.

McPartland, J. & Jeste, S. (2015). Connectivity in context: Emphasizing neurodevelopment in autism spectrum disorder. *Biological Psychiatry, 77,* 772–774.

Mehzabin, P. & Stokes, M. (2011). Self-assessed sexuality in young adults with high-functioning autism. *Research in Autism Spectrum Disorders, 5,* 614–621.

Meltzer, H., Gatward, R., Corbin, T., Goodman, R., & Ford, T. (2003). *The mental health of young people looked after by local authorities in England.* London: Office for National Statistics.

Melville, C., Cooper, S.-A., Morrison, J. .... Mantry, D. (2008). The prevalence and incidence of mental ill-health in adults with autism and intellectual disabilities. *Journal of Autism and Developmental Disorders, 38,* 1676–1688.

Menon, V. & Uddin, L. (2010). Saliency, switching, attention and control. *Brain Structure and Function, 214,* 655–667.

Mercer, J. (2013). Holding therapy: A harmful mental health intervention. *Focus on Alternative and Complementary Therapies, 18,* 70–76.

Mercer, J. (2015). Examining DIR®/Floortime™ as a treatment for children with autism spectrum disorders. *Research on Social Work Practice,* 1–11. doi:1049731515583062.

Mesibov, G. & Handlan, S. (1997). Adolescents and adults with autism. In D. Cohen & F. Volkmar (Eds.), *Handbook of Autism and Pervasive Developmental Disorders* (2nd edn) (pp. 309–322). New York: John Wiley.

Mesibov, G., Schopler, E., & Shea, V. (2004). *The TEACCH Approach to Autism Spectrum Disorders.* New York: Springer.

Meyer, J. & Hobson, R. P. (2004). Orientation to self and other: The case of autism. *Interaction Studies, 5,* 221–244.

Miles, J. (2011). Autism spectrum disorders – A genetics review. *Genetic Medicine, 13,* 278–294.

Miller, L. (1999). The savant syndrome. *Psychological Bulletin, 125,* 31–46.

Milne, E., Swettenham, J., & Campbell, R. (2005). Motion perception and autistic spectrum disorder: A review. *Current Psychology of Cognition, 23,* 3–36.

Mirenda, P. (2014). Augmentative and alternative communication. In F. Volkmar, S. Rogers, R. Paul & K. Pelphrey (Eds.), *Handbook of Autism and Pervasive Developmental Disorders* (Vol. 2, 4th edn) (pp. 813–825). Hoboken, NJ: Wiley & Sons.

Modahl, C., Fein, D., Waterhouse, L., & Newton, N. (1992). Does oxytocin deficit mediate social deficits in autism? *Journal of Autism and Developmental Disorders, 22*, 449–451.

Molteni, P., Guldberg, K., & Logan, N. (2013). Autism and multidisciplinary teamwork through the SCERTS model. *British Journal of Special Education, 40*, 137–145.

Montes, G. & Halterman, J. (2007). Psychological functioning and coping among mothers of children with autism. *Pediatrics, 119*, e1040–e1046.

Moore, D. J. (2014). Acute pain experience in individuals with autism spectrum disorders: A review. *Autism*, 1362361314527839.

Moss, P., Howlin, P., Savage, S., Bolton, P., & Rutter, M. (2015). Self and informant reports of mental health difficulties amongst adults with autism. *Autism, 19*, 832–841.

Mostofsky, S. & Ewen, J. (2011). Altered connectivity and action model formation in autism is autism. *The Neuroscientist, 17*, 437–448.

Mottron, L. & Belleville, S. (1993). A study of perceptual analysis in a high-level autistic subject with exceptional graphic abilities. *Brain and Cognition, 23*, 279–309.

Mottron, L., Bouvet, L., Bonnel, A. …. Heaton, P. (2013). Veridical mapping in the development of exceptional autistic abilities. *Neuroscience and Biobehavioral Reviews, 37*, 209–228.

Mottron, L. & Burack, J. (2001). Enhanced perceptual functioning in the development of autism. In J. Burack, T. Charman, N. Yirmiya & P. R. Zelazo (Eds.), *The Development of Autism: Perspectives From Theory and Research* (pp. 131–148). Hove: Lawrence Erlbaum Associates.

Mottron, L., Dawson, M., & Soulières, I. (2009). Enhanced perception in savant syndrome. *Philosophical Transactions of the Royal Society, 364*, 1385–1391.

Mottron, L., Dawson, M., Soulières, I., Hubert, B., & Burack, J. (2006). Enhanced perceptual functioning in autism: An update, and eight principles of autistic perception. *Journal of Autism and Developmental Disorders, 36*, 27–43.

Mottron, L., Peretz, I., Belleville, S., & Rouleau, N. (1999). Absolute pitch in autism: A case study. *Neurocase, 5*, 485–502.

Mouridsen, S. (2013). Mortality and factors associated with death in autism spectrum disorders. *American Journal of Autism, 1*, 17–25.

Mukaetova, E. & Perry, E. (2015). Molecular basis for cholinergic changes in autism spectrum disorders. In S. Fatemi & S. Hossein (Eds), *The Molecular Basis of Autism* (pp. 307–335). New York: Springer.

Mulloy, A., Lang, R., O'Reilly, M. …. Rispoli, M. (2010). Gluten-free and casein-free diets in the treatment of autism spectrum disorders: A systematic review. *Research in Autism Spectrum Disorders, 4*, 328–339.

Mundy, P. (1995). Joint attention and socio-emotional approach behaviour in children with autism. *Development and Psychopathology, 7*, 63–82.

Mundy, P. (2003). The neural basis of social impairments in autism: The role of the dorsal medial-frontal cortex and anterior cingulate system. *Journal of Child Psychology and Psychiatry, 44*, 793–809.

Murphy, D. & McMorrow, K. (2015). View of autism spectrum conditions held by staff working within a high-security psychiatric hospital. *Journal of Forensic Practice, 17*, 231–240.

Murray, D., Lesser, M., & Lawson, W. (2005). Attention, monotropism and the diagnostic criteria for autism. *Autism, 9*, 139–156.

Nation, K., Clarke, P., Wright, B., & Williams, C. (2006). Patterns of reading ability in children with autism spectrum disorder. *Journal of Autism and Developmental Disorders, 36*, 911–919.

National Research Council (US) (2001). *Educating Children with Autism*. Washington, DC: National Academies Press.

Nemeth, D., Janacsek, K., Balogh, V. .... Vetro, A. (2010). Learning in autism: Implicitly superb. *PloS One*, 5, e11731.

Newson, E. (1984). The social development of the young autistic child. Paper presented at the National Autistic Society Conference, Bath, UK.

Nguyen, M., Roth, A., Kyzar, E. .... Kalueff, A. (2014). Decoding the contribution of dopaminergic genes and pathways to autism spectrum disorder. *Neurochemistry International*, 66, 15–26.

NICE (National Institute for Clinical Excellence) (2013). The management and support of children and young people on the autism spectrum. http://publications.nice.org.uk/autism-cg170.

Nicholas, D. & Kilmer, C. (2015). Autism spectrum disorder and the family: Examining impacts and the need for support. In *Clinician's Manual on Autism Spectrum Disorder* (pp. 77–85). New York: Springer.

Nirje, B. (1969). The normalization principle and its human management implications. In R. Kugel & W. Wolfensberger (Eds.), *Changing Patterns in Residential Services for the Mentally Retarded* (pp. 179–195). Washington, DC: President's Commission on Mental Retardation.

O'Neill, M. & Jones, R. (1997). Sensory-perceptual abnormalities in autism: A case for more research? *Journal of Autism and Developmental Disorders*, 27, 283–293.

Oberman, L. & Ramachandran, V. (2007). The simulating social mind: The role of the mirror neuron system and simulation in the social and communicative deficits of autism spectrum disorders. *Psychological Bulletin*, 133, 310–327.

Oberman, L., Rotenberg, A., & Pascual-Leone, A. (2015). Use of transcranial magnetic stimulation in autism spectrum disorders. *Journal of Autism and Developmental Disorders*, 45, 524–536.

Oblak, A., Gibbs, T., & Blatt, G. (2013). Reduced serotonin receptor subtypes in a limbic and neocortical region in autism. *Autism Research*, 6, 571–583.

Ohan, J., Ellefson, S., & Corrigan, P. (2015). The impact of changing DSM-IV 'Asperger's' to DSM-5 'Autistic Spectrum Disorder' on stigma and treatment attitudes. *Journal of Autism and Developmental Disorders*, 45, 3384–3389.

Oliveras-Rentas, R., Kenworthy, L., Roberson III, R., Martin, A., & Wallace, G. (2012). WISC-IV profile in high-functioning autism spectrum disorders: Impaired processing speed is associated with increased autism communication symptoms and decreased adaptive communication abilities. *Journal of Autism and Developmental Disorders*, 42, 655–664.

Oller, D., Niyogi, P., Gray, S. .... Warren, S. (2010). Automated vocal analysis of naturalistic recordings from children with autism, language delay, and typical development. *Proceedings of the National Academy of Sciences*, 107, 13354–13359.

Onishi, K. & Baillargeon, R. (2005). Do 15-month-old infants understand false beliefs? *Science*, 308, 255–258.

Oppenheim, D., Koren-Karie, N., Dolev, S., & Yirmiya, N. (2009). Maternal insightfulness and resolution of the diagnosis are associated with secure attachment in preschoolers with autism spectrum disorders. *Child Development*, 80, 519–527.

Opris, I. & Casanova, M. (2014). Prefrontal cortical minicolumn. *Brain*, 137, 1863–1875.

Orekhova, E. V. & Stroganova, T. A. (2014). Arousal and attention re-orienting in autism spectrum disorders: Evidence from auditory event-related potentials. *Frontiers in Human Neuroscience*, 8, 34ff.

Orinstein, A., Helt, M., Troyb, E. .... Fein, D. (2014). Intervention history of children with high-functioning autism and optimal outcomes. *Journal of Developmental Behavioural Pediatrics*, *35*, 247–256.

Ornitz, E. & Ritvo, E. (1968). Neurophysiologic mechanisms underlying perceptual inconstancy in autistic and schizophrenic children. *Archives of General Psychiatry*, *19*, 76–98.

Ornitz, E. M. (1976). The modulation of sensory input and motor output in autistic children. In E. Schopler & R. Reichler (Eds.), *Psychopathology and Child Development* (pp. 115–133). New York: Springer.

Orsmond, G., Krauss, M., & Seltzer, M. (2004). Peer relationships and social and recreational activities among adolescents and adults with autism. *Journal of Autism and Developmental Disorders*, *34*, 245–257.

Ozonoff, S., Iosif, A.-M., Young, G. .... Rogers, S. (2011). Onset patterns in autism. *Journal of the American Academy of Child and Adolescent Psychiatry*, *50*, 796–806.

Ozonoff, S., Strayer, D., McMahon, W., & Filloux, F. (1994). Executive function abilities in autism and Tourette's syndrome. *Journal of Child Psychology and Psychiatry*, *35*, 1015–1032.

Page, J. & Boucher, J. (1998). Motor impairments in children with autistic disorder. *Child Language, Teaching, and Therapy*, *14*, 233–259.

Parish, S., Thomas, K., Rose, R., Kilany, M., & Shattuck, P. (2012). State Medicaid spending and financial burden of families raising children with autism. *Intellectual and Developmental Disabilities*, *50*, 441–451.

Parish, S., Thomas, K., Williams, C., & Crossman, M. (2015). Autism and families' financial burden. *American Journal on Intellectual and Developmental Disabilities*, *120*, 166–175.

Parish-Morris, J., Hennon, E., Hirsch-Pasek, K., Golinkoff, R., & Tager-Flusberg, H. (2007). Children with autism illuminate the role of social intention in word learning. *Child Development*, *78*, 1265–1287.

Park, C. C. (2001). *Exiting Nirvana: A Daughter's Life with Autism*. Boston, MA: Little, Brown & Co.

Pellicano, E. (2007). Links between theory of mind and executive function in young children with autism: Clues to developmental primacy. *Developmental Psychology*, *43*, 974.

Pellicano, E. (2010). Individual differences in executive function and central coherence predict developmental changes in theory of mind in autism. *Developmental Psychology*, *46*, 530–544.

Pellicano, E. (2012a). The development of executive function in autism. *Autism Research and Treatment* (Special Issue: Autism: Cognitive Control Across the Lifespan). Article ID 146132.

Pellicano, E. (2012b). Beyond weak central coherence. In J. Burack, J. Enns & N. Fox (Eds.), *Cognitive Science, Development, and Psychopathology* (pp. 153–187). Oxford: Oxford University Press.

Pellicano, E. (2012c). Do autistic symptoms persist across time? *American Journal on Intellectual and Developmental Disabilities*, *117*, 156–166.

Pellicano, E. & Burr, D. (2012). When the world becomes 'too real': A Bayesian explanation of autistic perception. *Trends in Cognitive Sciences*, *16*, 504–510.

Pelphrey, K., Shultz, S., Hudac, C., & Vander Wyk, B. (2011). The social brain and its development in autism spectrum disorder. *Journal of Child Psychology and Psychiatry*, *52*, 631–644.

Peppé, S., Cleland, J., Gibbon, F., O'Hare, A., & Castilla, P. (2011). Expressive prosody in children with autism spectrum conditions. *Journal of Neurolinguistics*, *24*, 41–53.

Périsse, D., Amiet, C., Consoli, A. .... Cohen, D. (2010). Risk factors of acute behavioural regression in psychiatrically hospitalized adolescents with autism. *Journal of the Canadian Academy of Child and Adolescent Psychiatry*, *19*, 100–108.

Perkins, M. (2007). *Pragmatic Impairment*. Cambridge: Cambridge University Press.

Perkins, M., Dobbinson, S., Boucher, J., Bol, S., & Bloom, P. (2006). Lexical knowledge and lexical use in autism. *Journal of Autism and Developmental Disorders, 36,* 795–805.

Perry, E., Lee, M., Martin-Ruiz, C. .... Wenk, G. (2001). Cholinergic activity in autism. *American Journal of Psychiatry, 158,* 1058–1066.

Persico, A. & Napolioni, V. (2013). Autism genetics. *Behaviour and Brain Research, 251,* 95–112.

Petalas, M., Hastings, R., Nash, S., Reilly, D., & Dowey, A. (2012). The perceptions and experiences of adolescent siblings who have a brother with autism spectrum disorder. *Journal of Intellectual and Developmental Disability, 37,* 303–314.

Pfeiffer, B., Kinnealey, M., Reed, C., & Herzberg, G. (2005). Sensory modulation and affective disorders in children and adolescents with Asperger's disorder. *American Journal of of Occupational Therapy, 59,* 335–345.

Philip, R., Dauvermann, M., Whalley, H. .... Stanfield, A. (2012). A systematic review and meta-analysis of the fMRI investigation of autism spectrum disorders. *Neuroscience and Biobehavioral Reviews, 36,* 901–942.

Pickles, A., Le Couteur, A., Leadbitter, K., Aldred, C. .... Green, J. (2016). Parent-mediated social-communication therapy for young children with autism: Long term follow up of a randomised control trial. *The Lancet,* October 25.

Pickles, A., Starr, E., Kazak, S., Bolton, P. .... Rutter, M. (2000). Variable expression of the autism broader phenotype: Findings from extended pedigrees. *Journal of Child Psychology and Psychiatry, 41,* 491–502.

Pinker, S. (1994). *The Language Instinct.* New York: Penguin Press.

Pinker, S. (1997). *How the Mind Works.* New York: Penguin Press.

Pinney, A. (2005). *Disabled Children in Residential Placements.* London: Department for Education and Skills (DfES) Reports.

Plaisted, K., O'Riordan, M., & Baron-Cohen, S. (1998). Enhanced visual search for a conjunctive target in autism. *Journal of Child Psychology and Psychiatry, 39,* 777–783.

Plaisted, K., Swettenham, J., & Rees, L. (1999). Children with autism show local precedence in a divided attention task and global precedence in a selective attention task. *Journal of Child Psychology and Psychiatry, 40,* 733–742.

Powell, S. & Jordan, R. (1993). Being subjective about autistic thinking and learning to learn. *Educational Psychology, 13,* 359–370.

Preece, D. & Jordan, R. (2007). Short breaks services for children with autistic spectrum disorders: Factors associated with service use and non-use. *Journal of Autism and Developmental Disorders, 37,* 374–385.

Preti, A., Melis, M., Siddi, S. .... Fadda, R. (2014). Oxytocin and autism. *Journal of Child and Adolescent Psychopharmacology, 24,* 54–68.

Pring, L. (2005). *Autism and Blindness: Research and Reflections.* London: Whurr.

Pring, L. (2008). Memory characteristics in individuals with savant skills. In J. Boucher & D. M. Bowler (Eds.), *Memory in Autism* (pp. 201–230). Cambridge: Cambridge University Press.

Prior, M., & Ozonoff, S. (2007). Psychological factors in autism. In F. Volkmar (Ed.), *Autism and Pervasive Developmental Disorders* (2nd edn., pp. 69–128). Cambridge: Cambridge University Press.

Prizant, B., Wetherby, A., Rubin, E., Laurent, A., & Rydell, P. (2006). *The SCERTS Model: A Comprehensive Educational Approach for Children with Autism Spectrum Disorders.* Baltimore, MD: Paul H. Brookes.

Quaak, I., Brouns, M., & Van der Bor, M. (2013). Dynamics of autism spectrum disorders: How neurotoxic compounds and neurotransmitters interact. *International Journal of Environmental Research and Public Health, 10,* 3384–3408.

Rai, D., Lee, B., Dalman, C. .... Magnusson, C. (2013). Parental depression, maternal antidepressant use during pregnancy, and risk of autism spectrum disorders. *British Medical Journal, 346,* f2059.

Ramachandran, V. & Oberman, L. (2006). Broken mirrors: A theory of autism. *Scientific American, 295*, 62–69.

Rapin, I. (1996). Neurological issues. In I. Rapin (Ed.), *Preschool Children with Inadequate Communication* (pp. 98–112). Cambridge: MacKeith Press.

Rapin, I. & Allen, D. (1983). Developmental language disorders: Nosologic considerations. In U. Kirk (Ed.), *Neuropsychology of Language, Reading and Spelling* (pp. 155–184). New York: Academic Press.

Rapin, I. & Dunn, M. (2003). Update on the language disorders of individuals on the autistic spectrum. *Brain and Development, 25*, 166–172.

Rapin, I., Dunn, M., Allen, D., Stevens, M., & Fein, D. (2009). Subtypes of language disorders in school-age children with autism. *Developmental Neuropsychology, 34*, 66–84.

Reichow, B., Barton, E., Boyd, P., & Hume, K. (2012). Early intensive behavioral intervention (EIBI) for young children with autism spectrum disorders. *Cochrane Database Systemic Review*, 10.

Renzaglia, A., Karvonen, M., Drasgow, E., & Stoxen, C. (2003). Promoting a lifetime of inclusion. *Focus on Autism and Other Developmental Disabilities, 18*, 140–149.

Rhode, M. (2009). Child psychotherapy with children on the autistic spectrum. In M. Lanyado & A. Horne (Eds.), *The Handbook of Child and Adolescent Psychotherapy: Psychoanalytic Approaches* (2nd edn) (pp. 287–299). London: Taylor & Francis.

Richa, S., Fahed, M., Khoury, E., & Mishara, B. (2014). Suicide in autism spectrum disorders. *Archives of Suicide Research, 18*, 327–339.

Richards, C., Oliver, C., Nelson, L., & Moss, J. (2012). Self-injurious behaviour in individuals with autism spectrum disorder and intellectual disability. *Journal of Intellectual Disability Research, 56*, 476–489.

Richdale, A. & Prior, M. (1992). Urinary cortisol circadian rhythm in a group of high-functioning children with autism. *Journal of Autism and Developmental Disorders, 22*, 433–447.

Riches, N., Loucas, T., Baird, G., Charman, T., & Simonoff, E. (2010). Sentence repetition in adolescents with specific language impairments and autism: An investigation of complex syntax. *International Journal of Language and Communication Disorders, 45*, 47–60.

Richler, J., Huerta, M., Bishop, S., & Lord, C. (2010). Developmental trajectories of restricted and repetitive behaviors and interests in children with autism spectrum disorders. *Development and Psychopathology, 22*, 55–69.

Ricks, D. & Wing, L. (1975). Language, communication, and the use of symbols in normal and autistic children. *Journal of Autism and Developmental Disorders, 5*, 191–221.

Rimland, B. (1964). *Infantile Autism*. New York: Appleton-Century-Crofts.

Rincover, A. & Ducharme, J. (1987). Variables influencing stimulus overselectivity and 'tunnel vision' in developmentally delayed children. *American Journal of Mental Deficiency, 91*, 422–430.

Rinehart, N., Bellgrove, M., Tonge, B. .... Bradshaw, J. (2006). An examination of movement kinematics in young people with high-functioning autism and Asperger's disorder. *Journal of Autism and Developmental Disorders, 36*, 757–767.

Risi, S., Lord, C., Gotham, K. .... Pickles, A. (2006). Combining information from multiple sources in the diagnosis of autistic spectrum disorders. *Journal of the American Academy of Child and Adolescent Psychiatry, 45*, 1094–1103.

Ritvo, E. & Freeman, B. (1977). National Society for Autistic Children definition of the syndrome of autism. *Journal of Pediatric Psychology, 2*, 146–148.

Ritvo, E., Freeman, B., & Scheibel, A. (1986). Lower Purkinje cell counts in the cerebella of four autistic subjects: Initial findings of the UCLA-NSAC autopsy research report. *American Journal of Psychiatry, 143*, 862–866.

Roberts, A., Koenen, K., Lyall, K., Ascherio, A., & Weisskopf, M. (2014). Women's post-traumatic stress symptoms and autism spectrum disorder in their children. *Research in Autism Spectrum Disorders, 8*, 608–616.

Roberts, A., Lyall, K., Hart, J. .... Weisskopf, M. (2013). Perinatal air pollutant exposure and autism spectrum disorder. *Nurses' Health Study II: Environmental Health Perspectives, 121,* 978–984.

Robins, D., Casagrande, K., Barton, M., & Fein, D. (2014). Validation of the Modified Checklist for Autism in Toddlers, Revised with Follow-up (M-CHAT-R/F). *Pediatrics, 133,* 37–45.

Robins, D., Fein, D., Barton, M., & Green, J. (2001). The Modified Checklist for Autism in Toddlers. *Journal of Autism and Developmental Disorders, 31,* 131–144.

Robinson, S. (2011). Teaching paraprofessionals of students with autism to implement pivotal response treatment in inclusive school settings using a brief video feedback training package. *Focus on Autism and Other Developmental Disabilities, 26,* 105–118.

Rodgers, J., Glod, M., Connolly, B., & McConachie, H. (2012). The relationship between anxiety and repetitive behaviours in autism spectrum disorder. *Journal of Autism and Developmental Disorders, 42,* 2494–2509.

Rojas, D., Singel, D., Steinmetz, S., Hepburn, S., & Brown, M. (2014). Decreased left perisylvian GABA concentration in children with autism and unaffected siblings. *NeuroImage, 86,* 28–34.

Ronald, A. & Hoekstra, R. (2011). Autism spectrum disorders and autistic traits: A decade of new twin studies. *American Journal of Medical Genetics, 156,* 255–274.

Rosenhall, U., Nordin, V., Sandstroem, M., Ahlsen, G., & Gillberg, C. (1999). Autism and hearing loss. *Journal of Autism and Developmental Disorders, 29,* 349–357.

Rubenstein, J. & Merzenich, M. (2003). Model of autism: Increased ratio of excitation/inhibition in key neural systems. *Genes, Brain and Behavior, 2,* 255–267.

Ruggeri, B., Sarkans, U., Schumann, G., & Persico, A. (2014). Biomarkers in autism spectrum disorder: The old and the new. *Psychopharmacology, 231,* 1201–1216.

Rumsey, J. (1985). Conceptual problem-solving in highly verbal, nonretarded autistic men. *Journal of Autism and Developmental Disorders, 15,* 23–36.

Russell, J., Mauthner, N., Sharpe, S., & Tidswell, T. (1991). The 'Windows task' as a test of strategic deception in preschoolers and autistic subjects. *British Journal of Developmental Psychology, 9,* 101–119.

Russo, N., Flanagan, T., Iarocci, G. .... Burack, J. (2007). Deconstructing executive deficits among persons with autism: Implications for cognitive neuroscience. *Brain and Cognition, 65,* 77–86.

Ruta, L., Mugno, D., D'Arrigo, D., Vitiello, B., & Mazzone, L. (2010). Obsessive-compulsive traits in children and adolescents with Asperger syndrome. *European Journal of Child and Adolescent Psychiatry, 19,* 17–24.

Rutgers, A., Bakermans-Kranenburg, M., Ijzendoom, M., & Berckelaer-Onnes, I. (2004). Autism and attachment: A meta-analytic review. *Journal of Child Psychology and Psychiatry, 45,* 1123–1134.

Rutter, M. (1968). Concepts of autism: A review of research. *Journal of Psychology and Psychiatry, 9,* 1–25.

Rutter, M., Bailey, A. & Lord, C. (2003). *The Social Communication Questionnaire.* Torrance, CA: Western Psychological Services.

Rutter, M., Bartak, L., & Newman, S. (1971). Autism – a central disorder of cognition and language. In M. Rutter (Ed.), *Infantile Autism: Concepts, Characteristics and Treatment* (pp. 148–171). London: Churchill-Livingstone.

Rutter, M., Greenfield, D., & Lockyer, L. (1967). A five to fifteen year follow-up study of infantile psychosis: II. Social and behavioural outcome. *British Journal of Psychiatry, 113,* 1183–1200.

Rutter, M., Le Couteur, A., & Lord, C. (2003). *Autism Diagnostic Interview—Revised.* Los Angeles, CA: Western Psychological Services.

Rutter, M. & Thapar, A. (2014). Genetics of autism spectrum disorders. In F. Volkmar, S. Rogers, R. Paul & K. Pelphrey (Eds.), *Handbook of Autism and Pervasive Developmental Disorders* (Vol. 2, 4th edn) (pp. 411–423). Hoboken, NJ: Wiley & Sons.

Sacks, O. (1995). *An Anthropologist on Mars.* London: Picador.

Sakamoto, A., Moriuchi, H., Matsuzaki, J., Motoyama, A., & Moriuchi, H. (2015). Retrospective diagnosis of cytomegalovirus infection in children with autism. *Brain Development, 37,* 200–205.

Santosh, P., Mandy, W., Puura, K., & Skuse, D. (2009). The construction and validation of a short form of the Developmental, Diagnostic and Dimensional Interview. *European Child and Adolescent Psychiatry, 18,* 521–524.

Scattone, D. & Billhofer, B. (2008). Teaching sign language to a nonvocal child with autism. *The Journal of Speech and Language Pathology—Applied Behavior Analysis, 3,* 78.

Scheuffgen, K., Happé, F., Anderson, M., & Frith, U. (2000). High 'intelligence', low 'IQ'? Speed of processing and measured IQ in children with autism. *Development and Psychopathology, 12,* 83–90.

Schneider, D., Slaughter, D., Bayliss, A., & Dux, P. (2013). A temporally sustained implicit theory of mind deficit in autism spectrum disorder. *Cognition, 2,* 410–417.

Schoen, S., Miller, L., Brett-Green, B., & Nielsen, D. (2009). Physiological and behavioral differences in sensory processing: A comparison of children with autism spectrum disorder and sensory modulation disorder. *Frontiers in Integrative Neuroscience, 3,* 29.

Schopler, E., Reichler, R., & Renner, B. (2002). *The Childhood Autism Rating Scale (CARS).* Los Angeles, CA: Western Psychological Services.

Schuh, J. & Eigsti, I. (2012). Working memory, language skills, and autism symptomatology. *Behavioral Sciences, 2,* 207–218.

Scott, F. & Baron-Cohen, S. (1996). Imagining real and unreal things: Evidence of a dissociation in autism. *Journal of Cognitive Neuroscience, 8,* 371–382.

Scott, F., Baron-Cohen, S., & Leslie, A. (1999). If pigs could fly: A test of counterfactual reasoning and pretence in children with autism. *British Journal of Developmental Psychology, 17,* 349–362.

Scott, J., Duhig, M., Hamlyn, J., & Norman, R. (2013). Environmental contributions to autism. *Journal of Environmental Immunology and Toxicology, 1,* 75–79.

Seal, B. & Bonvillian, J. (1997). Sign language and motor functioning in students with autistic disorder. *Journal of Autism and Developmental Disorders, 27,* 437–466.

Sebat, J., Lakshmi, B., Malhotra, D. …. Wigler, M. (2007). Strong associations with copy number mutations with autism. *Science, 316,* 445–449.

Selimoglu, O., Ozdemir, S., Toret, G., & Ozkubat, U. (2013). An examination of the views of parents of children with autism about their experiences at the post-diagnosis period. *International Journal of Early Childhood Special Education, 5,* 129–167.

Seltzer, M., Krauss, M., Shattuck, P. …. Lord, C. (2003). The symptoms of autism spectrum disorders in adolescence and adulthood. *Journal of Autism and Developmental Disorders, 33,* 565–582.

Senju, A., Southgate, V., White, S., & Frith, U. (2009). Mindblind eyes: An absence of spontaneous theory of mind in Asperger syndrome. *Science, 325,* 883–885.

Shah, A. & Frith, U. (1983). An islet of ability in autistic children. *Journal of Child Psychology and Psychiatry, 24,* 613–620.

Sharpe, D. & Baker, D. (2007). Financial issues associated with having a child with autism. *Journal of Family and Economic Issues, 28,* 247–264.

Shattuck, P., Narendorf, S. C., Cooper, B. …. Taylor, J. L. (2012). Postsecondary education and employment among youth with an autism spectrum disorder. *Pediatrics, 6,* 1042–1049.

Shavelle, R., Strauss, D., & Pickett, J. (2001). Causes of death in autism. *Journal of Autism and Developmental Disorders, 31,* 569–576.

Shelton, J., Geraghty, E., Tancredi, D. …. Hertz-Picciotto, I. (2014). Neurodevelopmental disorders and prenatal residential proximity to agricultural pesticides. *Environmental Health Perspectives (Online), 122,* 1103.

Shetreat-Klein, M., Shinnar, S., & Rapin, I. (2014). Abnormalities of joint mobility and gait in children with autism spectrum disorders. *Brain and Development, 36,* 91–96.

Shields, J. (2001). The NAS EarlyBird Programme: Partnership with parents in early intervention. *Autism, 5,* 49–56.

Shoffner, J., Hyams, L., Langley, G. N. …. Hyland, K. (2010). Fever plus mitochrondrial disease could be risk factors for autistic regression. *Journal of Child Neurology, 25,* 429–434.

Shriberg, L., Paul, R., MacSweeny, J., Klin, A., & Cohen, D. (2001). Speech and prosody characteristics of adolescents and adults with high-functioning autism and Asperger syndrome. *Journal of Speech, Language, and Hearing Research, 44,* 1097–1115.

Shtayermman, O. (2008). Suicidal ideation and comorbid disorders in adolescents and young adults diagnosed with Asperger's syndrome. *Journal of Human Behaviour in the Social Environment, 18,* 301–328.

Shulman, C. & Guberman, A. (2007). Acquisition of verb meaning through syntactic cues. *Journal of Child Language, 34,* 411–423.

Shute, N. (2010). Desperate for an autism cure. *Scientific American, 303,* 80–85.

Siegel, D., Minshew, N., & Goldstein, G. (1996). Wechsler IQ profiles in diagnosis of high functioning autism. *Journal of Autism and Developmental Disorders, 26,* 389–407.

Sigman, M. & Capps, L. (1997). *Children with Autism: A Developmental Perspective.* Cambridge, MA: Harvard University Press.

Sigman, M., Dijamco, A., Gratier, M., & Rozga, A. (2004). Early detection of core deficits in autism. *Mental Retardation and Developmental Disabilities Research Reviews, 10,* 221–233.

Silberman, S. (2015). *Neurotribes.* London: Allen & Unwin.

Siller, M. & Sigman, M. (2008). Modeling longitudinal change in the language abilities of children with autism: Parent behaviors and child characteristics as predictors of change. *Developmental Psychology, 44,* 1691.

Silverman, L., Bennetto, L., Campana, E., & Tanenhaus, M. (2010). Speech-and-gesture integration in high functioning autism. *Cognition, 115,* 380–393.

Simmons, D., McKay, L., McAleer, P. …. Pollick, F. (2007). Neural noise and autism spectrum disorders. *Perception, 36,* 119–120.

Simonoff, E., Pickles, A., Charman, T. …. Baird, G. (2008). Psychiatric disorders in children with autism spectrum disorders. *Journal of the American Academy of Child and Adolescent Psychiatry, 47,* 921–929.

Sinha, Y., Silove, N., Hayen, A., & Williams, K. (2011). Auditory integration training and other sound therapies for autism spectrum disorders. *Cochrane Database Systemic Review, 12.*

Skuse, D. (2011). The extraordinary political world of autism. *Brain,* awr111.

Skuse, D. (2013). Developmental, Dimensional and Diagnostic Interview. *Encyclopedia of Autism Spectrum Disorders,* 1–7.

Skuse, D., Warrington, R., Bishop, D. …. Place, M. (2004). The Developmental, Dimensional and Diagnostic Interview (3di): A novel computerized assessment for autism spectrum disorders. *Journal of the American Academy of Child and Adolescent Psychiatry, 43,* 548–558.

Slater-Walker, G. & Slater-Walker, C. (2002). *An Asperger Marriage.* London: Jessica Kingsley.

Smart, M. (2004). Transition planning and the needs of young people and their carers. *British Journal of Special Education, 31,* 128–137.

Smith, M., Fulcher, L., & Doran, P. (2013). *Residential Child Care in Practice: Making a Difference.* Bristol: Policy Press.

Smith, T., Scahill, L., Dawson, G. …. Wagner, A. (2007). Designing research studies on psychosocial intervention in autism. *Journal of Autism and Developmental Disorders, 37,* 354–366.

Snyder, A. (2010). Explaining and inducing savant skills: Privileged access to lower-level, less-processed information. In F. Happé & U. Frith (Eds.), *Autism and Talent* (pp. 75–88). Oxford: Oxford University Press.

Souders, M., Mason, T., Valladares, O. .... Pinto-Martin, J. (2009). Sleep behaviours and sleep quality in children with autism spectrum disorders. *SLEEP, 32*, 1566–1578.

Soulières, I., Hubert, B., Rouleau, N. .... Mottron, L. (2010). Superior estimation abilities in two autistic children. *Cognitive Neuropsychology, 27*, 261–276.

Sowden, H., Clegg, J., & Perkins, M. (2013). The development of co-speech gesture in the communication of children with autism spectrum disorders. *Clinical Linguistics and Phonetics, 27*, 922–939.

Sparrow, S. & Davis, S. M. (2000). Recent advances in the assessment of intelligence and cognition. *Journal of Child Psychology and Psychiatry, 41*, 117–132.

Spencer, L., Lyketsos, C., Samstad, E., & Chisolm, M. (2011). A suicidal adult in crisis: An unexpected diagnosis of autism spectrum disorder. *American Journal of Psychiatry, 168*, 890–892.

Spezio, M., Adolphs, R., Hurley, R., & Piven, J. (2007). Abnormal use of facial information in high-functioning autism. *Journal of Autism and Developmental Disorders, 37*, 929–939.

Spiker, D. & Ricks, M. (1984). Visual self-recognition in autistic children: Developmental relationships. *Child Development, 55*, 214–225.

Spiker, M., Lin, C., Van Dyke, M., & Wood, J. (2011). Restricted interests and anxiety in children with autism. *Autism, 16*, 306–320.

Spratt, E., Nicholas, J., Brady, K. .... Charles, M. (2011). Enhanced cortisol response to stress in children with autism. *Journal of Autism and Developmental Disorders, 42*, 75–81.

Stahmer, A., Akshoomoff, N., & Cunningham, A. (2011). Inclusion for toddlers with autism spectrum disorders: The first ten years of a community program. *Autism, 15*, 625–641.

Stahmer, A. & Ingersoll, B. (2004). Inclusive programming for toddlers with autism spectrum disorders: Outcomes from the children's toddler school. *Journal of Positive Behavior Interventions, 6*, 67–82.

Stahmer, A., Schreibman, L., & Cunningham, A. (2011). Toward a technology of treatment individualization for young children with autism spectrum disorders. *Brain Research, 1380*, 229–239.

Stahmer, A., Suhrheinrich, J., Reed, S., Bolduc, C., & Schreibman, L. (2010). Pivotal Response Teaching in the classroom setting. *Preventing School Failure: Alternative Education for Children and Youth, 54*, 265–274.

Stahmer, A., Suhrheinrich, J., Reed, S., & Schreibman, L. (2012). What works for you? Using teacher feedback to inform adaptations of pivotal response training for classroom use. *Autism Research and Treatment, 2012*. Article ID 709861.

Stamou, M., Streifel, K., Goines, P., & Lein, P. (2013). Neural connectivity as a convergent target of gene x environment interactions that confer risk for autism spectrum disorders. *Neurotoxicology and Teratology, 36*, 3–16.

Stanford, Ashley (2014). *Asperger Syndrome (Autism Spectrum Disorder) and Long-Term Relationships* (2nd edn). London and Philadelphia: Jessica Kingsley Publishers.

Stehli, A. (1992). *The Miracle of Silence*. London: Doubleday.

Steiner, A., Gengoux, G., Klin, A., & Chawarska, K. (2013). Pivotal response treatment for infants at-risk for autism spectrum disorders: A pilot study. *Journal of Autism and Developmental Disorders, 43*, 91–102.

Sterling-Turner, H. & Jordan, S. (2007). Interventions addressing transition difficulties for individuals with autism. *Psychology in Schools, 44*, 681–690.

Stevens, M., Fein, D., Dunn, M. .... Rapin, I. (2000). Subgroups of children with autism by cluster analysis. *Journal of the American Academy of Child and Adolescent Psychiatry, 39*, 346–352.

Stewart, H., Macintosh, R., & Williams, J. (2013). A specific deficit of imitation in autism spectrum disorder. *Autism Research, 6,* 522–530.

Stewart, P., Hyman, S., Schmidt, B. …. Manning-Courtney, P. (2015). Dietary supplementation in children with autism spectrum disorders: Common, insufficient, and excessive. *Journal of the Academy of Nutrition and Dietetics, 115,* 1237–1248.

Stiegler, L. & Davis, R. (2010). Understanding sound sensitivity in individuals with autism spectrum disorders. *Focus On Autism and Other Developmental Disorders, 25,* 67–75.

Stoit, A., van Schie, H., Slaats-Willemse, D., & Buitelaar, J. (2013). Grasping motor impairments in autism: Not action planning but movement execution is deficient. *Journal of Autism and Developmental Disorders, 43,* 2793–2806.

Stokes, M. & Kaur, A. (2005). High-functioning autism and sexuality. *Autism, 9,* 266–289.

Strain, P. & Bovey, E. (2008). LEAP preschool. In J. Handleman & S. Harris (Eds.), *Preschool Education Programs for Children with Autism* (pp. 249–280). Austin, TX: Pro-Ed.

Strain, P. & Bovey, E. (2011). Randomized, controlled trial of the LEAP model of early intervention for young children with autism spectrum disorders. *Topics in Early Childhood Special Education, 31,* 133–154.

Sukhodolsky, D., Bloch, M., Panza, K., & Reichow, B. (2013). Cognitive-behavioral therapy for anxiety in children with high-functioning autism: A meta-analysis. *Pediatrics, 132,* e1341–e1350.

Sullivan, K., Stone, W., & Dawson, G. (2014). Potential neural mechanisms underlying the effectiveness of early intervention for children with autism spectrum disorder. *Research in Developmental Disabilities, 35,* 2921–2932.

Surén, P., Gunnes, N., Roth, C. …. Stoltenberg, C. (2014). Parental obesity and risk of autism spectrum disorder. *Pediatrics, 133,* peds-2013.

Surén, P., Roth, C., Bresnahan, M. …. Stoltenberg, C. (2013). Association between maternal use of folic acid supplements and risk of autism spectrum disorders in children. *JAMA, 309,* 570–577.

Surian, L., Baron-Cohen, S., & Van der Lely, H. (1996). Are children with autism deaf to Gricean Maxims? *Cognitive Neuropsychiatry, 1,* 55–72.

Sussman, F. (1999). *More Than Words: Autism Spectrum Disorder.* Toronto: Hanen Centre.

Sutera, S., Pandey, J., Esser, E. …. Fein, D. (2007). Predictors of optimal outcome in toddlers diagnosed with autism spectrum disorders. *Journal of Autism and Developmental Disorders, 37,* 98–107.

Sztainberg, Y. & Zoghbi, H. Y. (2016). Lessons learned from studying syndromic autism spectrum disorders. *Nature Neuroscience, 19,* 1408–1417.

Szymanski, C., Brice, P., Lam, K., & Hotto, S. (2012). Deaf children with autism spectrum disorders. *Journal of Autism and Developmental Disorders, 42,* 2027–2037.

Tager-Flusberg, H. (2000). Language and understanding minds: Connections in autism. In S. Baron-Cohen, H. Tager-Flusberg & D. Cohen (Eds.), *Understanding Other Minds: Perspectives from Developmental Cognitive Neuroscience* (3rd edn) (pp. 124–149). Oxford: Oxford University Press.

Tager-Flusberg, H. (2005). What neurodevelopmental disorders can reveal about cognitive architecture: The example of theory of mind. In P. Carruthers, S. Laurence & S. Stitch (Eds.), *The Innate Mind: Structure and Contents* (pp. 272–288). Oxford: Oxford University Press.

Tager-Flusberg, H. & Joseph, R. (2005). How language facilitates the acquisition of false-belief understanding in children with autism. In H. Lohmann, M. Tomasello & S. Meyer (Eds.), *Why Language Matters for Theory of Mind* (pp. 298–318). New York: Oxford University Press.

Tajfel, H. (1981). *Human Groups and Social Categories.* Cambridge: Cambridge University Press.

Tang, G., Gudsnuk, K., Kuo, S. …. Yue, Z. (2014). Loss of mTOR-dependent macroautophagy causes autistic-like synaptic pruning deficits. *Neuron, 83,* 1131–1143.

Tanguay, P. (1984). Towards a new classification of serious psychopathology in children. *Journal of the American Academy of Child Psychiatry, 23,* 378–384.

Tarakeshwar, N. & Pargament, K. (2002). Religious coping in families of children with autism. *Focus on Autism and Other Developmental Disabilities, 16,* 247–260.

Tavares, P., Mouga, S., Oliviera, G., & Castelo-Branco, M. (2013). Preserved first-order and holistic face processing in high-functioning adults with autism: An EEG/ERP study. *Perception ECVP Abstract, 42,* 81–81.

Taylor, E., Target, L., & Charman, T. (2008). Attachment in adults with high-functioning autism. *Attachment & Human Development, 10,* 143–163.

Taylor, J. & Corbett, B. (2014). A review of rhythm and responsiveness of cortisol in individuals with autism spectrum disorders. *Psychoneuroendocrinology, 49,* 207–228.

Taylor, J. L. & Seltzer, M. (2011). Employment and post-secondary educational activities for young adults with autism spectrum disorders during the transition to adulthood. *Journal of Autism and Developmental Disorders, 41,* 566–574.

Theije, C. de, Wu, J., Lopez da Silva, S. …. Kraneveld, A. (2011). Pathways underlying the gut-to-brain connection in autism spectrum disorders. *European Journal of Pharmacology, 668,* S70–S80.

Thioux, M., Stark, D., Klaimann, C., & Schultz, R. (2006). The day of the week when you were born in 700 ms: Calendar computation in an autistic savant. *Journal of Experimental Psychology: Human Perception and Performance, 32,* 1155–1168.

Tordjman, S., Somogyi, E., Coulon, N., … & Ginchat, V. (2014). Gene x environment interactions in autism spectrum disorders: Role of epigenetic mechanisms. *Frontiers in Psychiatry, 5,* 53ff.

Treffert, D. & Tammet, D. (2011). *Islands of Genius.* London: Jessica Kingsley.

Trevarthen, C. & Aitken, K. (2001). Infant intersubjectivity: Research, theory, and clinical applications. *Journal of Child Psychology and Psychiatry, 42,* 3–48.

Tsai, L. (2014). Impact of DSM-5 on autism spectrum disorder. *Research in Autism Spectrum Disorders, 8,* 1454–1470.

Tsai, L. & Ghaziuddin, M. (2014). DSM-ASD moves forward into the past. *Journal of Autism and Developmental Disorders, 44,* 321–330.

Tuchman, R. & Rapin, I. (2002). Epilepsy in autism. *The Lancet Neurology, 1,* 352–358.

Tulving, E. (1995). Organisation of memory. In M. Gazzaniga (Ed.), *The Cognitive Neurosciences* (pp. 839–847). Cambridge, MA: MIT Press.

Turner, M. (1999). Generating novel ideas: Fluency performance in high-functioning and learning disabled persons with autism. *Journal of Child Psychology and Psychiatry, 40,* 189–202.

Tustin, F. (1981/1995). *Autism and Childhood Psychosis.* London: Hogarth Press. (Reprinted in 1995 and published by Karnac Books.)

Tustin, F. (1991). Revised understanding of psychogenic autism. *International Journal of Psychoanalysis, 72,* 585–591.

Tyson, K., Kelley, E., Fein, D. …. Helt, M. (2014). Language and verbal memory in individuals with a history of autism spectrum disorders who have achieved optimal outcomes. *Journal of Autism and Developmental Disorders, 44,* 648–663.

Uchiyama, T., Kurosawa, M., & Inaba, Y. (2007). MMR-vaccine and regression in autism spectrum disorders. *Journal of Autism and Developmental Disorders, 37,* 210–217.

Uddin, L. (2011). The self in autism. *Neurocase, 17,* 201–208.

Uljarevic, M. & Hamilton, A. (2013). Recognition of emotions in autism: A formal meta-analysis. *Journal of Autism and Developmental Disorders, 43,* 1517–1526.

Ullman, M. (2001). The declarative/procedural model of lexicon and grammar. *Journal of Psycholinguistic Research, 30,* 37–69.

Ullman, M. (2004). Contributions of memory circuits to language: The declarative/procedural model. *Cognition, 92*, 231–270.

Ullman, M. & Pierpont, E. (2005). Specific language impairment is not specific to language: The procedural deficit hypothesis. *Cortex, 41*, 399–433.

Umeda, S., Mimura, M., & Kato, M. (2010). Acquired personality traits of autism following damage to medial prefrontal cortex. *Social Neuroscience, 5*, 19–29.

Ung, D., Selles, R., Small, B., & Storch, E. (2015). A systematic review and meta-analysis of cognitive-behavioral therapy for anxiety in youth with high-functioning autism spectrum disorders. *Child Psychiatry and Human Development, 46*, 533–547.

Van der Meer, J., Oerlemans, A., van Steijn, D. .... Rommelse, N. (2012). Are autism spectrum disorder and attention-deficit/hyperactivity disorder different manifestations of one overarching disorder? *Journal of the American Academy of Child and Adolescent Psychiatry, 51*, 1160–1172.

Van der Meer, L., Sutherland, D., O'Reilly, M., Lancioni, G., & Sigafoos, J. (2012). A further comparison of manual signing, picture exchange, and speech-generating devices as communication modes for children with autism spectrum disorders. *Research in Autism Spectrum Disorders, 6*, 1247–1257.

Van Swieten, L., van Bergen, E., Williams, J. H. .... Mon-Williams, M. (2010). A test of motor (not executive) planning in developmental coordination disorder and autism. *Journal of Experimental Psychology: Human Perception and Performance, 36*, 493.

Vanvuchelen, M., Roeyers, H., & De Weerdt, W. (2011). *Research in Autism Spectrum Disorders, 5*, 89–95.

Vause, T., Hoekstra, S., & Feldman, M. (2014). Evaluation of individual function-based cognitive-behavioural therapy for obsessive compulsive behaviour in children with autism spectrum disorder. *Journal of Developmental Disabilities, 20*, 30–41.

Virues-Ortega, J., Julio, F., & Pastor-Barriuso, R. (2013). The TEACCH program for children and adults with autism: A meta-analysis of intervention studies. *Clinical Psychology Review, 33*, 940–953.

Vismara, L. & Lyons, G. (2007). Using perseverative interests to elicit joint attention behaviors in young children with autism. *Journal of Positive Behavior Interventions, 9*, 214–228.

Vivanti, G. & Hamilton, A. (2014). Imitation in autism spectrum disorders. In F. Volkmar, S. Rogers, R. Paul & K. Pelphrey (Eds.), *Handbook of Autism and Pervasive Developmental Disorders* (Vol. 2, 4th edn) (pp. 278–300). Hoboken, NJ: Wiley & Sons.

Vivanti, G., Paynter, J., Duncan, E. .... Victorian ASELCC Team. (2014). Effectiveness and feasibility of the Early Start Denver Model implemented in a group-based community childcare setting. *Journal of Autism and Developmental Disorders, 44*, 3140–3153.

Volden, J. & Lord, C. (1991). Neologisms and idiosyncratic language in autistic speakers. *Journal of Autism and Developmental Disorders, 21*, 109–130.

Volkmar, F. & Reichow, B. (2013). Autism in DSM-5: Progress and challenges. *Molecular Autism, 4*, 1.

Wakefield, A., Murch, S., Anthony, A. .... Walker-Smith, J. (1998). Ileal-lymphoid-nodular hyperplasia, non-specific colitis, and pervasive developmental disorder in children. *The Lancet, 351*, 637–641.

Walenski, M., Tager-Flusberg, H., & Ullman, M. (2006). Language in autism. In S. Moldin & J. Rubenstein, J. (Eds.), *Understanding Autism: From Basic Neuroscience to Treatment* (pp. 175–203). Boca Raton, FL: CRC Press.

Wallace, G., Dankner, N., Kenworthy, L., Giedd, J., & Martin, A. (2010). Age-related temporal and parietal cortical thinning in autism spectrum disorders. *Brain, 133*, 3745–3754.

Wallace, G., Robustella, B., Dankner, N. .... Martin, A. (2013). Increased gyrification but comparable surface area in adolescents with autism spectrum disorders. *Brain, 136*, awt:06.

Waltz, M. & Shattock, P. (2004). Autistic disorder in nineteenth-century London: Three case reports. *Autism, 8*, 7–20.

Wang, Z., Hong, Y., Zou, L. .... Wang, W. (2014). Reelin gene variants and risk of autism spectrum disorders. *American Journal of Medical Genetics Part B: Neuropsychiatric Genetics, 162,* 192–200.

Warren, Z., McPheeters, M., Sathe, N. .... Veenstra-VanderWeele, J. (2011). A systematic review of early intensive intervention for autism spectrum disorders. *Pediatrics, 127,* e1303–e1311.

Washington, S., Gordon, E., Brar, J. .... VanMeter, J. (2014). Dysmaturation of the default mode network in autism. *Human Brain Mapping, 35,* 1284–1296.

Waterhouse, L. (2013). *Rethinking Autism: Variation and Complexity.* London: Academic Press.

Watson, L., Crais, E., Baranek, G., Dykstra, J., & Wilson, K. (2013). Communicative gesture use in infants with and without autism: A retrospective home video study. *American Journal of Speech-Language Pathology, 22,* 25–39.

Webb, S., Jones, E., Kelly, J., & Dawson, G. (2014). The motivation for very early intervention for infants at high risk for autism spectrum disorders. *International Journal of Speech-Language Pathology, 16,* 36–42.

Wechsler, D. (1999). *Wechsler Adult Intelligence Scale (WAIS-III-UK).* Oxford: Harcourt Assessment.

Wechsler, D. (2004). *Wechsler Intelligence Scale for Children (WISC-IV-UK).* Oxford: Harcourt Assessment.

Wei, J., Yu, J., Shattuck, P., McCracken, M., & Blackorby, J. (2013). Science, Technology, Engineering, and Mathematics (STEM) participation among college students with an autism spectrum disorder. *Journal of Autism and Developmental Disorders, 43,* 1539–1546.

Weigelt, S., Koldewyn, K., & Kanwisher, N. (2013). Face recognition deficits in autism spectrum disorders are both domain specific and process specific. *PloS One, 8*(9), e74541.

Weiss, M. (2002). Hardiness and social support as predictors of stress in mothers of typical children, children with autism, and children with mental retardation. *Autism, 6,* 115–130.

Weitzman, E. (2013). More Than Words—The Hanen Program for parents of children with autism spectrum disorder: A teaching model for parent-implemented language Intervention. *SIG 1 Perspectives on Language Learning and Education, 20,* 96–111.

Werth, A., Perkins, M., & Boucher, J. (2001). 'Here's the weavery looming up': Verbal humour in a woman with high-functioning autism. *Autism, 5,* 111–127.

Wetherby, A., Guthrie, W., Woods, J. .... Lord, C. (2014). Parent-implemented social intervention for toddlers with autism: An RCT. *Pediatrics, 134,* 1084–1093.

Wetherby, A. & Woods, J. (2006). Early social interaction project for children with autism spectrum disorders beginning in the second year of life: A preliminary study. *Topics in Early Childhood Special Education, 26,* 67–82.

Wheelwright, S. & Baron-Cohen, S. (2011). Systemizing and empathizing. In D. Fein (Ed.), *The Neuropsychology of Autism* (pp. 317–338). Oxford: Oxford University Press.

White, B. & White, M. (1987). Autism from the inside. *Medical Hypotheses, 24,* 223–229.

Whitehouse, A., Mattes, E., Mayberry, M. .... Hickey, M. (2012). Perinatal testosterone exposure and autistic-like traits in the general population. *Journal of Neurodevelopmental Disorders, 4,* 1.

Wiggins, J., Peltier, S., Bedoyen, J. .... Monk, C. (2013). The impact of serotonin transporter genotype on default network connectivity in children and adolescents with autism spectrum disorders. *NeuroImage: Clinical, 2,* 17–24.

Wiggins, L. & Robins, D. (2008). Brief report: Excluding the ADI-R behavioral domain improves diagnostic agreement in toddlers. *Journal of Autism and Developmental Disorders, 38,* 972–976.

Wilcox, J., Tsuang, M., Schurr, T., & Baida-Fragoso, N. (2003). Case-control study of lesser variant traits in autism. *Neuropsychobiology, 47,* 171–177.

Will, D., Barnfather, J., & Lesley, M. (2013). Self-perceived autism competency of primary care nurse practitioners. *The Journal for Nurse Practitioners, 9,* 350–355.

Williams, D. (1994). *Somebody Somewhere.* London: Doubleday.

Williams, D., Botting, N., & Boucher, J. (2008). Language in autism and specific language disorder: Where are the links? *Psychological Bulletin, 134,* 944–963.

Williams, J., Whiten, A., & Singh, T. (2004). A systematic review of action imitation in autistic spectrum disorder. *Journal of Autism and Developmental Disorders, 34,* 285–299.

Williams, J., Whiten, A., Suddendorf, T., & Perrett, D. (2001). Imitation, mirror neurons and autism. *Neuroscience and Biobehavioural Reviews, 25,* 287–295.

Williams, K. & Wishart, J. (2003). The Son-Rise Program 1 intervention for autism: An investigation into family experiences. *Journal of Intellectual Disability Research, 47,* 291–299.

Williams, K., Wray, J., & Wheeler, D. (2012). Intravenous secretin for autism spectrum disorders. *Cochrane Database Systemic Review, 4.*

Wimpory, D., Nicholas, B., & Nash, S. (2002). Social timing, clock genes and autism: A new hypothesis. *Journal of Intellectual Disability Research, 46,* 352–358.

Windsor, J., Doyle, S., & Siegel, G. (1994). Language acquisition after mutism. *Journal of Speech Language and Hearing Research, 37,* 96–105.

Wing, L. (1981). Asperger's syndrome: A clinical account. *Psychological Medicine, 11,* 115–129.

Wing, L. (1996). *The Autistic Spectrum.* London: Constable.

Wing, L. & Gould, J. (1979). Severe impairments of social interaction and associated abnormalities in children: Epidemiology and classification. *Journal of Autism and Childhood Schizophrenia, 9,* 11–29.

Wing, L., Gould, J., Yeates, S., & Brierly, L. (1977). Symbolic play in severely mentally retarded and in autistic children. *Journal of Child Psychology and Psychiatry, 18,* 167–178.

Wing, L., Leekam, S., Libby, S., Gould, J., & Larcombe, M. (2002). The Diagnostic Interview for Social and Communication Disorders. *Journal of Child Psychology and Psychiatry, 43,* 307–327.

Wolff, J., Botteron, K., Dager, S. …. Zwaigenbaum, L. (2014). Longitudinal patterns of repetitive behavior in toddlers with autism. *Journal of Child Psychology and Psychiatry, 55,* 945–953.

Woodbury-Smith, M., Robinson, J., Wheelwright, S., & Baron-Cohen, S. (2005). Screening adults for Asperger syndrome using the AQ: A preliminary study of its diagnostic validity. *Journal of Autism and Developmental Disorders, 35,* 331–336.

World Health Organisation (1992). *International Classification of Mental and Behavioural Disorders: Clinical Descriptions and Diagnostic Guidelines* (10th edn) (*ICD-10*). Geneva: WHO.

World Health Organisation (1993). *The ICD-10 Classification of Mental and Behavioural Disorders: Diagnostic Criteria for Research.* Geneva: WHO.

Xu, G., Jing, J., Bowers, K., Kiu, B., & Bao, W. (2014). Maternal diabetes and the risk of autism spectrum disorders in the offspring. *Journal of Autism and Developmental Disorders, 44,* 766–775.

Yirmiya, N., Erel, O., Shaked, M., & Solomonica-Levi, D. (1998). Meta-analyses comparing theory of mind abilities of individuals with autism, individuals with mental retardation, and normally developing individuals. *Psychological Bulletin, 124,* 283–307.

Yirmiya, N., Kasari, C., Sigman, M., & Mundy, P. (1989). Facial expressions of affect in autistic, mentally retarded and normal children. *Journal of Child Psychology and Psychiatry, 30,* 725–735.

Yoshimasu, K., Kiyohara, C., Takemura, S., & Nakai, K. (2014). A meta-analysis of the evidence on the impact of prenatal and early infancy exposures to mercury on autism and attention deficit/hyperactivity disorder in childhood. *Neurotoxicology, 44,* 121–131.

Yoshimura, S. & Toichi, M. (2014). A lack of self-consciousness in Asperger's disorder but not in PDDNOS. *Research in Autism Spectrum Disorders, 8,* 237–243.

Young, G., Merin, N., Rogers, S., & Ozonoff, S. (2009). Gaze behavior and affect at 6 months: Predicting clinical outcomes and language development in typically developing infants and infants at risk for autism. *Developmental Science, 12,* 798–814.

Young, L. & Barrett, C. (2015). Can oxytocin treat autism? *Science* (New York), *347,* 825.

Zander, E. & Bölte, S. (2015). The new DSM-5 impairment criterion. A challenge to early autism spectrum disorder diagnosis? *Journal of Autism and Developmental Disorders, 45,* 3634–3643.

Zandt, F., Prior, M., & Kyrios, M. (2007). Repetitive behaviour in children with high-functioning autism and obsessive compulsive disorder. *Journal of Autism and Developmental Disorders, 37,* 251–259.

Zentall, S. & Zentall, T. (1983). Optimal stimulation: A model of disordered activity in normal and deviant children. *Psychological Bulletin, 94,* 446–471.

Zerbo, O., Iosif, A.-M., Walker, C. .... Hertz-Picciotto, I. (2013). Is maternal influenza or fever during pregnancy associated with autism or developmental delays? *Journal of Autism and Developmental Disorders, 43,* 25–33.

Zielinski, B., Anderson, J., Froehlich, A. .... Lainhart, J. (2012). scMRI reveals large-scale brain network abnormalities in autism. *PLoS One, 7:* e49172.

Zoghbi, H. & Bear, M. (2012). Synaptic dysfunction in neurodevelopmental disorders associated with autism and intellectual disability. *Cold Spring Harbour Perspectives in Biology, 4:* a009886.

Zwaigenbaum, L., Bryson, S., & Garon, N. (2013). Early identification of autism spectrum disorders. *Behavior and Brain Research, 251,* 133–146.

INDEX

Note: Page numbers followed by *gl* refer to terms in the glossary. Page numbers followed by "n" indicate footnotes and page numbers in *italics* refer to figures and boxes.